MAKING LIFE CHOICES

MAKING LIFE CHOICES

THE PSYCHOLOGY OF PERSONAL AND INTERPERSONAL GROWTH

First Edition

Edited by Steven L. Berman

University of Central Florida

SAN DIEGO

Bassim Hamadeh, CEO and Publisher
Jennifer McCarthy, Field Acquisitions Editor
Amy Smith, Project Editor
Jeanine Rees, Production Editor
Katie Zychowicz, Graphic Design Assistant
Stephanie Kohl, Licensing Coordinator
Natalie Piccotti, Director of Marketing
Kassie Graves, Vice President of Editorial
Jamie Giganti, Director of Academic Publishing

Printed in the United States of America.

CONTENTS

PREFACE

This book was created for a personal growth psychology course. It grew out of a project that began as my doctoral dissertation, under the mentorship of Dr. William M. Kurtines. I was interested in identity formation—how young people get a sense of direction and purpose in their lives. According to Erik Erikson, achieving a strong sense of personal identity is one of eight important developmental tasks across the life span. Based on both my personal observations and my review of the relevant psychological literature, I noted that for some people this task of figuring out who they are and what they want to do with life may be a bit anxiety provoking, but overall it is one of excitement and great possibilities. For others, however, the task can be fraught with overwhelming anxiety and debilitating depression as they are unable to master the challenge. My goal was to develop an intervention program to help people deal with their identity related distress and help them to make the best life decisions possible, considering their circumstances.

This goal led to the development of what my colleagues and I called the Making Life Choices Workshop. The workshop combined four processes. The first was Identity Exploration, as I (and my fellow group facilitators) helped the participants to explore and define their values and life goals. Part of this discussion was aimed at fears about the future and identifying the potential impediments to achieving goals. This led to choosing a particular issue to work on within the workshops. Issues might be related to career choice, overcoming procrastination, resolving a crisis of faith, sorting out relationship issues, etc. Once a problem or challenge was identified, the next process involved teaching the participants about the Steps of Problem-Solving and applying these steps to their particular issues. On top of this we also focused on the development of Critical Thinking. We challenge participants to be both more open-minded about new ideas and possible solutions and more skeptical, challenging and scrutinizing all ideas, including and especially one's own firmly held biases and self-imposed limitations. Critical thinking is a skill, but it is also a value. We are all capable of thinking critically, but we often choose not to do so. Thus, part of the workshop was focused on helping the participants to understand why it is so important to develop and use those skills in their daily lives. The group format is particularly helpful in this regard, as participants can call out and challenge each other for being too dogmatic and resistant at one extreme or too compliant and wishy-washy on the other. In this way, the critical discussion of the group fosters and reinforces critical thinking in the individual. The fourth and final process was Empowerment, getting participants to take active control and responsibility over their lives. Many people who feel stuck in their lives play the blame game for their life circumstances. And while others certainly may have contributed and even outright caused one's problems, sitting around complaining and focusing on blame will not change a thing. In short, you may not have chosen your life circumstances, but it is up to you to do something about it. Wallowing in self-pity will not change it, nor will focusing on others. This does not relieve others from their burden of blame, nor does it transfer the blame to the participant/victim. It is a matter of accepting that the situation was bad and unfair, but only they can choose to move forward. By actively taking control and responsibility for their life, they can start making decisions to grow and change their life circumstances to something more appealing.

The workshops were given on a college campus with undergraduate participants and were well received. The workshops were eventually brought by my fellow doctoral students (Laura Ferrer-Wreder, Carolyn Lorente, Ervin Briones) into an alternative high school for teens at high risk for dropout, to help them make better life choices. These participants were quite used to parents, teachers, and administrators telling them exactly what they should be doing to live a more productive life, but the workshops took a different route by encouraging young people to think critically about their lives in line with their own self-chosen values, to create solutions which came from them, guaranteeing greater personal investment, commitment, and, of course, empowerment. Meanwhile back at the university, I started developing a course for the psychology undergraduate curriculum that combined my workshop with the application of other psychological principles for maximizing personal growth and self-actualization. We met twice each week. During one weekly session I would lecture and assign readings on various topics of common concern, such as overcoming procrastination, managing time and stress, improving communication, enhancing relationships, developing effective coping skills, resolving conflict, etc. At the other weekly meeting, I broke them into small groups to do the workshop by identifying a personal issue and working it through the steps of problem-solving with the help of their group. In the beginning I used graduate students from our Clinical Psychology Masters Degree Program as facilitators of the groups. But as I refined the directions and tasks involved (and as class enrollment continued to rise beyond my ability to provide a sufficient number of facilitators), I found that I could create leaderless groups. The groups were tasked each week with facilitating themselves, and I could circulate between groups to do any troubleshooting. Eventually I created a totally online version of this course whereby the small group work was done asynchronously using a discussion board.

This book is an outgrowth of that work and my program of research on identity and identity distress. It includes a collection of readings on topics related to personal growth, as well as the list of activities that made up the Life Choices Workshops. Of course, an instructor could choose to use the readings without the activities, or the activities without the readings, but I have found the combination to be quite fruitful. It is compatible with various class formats, including face-to-face class, mixed mode, or totally online. The activities could be redesigned as individual assignments if necessary, but I believe they are most powerful when done in groups that promote critical discussion. I hope that the professors and students who use this book will find it as engaging and rewarding as have I and my students!

CHAPTER 1

Introduction to Working in Groups

This book of readings is geared toward applying psychological principles toward personal and interpersonal growth. Its purpose is to help you in identifying the roles, goals, and values that have the potential to give your life meaningful direction and purpose. It also aims to help you make important life choices so that you might achieve your goals and become the person you would like to be.

This program is not for everyone. If you have no goals to attain, no challenges to overcome, and you don't want to change a thing about your life, then this is not for you. However, if you're up for a challenge and you believe that life could always be better, then I believe you will find these readings and associated activities to be extremely rewarding.

This book is designed to include a significant experiential component. Although you can read about personal and interpersonal growth, and engage in critical thinking and problem-solving as an individual activity, it has been my experience that much greater progress can be made if you work in a small group that can provide you with important feedback. I have been teaching this course at the college level for many years. I have also conducted similar workshops with high school students and older nontraditional students looking to make important changes in their lives. I have led these groups, trained and supervised graduate students as group leaders, and also conducted leaderless groups whereby undergraduates are given instructions on how to run their own group. After doing this face-to-face for years, I also created a totally online version of this course where a class of 125 students would be divided into small groups of 4 to 6 people in order to complete the associated activities with an asynchronous online discussion board.

In addition to hearing different perspectives and receiving valuable feedback on your issues by participating in groups, you will also learn about group process by experiencing it.

Some of the exercises will be aimed at analyzing your group, how it works, how it could work more effectively, and the role that you and others play in your group.

What You Will Be Asked to Do

Within the small group to which you will be assigned, you will be asked to identify and share a personal goal which you will work on, and follow through the steps of problem-solving, with the assistance of the group. Expect the others to ask you questions and challenge your ideas. You will be expected to do the same for them. You will give each other feedback on how well each of you are fulfilling your role as a group member. In addition to teaching you the steps of problem-solving, we will be fostering your critical thinking and critical discussion skills as well as encouraging you to take personal responsibility for making life choices. You will be learning about things like relationship skills, coping skills, and how to deal with anxiety. Rather than just learning about theories of group work, you will experience it in action as a participant. Don't worry, you don't have to have a deep-seated psychological issue to work on, nor do you have to share anything about yourself that you don't want to. You will, however, have to choose some issue to work on (we all have goals and challenges), and it should be a real issue that is important to you. If you are extremely uncomfortable talking about your life in front of others, then you should discuss your discomfort with your professor to determine the degree to which group participation will be required and whether or not this course is right for you. This book is written to include a group experiential component, but ultimately it will be up to your professor to establish the extent to which such a component is used and enforced.

Working in Groups

As we prepare to start working in a small group, it would be good to start thinking about group process and your expectations for group work. You have probably worked on group projects in school before, but this will be a very different group experience. If you have ever participated in group therapy or a support group, this will be closer to your experience, but still not the same. This is NOT a therapy group and it will not solve all your life issues. We will attempt to tackle ONE issue that you have identified. This is a time-limited group so we cannot promise that you will "solve" your issue, or even make significant progress. However, the skills that you will be learning in group should prove valuable for the rest of your life as you continue to tackle the challenges that life presents. You will NOT be asked to talk about anything you do not want to discuss. What you choose to talk about is totally up to you. On the other hand, you will need to stay focused. This is not the place to discuss all your problems and/or the difficulties that you have recently encountered. It will be a highly focused group, taking you through the steps of problem-solving in regard to the issue you have selected for yourself. Your group mates are there to help you through the process, as you will be expected to help them.

Individual Assignment

In preparation for what you will soon be doing in your small group, I would like you to start thinking about the direction of your life; where have you come from and where are you going. Think about the high points, low points, and turning points in your life. Make a chart that highlights these important events; draw a time line (age) along the bottom of a piece of paper in landscape orientation and place a life satisfaction rating along the left side (running from −5 to +5). Put an X on your chart for each high point, low point, and turning point (high and low points can also be turning points but not necessarily), then write a description of each of these important markers in your life.

Think about where your life might go next. Where would you like it to go and where do you not want it to go, or fear that it might possibly go? What are some of the reasons it may or may not go as planned and hoped? Which of these reasons are under your control and which are not? Write down the answers to these questions.

The Weekly Reading

Your reading for this week is about the stages of small group development. In addition to using a group to work on your issue, you will also be learning about group process, or how groups work. The purpose of this reading is to get you to begin to think about what goes on in groups when working toward common goals.

Pre-Reading Questions

The reading for this chapter is on the development of small groups.

1. What are the different types of groups in which you have participated? Were they positive or negative experiences? Why?
2. How have your past experiences in groups shaped your expectations for the group you are about to join for this class? Why do you think it might be similar, and why might it be different?

READING 1

Stages of Small-Group Development Revisited[1]

Bruce W. Tuckman and Mary Ann C. Jensen

Editor's Note

Thinking today about the phases of group development, a group facilitator is hard pressed to not hear the famous words of Bruce Tuckman's 1965 seminal work *Developmental Sequence in Small Groups*[2] that hypothesized his *forming, storming, norming* and *performing* model of group development. Tuckman's 1965 article was reprinted in a Special Issue on Group Development in *Group Facilitation: A Research and Applications Journal* in 2001[3]. What many facilitators may not be aware of is that Bruce Tuckman and Mary Ann Jensen conducted a follow-up review thirteen years later, to discover what empirical testing of the model had been conducted by others. The following article, originally published in 1977 in *Group & Organization Studies*, noted that several subsequent empirical studies suggested a termination stage, which Tuckman and Jensen then integrated into the model of group development as a fifth stage named *adjourning*. While many have argued that there are limitations of "stage models" such as this, the wide use and popularity of the Tuckman model means this article is suggested reading for every group facilitator. – Stephen Thorpe, Editor

The purpose of this review was to examine published research on small-group development done in the last ten years that would constitute an empirical test of Tuckman's (1965) hypothesis that groups go through the stages of "forming," "storming," "norming," and "performing." Of the twenty-two studies reviewed, only one set out to directly test this hypothesis, although many of the others could be related to it. Following a review of these studies, a fifth stage, "adjourning," was added to the hypothesis, and more empirical work was recommended.

Tuckman (1965) reviewed fifty-five articles dealing with stages of small group development in an attempt to isolate those concepts common to the various studies and produce a generalizable model of changes in group life over time. He examined studies of (1) Therapy Groups, (2) human relations training or T-groups, and (3) natural and laboratory-task groups in terms of two realms—task and interpersonal. The way members acted and related to one another was considered group-structure or the interpersonal realm: the content of the interaction as related to the task was referred to as the task-activity realm. Both realms represented simultaneous aspects of group functioning because members completed tasks while relating to one another.

The Model

As a result of the literature reviewed, Tuckman proposed a model of developmental stages for various group settings over time, labeled (1) testing and dependence, (2) intragroup conflict, (3) development of group cohesion, and (4) functional role relatedness. The stages of task activity were labeled (1) orientation to task, (2) emotional response to task demands, (3) open exchange of relevant interpretations, and (4) emergence of solutions. An essential correspondence between the group-structure realm and the task-activity realm over time caused Tuckman to summarise the four stages as "forming," "storming," "norming," and "performing." He acknowledged, however, that this was "a conceptual statement suggested by the data presented and subject to further test" (p. 5).

Tuckman cited several limitations of the literature, e.g., that the literature could not be considered truly representative of small-group developmental processes because there was an overrepresentation of therapy and T-group settings and an underrepresentation of natural or laboratory groups, indicated the need for more rigorous methodological considerations in studying group process, and criticized the use of a single group for observation because it made control and systemic manipulation of independent values impossible.

Tuckman provided a developmental model of group process by organizing and conceptualizing existing research data and theoretical precepts rather than by presenting original empirical data to support a particular model. He stated, however, that his model was in need of further testing.

Purpose and Methodology of This Review

The purpose of this follow-up study is to discover whether anyone has empirically tested the model of group development proposed by Tuckman in 1965, to investigate any new models in light of Tuckman's hypothesis, and to determine whether any alternative models have been conceived.

To locate any studies referencing the 1965 Tuckman article, the *Science Citation Index* from 1965 and the *Social Science Citation Index* from 1970 were consulted and a list of fifty-seven articles was compiled. Of these, only those studies concerned primarily with empirical research (approximately twenty-two) were reviewed.

Review of the 'New' Literature

Only one study could be found that set out to test Tuckman's hypothesis. Runkel et al. (1971) studied three groups of fifteen to twenty college students in a classroom setting. The task of each group was to decide on a project, collect and interpret data, and write a final report. During meetings of the work group, sixteen observers, armed with descriptions of the Tuckman model of stage development, observed the group "until something happened that fitted a behavior described by Tuckman as belonging to one of the four stages of group structure or task activity" (p. 186). The observers rotated among groups in an effort to reduce observer bias. Ratings from observers supported Tuckman's theory of group development.

Although this empirical test of Tuckman's hypothesis supported his suggested developmental sequence, observers were given only descriptions of Tuckman's four stages and asked to "fit" their observations to that model. A methodology less prone to observer bias would have been to have observers record particular behaviors apparent in the group; at a later time, these could have been reviewed in light of particular models. Runkel et al. did, however, provide an empirical base for further testing of the Tuckman model.

Several articles from the literature contained elements of the Tuckman model. Zurcher (1969) offered some explanation of the developmental sequence in natural groups, an area Tuckman described as underrepresented in the literature. Data were obtained from 174 meetings of twelve poverty programme neighborhood action committees in Topeka, Kansas, over a nineteen-month period. Results from a team of participant-observers indicated that the stages of development for these neighborhood committees included (1) orientation, (2) catharsis, (3) focus, (4) action, (5) limbo, (6) testing, and (7) purposive. Zurcher stated that these seven stages "could parisimoniously have been reduced to four stages suggested by Tuckman" (p. 245) as shown below.

Orientation	Forming
Catharsis	Storming
Focus, Action	
Limbo, Testing	Norming
Purposive	Performing

Although Zucher's results would serve to support the Tuckman model, he did not specifically set out to test any particular model of group development and did not present any statistical treatment of his data.

Smith (1966) observed, over a period of approximately four months, a group of seven man stationed in Antarctica and collected data on technical-task activities as well as on behavioral dimensions of informal structure. He reported on only two developmental stages rather than on the four listed by Tuckman. However, Smith's two developmental *stages* appear to be task-activity behavior and interpersonal behavior, both of which were identified by Tuckman as the *realms* of group behavior. Smith's results serve to reinforce the hypothesis that task and interpersonal dimensions play a substantial role in the way groups develop.

Smith also concluded that the order of development would be different for various groups. Although the interpersonal "stage" seemed most important for therapy or training groups, task activity was stressed by the men in Antarctica. That the content or task activity appeared prior to development of a group structure might be due to the specific nature of the group assignment and to the well-defined roles of the participants, which suggest that those aspects related to the primary purpose of the group develop first. Due to the uniqueness of his group in terms of task and setting, Smith's results might not be applicable to other types of groups.

Shambaugh and Kanter (1969) described the evolution of a therapy group for spouces of patients on hemodialysis machines. A group of six spouses met weekly for a period of eight months. As observed by the group leader/psychiatrist, the stages of group development included (1) initial experience, (2) formation of the group, (3) optimism and partial separation, and (4) final stage.

The authors believed that this group was a "paradigm of the unconscious forces inherent in group structure and process" and that "the overall developmental sequence was that of the usual small group" (p. 936). They did not attempt to "test" any particular model of group development; however, their observations appear to fit the behaviors characterizing Tuckman's stages of "forming," "storming," "norming," and "performing" (i.e., dependence on leader, criticism among members, optimism and cohesiveness). Shambaugh and Kanter did not describe behaviors characteristic of each stage clearly, which made it difficult to differentiate among them. The authors did observe, however, that their observations supported Tuckman's four-stage theory.

A second problem with this study was the introduction of new members into the group prior to the final stage, which made identification of the four stages and the characteristic behaviors pertinent to each difficult.

Lacoursiere (1974) observed stage development while using a group method to facilitate learning for student nurses involved in a psychiatric setting. The student nurses, in their twenties, single and female (except for one male student in each of the three groups observed), worked in a state mental hospital and met as a group for one and one-half hours each week to discuss their concerns. Over a ten-week period, Lacoursiere observed four stages of group development:

1 Orientation, characterized by fears and anxieties and fairly strong positive expectations;

2 Dissatisfaction, characterized by an increasing sense of frustration, along with depression and anger;

3 Production, demonstrated by a more realistic appraisal of what could be accomplished; and

4 Termination, concerned with sadness and some self-evaluation.

Lacoursiere's four stages differed from Tuckman's in three respects. First, in stage 2, dissatisfaction, there was a lack of intragroup conflict among the student nurses. Any anger and hostility present was directed toward the hospital, the staff, and psychiatry in general rather than toward group members. Second, Lacoursiere combined "norming" and "performing" into stage 3, production, at which tome students' expectations became more realistic and they desired "to learn what can be learned and to do what they can reasonably do as student nurses" (p. 348). Third, and the major difference between models, was the addition of the termination stage.

Another article dealing with the training of nursing students was one by Spitz and Sadock (1973), who observed twenty-one second-year nursing students, all white females from twenty to forty years old, using techniques such as role playing, video taping, and analysis of dreams. Spitz and Sadock categorized group life into three phases:

1 Stage One, characterized by anxiety, guardedness, dependency, and a mixture of curiosity and confusion;

2 Stage Two, the period of beginning trust, cohesiveness, interdependence, and group interaction;

3 Stage Three, the final phase of disengagement, anxiety about separation and termination, and positive feelings toward the leader.

Stages one and two contain elements of Tuckman's "forming" and "norming" stages, respectively. Tuckman's second stage, "storming," has for the most part been eliminated. Although Lacoursiere's group demonstrated anger and hostility toward an outside force, Spitz and Sadock's group appeared to touch on themes of anger and discontent in their group discussions. It is of significance that neither student-nurse group demonstrated noticeable characteristics of intragroup conflict. Possibly the close association experienced by nursed unites them in a cohesive, personal group. Also, the groups' composition—overwhelmingly female—might be a factor, as women have traditionally been socialized to be more passive and trusting. Spitz and Sadock also observed third-year medical students and found them to be more guarded and "overtly hostile." Group composition, therefore, may be one of the variables that influence appearance of stages in the developmental process.

A second variation in Spitz and Sadock's model, which also was found in the Lacoursiere model, was the addition of a stage concerned with termination and separation, a significant departure from the Tuckman model.

Braaten (1975) compiled an interesting review of fourteen models of the developmental stages of groups. Several of the more recent models not reviewed in the 1965 tuckman article demonstrated a resemblance to his four-stage model. For example, Yalom (1970) presented a four-stage model, including an initial phase of orientation and hesitant participation; a second phase of conflict, dominance, and rebellion; a third phase of intimacy, closeness, and cohesiveness; and a final phase of termination (differing from Tuckman).

Braaten presented a composite model of the fourteen theories and also set fourth his own model. His composite model utilized the three stages identified by Tuckman as "forming," "storming," and "performing" (which incorporated "norming") and added a final stage of termination. Braaten's own model followed the composite model fairly closely:

1 Initial phase lacking in structure;

2 An early phase characterized by hostility and conflicts between subgroups;

3 The mature work phase in which norms are resolved and interdependency and trust formation are apparent;

4 Termination, concerned with disengagement and ending.

Braaten concluded, as did Tuckman, that there appeared to be substantial agreement among authors on the aspects of a developmental phase but that systemic research was needed to verify the theoretical concepts. Braaten's review of the literature suggests that empirical research in stages od small group development is sparse and inconclusive.

Only two of the journal articles reviewed substantially deviated from the four-stage Tuckman model. Dunphy (1968) conducted an empirical study of the developmental process in self-analytic groups (therapy and T-groups). He observed two sections of a Harvard Social Relations 120 course for a period of nine months. Though the use of a computer system of content analysis, Dunphy identified six developmental phases for the group:

1 Maintenance of external normative standards;

2 Individual rivalry;

3 Aggression;

4 Negativism;

5 Emotional concerns;

6 High Affection.

Individual rivalry, aggression, and negativism parallel Tuckman's second stage, "storming." Emotional concerns and high affection might be viewed in terms of the "norming" stage. However, Dunphy's model does not include any stage resembling "performing." Dunphy acknowledged that his results might not be generalizable to all self-analytic groups and that further testing was needed to establish the extent of their validity.

A study by Heckel, Holmes, and Salzberg (1967) examined whether distinct verbal behavioral phases occur in group psychotherapy. Seventeen neuropsychiatric male and female patients were observed over eighteen sessions of group therapy.

Verbal responses of participants were recorded and grouped according to type of response and specific category (i.e., therapist-directed response, etc.). Results revealed a significant change between the seventh and eighth and twelfth and thirteenth sessions. Therapist-directed responses were most noticeably affected, going from fifty-nine to twenty-three; group-directed responses went from twenty-one to thirty-nine. On the basis of these results, Heckel et al. believed their findings were "somewhat supportive" of a two-stage hypothesis of group development. The authors did not describe characteristics of the two stages, however, nor did they attempt to propose their own theoretical model for further testing.

Another study by Heckel, Holmes, and Rosecrans (1971) employed a factor-analytic approach for analyzing verbal responses of group-therapy members. Utilizing the theory of two-stage development derived from the 1967 study, the authors rated responses from approximately thirty male neuropsychiatric patients during their second and third sessions and from seventeen of these patients during the twelfth and thirteenth sessions. The authors reported that combined results from sessions two and three indicated low group cohesiveness, high defensiveness and superficial verbal interaction and a pattern of personal and group-building responses. An obvious change had occurred by the twelfth and thirteenth sessions, but the loss of almost half the members of the group by this time also may have had an impact on changes in their verbal responses. Without observing interactions over the life of the group, the suggestion that these four sessions represent the *only* changes taking place seems premature.

Mann (1967) offered a third variation to the four-stage model. Through the use of factor analysis, he categorized five stages of group development: (1) initial complaining, (2) premature enactment, (3) confrontation, (4) internalization, (5) separation and terminal review. This model appears to incorporate characteristics of Tuckman's "forming," "storming," "norming," and "performing" stages, with the addition of stage 5—termination.

Braaten (1975) included an updated version of Mann's (1971) developmental model:

1 Dependency upon trainer;

2 Initial anxiety and/or resistance;

3 Mounting frustration, hostility;

4 Work phase, intimacy, integration, mutual synthesis;

5 Separation.

Discussion

This review of articles was undertaken to discover whether the Tuckman (1965) model of group development had been empirically tested. Only Runkel et al. (1971) set out to test this model. Their conclusions were supportive of Tuckman's four-stage model, but their results may not be reliable because of the researchers' methodology.

The bulk of the literature from 1965 to present has been theoretical in nature; those articles describing empirical research were not primarily concerned with testing already existing models. Many of the authors described a group's behavior and offered their own models of group development, however similar to models already described in the literature.[4] Two studies and a review did identify termination as an important final stage overlooked by Tuckman. Braaten's (1975) review of fourteen models led to a composite model incorporating "forming," "storming," and "performing" stages and including a termination stage.

Gibbard and Hartman (1973) introduced the concept of a "life cycle" model as developed by Mills (1964). Proponents of a life cycle approach recognize the importance of separation concerns as an issue in group development. Although Tuckman saw performing as the final stage of group evolution, those who agree with a life cycle model view separation as an important issue throughout the life of the group and as a separate and distinct final stage. With a substantial amount of activity taking place in training and therapy groups in which presumably strong interpersonal feelings are developed, the "death of the group" becomes an extremely important issue to many of the group members. As a reflection of the recent appearance of studies postulating a life cycle approach (Mann, 1971; Gibbard & Hartman, 1973; Spitz & Sadock, 1973; Lacoursiere, 1974; Braaten, 1975), the Tuckman model is hereby amended to include a fifth stage: adjourning.

Conclusion

It is noteworthy that since 1965 there have been few studies that report empirical data concerning the stages of group development. It is also of interest that most authors, although writing from a theoretical framework, call for further research to verify their hypotheses. A virtually untapped field is the empirical testing of existing models of group-stage development. There is a need to supply statistical evidence as to the usefulness and applicability of the various models suggested in the literature.

A major outcome of this review has been the discovery that recent research posits the existence of a final discernible and significant stage of group development—termination. Because the 1965 model was a conceptual statement determined by the literature, it is reasonable, therefore, to modify the model to reflect recent literature. The model now stands: forming, storming, norming, performing, and adjourning.

References

Adelson, J. Feedback and group development. Small Group Behavior, 1975 6(4), 389–401.

Braaten, L. J. Developmental phases of encounter groups and related intensive groups: A critical review of models and a new proposal. Interpersonal Development, 1974–75, 5, 112–129.

Dunphy, D. Phases, roles and myths in self-analytic groups. Journal of Applied Behavioral Science, 1968, 4(2), 195–225.

Gibbard, G., & Hartman, J. The oedipal paradigm in group development: A clinical and empirical study. Small Group Behavior, 1973, 4(3), 305–349.

Heckel, R., Holmes, G., & Salzberg, H. Emergence of distinct verbal phases in group therapy. Psychological Reports, 1967, 21, 630–632.

Heckel, R. V., Holmes, G. R., & Rosecrans, C. J. A factor analytic study of process variables in group therapy. Journal of Clinical Psychology, 1971, 27(1), 146–150.

Lacoursiere, R. A group method to facilitate learning during the stages of a psychiatric affiliation. International Journal of Group Psychotherapy, 1974, 24, 342–351.

Liebowitz, B. A method for the analysis of the thematic structure of T-groups. The Journal of Applied Behavioral Science, 1972, 8(2), 149–173.

Lundgren, D. C. Trainer style and patterns of group development. The Journal of Applied Behavioral Science, 1971, 7(6), 689–709.

Lundgren, D. C. Attitudinal and behavioral correlates of emergent status in training groups. The Journal of Social Psychology, 1973, 90, 141–153.

Mann, R. D. The development of the member-trainer relationship in self-analytic groups. In C. L. Cooper & I. L. Mangham (Eds.), T-groups: A survey of research. London: Wiley-Interscience, 1971.

Mann, R. D. Interpersonal styles and group development. New York: John Wiley, 1967.

Mills, T. M. Group transformation. Englewood Cliffs, N. J.: Prentice-Hall, 1964.

Runkel, P. J., Lawrence, M. Oldfield, S., Rider, M., Clark, C. Stages of group development: An empirical test of Tuckman's hypothesis. The Journal of Applied Behavioral Science, 1971, 7(2), 180–193.

Shambaugh, P., & Kanter, S. Spouses under stress: Group meetings with spouses of patients on hemodialysis. American Journal of Psychiatry, 1969, 125, 928–936.

Smith, W. M. Observations over the lifetime of a small isolated group; structure, danger, boredom, and vision. Psychological Reports, 1966, 19, 475–514.

Spitz, H., & Sadock, B. Psychiatric training of graduate nursing students. N. Y State Journal of Medicine, June 1, 1973, pp. 1334–1338.

Tucker, D. M. Some relationships between individual and group development. Human Development, 1973, 16, 249–272.

Tuckman, B. W. Developmental sequence in small groups. Psychological Bulletin, 1965, 63(6), 384–399.

Yalom, I. The theory and practice of group psychotherapy. New York: Basic Books, 1970.

Zurcher, L. A., Jr. Stages of development in poverty program neighborhood action committees. The Journal of Applied Behavioral Science, 1969, 5(2), 223–258.

Authors

Bruce W. Tuckman was professor of education and director of the Bureau of Research and Development of the Rutgers University Graduate School of Education. He completed his masters and doctoral training in psychology at Princeton University in 1963 and, after two years at the Naval Medical Research Institute, joined the Rutgers faculty as an associate professor. He has published extensively, including two textbooks, and has developed several instruments in use today on teacher style and on personality. In 1977 he was a Fellow of the American Psychological Association and an active member of both the American Educational Research Association and Phi Delta Kappa.

Mary Ann Conover Jensen was a doctoral candidate in counseling psychology at the Rutgers University Graduate School of Education. She has been involved in counseling both residential and commuting students at a four-year college, served as a small-group facilitator for a series of "life-skills" workshops, and has conducted research in the area of small-group development. In 1977 she was an intern at a community guidance center, participating in child psychotherapy, family therapy, and individual and group counseling.

Notes

1 Tuckman, Bruce W. & Jensen, Mary Ann C. (1977). Stages of Small-Group Development Revisited. *Group & Organization Management, 2*(4), 419–427. Copyright 1977 by Sage Publications. Reprinted by permission of Sage Publications.

2 Tuckman, Bruce W. (1965). Developmental Sequence in Small Groups, *Psychological Bulletin, (63)*6, 384–399.

3 Group Facilitation: A Research and Applications Journal (3), 66–81. 2001.

4 Other studies examined but not cited because of their limited relevance to the discussion are Lundgren (1971), Liebowitz (1972), Tucker (1973), and Adelson (1975).

Chapter 1: Post-Reading Questions

After you have read the article, think back to the sorts of groups to which you have been a member—the groups you identified in the Pre-Reading Questions.

1. Did the groups of which you were a member follow the proposed model? If not, how and why do you think they differed?
2. How has reading this article influenced your anticipation of what might transpire within your group for this class?

CHAPTER 2

Stress Management

This week we start working in our small group. In order for your group to run smoothly and effectively, we need to establish and follow some basic rules.

Group Rules

Respect

Be kind and considerate. If you are doing the group work online, be *extra* kind and considerate in your postings. When people are sitting behind a computer screen they sometimes forget the rules of propriety and can easily become more brazen than they would when talking face-to-face. Be careful not to slip into that. Always conduct yourself appropriately. Remember, your professor can see everything you type!

Body language and intonation are completely lost in an online medium, so be extra careful that your meaning will not be misconstrued. What was meant as a joke or gentle teasing might be read as an accusation or an insult. Reread what you write before you hit send, and think about whether the tone of your message could be misread.

You will be asked to give each other feedback, but always do it politely and gently. You don't want to come off sounding accusatory, demeaning, or preachy. Remember that it is not always easy to hear feedback, so give it in a way that it would best be received. And if it is not received well, don't press it. Allow each person to accept or reject the feedback you have given to them.

Be nonjudgmental. We come from different walks of life with different life circumstances, and with that come different values and belief systems. Be open to the fact that not everyone sees things the way you do, and try to respect that fact. Some people are very open and discuss behaviors you do not approve of. Others are very guarded and may not be as open and forthright when talking about their issues as you might wish them to be. Recognize that everyone is doing the best they can with the interpersonal tools they have available to them at any particular moment, and try not to expect people to deal with life the same way you do.

Also keep in mind that several times throughout the semester you will be asked to rate your fellow group members, and they will be rating you in regard to your group behavior; depending on your professor, this might enter into your course grade. It makes no sense to create superfluous enemies. Be kind and friendly at all times.

No Advice

We do not tell others what to do. We do not assume that we know their life and circumstances better than they themselves, even if we have been in similar situations. We can share our own situation and what we did about it, and we can suggest options in the form of "What I might do if I were in your situation," but we never say, "This is what you *should* do." We will respect everyone's right to make their own decisions about their own life, no matter how much we agree or disagree with them.

Be Prompt and Present

A group can only function effectively if its members are present. Try to avoid unnecessary absences and always be on time. If you are part of an online group, don't wait until the end of the week to get involved in the discussion; it delays other people's ability to do the assignments and interrupts the flow of the discussion. Post your thoughts early in the week and check back periodically to respond to others.

Actively Participate

You are expected to give others feedback and help them problem-solve. Show concern and empathy for other people's issues. When you don't respond to what people write, they may think you don't care. The group will only help if all members work together!

Accept Feedback

Just as you must give others feedback, you must accept that they are tasked with giving you feedback. Try to listen with an open mind to what others have to say. The biggest block to solving any problem is a closed mind. The group is here to help. Use them!

Be Psychologists

This course is typically part of a Psychology, Counseling, or Social Work class. Most of you are considering going into the helping profession, so act like a helping professional. And by that I don't mean psychoanalyze your group members, but rather, be diplomatic. Don't pick fights and don't rise to the bait. Learn how to sidestep confrontation and say things in ways that they will be best received. If two group members don't seem to be getting along, try to facilitate an understanding and working relationship between them. Apply the tools you are reading about in your text to your own group.

Confidentiality

What goes on in group, stays in group. Do not discuss it with others or let others read the postings. It is important to build a level of trust in the group so that you all feel free to talk openly with each other and seek out support. On the other hand, while I ask you all to promise confidentiality, I cannot guarantee what your group members will or will not do. Once you reveal something personal, you risk exposure. I would hope that no one in your group would disclose anything said or written, but you must be aware of the possibility when you consider what you feel comfortable revealing. This is always the situation in group therapy. And while this is not exactly group therapy, it is a quasi-group counseling experience. Keep this in mind.

Report Problems

While it would be preferable that the group handle problems and work things out together, it is important to let the professor know if flagrant abuses are occurring. If you are in a leaderless group, s/he can step in if needed. The professor might encourage you to work it out within the group, but being aware allows him or her to intervene if necessary.

Group Assignment

After being assigned to a group, on your first meeting (or on a discussion board if you are in an online class) you should go around and introduce yourself. A useful "icebreaker" activity I like to use on the first meeting is to play two truths and a lie. List three interesting facts or anecdotes about yourself, two of which are true, and one that you just made up. Take a guess on each of your group members as to which was their lie. When all have taken a guess, let them know which one you made up. This activity will help you to get to know each other just a bit. It would also be a good idea to go over the group rules together so everyone is on the same page and understands the expectations and responsibilities of being a group member.

Individual Assignment

In the previous chapter, you wrote about the high points, low points, and turning points in your life, as well where you would like to go from here. Now think over your life in terms of where you have been and where you are going, and describe three of your most important life goals. Why are they important to you? Be prepared to discuss these goals at the next meeting of your small group.

The Weekly Reading

Pre-Reading Questions

The readings for this chapter are on stress management.

1. What physical and psychological symptoms do you typically experience when you are under stress?
2. What are your typical triggers for stress reactions?
3. How do you usually deal with stress?

READING 2

Manage Stress Before it Manages You

Laura Crooks

In today's culture we assume that living with large amounts of stress is perfectly normal. We have forgotten what it is like to be relaxed, but we don't need to live that way. Although stress is all around us, we can and should learn to manage it.

Not all stress, however, is negative. Small amounts can be beneficial. It can keep us engaged—learning something new, trying a new food, organizing a party, planning a trip. Overcoming challenges can add to our skills and confidence—repairing or building something, finding a new route to work, changing your lifestyle to manage high blood pressure or diabetes.

What Is Stress?

Stress is your body's response to your perception of an event. It is less about the specific event and more about your response and the resulting feelings of being overwhelmed and hopeless.

Although stress can involve happy events (such as getting married, buying a house, getting a promotion, having children, winning the lottery), we tend to think of stress as coming from sudden, overwhelming, catastrophic events such as losing a job, getting divorced, having an accident, experiencing a house fire. Such events are acute stressors. They occur suddenly or have a limited time span, and eventually life calms down. Our nervous system is actually designed to handle acute stresses well.

Chronic stress, on the other hand, can wear us down, makes us sick, and even has the potential to kill us. Chronic stressors are constant stressors; they include the daily occurrences that drive us crazy—traffic jams, endless phone trees, scheduled appointments running late, rude people, being understaffed, poorly run meetings, hostile coworkers, illness, lack of sleep ... and the list goes on. Ironically, our nervous system produces the same responses to these annoying daily stressors as it does for the large, acute ones. Because chronic stressors continue to occur, our bodies never fully relax.

Unfortunately, acute stress can also transform into chronic stress with the occurrence of such situations as a job loss, prolonged financial hardship, a sudden health issue turned chronic, or the burden of an adult child.

Even though our lifestyles and stressors have changed dramatically from our caveman days, our neurochemicals have not. Whether experiencing physical, mental, or emotional stress, our bodies produce the same neurochemical response. Whether the stressor is large or small, the same response is elicited.

The Nervous System

The nervous system automatically regulates our involuntary body functions, such as heart beat, digestion, and sweating—without us consciously thinking about it. The two better-known components of the nervous system are the sympathetic nervous system and parasympathetic nervous system. Less well-known is the enteric nervous system.

The sympathetic nervous system is responsible for the arousal and activation needed for "flight or fight," or emergency mode. This state is marked by increased heart rate and blood pressure and the diversion of blood away from digestion to the large muscles for running, breathing, and fighting. The neurochemicals cortisol and adrenaline are secreted to begin the process of getting your body ready to react.

The parasympathetic nervous system is the counterbalance and is responsible for the "rest and digest," nonemergency or relaxation activities. It is characterized by slower heart rate, slower breathing, stronger immune system, improved creativity, sense of calm. The ventral vagal complex falls within the parasympathetic nervous system. It is responsible for social engagement. Simply being engaged with others can be calming. Smiling and making eye contact can trigger the parasympathetic nervous system.

The enteric nervous system is an intricate and extensive network of nerves in our gastrointestinal tract, sometimes referred to as our second brain. The nerves in our gut outnumber the nerves in our skin and muscles. Most of the enteric nerves send signals to our brain as opposed to receiving information from the brain. What we "feel" in our gut is sent to our brain for translation. The "gut feeling" we sometimes experience is generally accurate and should not be summarily dismissed.

Unique to the Individual

Stress is unique. What one person finds stressful, another may not. For example consider the effect of a snowstorm. One person worries about having no power, no computer, or no television. If the outage lasts too long, the food in the refrigerator goes bad. Another person facing the same storm sees it as a gift that allows him or her to spend a few days with family playing games, reading, helping neighbors shovel driveways, and going to bed early. This person simply accepts that food may spoil.

What stresses an individual also changes over time. Stressors change day to day and year to year. Stressors today may not be a stressor in a few years. Situations that you had difficulty coping with a decade ago may not pose a problem now.

Matter of Control

Stress is inversely related to our perceived amount of control in a given situation. The less control we feel we have, the more stress we feel. Although you may have no control over specific events, you always have control over your response. Our feeling of lack of control is simply our perception of the entire event and the possible outcomes. However, at each small decision point, you have the power to make choices. When the washing machine overflows, you can rant and rave or decide to take constructive action. You can choose to resolve the washer problem now or later. You can choose to clean up the mess yourself or delegate it. You can choose to fix the washer yourself, hire a repairman, or buy a new washing machine. You can choose to take clothes to a laundromat or a neighbor, or rewear a few outfits. Breaking the event into small steps or choices allows you to feel in control and lessens your sense of being overwhelmed, thus dramatically reducing your stress level.

Effects of Stress

Stress takes a toll on us physically, mentally, and emotionally. Symptoms include:

- Increased heart rate.
- Elevated blood pressure.
- Chest pain.
- Elevated blood sugar levels.
- Changes in metabolism.
- Hormonal changes.

- Increased belly fat.
- Headaches.
- Depressed immune system.
- Muscle tension.
- Gastro-intestinal distress.
- Increased pain.
- Increased fatigue.
- Panic attacks.
- Sense of being overwhelmed.
- Sense of hopelessness.

As an underlying common denominator, chronic stress can play a role in such diseases as asthma, arthritis, multiple sclerosis, cancers, skin conditions, and heart disease. Not only can it lessen the quality of a person's life, it can lessen life expectancy itself. It can produce depression and anxiety. It is often the reason for health care visits and for employee sick leave.

Your personality may determine how you manage stress including your past experience with stress and its challenges, coping strategies or style, and social support. Some people by nature are more positive and accept change better than others. People who are more rigid and resistant to change have a more difficult time coping with stress. If you have successfully managed a stressful event in the past, then you have gained some experience and a level of confidence to handle it again. Additionally, some people have better coping mechanisms than others. People who seek out the company of friends generally fare better than those who isolate themselves and self-medicate with drugs or alcohol. People who ask for help and allow friends to support them during stressful times tend to have better outcomes.

What to Do About Stress

Stress can be managed with these five steps:

- Identify your personal symptoms.
- Identify your triggers.
- Plan ahead for possibly stressful times.
- Learn techniques that can help in the moment.
- Create a daily relaxation routine (a lifestyle that incorporates stress management).

Identify Symptoms

The first step to managing stress is to recognize what stress feels like to you. If you do not know your symptoms, ask your family or coworkers ... they know. The signs of stress can vary greatly from person to person but may include:

- Irritability/anger.
- Worry/nagging thoughts that something is not right.
- Depression.
- Panic/fear.
- Constipation, diarrhea, and/or nausea.
- Overeating (especially common with chronic stress).
- Undereating (more common in times of acute stress).
- Heaviness or uneasiness in the belly.
- Jittery feeling/difficulty focusing/indecision/forgetfulness.
- Impatience/defensiveness/rash judgments.
- Clumsiness.
- Decreased creativity/productivity.
- Muscle tension and/or increased aches and pains.
- Jaw clenching/grinding teeth.
- Increased use of cigarettes, alcohol, drugs.
- More pronounced obsessive/compulsive behaviors.
- Twitching/trembling.
- Skin disorders/itching.
- Racing/pounding heart, skipped heart beats, and/or high blood pressure.
- Chest pain and/or headache.
- Fatigue/trouble sleeping/nightmares.
- Dry mouth.
- Sweating.
- Crying.
- Labored breathing.
- Nervous laughter/nervous chatter/talking quickly.

Identify Triggers

The next step is to recognize what triggers your stress. Stress is often triggered by:

- People (specific people, certain combinations of people, crowds).
- Structured, formal events (may involve public speaking) or unstructured events such as holiday or birthday gatherings.
- Noises (loud, sudden, irregular, irritating).
- Poor health (including lack of sleep, nutritious food, exercise, personal time).
- Deadlines.
- Work/career issues involving coworkers/management, low job satisfaction, burnout, travel, and lack of resources.
- Finances.
- Changes in routine.
- Boredom/understimulation/lack of structure.
- Hunger.
- Life imbalance (unsatisfying balance between personal-professional-family time and/or living a lifestyle that does not match your beliefs and values).
- Sense of no control.
- Unrealistic fears or expectations.
- Perfectionism/all-or-nothing thinking.
- Poor time management (overcommitting yourself/putting your needs last/being available 24/7).

Stress from one area in your life can spill into other areas. For example, your elderly parent is sick. Your options are either to go to work, but then spend the day worrying; or stay home to provide care and then worry about work. A busy workload can cause stress at home. Working overtime can affect the time with your family and friends. In all, you become less available and less effective.

Stress can spiral out of control even as we think we are solving the problem. We attempt to buy more time by staying up late and getting up early. We skip workouts. We don't cook. We order takeout or visit the nearby vending machine. These behaviors leave us feeling run down and less able to handle stress. We become grouchier, less focused, and less productive. As counterintuitive as it feels, we need to step away from our stress and restore ourselves. It could be as simple as taking 20 minutes to soak in a hot bath, work a puzzle, or go for a walk.

Management Techniques

Acknowledge your feelings of stress as soon as you recognize them, then begin to actively manage them. Because stress is your response to a perceived event, you have the power to change how you react. You can teach yourself to see things differently. You can change your situation to minimize or decrease the chance of certain events happening. You can improve your coping skills. Look ahead and note when you could encounter stressful situations and plan accordingly.

Stress management needs to be fluid and dynamic. One stress-reducing technique will not work for every situation or for every person. Try several until you find a few that work. Build a toolbox of stress reducers. Some techniques may not be appropriate or available in all situations. Having only a hammer is not foolproof, because not everything in life is a nail.

Stress management is a skill. It takes commitment and practice.

Two-Minute Stress Relievers

- Sit quietly and follow your breath.
- Sit quietly and notice your heartbeat.
- Identify six things for which you are grateful.
- Watch the clouds overhead.
- Observe a candle flame.
- Watch fish swim.
- Dance or sing.
- Roll your feet over a golf ball to relieve tension.
- Listen to sounds of nature or water.
- Laugh.
- Go outside.
- Do something mindfully.
- Sip tea.
- Blow bubbles and watch them float.
- Massage your outer ear. (There are more than 100 acupressure points in your outer ear, many of which reduce pain and anxiety.)

Stress Relievers When You Have More than Two Minutes

- Yoga.
- Meditation.
- Qi gong.
- Tai chi.
- Breath work.
- Walking a labyrinth.
- Practicing mindfulness.
- Visualization or guided imagery exercises (free exercises can be found on the Internet).
- Progressive muscle relaxation.

It can be done in the moment or prophylactically. As soon as you recognize your stress level rising, do a stress management technique. In addition, take time every day for a soothing and calming strategy that restores the balance to your nervous system. It is like building a bank account of calm so that you don't explode over each stressful thing.

There are a plethora of stress management and relaxation techniques. Because it can be intimidating to suddenly sit still for 20 minutes, start small and slowly. Try relaxing for two minutes and then gradually increase your time. It is important to note that practicing relaxation is not the same as physically relaxing. You can be lying comfortably on the couch, but your mind may be whirling with worries and things to do. When practicing relaxation, you become very focused on one thing; your mind is not blank. Some people enter a relaxed state by running, painting, or playing an instrument. As you are learning to focus your mind, it is normal for your mind to wander. You can gently escort your other thoughts to the edge of your mind and refocus your thoughts.

One of the best and quickest ways to begin to relax is to stop what you are doing and take three or four slow, full-belly breaths. Breathe in through your nose, expanding your ribs and filling your chest and belly. Then slowly release all the air through your nose, feeling your abdomen and ribs retract. As you breathe imagine clean, pure, refreshing air soothing and nourishing every cell. As you breathe, you can also repeat a comforting phrase such as "I can do this," "let it go," or "this will pass."

Slow breathing can be done both in the moment and throughout every day. It is easiest to create the habit of regularly pausing to take slow, full breaths by linking it to an existing habit or something you do regularly throughout your day, such as each time you wash your hands or pass through a certain doorway. Initially you need to remind yourself to breathe, but over time it will become a habit and you will have built some stress release into each day.

Reducing Stress at Work

- Reduce the clutter in your work areas. Unnecessary items, even if beautiful or functional, can become distractions and add to chaos. Physical clutter can lead to mental clutter.
- Reduce the clutter in your head. You can remember only so many things. Free up some brain space by making notes and to-do lists.
- Try dimming the lights throughout the facility at set times for 5 to 30 minutes as a visual reminder to slow down, take a breath, and be mindful of what you are doing.
- Start each shift with a few slow, deep breaths. Make it a change-of-shift ritual.
- Begin meetings with a short relaxation exercise. When people are relaxed, they are more positive, open-minded, productive, and creative.
- Play soothing music in certain areas.
- Change the lighting if it is harsh or flickering.
- Arrange for regular onsite chair massages. Taking 10 to 15 minutes to relax and unwind can have immense payoffs in happiness, productivity, and lowering stress.
- Set a chime sound on your watch, phone, or computer. Or have the chime sound throughout the institution as a periodic reminder to slow down and breathe.
- Consider establishing or using an onsite gym. Or have your institution contribute toward a gym membership for employees. Exercise is good for your body, mind, and attitude.
- Create a relaxation room, a retreat space that can be an oasis of calm. Paint the room a wonderful color; bring in a fish tank, CDs of soothing music, a waterfall sound machine, and an easy chair. Allow employees to use the room for a few minutes when they need an escape or to calm down.
- Have nutritious food and snacks available on-site. You can also pack healthy foods. Eating refined and processed foods, whether sugary or salty, does not allow for optimal health. The metabolic byproducts of digesting poor food choices create stress and wear and tear on your body. Your body functions better when fed better foods.
- Swap out the coffee pot for a pitcher of water. You can add different fruit slices daily to flavor the water. You may feel calmer by giving up some caffeine. (If you drink a lot of caffeine, consider slowly decreasing your daily amount to minimize caffeine withdrawal.)
- Update the ventilation system.
- Ensure the work temperature is within a normal and comfortable range.
- Paint the walls nice colors.

- Add live plants where you can. People who work near potted plants report feeling happier than those who do not see green plants.
- Shift the work culture to one that supports collaboration and knowing your coworkers.
- Make eye contact and smile at each other.

Avoid, Alter, Accept, Adapt

Avoid. There may be people, places, or situations you can avoid altogether.

Alter. For those events you can't avoid, change some aspect so they are less troubling. Example: Hold meetings in a more neutral territory, schedule your most pressing tasks in the morning, or allow buffer time for unexpected delays and emergencies.

Accept. Sometimes you can find relief in just accepting that things are as they are and moving forward. You do not need to agree with or approve of the situation. Example: You are short-staffed and know it will be a horrendous day. Instead of complaining to everyone, accept that this may not be your best day and do your best.

Adapt. Consciously change your perspective of the occurrence or see it from another view point. Example: Perhaps the person who always takes a particular seat and speaks loudly has a hearing problem. Perhaps the person you interpret as being rude is very shy, or the meanest coworker is actually dealing with a serious illness or death. Assume there may be a piece of the story unknown to you that could explain some of the behaviors.

Change Your Perception

Eleanor Roosevelt stated, "A stumbling block to the pessimist is a stepping stone to the optimist." The way you mentally frame a situation creates your reaction to it. We may initially see situations as threats to stability. Accept that as one interpretation, but then look for others. View the event as a challenge to solve instead of an insurmountable obstacle to overcome. Threats feel negative, where challenges feel more positive and are open to creativity.

Change your vocabulary from "should" to "could." I should go home and mow the grass or go grocery shopping sounds more dreadful than I could mow the grass or grocery shop. "Should" suggests that we have no control. The duty has been placed upon us by an outside source, and we have no say in the matter. "Could" on the other hand says that we do have a choice. When we choose to do something, we develop a different attitude.

Not only change your perception, try letting go of some control and embracing small changes. For example, sleep on the other side of your bed, take a new route to work, read a different type of book, eat lunch with new people, brush your teeth with your opposite hand. Handling change is a skill that with practice becomes less stressful.

Stress Statistics

- More than 40 percent of employee work absences are related to stress (Bureau of Labor Statistics).
- 75 to 90 percent of health care visits are due to stress (Harvard Business Review).
- 45 percent of Americans manage their stress with alcohol, cigarettes, pills, TV, food (American Psychological Association).
- According to HeartMath, many people are so accustomed to their stress they think it is normal.
- Work-related stress causes health problems more frequently than family or financial stresses (National Institute for Occupational Safety and Health).
- Stress is the number one cause of chronic illness (American Psychological Association).
- Job stress costs American business more than $300 billion a year (American Psychological Association).
- The American Psychological Association reports that in 2012 the top five sources of stress for adults were:

    1. Job (tension with coworkers or boss, heavy workload, feeling powerless at work).
    2. Money (bills exceed income, loss of job, medical expenses).
    3. Health (chronic or terminal illness, health crises).
    4. Relationships (divorce, arguments, loneliness).
    5. Poor nutrition (caffeine, sugar, refined and processed foods).

- The life expectancy of corrections officers is 17 years less than the national average (National Institute of Corrections).
- One in three prison officers show signs of PTSD (post-traumatic stress disorder) according to an Oregon Correction Department survey. This rate of PTSD is even higher than firefighters and deployed military personnel.

Although many stress management techniques are simple, they are not always easy. The key to maximizing the results is to practice consistently. The mind and body have a powerful connection. Something as simple as changing your self-talk from negative to positive can have a profound effect.

You own your stress, but it affects everyone around you. When you arrive at work angry, your coworkers will react to you less positively. When feeling pressured, you are less likely to be polite, make eye contact, or smile. Conversely, when you manage your stress well, you arrive at work feeling upbeat and are able to work collaboratively. Your positive mood spreads and makes a better day for everyone.

Stress Toolkit

As mentioned earlier, building a stress toolkit provides you with a variety of techniques upon which to draw. Some techniques require more time than others; some are portable; some you may do only at home. Some techniques can be done in the heat of the moment; others are best accomplished when you have time and space to relax away from the issue.

How do you decide on what to place in your stress kit? If you are very tactile, have something cozy or soft to wear or touch. You may relax by rubbing a polished stone, squeezing putty, stroking your pet, or playing with a Slinky®. Kinesthetic types may prefer sitting in a swing or rocking chair, walking, knitting, or doodling. A scented candle, lotion, or essential oils can appeal to those who are olfactory-oriented. Visual people may find peace in watching fish or a lava lamp, or looking at a beautiful or meaningful picture.

Do you know what motivates you, calms you, gives you happiness? Build time for these things into your day, week, or month. A four-hour fishing trip cannot be done every day or even every week; however, you can spend a few minutes each day planning, preparing your equipment, and deciding where to go for your next fishing trip. For pleasure, you can read a book or magazine 10 minutes every day, but on the weekend reserve an hour for uninterrupted reading.

Conclusion

Chronic stress is associated with physical, mental, and emotional problems: heart disease, obesity, pain, illness, fatigue, depression, unhappiness, insomnia, and mood swings to name only a few. Stress is all around us. We can't avoid it, but we can lessen its impact. Breathing slowly and deeply is the easiest and quickest way to tame your stress. Your stress toolkit can be your unique assortment of items to use in the heat of the moment as well as daily. By having a regular relaxation practice, you can improve your health and feel better.

Tune in to Your Breath to Find Inner Peace

Meditating on Your Breathing Can Help You Feel Calm, Grounded, and Connected

Richard Miller

Your breath is one of your most powerful healing resources. For instance, deep, slow, and rhythmic whole-body breathing can reduce anxiety, fear, pain, and depression; activate your immune system; increase your ability to concentrate; and release healing and "feel-good" hormones, such as serotonin and oxytocin. Deep breathing does this by activating your parasympathetic nervous system and a rest-renew-heal response, ultimately helping you feel relaxed, in control of your experience, and connected with yourself and the world.

The practice of "breathsensing," a meditation technique that teaches you to observe, experience, and regulate your breathing patterns, offers a way to access the benefits of deep, rhythmic breathing any time you'd like. By mindfully following and observing your breath, you develop a relationship with it and start to think of it as a moment-to-moment flow of sensation, energy, and feedback. Focusing on the breath in this way helps to deactivate your brain's default network, which allows you to locate yourself in space and time. (*For more, see my Meditation column in the June issue, online at* yogajournal.com/meditationpractice.) Turning off this network enables you to release obsessive thinking; it also activates your parasympathetic nervous system, encouraging your mind and body to relax.

Once you become aware of your breathing patterns, you can start to make changes that help you stay balanced. For example, practicing exhalations that are longer than your inhalations supports your nervous system in maintaining a healthy equilibrium between your sympathetic response—a fight-flight-freeze pattern in the face of stress—and the calming parasympathetic response. This, in turn, helps you feel balanced and at ease as you move through your day; it also enhances your ability to sense and respond to the critical information your body is constantly sending you.

Attuning to your breath can help you recognize subtle sensations of irritation, fatigue, and more that may be early-warning signs that you need to set a boundary with something or someone, or that you need to take time to rest, change your diet, or take actions to reduce your stress.

Experience Breathsensing

Introduce breathsensing during the first several minutes of your daily meditation practice. Start with Practice 1, below; as you feel calmer and more comfortable, move on to the more advanced second and third practices. Then, interweave breathsensing into your daily life by remembering to tune in to your breathing patterns throughout the day. If you wish, set your watch or phone to beep at regular intervals, such as every hour, as a reminder to stop whatever you're doing and check that your exhalation is smooth, steady, and slightly longer than your inhalation.

Practice 1: Observe Your Inhalations and Exhalations

During the following practice, note the natural flow of your inhalations and exhalations, and the feelings of well-being that naturally arise. Rather than thinking about your breath, be fully engaged with the sensation of each breath.

Sit or lie in a comfortable position. With your eyes open or closed, scan your body and note any unnecessary tension. Bring attention to the sensation of your breath. Without thinking, simply note and feel the sensation of each inhalation and exhalation. During inhalation, note your belly gently expanding; during exhalation, sense it gently releasing. Feel yourself settling, relaxing, and letting go with each breath. When your mind wanders, gently and nonjudgmentally bring it back to noting and feeling the breath-driven expansion and release of your belly.

Welcome and nourish the feelings of well-being, ease, peace, and groundedness that naturally arise with each breath. Remain here as long as you feel comfortable, being at ease with each breath.

When you're ready, allow your eyes to open and close several times as you return to a wide-awake state of mind and body.

Practice 2: Observe Flows of Sensation and Energy

Stress can disconnect you from feeling the natural flow of the life force within your body that supports health, harmony, and well-being. However, the meditative practices of breathsensing can help you stay connected to it. Set aside 10 minutes at the beginning of your daily meditation for the following practice, which will help you experience your breath as a flow of sensation and energy.

Sit or lie in a comfortable position. With your eyes open or closed, scan your body and note any unnecessary tension. Bring your attention to your breath. During inhalation and exhalation, note your belly gently expanding and releasing. Feel yourself settling, relaxing, and letting go with each breath.

With each breath, note a circulating current of sensation and energy flowing throughout your body: With each inhalation, sensation and energy flow down the front of your body, from head to feet. With each exhalation, sensation and energy flow up the back of your body, from feet to head.

As the sensation and energy continue to circulate, allow every cell in your body to welcome feelings of ease and well-being.

When you're ready, allow your eyes to open and close several times as you return to a wide-awake state of mind and body.

Practice 3: Count Your Breaths

You can also practice breathsensing by counting your breaths—a practice that's useful in developing focused attention and concentration. To succeed at anything, be it meditation, a work-related task, getting a good night's sleep, or developing a sense of well-being, you need to maintain single-pointed focus for the duration necessary to accomplish your goal. Breath counting helps strengthen this ability for as long as a task needs your complete attention.

When counting breaths, you'll find yourself distracted by random thoughts. When this occurs, gently and nonjudgmentally refocus and begin counting again. Each time you refocus, you're strengthening your ability to remain undistracted during breath counting, as well as in your daily life. At first, breath counting can feel challenging, like simultaneously trying to rub your stomach and pat your head. I encourage you to patiently continue practicing; in time, you'll discover the physical, mental, and spiritual benefits that come as a result of doing this simple yet powerful practice.

Sit or lie in a comfortable position. With your eyes open or closed, scan your body and note any unnecessary tension. Bring your attention to your breath while noting the natural flow of sensation. Let your belly expand as air flows in, and release as air flows out. As you breathe, count each breath from 1 to 11 like so: Inhaling, belly expanding 1; exhaling, belly releasing 1. Inhaling, belly expanding 2; exhaling, belly releasing 2. And so on.

When you recognize that you've become distracted, gently and nonjudgmentally bring your attention back to your breath, starting your counting again at 1. Continue counting while noting tension throughout your body.

When you're ready, allow your eyes to open and close several times, returning to a wide-awake state of mind and body.

Move Forward

How do your body and mind feel at the end of breathsensing? I think you'll be amazed how only a few minutes of breathsensing can leave you feeling grounded and refreshed—and able to respond to each moment, no matter what your situation. Can you imagine how you might use these practices on the fly, during your daily life? Make it your intention to practice breathsensing whenever you feel the need to relax, rest, and renew. As you engage these meditative practices, you're laying the foundation that will enable you to thrive. Be aware that as you practice breathsensing, it's natural to encounter the emotions that are present in your body. Tune in to the November issue, in which I'll focus on how to respond to these emotions with actions that empower you to feel in harmony, both with yourself and the world around you.

Chapter 2: Post-Reading Questions

1. Did you find any new ideas for how to deal with stress in the Crooks article? Which of the ideas listed did you like best and why? Which ones did you like least and why?
2. Do the breathing exercise outlined in the Miller article. How did you feel afterwards? Breathing and meditation exercises often take time to be effective (practice makes perfect in all things!), so if you did not obtain the immediate results you had hoped for, don't give up. Keep practicing!

CHAPTER 3

Time Management

In this chapter, we will go over the steps to problem-solving. These are the steps you will follow in your small group when working on the issue you will eventually select. Hopefully you will not just find them useful in this group but will also find that it is a useful format to use on all your issues in the future.

Steps to Problem-Solving

Before you can solve a difficult problem, it helps to systematically take it through several steps. These steps have been developed through research and demonstrated to be effective. During this course you will be asked to take one of your issues/problems/challenges through these steps. There might be a tendency to rush through them thinking "Yeah, yeah, I know all that," but to truly be effective, you have to take them slowly and make sure you have totally and completely explored each one. Thus, we will be taking them at the rate of about one step per week. But first, I want to give you an overview so you will know where we are headed.

We use the acronym "ICECRM" to help you remember the steps.

(I) Identify the Problem

This might seem silly. Many people will say, "I know what the problem is. What I don't know is the solution!" But the fact is, we are often focusing on the wrong part of the problem, which makes finding a solution more difficult. Take for example a person who says, "I can't figure out what to major in." On further inquiry we might learn that he is thinking about going into political science, but his father really wants him to do pre-med and become a doctor. The real problem, then, is not what to major in, but rather whose life is he going to lead. Once he works out his issues with his father, the major will probably fall into place.

After you have identified your life goals, we will ask you about any obstacles or challenges that might interfere with you achieving your goals. This is part of identifying the problem. We will ask you to share your challenge statements (the issue you would like to work on/overcome) with your small group. They should ask you questions to help determine if you are focused on the real problem or if there are underlying issues that should be dealt with first. For instance, one person's challenge statement might read something like: "I want to reduce my tendency to procrastinate." The immediate question that should come to mind is "Why do you procrastinate?" Solving the problem successfully really depends on knowing what we're up against.

Another issue in identifying the problem is limiting your options. For instance, the person struggling with whether to major in political science or pre-med has already limited his options. A better question than "Should I do A or B?" would be "What should I do?" or, in this case, "What should I major in?" Sometimes there are many other options that might better resolve the issue than the ones you have been considering. In this course we don't want you to limit your options. So in your challenge statements don't let your group mates get away with option-limiting statements! Your challenge statements should be open ended, not multiple choice.

Finally, think about whether you can make progress on your challenge in one semester. The journey of a thousand miles begins with one step, and you will be more successful if you focus on your steps rather than on the end point. If you have a lofty goal that will take years to achieve, think about what you could achieve in one semester to help move you toward that bigger goal; focus on that. Success is increased and frustration decreased when we focus on shorter term goals.

In each of these things (focus on the real problem, don't limit your options, have short-term goals) ask your group mates if they think you are doing these things, and give them feedback on how well their challenge statements align with these principles.

(C) Create Alternatives

Having resisted the temptation to limit your options in the previous step, you are now ready to move on to the next step: brainstorming for alternative potential solutions. The key here is to be totally open-minded. Nothing should be rejected at this step. One of the biggest resistances to problem-solving is our tendency to say, "I could never do that!" or "That would never work!" Our tendency to shoot ideas down before they're even fully developed blocks us from ever trying anything new (and we already know the old attempted solutions didn't work). The key is to get out of that negativity, and to do that, it helps to put down some utterly ridiculous ideas! Have fun with this step. Be silly. Amazing breakthroughs have come from the wildest of ideas. You can't think out of the box if you try too hard to be realistic. We'll worry about being realistic and practical at a later step. For right now, it is anything goes! So do not reject anything that someone suggests for your list of alternatives, and don't be afraid to give outlandish ideas to others (or yourself).

(E) Evaluate Alternatives

OK, here is the step where we begin to get more practical and realistic. But to make sure we don't "throw out the baby with the bathwater," we need to evaluate both the good and the bad of each idea. Once we have separated this out, we might see ways to maximize the positive aspects while minimizing the negative aspects. Thus, what first seemed like a silly idea might be transformed into a dynamite idea! Also, by formally separating out the good from the bad of each idea, we will be developing our critical thinking skills, which are essential to successful problem-solving. We'll talk more about critical thinking in the next chapter, but at this point, let's just say that critical thinking involves being willing to consider all competing ideas with an open mind while at the same time being skeptical enough to not accept anything without thorough examination. It is tough to do both at the same time, so first we'll be completely open-minded, and then we will be super skeptical.

Once we have thoroughly examined the pros and cons of each potential solution, we will look for a completely new idea that builds on and combines the best parts of the preceding ideas while eliminating, or at least minimizing, their negatives.

(C) Construct a Plan

Once we have identified and developed a potential solution that we would like to put to the test, we need to start working it. That means figuring out the first step and taking it. We need a game plan and it needs to be specific. Instead of saying, "I am going to work on being more assertive," one might choose a task such as "I am going to the gym this week and strike up a conversation with a perfect stranger." It is important to be very concrete and specific. State exactly what you are going to do with whom, when, where, and how long. Don't give yourself any wiggle room to "sort of" do it, and don't allow your group mates to give themselves any wiggle room either. The best plans are specific and achievable. Take baby steps. If you are working on your fear of water, your task should be to stick your toe in the pool, not to jump into the deep end without a life preserver. Don't allow your group mates to get in over their heads. Being successful is more important than mastering the problem on your first outing.

(R) Run the Plan

The next step is to do the thing you said you would do. We make tons of New Year's resolutions each year that we never put into action. Your group mates will be wanting to hear how it went, so don't procrastinate (especially if eliminating procrastination is your challenge!) and don't let excuses get in your way. Just do it! Do it quickly. Do it the way you said you would do it. Failing IS acceptable. Not trying is not!

(M) Measure Your Success

After you have run your plan, you will report back to the group about how it went. If it went great, congratulations! If it went sort of OK, then semi-congratulations. If it was a complete disaster, do not despair. The greatest home-run hitters first had to strike out before they became great. Every toddler falls when taking their first steps, but they pull themselves up and try again. For us, rather than just going out and falling on our face again (which will eventually lead to success, but there might be less painful ways), we will evaluate what happened. Why were we not successful? Was the task too big? Were there unforeseen circumstances that interfered? By identifying the blocks to success, we can formulate a new plan that addresses those blocks and helps to better insure success the next time. Help your group mates identify those blocks and write a new plan that increases the likelihood for success next week. They will re-run the plan and report back again.

If you were successful on the first try, then maybe you need to take a bigger step, or maybe you just need to do the same thing again until you start to feel more comfortable doing it. Each case is different. Let your group mates help you decide what to do next.

So that's it in a nutshell. ICECRM

Hopefully, by now you are looking forward to implementing these steps in your own life!

Group Assignment

In this week's small group discussion, please share your life chart and your life goals (created in your previous individual assignments) with your small group members and learn about theirs. Ask questions, find out more about your group mates, and offer support and encouragement. Feel free to show empathy by discussing similar experiences you might have had, but do not attempt to give any advice or tell people what they should or shouldn't be doing. We are information seeking at this point, not problem-solving. Maintain an accepting and nonjudgmental tone and attitude.

Individual Assignment

What challenges or obstacles might interfere with your ability to meet any and all of the life goals that you previously identified and discussed with your group? Select one of the challenges or obstacles identified (in the previous question) that you would like to work on or overcome this semester and re-write it in the form of a specific problem statement to be solved. Be prepared to discuss it at the next meeting of your small group.

The Weekly Reading

Pre-Reading Questions

The reading for this chapter is on time management—a skill which we all could probably afford to improve.

1. What are your typical time wasters?
2. What strategies do you use to save time?
3. Do you have any time management tricks?

READING 4

Optimize Your Time Management

Gary R. Martin

When seasoned professionals review this book, they frequently comment that even *they* found this section helpful. Personal productivity and efficiency have become such strong sciences that most people can benefit by at least reviewing the following principles occasionally. Good time management boils down largely to working smart. The most productive people operate under the strictest codes of setting priorities and living by them. They put one hundred percent into everything they do, whether it is solving a problem at work, training at the gym, or taking a break. "Focus" is their middle name. They strive for balance. And they set their sights on outcomes.

Living by priorities inherently means learning to say "no" to countless requests. **To say 'yes' to one thing is to say 'no' to another**. (Think about it.) Or another way to view this is, "To 'stretch yourself too thin' is to compromise your priorities." Nobody likes to disappoint other people by having to say no, but again, good time managers will protect their higher priorities.

The science of Time Management consists predominantly of countless specific tips. Consequently, I shall present the majority of this chapter in the form of bullets and lists. Remember that you are an individual; you are unique. You can learn from others, but you should do what works best for you.

Time Wasters and Savers

The following is a list of some of the most common Time Wasters and Time Savers suggested by a cross-section of business executives.

Time Wasters

1. Unnecessary paperwork
2. Clutter
3. Excessive record-keeping
4. Unclear communication
5. Indecisiveness
6. Poorly planned meetings
7. Telephone calls that last too long
8. Mental blocks
9. Perfectionism
10. Backlogs of unfinished projects

Time Savers

1. Goal setting and goal making, as well as keeping deadlines
2. Setting priorities for tasks, goals, and projects
3. Saying no to protect and preserve your priorities
4. Establishing routines
5. Delegating responsibility
6. Segmenting (breaking up into manageable parts) large tasks
7. Concentrating on one thing at a time
8. Keeping a follow-up file and referring to it on a regular basis

Time Management: A Collection of Individual Responses

I collect responses from people to the question, "What are your Time Management tricks?" While I do not necessarily subscribe to all of the following, these are the ones I find at least bear reporting.

1 I listen to NPR (National Public Radio) when I am driving, and I listen to audiobooks when I am exercising.

2 I count all my time as on-time and try to get satisfaction (not necessarily accomplishment) out of every minute.

3 I try to enjoy whatever I am doing.

4 I am a perennial optimist.

5 I build on successes.

6 I don't waste time regretting my failures.

7 I don't waste my time feeling guilty about what I don't do.

8 I remind myself: There is always enough time for the important things. If it is important, I will make the time to do it.

9 I get up at 5 a.m. during the week (and I go to bed early).

10 "To be early is to be on time. To be on time is to be late."

11 I don't carve my to-do list in stone—I try to remain flexible.

12 I have a light lunch so I don't get sleepy in the afternoon.

13 I don't read newspapers or magazines very thoroughly.

14 I skim books quickly looking for ideas.

15 I don't own a television set.

16 I have my home close to my office.

17 I examine old habits for possible elimination or streamlining.

18 I have given up forever all waiting time. If I have to wait, I consider it a gift of time to relax, plan, or do something I would not otherwise have done.

19 I keep my watch three minutes fast to get a head start on everything.

20 I jot down notes on my smart phone when I think of things important to remember.

21 I revise my lifetime goal list once a month.

22 I review my lifetime goal list every day and identify activities to do each day to further my goals.

23 I put signs in my office reminding me of my goals.

24 I keep my long-term goals in mind even while doing the smallest task.

25 I always plan first thing in the morning and set priorities for the day.

26 I schedule actual appointments in my calendar for working on specific assignments.

27 I keep a list of specific items to be done each day, arrange them in priority order, and then do my best to get the important ones done as soon as possible.

28 I schedule my time months in advance in such a way that each month offers variety and balance, as well as open time reserved for hot projects.

29 I give myself time off and special rewards when I have done the important things.

30 I do first things first.

31 I work smarter rather than harder.

32 I try to do only A's, never B's or C's.

33 I have confidence in my judgment of priorities and stick to them in spite of difficulties.

34 I ask myself, "Would anything terrible happen if I didn't do this priority item?" If the answer is no, I don't do it.

35 If I seem to procrastinate, I ask myself, "What am I avoiding?" Then I try to confront that thing head-on.

36 I always use the 80/20 rule. (Most people spend eighty percent of their time doing low-priority items, and twenty percent doing high-priority items. The 80/20 rule reverses this.)

37 I start with the most profitable parts of large projects and often find it not necessary to do the rest.

38 I cut off nonproductive activities as quickly as possible.

39 I give myself enough time to concentrate on high-priority items.

40 I have developed the ability to concentrate well for long stretches of time, sometimes with the aid of coffee. (Starbucks employees know my name.)

41 I concentrate on one thing at a time.

42 I focus my efforts on items that will have the best long-term benefits.

43 I keep pushing, and am persistent when I sense I have a winner.

44 I have trained myself to go down my to-do list without skipping over the difficult items.

45 I do much of my thinking on paper.

46 I do work alone creatively in the morning and use the afternoon for meetings, if necessary.

47 I set deadlines for others and myself.

48 I try to listen actively in every discussion.

49 I try not to waste other people's time (unless it is something that really matters to me).

50 I delegate everything I possibly can to others.

51 I make use of specialists to help me with special problems.

52 I have someone screen my email and phone calls and handle all routine matters.

53 I generate as little paperwork as possible and throw away anything I possibly can.

54 I handle each piece of paper only once.

55 I keep my desktop cleared for action, and put the most important thing in the center of my desk.

56 I have a place for everything (so I waste as little time as possible looking for things).

57 I try not to think of work on weekends.

58 I relax and do nothing rather frequently.

59 I recognize that inevitably some of my time will be spent on activities outside my control and don't fret about it.

60 I keep small talk to a minimum during work hours.

61 I look for action steps to be taken now to further my goals.

62 I am continually asking myself, "What is the best use of my time right now?"

63 I use the Swiss cheese method when I am avoiding something, by breaking it into smaller tasks and just doing one of the smaller tasks for fifteen minutes.

64 I practice the art of intelligent neglect, eliminating trivial tasks from my life as much as possible.

65 I look ahead in my month and try to anticipate what is going to happen so I can better schedule my time.

66 I manage the amount of time I spend in meetings. I find out which ones are mandatory or really important. I sometimes skip meetings if it might be more valuable to complete an assignment.

67 I note deadlines in my calendar, and I add a second note a few days before the deadline reminding me it's coming.

68 I try to be an optimist and seek out the good in my life.

69 I take breaks as reward for work. Not only are the breaks good motivation to help me complete something, I also am more refreshed to tackle the next bit of work after a break.

Key Points from Various Studies on Time Management

1. Getting less than eight hours of rest seriously compromises our ability to concentrate and solve problems.
2. Creativity rarely strikes in a flash, but more typically results from steady cogitation.
3. Multitasking, for all its seeming efficiency, can exact a heavy toll on the quality of our output.
4. Daily meditation physically transforms the cerebral cortex.
5. Physical exercise may be as important as mental gymnastics in keeping Alzheimer's disease at bay.
6. The human brain retains an astonishing degree of plasticity and capacity for learning throughout life. Doesn't peak until midlife.
7. Don't stress too much; relaxation is a balm for the overtaxed brain.
8. Dangerous attitudes:
   a. "I never do just two things at once if I can possibly do four or five."
   b. "I feel anxious when my in-box is full; but I feel no better when it is empty."
9. Dr. Edward Hallowell, a psychiatrist in Sudbury, Massachusetts, and author of best-selling books, including *Driven to Distraction and Overbooked and About to Snap: Strategies for Coping in a World Gone ADD.*

a. Has seen a tenfold rise in the number of patients showing up with symptoms that closely resemble those of attention-deficit disorder (ADD), but of a work-induced variety. Attributes this to attempts by working professionals to multitask.
   i. More irritable.
   ii. Productivity declining.
   iii. Couldn't get organized.
   iv. Making decisions in black-and-white, shoot-from-the-hip ways due to pressure to get things done quickly.
   v. Leads to distractibility, impulsiveness and haste, guilt, and inadequacy.
b. Recommendations
   i. Prioritize ruthlessly.
   ii. Cultivate the lilies or the things that fulfill you.
   iii. Cut the leeches, those that deplete you.
   iv. Allot thirty minutes a day for thinking, relaxing or meditating.
   v. Get significant doses of "Vitamin C": the live Connection to other people.

10 Multitasker's Glossary

a. Screen sucking—Wasting time online long after you have finished what you signed on to do.
b. Frazzing—Frantic, ineffective multitasking, typically with the delusion that you are getting a lot done.
c. Pizzled—How you feel when someone you're with pulls out a cell phone and uses it without an explanation or apology. (Cross between p____off and puzzled.)
d. Doomdart—The internal distraction of a forgotten task that pops into your mind when you are doing something else. A side effect of frazzing.

11 Report entitled *The Cost of Not Paying Attn.* (Basex, an information-technology research firm in NY)

a. Interruptions now consume an average of 2.1 hours a day, or 28% of the workday.
b. This includes the recovery time associated with getting back on task.
c. Workplace interruptions cost the U.S. economy $588 billion per year.
d. Biggest causes of interruptions in descending order
   i. Colleague stops by
   ii. Being called away from the desk
   iii. Arrival of new email: Fifty-five percent of workers open email immediately or shortly after it arrives, no matter how busy they are. Most people don't even think about turning off the dinger.
   iv. Switching to another task on the computer
   v. Phone call

12 Research shows breakfast provides the day's most vital brain food.

13 Keep cell phones and iPods off or away when in transit so you can use the downtime for thinking.

14 How racehorses win: They come out of gate with blinders on and go for the finish line. They don't care what the competition is doing.

15 Some companies give employees *Do not interrupt* signs to put up as needed.

16 Scientists used to think intellectual power peaked at age forty. Hooey!

   a. Brain brings new cognitive systems online and cross-indexes existing ones as you get older.
   b. Short- and long-term memory may not be as strong, but you manage info and parse meanings better.
   c. Women's highest inductive reasoning abilities range from ages forty to early sixties. (Presumably similar for men?)

17 Athlete Paradigm

   a. Athletes talk a lot about getting in and staying in the zone.
      i. Magical place where mind and body work in perfect synch and movements seem to flow without conscious effort.
      ii. Athletic nirvana.
   b. Set-backs (From Michael Johnson—Olympic sprinter)
      i. "If you have disappointments, you need to ask yourself, 'Why did I not perform well today? Was it the preparation? A mistake in execution?' Then you need to get yourself at peace with that situation."
      ii. "Achieving that peace is the key to avoiding a full-fledged slump—that downward spiral that only gets worse the harder you try."
   c. Training is about strengthening the mind–body connection. Athletes need to train their mind with the same discipline that they train their bodies.
   d. One way experts help athletes control the jitters is by teaching them to take command of the interior monologues that psychologists call self-talk.
      i. This is the endless conversation that we all have with ourselves, processing events as they pass before our eyes.
      ii. The average person speaks to himself at a rate of 300–1,000 words a minute.
      iii. You must replace any negative self-talk with positive self-talk.
   e. The first thing an athlete has to realize is that he or she always in control.

18 Sleeping your way to the top

a. Eight hours/night; nine for adolescents; seventy-one percent of American adults and eighty-five percent of teens do not get this.
b. Purpose is more to rest the mind than the body.
c. Helps consolidate memory, improve judgment, promote learning and concentration, boost mood, speed reaction time and sharpen problem-solving and accuracy.
d. Wake up each day at the same time; but if you need extra rest, sleep late on Saturday rather than Sunday, because that way the work week won't start with Monday morning blues.
e. Avoid late-night snacks and alcohol, since digestion prevents quality rest.
f. Exercising early in the morning increases the risk of injury since the body is not warmed up and is less coordinated; too late at night may keep you from falling asleep quickly.

19 Creativity

a. Many people believe creativity comes in a sudden moment of insight and that this magical burst of an idea is a different mental process from everyday thinking. Not true. Just uses same building blocks you use every day—like when you figure out a way around a traffic jam.
b. Three B's—bathtub, bed, and bus—places where ideas have emerged. When we take time off from working on a problem, and we change what we're doing and our context, that can activate different areas of our brain. If the answer is not in the part of the brain we were using, it might be in another.
c. People who are creative have tons of ideas, many of them bad. But even bad ideas can be useful.
d. Take risks and expect to make lots of mistakes. Creativity is a numbers game. Work hard and take frequent breaks, but stay with it over time. Do what you love, because creative breakthroughs take years of hard work.
e. Develop a network of colleagues.
f. Schedule time for freewheeling.
g. Forget romantic myths that creativity is all about being artsy and gifted.
h. Other myths. Creative people
    i. get a great idea in a flash and then execute it
    ii. always have great ideas
    iii. have radical new ideas that come out of nowhere
    iv. blindly ignore convention because their inspiration springs full-blown from their subconscious

20 Meditation

a. Scientists find that meditation not only reduces stress but also reshapes the brain.
b. Some evidence that the daily practice of meditation increases attention span, sharpens focus, and improves memory.
c. Seems to help regulate emotions, which in turn helps people get along—emotional intelligence.

21 Caffeine

a. Makes more alert, focused, quick-witted, clever. Enhances short-term memory. Improves reaction time and mental acuity. (Wellness Letter, 2013)
b. Appears to have some protective effect against liver damage, Parkinson's disease, diabetes, Alzheimer's, gallstones, depression, and maybe even some forms of cancer.
c. Only proven medical down side appears to be a temporary elevation in blood pressure, which is a problem only if you already suffer from hypertension. Small evidence also for miscarriage and benign breast cysts, but this is highly controversial.
d. If well rested, tends to improve rudimentary brain functions, like keeping your attention focused on boring, repetitive tasks for long periods. Also tends to improve mood, and makes people feel more energetic.
e. When sleep-deprived and you take caffeine, pretty much anything you measure will improve: reaction time, vigilance, attention, logical reasoning, most of the complex functions you associate with intelligence (remember that most Americans are sleep-deprived most of the time) (*Time* 2006).

Striking A Balance Between Your Professional and Personal Goals

This may be the most important subject in this book. The old question of, "Are you living to work or working to live?" depicts the range in values and attitudes different individuals live out. Are you working as hard as you should to increase your job and financial security? Are you taking good care of your body? Are you being a good family member and friend? Are you making a positive difference in the world? And are you having some fun along the way? Senior citizens frequently reflect back on their lives with such comments as wishing they could do it again, so that they could put *more* time in one of these areas, or *less* in another. So how do you look at the big picture to set, and live out, your priorities? This is called work–life balance.

Jack Welch, former CEO for General Electric (GE) wrote a book called *Winning*, in which he makes three suggestions regarding work–life balance:

1. Focus on the task at hand. If you are at work, focus on your work, and do not do such personal things as plan family vacations. When you are home, focus on your family or personal things. Do not conduct business phone calls in the middle of your golf game.
2. Say no to opportunities outside your work–life plan. If your plan calls for taking your spouse out for dinner every Tuesday evening, do not allow other opportunities that may arise to challenge this commitment.
3. Take care of yourself, including rest, exercise, and fun. (2007)

A healthy work–life balance optimizes your overall fulfillment. It also contributes immediately to your productivity.

So after determining the broader parameters for yourself, such as how many hours you should work each week, a subsequent important key is learning to make the best possible use of the time that is left over. Many students work so hard during their school years that they do not feel like they have very much free time. And it is sort of chopped up, rather than existing in solid blocks of time. Working professionals have lives that are quite different from the world of school. Their lives tend to revolve around an eight- to nine-hour workday, with evenings and weekends off. More dedicated employees may spend much more time on work, leaving that much less time available in the balance. Regardless, how do you get the most of this remaining leisure time?

Your leisure time presents an invaluable opportunity for personal growth, increased health, and overall happiness and fulfillment. You should approach the question of how to use your spare time like you'd approach any topic of importance in your life. That means taking the time to consider what you'd like to do in a constructive manner. Ask yourself:

> What are the other priorities in my life outside of my career? What would I like to get out of my leisure time?

Some obvious examples are regular physical conditioning, pleasure reading, intellectual stimulation, and maintaining personal relationships with family and friends.

Sit down and think about it. Brainstorm on a sheet of paper some of the ideas that come to mind. Maybe even ask some friends what they do with their leisure time that is important to them. Think about which ones are realistic and affordable. Whatever you come up with, write it down someplace. If you keep any kind of a personal journal, that might be a good place to record it. If your goals can be measurable, you will enjoy looking back over your journal entries over time to see how you did.

Intellectual Ideas for Your Spare Time

1 Read or at least skim:
   a. Job-related texts or manuals
   b. Professional journals
   c. Periodicals such as the *Wall Street Journal*, *Newsweek*, or your local daily newspaper

2 Take an evening class
   a. On financial planning
   b. Related to your job
   c. About something that just interests you

3 Look into graduate programs

4 Tutor local high school students

5 Learn a new language

6 Join a professional society/organization

7 Professional registration preparation (e.g., EIT—Engineering in Training exam)

8 Write research paper on a subject of interest

9 Travel more

Be interesting!

In order to be interesting, you have to do interesting things. You only go around once in life, so take advantage of it. Travel to other countries. Try different parties. Accept unique challenges. Don't do anything that is dangerous, but the only way you can have interesting things to share at Thanksgiving is if you do things out of the ordinary. So don't be boring—be interesting!

This is the shortest chapter in the book, but again, it may be the most important. The level of success you attain in your career will be a function of your

- Physical well-being
- Mental or emotional health
- Intellectual strength

Body, soul, and mind. These three areas will *rely* on good use of your non-working hours. Get good exercise and rest on top of a sensible diet. Find means for personal fulfillment. And stretch your mind through reading and other forms of mental exercise and stimulation. You will see the pay-off.

Time Management Self-Analysis (10 Minutes)

The following questions are designed to help you determine how strong your Time Management skills are. Rate each of the questions below according to the following scale:

0 This is not true for me
1 This is rarely true for me
2 This is seldom true for me
3 This is somewhat true for me
4 This is usually very true for me
5 This is absolutely true for me

**Place an X in the box that best corresponds to you.

		0	1	2	3	4	5
1.	I take time each morning before I start the day to plan each day's activities and consider my priorities.						
2.	I place myself in a situation conducive to creativity every day.						
3.	I am an optimist.						
4.	I spend an average of four hours/week improving my capabilities.						
5.	I do what the boss says to do first.						
6.	It is almost impossible to interrupt me when I am in the middle of focusing on a serious project.						
7.	I control my time all day every day (as opposed to letting circumstances and other people control it).						
8.	I tackle and complete the most important tasks first, and/or during the best part of my working day. (Be honest.)						
9.	I write everything down that I am responsible for remembering to do. (This includes major assignments from the boss, as well as minor types of tasks, such as when a colleague requests a copy of something I have. It also includes personal kinds of things such as getting the dog updated on his vaccines).						
10.	I set deadlines for myself and for the people who report to me.						
11.	I make minor decisions quickly.						
12.	I delegate jobs to others when practical.						

		0	1	2	3	4	5
13.	I make constructive use of my commute time and the time I spend waiting for appointments.						
14.	I write down a set of short-term and long-term goals for my life at least once a year.						
15.	I have the courage to be effective and to say no when appropriate.						
16.	I understand the meaning of "Work smarter, not harder" and how to implement this concept.						
17.	I know the difference between effectiveness and efficiency and, given a choice, which one is more important.						
18.	I approach every major project by establishing goals and setting objectives.						
19.	I take the time to analyze my job and tasks to determine how I can combine things or eliminate things to be more effective.						
20.	I do work that demands more creativity during those times when I will be disturbed the least and when I have the most energy.						
21.	I know my major time-wasters and have some ideas of how to overcome them.						
22.	I handle each piece of paper only once.						
23.	I communicate clearly. This includes proof-reading everything I send out, including emails. I rehearse oral presentations.						
24.	I do a good job of thinking out issues and questions before presenting them to anybody.						
25.	I take time with my people to train, understand, commit, encourage, appreciate, assist, involve, and promote.						
26.	I know how to plan and conduct, as well as follow up on effective meetings. I always prepare agendas.						
27.	I focus on one task at a time.						
28.	My desk and work area are neat and orderly all day, every day.						
29.	I spend some time in some form of meditation each day.						
30.	I know how to get out of slumps.						
31.	I am familiar with the effects of caffeine and use it to my greatest personal advantage.						
32.	I live a balanced life.						
33.	I get enough rest. (Most people need about eight hours of sleep each night.)						
34.	I do not think about work responsibilities when I am doing non-work kinds of things, such as spending time with my family or playing tennis.						

(Continued)

		0	1	2	3	4	5
35.	I enjoy a reasonable amount of leisure or down time for relaxing and doing unimportant things.						
36.	I am a good family member (e.g., as a wife/husband, mother/father, daughter/son).						
37.	I get enough physical exercise each week. (The CDC says that you need a minimum of 150 minutes of elevated heart rate each week.)						
38.	I eat a balanced diet every day.						
39.	I have a healthy breakfast every morning.						
40.	I am not a Time Management nut.						

Totals						
	x0	x1	x2	x3	x4	x5
equals						

Now total up all the points______

Scoring: How Good of A Time Manager Are You?

200–150 Points:	Time Management Expert
149–100 Points:	Improvement Warranted
99–50 Points:	A Good Start
49–0 Points:	You Need Lots of Help!

Weekly Time Management Matrix

You can use this for planning some structure in your week such as exercise, meditation, and personal development.

	MONDAY	TUESDAY	WEDNESDAY	THURSDAY	FRIDAY	SATURDAY	SUNDAY
6:00–7:00							
7:00–8:00							
8:00–9:00							
9:00–10:00							
10:00–11:00							
11:00–12:00							
12:00–1:00							
1:00–2:00							
2:00–3:00							
3:00–4:00							
4:00–5:00							
5:00–6:00							
6:00–7:00							
7:00–8:00							
8:00–9:00							
9:00–10:00							
10:00–11:00							
11:00–12:00							
12:00–1:00							
1:00–2:00							
2:00–3:00							
3:00–4:00							
4:00–5:00							
5:00–6:00							

Chapter 3: Post-Reading Questions

1. What new strategies for time management in this article most intrigued or inspired you? Why?
2. How likely are you to implement any of them?
3. Take the Time Management Self-Analysis Survey. How did you score? Were you surprised by the results?

CHAPTER 4

Procrastination

Critical Thinking

Critical Thinking and Discussion

What Is Critical Thinking?

People throw around the term critical thinking rather loosely and they mean different things. For many, it means the ability to be critical—to criticize, to challenge, and to discredit. That can be one aspect, but some people can be very critical without being critical thinkers. Some professors (we won't mention any names) think being critical means to think like they do. They hold certain opinions as to what is right and wrong with the theories and paradigms within their discipline. If you agree with them, clearly you are thinking critically and effectively. If you don't agree with them, then clearly you are deluded and unable to distinguish fact from fiction. This is probably not the best definition.

We operationalize our definition of critical thinking as the use of two somewhat opposing tendencies: open-mindedness and skepticism. Being open-minded to new and different ideas without a healthy dose of skepticism can result in one being naïve, gullible, and generally wishy-washy. Being overly skeptical without open-mindedness can result in one being dogmatic, argumentative, and unable to learn. We need to do both.

Open-Mindedness

Being open-minded means being willing to consider new ideas, even, and especially, ideas that might challenge the way you traditionally think and feel on a particular issue. This is partly a personality trait. Some of us are just more open to new experiences and ideas, and others prefer the comfort of familiarity and don't like to be challenged. However, just because it is part of our personality (and may have been for many years) doesn't mean it can't be changed. One of the things I would like you to do in this course is try to be more open-minded. But to do this, first you have to value it. You have to want to be more open-minded. Why should you want it? Because as we discussed in the previous module, you cannot find new solutions to complex life challenges if you are not willing to think out of the box. Many people are "help-rejecting complainers." They go on and on about all their unsolvable problems, sounding desperate for help, but whenever anyone does give them suggestions, they immediately reject them out of hand. The biggest block to creative thinking and creative problem-solving is an unwillingness to consider new ideas! So we are going to ask you to consider the possible solutions that other group members offer you. We are going to ask them to confront you when they think you are being closed-minded. And we expect you to confront them when they are being closed-minded. We don't always recognize when we are doing it, so it helps to have people we trust to call us on it when they see it.

Skepticism

Being skeptical means being willing to question and challenge all competing ideas and opinions (and this includes our own deeply held convictions). Before we can decide the best course of action, we have to consider all alternatives with an open mind, but we also have to vigilantly explore the shortcomings of each idea. We don't want to go off half-baked, and we don't want to pursue a course of action that would do more harm than good. No claim goes unquestioned. Nothing is off limits for discussion.

Once again, before you can become more skeptical, you need to value and recognize the importance of being skeptical. It is easy to see it in the abstract, but when someone is challenging your deeply held convictions, you need to resist the urge to get defensive by verbally attacking or cutting off the communication. So we are going to ask you not to be afraid to question and challenge your group mates as they consider their ideas, and we are likewise going to ask you not to get overly defensive when they question and challenge your ideas. Together we can come up with wonderful new ideas!

Self-Deception

It is all well and good to say "I am going to be a critical thinker. I'm going to approach all ideas with both an open mind and a healthy skepticism." But how do we know that we really are being critical? Imagine the person who questions her religion. She has been taught that her religious beliefs represent the truth—that all other religions are wrong. She does some exploration into comparative religions and spiritual beliefs and determines that all other religions truly are wrong and that she had been taught the one true and right religion all along. She really does think that she has been open-minded and skeptical and come up with the truth. Others might suspect the deck was stacked from the beginning. None of us can totally break through our own egocentric point of view. We see the world in a certain way, and it is very difficult to understand how others might see it differently. For some of us these issues might be religious, or political, or moral. We all come from different circumstances with different experiences and value systems. In short, we all have our "hot buttons," the places where those that know us best know not to go. So the question remains: how do we know that we have thought about some issue critically and we haven't been a victim of self-deception? Since the mind is a tricky thing, and I can't totally overcome my own biases, the best way I know to avoid self-deception is to open up my thought processes to someone else. Can I defend my ideas to someone who I know will call me out if they think I am deluding myself—someone who is willing and able to question and challenge my ideas? In short, I must engage in critical discussion.

Critical Discussion

Critical discussion is a lot like critical thinking. It involves open-mindedness and skepticism. However, while critical thinking takes place in my head, critical discussion requires other people. The nice thing about the small groups in this course is that we have three to five other people from completely different perspectives who should all be working to help each other avoid self-deception. If you let them, they will help you to see things from new angles and will offer contrary opinions. You are charged with the responsibility to do the same for them. If you all humor each other by agreeing all the time and never challenging each other to look at yourselves differently, then you are doing each other a disservice. Your group will cease to function effectively. An effective group will offer new ideas and challenge each other, but in a friendly and supportive manner. How the feedback is given is just as important (if not more so) than the feedback itself. Challenge, but don't attack. Know when to push and when you are pushing too hard. Make all your feedback to others from a place of caring and concern, and try to take everyone else's feedback to you from the same place. This is how we will grow and change for the better! (And if that is not what you want, why are you taking this class??)

Group Assignment

Share with your group the specific challenge that you are considering to undertake this semester as part of this course, as recorded on last week's individual assignment. As discussed in the Steps to Problem-Solving in the previous chapter, try to determine if everyone in your group is (a) focusing on the *real* problem, (b) likely to be able to make progress in one semester, and (c) not limiting their options (no multiple choice!). Thus we should not use challenge statements such as "Should I get divorced now or later?" Rather, we might ask "What should I do about my marital problems?" Also, a challenge statement should be written as a question ("How can I lose weight?") not a statement ("I am going to do the Atkins diet for the next 16 weeks"). On the next step we are going to brainstorm for strategies and solutions, so we don't want to put the cart before the horse by trying to solve our issue before we have considered all our options.

Individual Assignment

Based on feedback from your small group on the discussion board this week, re-write your challenge statement. Did the group think you were totally focused on the real problem, and if not, how did you modify your challenge statement? Did the group think you were able to make good progress on solving or meeting this challenge in one semester, and if not, how did you modify your challenge statement? Is your challenge statement written in the form of a question (How can I lose weight?) rather than a statement (I will go on the Atkins Diet.)? If not, fix it now. Is your challenge statement written in a way that does not limit your options (What can I do about my marital situation?) rather than multiple choice (Should I get divorced now or later?)? If necessary, fix it now. Without discussing individuals, how do you feel your group as a whole is functioning?

The Weekly Reading

Pre-Reading Questions

The readings for this chapter are on procrastination, the bane of many an undergraduate student!

1. Are you a habitual procrastinator?
2. What strategies have you attempted to employ to overcome procrastination and how effective have they been?

You'll Read This Later ... Maybe

Peter de Jager

We procrastinate; some of us suffer from this "affliction" more than others. For the most part, putting something off until later isn't a big deal. But, when we start missing deadlines, letting people down, letting ourselves down ... then, it becomes a problem we must either avoid, overcome, or mitigate.

Why put things off? We all know why. For starters, there are some things we simply don't like doing (my personal nemesis is office administrivia). Since we'd much rather do something we *like* doing, we do one of those enjoyable things instead.

Then, there's the task we should do, but frankly don't think is that important. Our boss, or organization, might think that it's important—but not us. So, it sits and waits until it becomes a crisis of some sort; then, we get to it, under increased pressure and stress.

There's another type of task that poses a greater, though often unseen, problem. Those tasks that determine whether or not we are any good at something: the tasks we don't attempt because we might fail; the tasks well and truly outside of our comfort zone. I suspect that many bestsellers are never written because the person who had a great work within them never started, because they didn't believe they could deliver anything of worth. It's called the "fear of failure."

For the first two examples, here are some solutions that sometimes work. Unfortunately for us, there are no perfect, one-size-fits-all solutions.

Deadlines—If something doesn't have a delivery deadline, then, almost by definition, it isn't important; and, it's never going to rise to the top of the priority list. If *Municipal World* did not impose a monthly deadline for this column, it would never get written. (As it is, I miss that deadline from time to time—sorry, Susan!)

Peter de Jager, "You'll Read This Later ... Maybe," *Municipal World*, vol. 125, no. 11, pp. 29–30.

Decide to just do it—If we accept that we *decide* to procrastinate, then we should be able to make a different decision. It is possible for a person with free will to decide, "Tomorrow, at 9:00 a.m. sharp, I will sit down and do X. I won't do anything else until X is complete!" Surprisingly, this tactic works. When the alarm rings in the early morning, just decide the night before, that *when* the [expletive deleted] alarm goes off, you'll roll out of bed. You won't think about options ... you'll just roll out of bed. It is possible to challenge ourselves, and then rise to the challenge.

Reward yourself—If the "personal challenge" approach fails, then rewards nearly always do the trick. I suspect nearly everyone learnt this trick when they were very young. "No dessert for you kiddo, until you finish those Brussels sprouts!" Sound familiar?

The reward strategy doesn't lose effectiveness as we grow older. It might even work better, since we get to choose our own rewards. Examples: As soon as I get this report done, I'll go get a coffee; once I do the banking, then I'll spend an hour reading; once I do X, I'll treat myself to Y. This strategy does have one flaw. If it works *really* well for you, you can go bankrupt on the "reward" part ...

Tiny steps—If completing the entire task all at once is too much to contemplate, then compromise with yourself—break it down to smaller bits. We climb mountains in measured steps, not giant leaps. Start small; a string of little achievements builds confidence.

Sprints—This is a variation of the "tiny steps" approach. Decide that you will work on X for a set amount of time (e.g., 20 minutes), and then you can stop and return later.

Go easy on yourself—The guilt you build when you procrastinate only makes things worse.

The last strategy points to the very best reason to break the habit of putting things off until "later." Procrastinating is mentally exhausting; the undone tasks hover over you like a squadron of vultures waiting for a warm meal. Procrastinating saps your energy and almost certainly ensures you don't look forward to getting up in the morning.

We have many readily accessible, and reasonably effective, solutions to the first two categories of chronic delayitis. It's the last variation of the affliction—fear of failure—that is more difficult to solve.

In everyday procrastination, the consequences are minimal—without a doubt cumulative, but minimal at the start. Now and then, putting off tasks until later (and then getting to them later) isn't the end of the world. If it is a long-term habit, however, then it is unnecessarily pegging our performance at "normal," which is a polite way of saying "average."

When we put off tasks until the future, because we're *afraid* that attempting the task will prove conclusively that we don't have the desirable talent, then we've entered the dreaded zone of eternal regret. One consolation: it's not lonely in there; the last time I checked, it was definitely crowded.

I don't think there's a simple solution for this form of delayitis. In the end, it requires that we just *decide* to get on with it—despite the fear of possible failure. Yes, indeed, that's much easier said than done; but, it is what it is.

Here's a trick that makes the above decision "easier." I learned it from Gerald Weinberg a long time ago. We need to ask ourselves three questions:

1. What's the absolute worst that could happen if we fail? (i.e., Will you lose body parts?)
2. How likely is that?
3. Can we live with the risk?

With our answers in hand, we'll make a rational, instead of an emotional, decision. (Of course, if your gut says go for it, then go for it!)

Here's another perspective on delayitis, with apologies to Henry Ford: "One of the greatest discoveries a person makes, one of their great surprises, is to find they can do what they were afraid they couldn't do."

READING 6

Introduction: Eat That Frog

Brian Tracy

This is a wonderful time to be alive. There have never been more possibilities and opportunities for you to achieve more of your goals than exist today. As perhaps never before in human history, you are actually drowning in options. In fact, there are so many good things that you can do that your ability to decide among them may be the critical determinant of what you accomplish in life.

If you are like most people today, you are overwhelmed with too much to do and too little time. As you struggle to get caught up, new tasks and responsibilities just keep rolling in, like the waves of the ocean. Because of this, you will never be able to do everything you have to do. You will never be caught up. You will always be behind in some of your tasks and responsibilities, and probably in many of them.

The Need to Be Selective

For this reason, and perhaps more than ever before, your ability to select your most important task at each moment, and then to get started on that task and to get it done both quickly and well, will probably have more of an impact on your success than any other quality or skill you can develop.

An average person who develops the habit of setting clear priorities and getting important tasks completed quickly will run circles around a genius who talks a lot and makes wonderful plans but who gets very little done.

The Truth About Frogs

It has been said that if the first thing you do each morning is to eat a live frog, you can go through the day with the satisfaction of knowing that that is probably the *worst* thing that is going to happen to you all day long.

Your "frog" is your biggest, most important task, the one you are most likely to procrastinate on if you don't do something about it. It is also the one task that can have the greatest positive impact on your life and results at the moment.

The first rule of frog eating is this:
If you have to eat two frogs, eat the *ugliest* one first.

This is another way of saying that if you have two important tasks before you, start with the biggest, hardest, and most important task first. Discipline yourself to begin immediately and then to persist until the task is complete before you go on to something else.

Think of this as a test. Treat it like a personal challenge. Resist the temptation to start with the easier task. Continually remind yourself that one of the most important decisions you make each day is what you will do immediately and what you will do later, if you do it at all.

The second rule of frog eating is this:
If you have to eat a live frog at all, it doesn't pay
to sit and look at it for very long.

The key to reaching high levels of performance and productivity is to develop the lifelong habit of tackling your major task first thing each morning. You must develop the routine of "eating your frog" before you do anything else and without taking too much time to think about it.

Take Action Immediately

In study after study of men and women who get paid more and promoted faster, the quality of "action orientation" stands out as the most observable and consistent behavior they demonstrate in everything they do. Successful, effective people are those who launch directly into their major tasks and then discipline themselves to work steadily and single-mindedly until those tasks are complete.

"Failure to execute" is one of the biggest problems in organizations today. Many people confuse activity with accomplishment. They talk continually, hold endless meetings, and make wonderful plans, but in the final analysis, no one does the job and gets the results required.

Develop the Habits of Success

Your success in life and work will be determined by the kinds of habits that you develop over time. The habit of setting priorities, overcoming procrastination, and getting on with your most important task is a mental and physical skill. As such, this habit is learnable through practice and repetition, over and over again, until it locks into your subconscious mind and becomes a permanent part of your behavior. Once it becomes a habit, it becomes both automatic and easy to do.

This habit of starting and completing important tasks has an immediate and continuous payoff. You are designed mentally and emotionally in such a way that task completion gives you a positive feeling. It makes you happy. It makes you feel like a winner.

Whenever you complete a task of any size or importance, you feel a surge of energy, enthusiasm, and selfesteem. The more important the completed task, the happier, more confident, and more powerful you feel about yourself and your world.

The completion of an important task triggers the release of *endorphins* in your brain. These endorphins give you a natural "high." The endorphin rush that follows successful completion of any task makes you feel more positive, personable, creative, and confident.

Develop a Positive Addiction

Here is one of the most important of the so-called secrets of success. You can actually develop a "positive addiction" to endorphins and to the feeling of enhanced clarity, confidence, and competence that they trigger. When you develop this addiction, you will, at an unconscious level, begin to organize your life in such a way that you are continually starting and completing ever more important tasks and projects. You will actually become addicted, in a very positive sense, to success and contribution.

One of the keys to your living a wonderful life, having a successful career, and feeling terrific about yourself is to develop the habit of starting and finishing important jobs. When you do, this behavior will take on a power of its own and you'll find it easier to complete important tasks than not to complete them.

No Shortcuts

You remember the story of the man who stops a musician on a street in New York and asks how he can get to Carnegie Hall. The musician replies, "Practice, man, practice."

Practice is the key to mastering any skill. Fortunately, your mind is like a muscle. It grows stronger and more capable with use. With practice, you can learn any behavior or develop any habit that you consider either desirable or necessary.

The Three Ds of New Habit Formation

You need three key qualities to develop the habits of focus and concentration, which are all learnable. They are decision, discipline, and determination.

First, make a *decision* to develop the habit of task completion. Second, *discipline* yourself to practice the principles you are about to learn over and over until they become automatic. And third, back everything you do with *determination* until the habit is locked in and becomes a permanent part of your personality.

Visualize Yourself as You Want to Be

There is a special way that you can accelerate your progress toward becoming the highly productive, effective, efficient person that you want to be. It consists of your thinking continually about the rewards and benefits of being an action-oriented, fast-moving, and focused person. See yourself as the kind of person who gets important jobs done quickly and well on a consistent basis.

Your mental picture of yourself has a powerful effect on your behavior. Visualize yourself as the person you intend to be in the future. Your self-image, the way you see yourself on the inside, largely determines your performance on the outside. All improvements in your *outer* life begin with improvements on the *inside*, in your mental pictures.

You have a virtually unlimited ability to learn and develop new skills, habits, and abilities. When you train yourself, through repetition and practice, to overcome procrastination and get your most important tasks completed quickly, you will move onto the fast track in your life and career and step on the accelerator of your potential.

Eat That Frog!

READING 7

Conclusion: Putting It All Together

Brian Tracy

The key to happiness, satisfaction, great success, and a wonderful feeling of personal power and effectiveness is for you to develop the habit of eating your frog first thing every day when you start work.

Fortunately, this is a learnable skill that you can acquire through repetition. And when you develop the habit of starting on your most important task before anything else, your success is assured.

Here is a summary of the 21 great ways to stop procrastinating and get more things done faster. Review these rules and principles regularly until they become firmly ingrained in your thinking and actions, and your future will be guaranteed.

1 **Set the table:** Decide exactly what you want. Clarity is essential. Write out your goals and objectives before you begin.

2 **Plan every day in advance:** Think on paper. Every minute you spend in planning can save you five or ten minutes in execution.

3 **Apply the 80/20 Rule to everything:** 20 percent of your activities will account for 80 percent of your results. Always concentrate your efforts on that top 20 percent.

4 **Consider the consequences:** Your most important tasks and priorities are those that can have the most serious consequences, positive or negative, on your life or work. Focus on these above all else.

Brian Tracy, "Conclusion: Putting It All Together," *Eat That Frog!: 21 Great Ways to Stop Procrastinating and Get More Done in Less Time*, pp. 105–108. Copyright © 2017 by Berrett-Koehler Publishers. Reprinted with permission.

5 **Practice creative procrastination:** Since you can't do everything, you must learn to deliberately put off those tasks that are of low value so that you have enough time to do the few things that really count.

6 **Use the ABCDE Method continually:** Before you begin work on a list of tasks, take a few moments to organize them by value and priority so you can be sure of working on your most important activities.

7 **Focus on key result areas:** Identify those results that you absolutely, positively have to get to do your job well, and work on them all day long.

8 **Apply the Law of Three:** Identify the three things you do in your work that account for 90 percent of your contribution, and focus on getting them done before anything else. You will then have more time for your family and personal life.

9 **Prepare thoroughly before you begin:** Have everything you need at hand before you start. Assemble all the papers, information, tools, work materials, and numbers you might require so that you can get started and keep going.

10 **Take it one oil barrel at a time:** You can accomplish the biggest and most complicated job if you just complete it one step at a time.

11 **Upgrade your key skills:** The more knowledgeable and skilled you become at your key tasks, the faster you start them and the sooner you get them done. Determine exactly what it is that you are very good at doing, or could be very good at, and throw your whole heart into doing those specific things very, very well.

12 **Identify your key constraints:** Determine the bottlenecks or choke points, internal or external, that set the speed at which you achieve your most important goals, and focus on alleviating them.

13 **Put the pressure on yourself:** Imagine that you have to leave town for a month, and work as if you had to get your major task completed before you left.

14 **Motivate yourself into action:** Be your own cheerleader. Look for the good in every situation. Focus on the solution rather than the problem. Always be optimistic and constructive.

15 **Technology is a terrible master:** Take back your time from enslaving technological addictions. Learn to often turn devices off and leave them off.

16 **Technology is a wonderful servant:** Use your technological tools to confront yourself with what is most important and protect yourself from what is least important.

17 **Focus your attention:** Stop the interruptions and distractions that interfere with completing your most important tasks.

18 **Slice and dice the task:** Break large, complex tasks down into bitesized pieces, and then do just one small part of the task to get started.

19 **Create large chunks of time:** Organize your days around large blocks of time so you can concentrate for extended periods on your most important tasks.

20 **Develop a sense of urgency:** Make a habit of moving fast on your key tasks. Become known as a person who does things quickly and well.

21 **Single handle every task:** Set clear priorities, start immediately on your most important task, and then work without stopping until the job is 100 percent complete. This is the real key to high performance and maximum personal productivity.

Make a decision to practice these principles every day until they become second nature to you. With these habits of personal management as a permanent part of your personality, your future success will be unlimited.

Just do it! *Eat that frog!*

Chapter 4: Post-Reading Questions

1. Were any of the suggestions in the de Jager article helpful? Which ones do you already do, and how helpful has it been? Which ones do you not do, and how useful do you think they would be?
2. What did you think of the frog-eating analogy used in the Tracy article? Of the 21 ways he lists to stop procrastinating, which do you think would be most useful to you and why?

CHAPTER 5

Decision-Making

Working in Groups

Working in groups is a mixed bag. It provides opportunity for social support and sharing the load, but it can also be frustrating, especially when members don't pull their own weight. In the groups for this course, some of you are probably feeling lucky that you have such a great group. Everyone is responsive and supportive and you're really enjoying the discussions, giving and receiving feedback. Others of you are probably feeling frustrated with your groups. In online groups, people may not be participating, you're not getting feedback, or they're waiting until the last minute to respond so you are always stuck waiting for them before you can progress. In some groups you might have a member who is bossy, or judgmental, or otherwise not very polite/understanding. Some of you feel very connected to your group, and others feel disconnected. How do you get your group to work effectively? You need to start by Identifying the Problem. Hmm. That should sound familiar. In fact it was the first step in problem-solving. The second step, however, will be a little different. The second step here is to communicate to your group what you see as the problem. Rather than accusing other people of things ("You never give your opinion!"; "You are too critical"), it is better to use what we call I-Statements.

I-Statements use this format: "I feel __(state your feeling)__ when __(state the behavior)__, because__(state the reason)__."

Some examples:

- "I feel hurt when no one responds to my discussion prompts, because it makes me think that no one cares about me."

- "I feel frustrated when people wait until the last minute to post their discussion prompts, because I can't get my work accomplished on time."
- "I feel angry when you give me feedback, because your tone sounds like you are scolding me."

This week I want you to practice using I-Statements with your small group. Provide feedback both to individuals and the group as a whole. Give both positive and negative feedback. I-Statements can also be used to give positive feedback ("I feel happy when I get support from the group, because it makes me think people care about me.")

In your last individual assignment you were asked to report how your group as a whole is functioning. Now I would like you to share your feelings with the group. Remember, the point is not to attack the others, but to communicate your needs to them. Likewise, you should want to know if you are meeting their needs. So begin with some comments about the group as a whole and how well (or not) you think you all are functioning as a group. Then give individual feedback to each and every group member. Try to say something positive to each member, and try to give each member something to work on. When you hear what others have to say about you, try not to be defensive, but rather, think about how you can use this information to better yourself. Remember, that is what this course is about, and that is what you agreed to when you decided to continue with this course after reading the introduction. (It might be a good idea to go back and read it again!) Respond to everyone's comment about you. Thank them for any positive feedback, and discuss the ways in which you will attempt to address the need for improvement. This is where both your critical discussion skills and your budding psychologist skills will really come in handy. Try to make this a positive corrective experience, not a negative gang up and gotcha experience.

Group Assignment

This week in your group you will practice giving and taking feedback. Discuss your assessment of how your group is functioning as a whole, then give individual feedback to each and every group member. Try to say something positive to each member, and try to give each member something to work on. Make sure to practice using some I-Statements. Make sure to respond to everyone's comment about you. Thank them for any positive feedback, and discuss the ways in which you will attempt to address the need for improvement. It is helpful for everyone to write down their intended feedback for others before anyone begins to speak. If this is not done, there is a tendency for people to repeat each other's comments. If all comments for an individual are similar even after everyone wrote down their comments before anyone spoke, that suggests the feedback is even more valid as everyone came up with it independently rather than just tagging on.

Individual Assignment

You are on the beginning of a journey to make some major changes in your life. James Prochaska and Carlo DiClemente created a Stages of Change model that suggests people go through five stages when they attempt to make a major change in their life. The first stage is called Precontemplation—the person is not even aware that they have a problem to solve. Next is Contemplation—a person becomes aware of the issue but is not yet ready to do anything about it. Then comes Preparation—actively thinking about and planning for change. This is followed by Action—the stage at which changes are made. And finally there is Maintenance—the person engages in the work of keeping up with and maintaining those changes (think about how many diets fail at the maintenance stage). Think about the challenge you have identified in a historical perspective. How long has this been an issue? Was it an issue before you even identified it as a potential problem? How long, if at all, have you been trying to address it? Do you feel ready to address it now? Do you anticipate being successful this time? Map out a time line through the stages of change. Where have you been and where are you now?

The Weekly Reading

Pre-Reading Questions

The reading for this chapter is on decision-making and problem-solving in organizations, but we will be doing similar things in your small group.

1. What do you think are some of the pros and cons of using group decision-making instead of making decisions individually?
2. Which type of decision-making (group vs. individual) do you prefer and why?

READING 8

Decision-Making and Problem-Solving Processes

Joseph E. Champoux

After Reading This Chapter, You Should Be Able To

- Describe decision-making and problem-solving processes in organizations.
- Discuss the relationship between problem solving and decision making in organizations.
- Compare the decision strategies that managers can use for decision making.
- Analyze several decision-making models and the perspectives they bring to the decision process.
- List the assets and liabilities of group decision making.
- Distinguish between individual and group decision making and identify the situations for which they are best suited.
- Discuss the sources of decision-making bias and error.
- Describe the process of escalation of commitment to a losing course of action.
- Recognize groupthink and how to avoid it during group decision making.
- Explain several methods of improving decision processes in organizations.
- Appreciate some international and ethical issues that surround decision making in organizations.

Chapter Overview

The **decision-making process** defines a decision problem, creates alternative courses of action, and chooses among them using decision criteria. The criteria for choosing among alternatives can include the cost, profit, danger, or pleasure of each alternative. Although decision making focuses on choice, it also intends to reach a goal.[1]

Decision making fits within the larger context of problem-solving activities in organizations. Individuals in organizations, especially managers, face problems, opportunities, and events that require action. The **problem-solving process** identifies the problem, tries to find root causes, and creates options that become input to a decision-making process. Decision making is the part of the problem-solving process that chooses a course of action.[2]

Both individuals and groups can make decisions. Individuals do a good job with well-structured problems that have several tightly coupled parts. Groups do a better job with ill-defined problems with loosely coupled parts. They work well with problems too complex for a single person to solve. Such decisions include those affecting multiple constituencies and decisions needing the commitment of those affected to get effective execution.[3]

Although decision making is a basic function of a manager's role, nonmanagers also make decisions.[4] Organizations that embrace quality management or use self-managing teams involve many nonmanagers in decision processes. Throughout this chapter, the term decision maker refers to a person at any organizational level who chooses a course of action when faced with a decision situation.

Decision Strategies

The two major **decision strategies** are programmed and unprogrammed.[5] Three dimensions define the characteristics of each strategy. The **routine–nonroutine dimension** describes whether the decision is common or unusual. The **recurring–nonrecurring dimension** describes whether the decision happens often or infrequently. The **certainty–uncertainty dimension** describes the degree of predictability of the decision. Risk embraces a large part of the certainty–uncertainty dimension. Situations with complete certainty or uncertainty are not as common as risky situations. When making decisions under risk, the decision maker assesses the probability of the alternatives during the decision process.[6]

Decision makers use a **programmed decision strategy** for routine, recurring, and predictable decisions. This strategy relies on existing rules and standard procedures, uses well-known decision criteria, and applies uniform processing to a decision problem.[7] Examples include handling exchanges and returns after Christmas and recording and processing accrued vacation and sick leave time.

Decision makers use an **unprogrammed decision strategy** for nonroutine, nonrecurring, and unpredictable decisions. Decision makers use this strategy when faced with novel or unusual events that they have not encountered in the past. Such unstructured events require creative problem solving for effective decision making.

The Decision-Making Process

The decision-making process is much more than choosing from alternative courses of action. The process involves several interrelated phases, only one of which is choice. Figure 5.8.1 shows those phases.[8]

Decision processes are dynamic. They can unfold linearly or restart at an earlier phase. A decision maker can also repeat or restart the entire process, depending on the conditions that unfold during the process. Decision makers can move in both directions in the sequence and even stop for an extended time at one phase.[9]

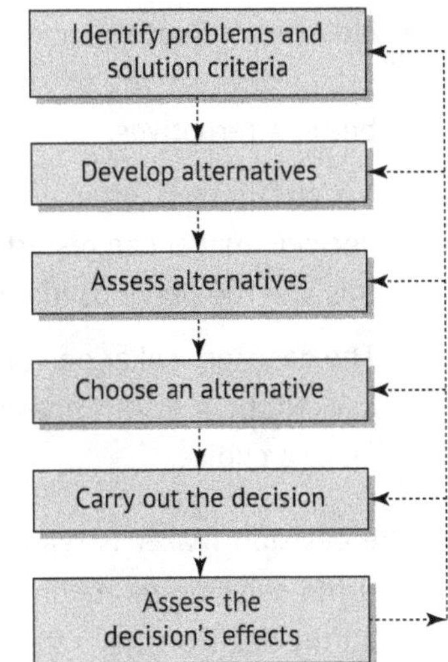

Figure 5.8.1 The Decision-Making Process

The first phase is **problem identification and diagnosis.** The organization faces an issue or problem that needs a solution. The issue or problem could be as simple as a request by a customer or an employee to do something not covered by existing policies or as major as widespread unethical behavior in the organization. Whether the problem is simple or difficult, its presence starts the decision process.

The first phase includes **identification of criteria** that will show that the issue is resolved or the problem is solved. This element is important, because it ties directly to the last phase, which is assessing the decision's effects. The criteria should be as explicit and as measurable as possible so managers can determine the success or failure of the decision.

The second phase focuses on **developing alternatives** for dealing with the issue or solving the problem. The decision maker searches for alternatives and information about the alternatives. The search can be informal, such as a telephone call for advice on a simple but unusual issue, or formal, such as a marketing survey to find out why the company's product is losing market share.

When faced with a complex problem, the decision maker might look at many different alternatives and consider them simultaneously. During the search, the decision maker often faces time and cost constraints, which can lead to imperfect or incomplete information about each alternative.

Decision makers discard alternatives they view as unacceptable solutions to the problem or issue, based on the criteria developed in the first phase. Acceptability, of course, is a judgment based on the decision maker's perception of the alternatives. Acceptable alternatives then become part of the decision maker's set of possible alternatives that move to the assessment phase of the decision process.

The decision maker now **assesses the alternatives** in the feasible set. She examines each alternative to see what desirable and undesirable results it is likely to have. The decision maker considers whether those affected by an alternative are likely to accept it. How well the decision is accepted can affect its success. The decision maker also considers the amount of risk each alternative involves and the certainty of its results.

After the decision maker completes the assessment, she must **choose an alternative.** Although people commonly associate decision making only with this phase, the decisions are actually made by means of the entire dynamic and interdependent process just described.

Decision makers may face several dilemmas, including the following:

- Two or more alternatives appear equally good. If the decision maker is truly indifferent, a random process such as a coin toss can make the choice.

- No one alternative can solve the issue or problem. Here the decision maker can use a set of alternatives to solve the problem or restart the decision process to search for better alternatives.
- No alternatives offer enough positive results to offset expected negative effects. The decision maker can restart the process to see if better alternatives exist. Note that, in both this and the previous dilemma, a decision has been made—the decision not to decide.[10]
- The decision maker perceives many alternatives as acceptable. The decision maker can go back to the previous phase to get more information about the alternatives and then try to make a choice.

The decision maker is ready to **carry out the decision** after she has chosen an alternative. Moving the decision to action is often as complicated as making the decision. Those asked to carry out the decision may accept decisions about simple issues but resist tough decisions about complex problems. The major issues in this phase go beyond the quality of the decision. They focus squarely on managing a successful implementation.

The last phase in the decision process **assesses the decision's effects**. The criteria for assessing the decision come from the first phase. The people asked to carry out the decision measure the results and compare them to the criteria. If the results are not as desired, corrective action may be required. If it becomes clear that the criteria need revision, the entire process begins again.

Decision-Making Models

Problem-solving and decision-making processes can follow several models. Each model describes variations in the decision process and includes different assumptions. These assumptions imply that the models apply to different types of decisions in modern organizations.

The Rational Model

The **rational model** of decision making has its roots in the classical economic theory of the firm and statistical decision making. According to this model, a decision maker approaches a decision problem in the following way:[11]

1. The decision maker has a goal she wants to maximize or minimize. That goal can be profit, revenue, market share, cost, and so on.
2. The decision maker knows all alternatives and their results. She has complete information about each alternative. The decision maker is also fully knowledgeable about the degree of risk and uncertainty associated with each alternative.

3 The decision maker uses some function to give a preference ordering to the alternatives under consideration. The decision maker knows that function at the beginning of the decision process.

4 The decision maker applies the preference ordering function to the set of alternatives and chooses the alternative that maximizes the goal.

The rational model sees decision making as proceeding sequentially from beginning to end. This model does not have dynamic properties such as revising the goal or extending the search for new alternatives.

The Bounded Rationality Model

The **bounded rationality model** assumes decision makers have limitations that constrain rationality in the decision process. Those limits include the absence of complete information about alternatives and their results, cost constraints, time constraints, and limitations in dealing with complex problems.[12]

Because of these limitations, decision makers might not consider all possible alternatives and therefore might not choose the alternative that maximizes a goal. Instead, the decision maker picks an alternative that is good enough to reach the goal. Selecting a satisfactory, but not optimal, alternative is known as **satisficing behavior**, a term that emphasizes the decision maker's search for satisfactory, not optimal, solutions. The following classical analogy shows the distinction between optimizing and satisficing: "An example is the difference between searching a haystack to find the sharpest needle in it and searching the haystack to find a needle sharp enough to sew with."[13]

The bounded rationality model is both open and dynamic. Decision makers attend to forces and constraints imposed by the environment of the decision. As new information comes into the decision process, they can change both the goal of the decision problem and the set of alternatives. If the decision maker does not find a satisficing alternative in the set under consideration, she broadens the search for more alternatives.

Unstructured Decision-Making Models

Unlike the two models just described, many decisions do not have a structure that allows orderly progression from identifying the decision problem to selecting an alternative. **Unstructured decisions** often are unprecedented, significant, and complex events that defy program-like decision processes.[14] To put it more dramatically, unstructured decision making is a process characterized by novelty, complexity, and openendedness, by the fact that the organization usually begins with little understanding of the decision situation it faces or the route to its solution, and only a vague idea of what the solution might be and how it will be evaluated when it is developed.[15]

Decision makers solve such complex, unstructured, and ambiguous problems by breaking them into manageable parts to which they apply more structured approaches to decision making.

The novelty of such problems usually does not allow an optimizing approach to selecting an alternative. Decision makers rely on satisficing approaches for finding solutions to unstructured problems.[16]

Unstructured decisions are especially vulnerable to factors that can disturb orderly movement through the decision process. The process can encounter political forces trying to stop a decision, make false starts because of inadequate information about the problem, or run into blank walls when an alternative does not solve the unstructured problem.[17] The decision maker assesses many alternatives simultaneously using a series of cycles for finding and assessing them.[18] During the process of finding and assessing alternatives, one alternative can emerge as the preferred choice. Such an "implicitly favored" alternative emerges during the decision process, not just at the end of the process. During the search for alternatives, the decision maker rejects those alternatives that are unacceptable and adds those that are acceptable to the set, even though she has already identified a preference.

The decision maker then moves to a stage of confirming the implicitly chosen alternative. During this stage, she tries to arrive at the belief that her implicit preference was the right choice. Many aspects of selective perception, distortion, and attribution discussed in Chapter 5, "Perception, Attitudes, and Personality," operate during this phase. The task for the decision maker is to believe that her implicit favorite is better than at least one alternative to which it is compared.

The Garbage Can Model of Decision Making

The **garbage can model** of decision making was developed to explain decision making under highly ambiguous conditions. Ambiguous conditions arise in organizations when goals are not clear, organizational participants change fast, and the technologies of the organization are either poorly understood or swiftly change. The fast-changing global environments of many organizations also add ambiguity.[19]

Decision making under ambiguity does not lend itself to the more rational, structured approaches described earlier. In ambiguous situations, a decision maker might not know all the alternatives available and the results of each alternative. She also might not have a clear set of rules to guide her as she chooses from the alternatives.

The garbage can model sees decision making under ambiguity as a time-sensitive process of four almost independent streams or flows: problem streams, solution streams, participant streams, and choice opportunity streams. These streams are constantly moving through an organization. The convergence of the streams at some point results in a decision.

Problem streams are the issues or problems facing the organization or part of the organization at a particular time. **Solution streams** are the solutions available to a decision maker, even though these solutions might have no direct connection to the problems. **Participant streams** are the decision makers and others who are available to decide. The **choice opportunity streams** are the chances to decide.

The garbage can metaphor was chosen deliberately and is not an attempt at humor. The contents of a real garbage can consist of whatever people have tossed into the can. A decision-making garbage can is much the same. The four streams flow toward the garbage can. Whatever is in the can when a decision is needed contributes to that decision. The garbage can model sees decision making in organizations as chaotic: Solutions look for problems to solve, and decision makers make choices based on the arbitrary mix of the four streams in the garbage can.

Political Decision-Making Models

Political decision-making models assume that individuals and groups in organizations pursue their self-interests and try to reach decisions that serve those interests. These models see decision making as a power- and conflict-based process featuring bargaining and compromise as ways of reducing conflict. The decisions that emerge from this process usually do not satisfy everyone involved.[20]

Political decision-making models view power as a central feature of the decision process. Such models define power as the ability or capacity of an individual or group to overcome an opponent. According to the model, individuals or groups try to gain power and affect decisions by developing strategies such as controlling information that is critical to a decision and building coalitions within the organization to gain support for a position. Political forces within an organization are most likely to affect resource allocation decisions, such as budget decisions (see Chapter 15, "Power and Political Behavior").

Assets and Liabilities of Group Decision Making

Group decision-making processes have both **assets and liabilities.**[21] Recognizing these assets and liabilities can help you understand what group decision making can and cannot do.

Assets

Groups of people can bring more knowledge, information, skills, and abilities to a problem than individuals working alone. The heterogeneity of a decision-making group can stimulate discussion and debate about how to solve the problem. Each person contributes a piece of information or knowledge to the decision process. Some research shows that groups with goals of cooperation manage their discussions more effectively than groups with goals of competition.[22]

When groups make decisions, everyone in the group understands more about the decision. Participants in the process know which alternatives were reviewed and why one was selected and others rejected.

Participation in a decision-making group can lead to increased acceptance of the decision. If they perceive their participation as legitimate, participants can develop a sense of ownership of decisions, reducing resistance while carrying out the decision.

Group decision making also helps the personal development of participants, letting them work on more complex problems in the future. Group decision making can improve collaborative problem-solving skills, develop trust among those who participate, enhance interpersonal skills, and increase job satisfaction.[23]

Liabilities

Group decision making also has liabilities. Individuals who participate in group decision making might feel strong social pressures to conform to an emerging norm. Pressure is placed on those who disagree to get them to accept the favored alternatives.

Often one person dominates a group, especially if the group had no appointed leader from the start. Such people become dominant by participating more, being particularly persuasive, or persisting in their position.

As the group uncovers alternatives, individuals can develop strong preferences for a particular alternative. Although that alternative might not be the best solution to the problem, attention may shift to converting those who do not agree with the favored alternative.

Group decision making takes time and is ill suited for problems that require quick decisions. The time liability of group decision making includes not only the time of the principal decision maker, but also the time of everyone involved in the process.

Choosing Between Individual and Group Decision Making

Managers can choose from several **alternative social processes for decision making**. This section describes the approaches and briefly discusses a normative model that guides choices among them.[24]

Alternative Social Processes for Decision Making

Table 5.8.1 shows several approaches to decision making. The table identifies the approaches with a combination of letters and Roman numerals. The letters represent the major characteristics of a process; the Roman numerals are variants of a process. The approaches labeled with an "A" are **authoritative** in character, which means the decision maker alone makes the decision. The "C" approaches are **consultative**, with the decision maker getting information and advice from others before deciding. The "G" approach uses **group** processes for decision making and tries to get consensus among group members.

Table 5.8.1 Different Approaches to Decisions Affecting Individuals and Groups

SYMBOL	DEFINITION
AI	You solve the problem or make the decision yourself using information available to you at the present time.
AII	You obtain any necessary information from subordinates, then decide on a solution to the problem yourself. You may or may not tell subordinates the purpose of your questions or give information about the problem or decision on which you are working. The input provided by them is clearly in response to your request for specific information. They do not play a role in the definition of the problem or in generating or evaluating alternative solutions.
CI	You share the problem with relevant subordinates individually, getting their ideas and suggestions without bringing them together as a group. Then you make the decision. This decision may or may not reflect your subordinates' influence.
CII	You share the problem with your subordinates in a group meeting in which you obtain their ideas and suggestions. You make the decision, which may or may not reflect your subordinates' influence.
GII	You share the problem with your subordinates as a group. Together you generate and evaluate alternatives and attempt to reach agreement (consensus) on a solution. Your role is much like that of [a] chairperson, co-ordinating the discussion, keeping it focused on the problem, and making sure that the critical issues are discussed. You can provide the group with information or ideas you have, but you do not try to "press" them to adopt "your" solution, and you are willing to accept and implement any solution that has the support of the entire group.

Source: Table 2.1."Decision Methods for Group and Individual Problems" from *Leadership and Decision-Making*, by Victor H. Vroom and Philip W. Yetton, © 1973. Reprinted by permission of the University of Pittsburgh Press. There is no GI approach for decisions affecting groups.

You can view the approaches as social processes for decision making. These approaches have several characteristics as you move from the "A" approaches to the "G" approaches:

- Social interaction increases between the decision maker and others involved in the decision.
- Participants in the decision process have increased involvement, which can lead to more influence on the decision and increased commitment to the decision. They also have a better understanding of the problem because of their involvement in making the decision.
- The social processes for making a decision become increasingly complex and feature increased potential for conflict.
- The time to make a decision increases.

The Vroom–Yetton Model

A normative decision-making model has been proposed that guides a person's choices among the alternative approaches to decision making just described. The **Vroom–Yetton model** uses a set of rules that protects a decision's acceptance and quality. The model picks the approach indicated by the rules as best for the decision problem under consideration.

The Vroom–Yetton model considers decision problems to have certain characteristics. The decision maker assesses the characteristics of the decision problem by asking some diagnostic questions. The answers to those questions guide the decision maker to the model's recommended approach for that decision problem. For example, if the decision maker has enough information to decide, the model selects AI. If high conflict about decision alternatives is likely, the model selects CII or GII.

The model has received broad general support from several research efforts.[25] No one suggests the model guarantees perfect decisions; however, research evidence says that decisions made by processes that the model selects are consistently higher-quality than decisions made by processes the model does not select. The decision's effectiveness, quality, and acceptance decline as the number of rule violations increases.[26] One study focused on the model's prescription of group processes (CII and GII) when conflict is likely to occur among subordinates and acceptance of the decision is important. That study showed that subordinates were more likely to accept a decision from a group decision process than an individual one.[27]

Judgment Biases

The description of decision-making models started with models that see the process as rational and ended with models that have a less rational view. Those models see decision makers using less than optimal judgment. Many factors can affect human judgment during the decision-making process.

Heuristics

Decision makers use several **heuristics** or guidelines to simplify the task of processing an often bewildering array of information developed during decision making. These strategies let them move quickly through the process, but also limit the information to which they attend. Although heuristics can lead to accurate decisions, they often introduce biases in human judgment. People are not always aware that they use heuristics. The next paragraphs describe three heuristics. Which do you tend to use when faced with a decision?

The **availability heuristic**[28] is the tendency to recall and use information that is easily retrieved from memory. Such information usually is vivid, emotional, specific, and recent. Information without those characteristics might apply to the decision problem, but is less available to the decision maker. For example, managers who do performance appraisals often recall recent events better than earlier events. As a result, they do not have a continuous stream of information for the entire performance period. The result could be an unbalanced and possibly unfair performance appraisal.

The **representativeness heuristic**[29] leads a decision maker to compare a current event to past events about which the person has knowledge or beliefs. If the current and past events are not comparable or if the decision maker's beliefs are incorrect, the decision might not be accurate. This heuristic includes stereotypes. Using stereotypes with an increasingly diverse workforce can lead to inaccurate or discriminatory hiring and promotion decisions.

Anchoring and adjustment[30] is a heuristic decision makers use to get a starting point for a decision and then adjust beyond that point. This heuristic can play a big role in setting a person's hiring salary or developing a budget. For example, a manager might set a new employee's salary by increasing the person's present salary by some percentage. The salary offer will not necessarily reflect the new employee's true value to the organization. The anchoring and adjustment heuristic is tenacious, tying the decision maker to the original anchor even when other information indicates that the behavior is irrational.

Judgment Biases

When heuristics are right for the decision problem, they can help managers make good decisions. They help the person process information and simplify complex decisions. When the heuristic is not right for the decision, it can introduce systematic **judgment biases** that lead to wrong or irrational decisions. Heuristics can work alone or in combination to bias a person's judgment.[31]

The availability heuristic leads to judgment biases that adversely affect the accuracy of the information used in a decision process. Inaccuracies come from the recalled information, estimates of the frequencies of events, and errors in association. The **ease of recall bias** occurs when people recall vivid, recent events more easily than other events. A person perceives easily recalled events as happening more often than less easily recalled events. This bias can affect a supervisor's judgment in a performance appraisal. Recent, dramatic events can have more effect on a performance appraisal than older, less remarkable events.

The representativeness heuristic yields judgment biases that affect estimates of events that occur and misperceptions about whether a series of events is random or not. A **misconception of chance bias** occurs when people judge the randomness of a sequence of events from its appearance, although the number of events is statistically too small for that conclusion. A manufacturing manager could question the randomness of a sampling process that resulted in good, good, good, good, bad, good, bad, bad, bad, good. Statistical theory says that one sequence is equally likely as any other sequence when drawn randomly.[32]

The anchoring and adjustment heuristic affects a decision maker's ability to make accurate estimates that can affect project completions or budgets. An **overconfidence bias** can lead to inaccurate judgments when answering questions about which the person has little knowledge. For example, a manager firmly believes her sales estimate for Gillie's Hatch Valley Chile

Company in Hatch, New Mexico, is accurate. Gillie's is a real, but little known, company that does not publish sales figures.

Some judgment biases stem from multiple heuristics. A **confirmation trap bias** can lead to behavior that avoids disconfirming and uncomfortable information. People tend to search for information that supports what they believe is true. They tend not to seek information that challenges their views. For example, a manager tentatively decides to introduce a product and seeks only confirming evidence to reach a decision.

Framing Effects

The presentation of a decision problem can lead to **framing effects**, a form of judgment bias that affects decision makers. Differences in presentation or framing of the problem affect their choices.[33] As an illustration, read Decision Problems 1 and 2 in Table 5.8.2 and choose an alternative for each.

Psychological research on decision making has consistently shown that people prefer Program A for Decision Problem 1 and Program D for Decision Problem 2. Perhaps you did the same. Now look closely at the problems. The only difference between them is the wording. The programs in Problem 1 are phrased as gains and those in Problem 2 as losses. People prefer to avoid risks (**risk-averse** behavior) when facing decisions involving gains. They prefer to take risks (**risk-seeking** behavior) in decisions involving losses.

Framing decisions as losses can contribute to excessively risky decision behavior. Hoping to regain losses through the risky alternative, decision makers might engage in excessive and possibly inappropriate risky decision behavior. Such decision behavior can be associated with high levels of decision failures.[34]

Table 5.8.2 Framing Effects and Decision Problems

PROBLEM 1
Assume you are a plant manager faced with the prospect of laying off 600 workers. You are considering two programs to reduce the number of people laid off: • If you choose Program A, you will save 200 jobs. • If you choose Program B, a 33 percent chance exists to save the jobs of all 600 workers and a 67 percent chance exists to not save any workers' jobs.
PROBLEM 2
Assume that you are a plant manager faced with the prospect of laying off 600 workers. You are considering two alternative programs to reduce the number of people laid off: • If you choose Program C, you will lay off 400 workers. • If you choose Program D, you have a 33 percent chance of no layoffs and a 67 percent chance of laying off all 600 workers.

Source: Tversky, A., and D. Kahneman. 1981. The Framing of Decisions and the Psychology of Choice. *Science* 211: 453–58. Problems 1 and 2 are based on page 453. Problem 3 comes from page 454.

Decision makers also should view a decision problem from different frames to see whether they get contradictory results.[35] Some research points to success from reframing decision problems. Although such efforts add time to the decision process, better decisions can result.[36]

Escalation of Commitment

Decision makers face a common dilemma: Should they end a losing course of action or increase their commitment to it in the hope of getting future positive results and recovering past losses? Research evidence suggests they are likely to commit more resources, a process called **escalation of commitment**, to a losing course of action.[37] Some evidence suggests this result varies among cultures. Managers from low uncertainty avoidance cultures such as Singapore are less likely to follow a losing course of action.[38]

Commitment escalation typically happens when decisions can have strong effects on an organization. Such decisions include capital investments, major research and development investments, plant expansions, and the like. Decision makers watch the effects of their decisions to see whether intended results occur. Some decisions succeed and others fail—it is when they fail that irrational decision behavior happens.

Rational decision theory emphasizes using future costs and benefits, not past or sunk costs, to assess alternatives.[39] Economists argue that sunk costs should play no role in a present decision, but decision makers often do not see them as psychologically sunk. As a result, past decisions can have negative effects on present ones.

Several factors contribute to escalating commitment.[40] The decision maker might feel a need to justify past actions to self for ego protection or to others who assess her performance. Pressures for decision behavior consistency and the desire to appear as a rational decision maker can result in irrational escalation. Decision makers with confidence in their skills and abilities appear more likely to escalate commitment than those with less confidence.[41]

Recall from the framing effects discussion that decision makers tend to avoid risk for positively framed problems and seek risk for negatively framed problems. The latter tendency can contribute to commitment escalation, which leads to failure. A failing project appears to the decision maker as a choice between losses. The first choice is to stop the project and accept the sunk costs. That option has a 100 percent chance of happening if the action is taken. The second choice is to consider an option with some probability of loss and some probability of success. This is the risky choice a decision maker will likely take when she frames the problem as a loss.

Groupthink

Groups can make bad, even disastrous, decisions. A major example is the space shuttle Challenger tragedy. Despite evidence of safety hazards, senior managers at the National Aeronautics and Space Administration (NASA) pressed for the launch.[42] Why do group decision processes go awry?

One prominent and popular explanation is the groupthink phenomenon, an ugly disease presumed to infect cohesive decision-making groups. Members of such groups have worked closely together for some time and share a common set of values. These groups often operate during times of crisis, putting stress on their members to reach a commonly agreed-upon decision.[43]

Groupthink involves excessive conformity to a group norm that supports agreement among group members. Decision-making groups with groupthink have lost their ability to critically assess alternative solutions to a problem. They also have lost the ability to examine the effects of past decisions critically, especially decisions that have become dysfunctional for the organization. Another major feature of groupthink is the absence of ethical concerns for the effects of the group's decisions.

Groupthink does not affect decision-making groups simply because they are cohesive. The nature of the norms of such groups is the key to groupthink. If those norms have the qualities just described, then the decision process becomes seriously dysfunctional. If those norms support continuously and critically examining alternatives, the decision-making group will not suffer from groupthink.

The group leader can head off the dysfunctional effects of groupthink in several ways. She can encourage critical appraisals of issues, ideas, and alternatives that the group considers. She should deliberately stimulate conflict during the decision process to get the information the group needs for a quality decision.[44] The group leader can assign one member to play devil's advocate for each group meeting. It also helps to invite knowledgeable outsiders to the group's meetings and to encourage them to analyze and comment on the group's deliberations.

Groupthink theory has received extensive research attention since its introduction in the early 1970s. Existing research evidence does not support all parts of the theory. Despite its lack of clear empirical research support, it remains an intuitive explanation of group decision-making failure.[45]

Improving Decision Making in Organizations

Many methods exist to **improve decision making** in organizations. Some are human-based methods; others use computers and related technologies.

Human-Based Methods

The human-based methods for improving decision making are designed to generate more decision alternatives or to increase the criticism of the alternatives. Some methods also increase conflict in a decision-making group to offset the liabilities of such groups.

Brainstorming is a method of improving decision making that involves spontaneously generating ideas while deferring critical evaluation of those ideas. Its role in the decision process is to create a set of decision alternatives, not to pick the final alternative.

Four rules guide brainstorming. First, group members generate ideas in a freewheeling fashion. Wacky ideas are welcome. Second, at this stage there is no criticism of any idea, no matter how bizarre or bland. Third, many ideas are desired. The assumption is that, if people suggest many ideas, some will be good ones. Fourth, after ideas are presented, group members suggest ways to combine or improve them. At the end of a brainstorming session, decision makers should have many alternative solutions to a problem or issue.[46]

A new approach to brainstorming uses computer technology to improve the results of the process.[47] Some research has shown that face-to-face brainstorming does not always yield as many good alternatives as people working alone. The lack of anonymity in a face-to-face group inhibits some people from offering their ideas. **Electronic brainstorming** links people by computers so they do not interact directly. Participants behave anonymously in the process, letting them offer ideas without fear of social pressure from a dominant person. Electronic groups, described in detail in Chapter 10, "Groups and Intergroup Processes," are the broader example of using technology in decision-making groups.

The **nominal group technique (NGT)** is a procedure for generating large amounts of information about a decision problem. The NGT uses a structured approach to decision making that is useful for generating, evaluating, and choosing alternative courses of action. It is a special case of brainstorming that does not include direct interaction. Research evidence shows NGT as outperforming the interactive brainstorming just described. NGT usually creates more ideas of at least equal quality.[48]

During the early stages of the NGT, members of the decision-making group do not interact or talk with each other. Instead, they write their ideas about the decision problem on paper. After about 20 minutes, each person reads one idea from her list. Another person records each idea on a flip-chart in full view of all members of the group. The reading and recording continue with each member presenting one idea at a time, until all ideas are recorded.

During the reading and recording phase, no discussion takes place. By the end of this phase, the group has generated its set of ideas for the decision problem. The group then discusses the ideas on the flip-chart. After the discussion, each group member votes privately on the ideas. Finally, the individual votes are pooled to arrive at a decision about the problem.

The **Delphi method** is a structured technique for making decisions that are surrounded by uncertainty or that are conflicting values laden. This method also is used when group members are geographically scattered. Forecasting future events and determining public policy are examples of the types of decisions that can use the Delphi method.[49]

Several people anonymously contribute to a group's decision when made by the Delphi method. Such people often are experts in their fields. They do not have any face-to-face contact. Members of a Delphi group interact through paper-and-pencil questionnaires or through computers.

The Delphi method follows a sequence of interrelated steps. The person managing the Delphi summarizes the outcomes of those steps using frequency distributions, the median, the quartile, or other appropriate statistics. The summary then becomes the input to the next step.

The Delphi method avoids some liabilities of group decision making. The lack of face-to-face interaction decreases the chance of one person becoming dominant. The controlled feedback from the summaries of each stage helps ensure the information accuracy passed from step to step.

The **devil's advocate technique** starts with one decision maker, or a group of decision makers, advocating and arguing forcefully for a decision alternative. Another person or group plays the role of critic, finding fault with the alternative and arguing for its rejection. The devil's advocate technique assumes a good decision alternative will withstand harsh criticism.[50] Research evidence suggests the technique helps in reaching high-quality decisions.[51]

Dialectical inquiry is a structured, logical, and analytical method of examining decision alternatives. The process begins by describing the favored decision alternative and the data used to select it. The process analyzes the assumptions held by the decision makers when choosing the alternative. Another decision alternative is then selected for consideration. That alternative could be a new one or one rejected earlier in the decision process. The assumptions underlying the choice of the counter-alternative are also derived logically.[52] Research evidence suggests this technique can also help in reaching high-quality decisions.[53]

Other human-based methods exist for improving group decision making. These diverse methods have many names, including "appreciative management" and "Technology of Participation." They recognize that decision-making groups are increasingly diverse, with many different viewpoints. The goal of these methods is to harness differences, decrease dysfunctional conflict, and focus diverse members on the organization's goals.[54]

Computer-Based Methods

Computer-based methods of improving decisions in organizations include management information systems, decision support systems, and expert systems. The rapid spread of computer-based methods means you will likely encounter some of these systems in your work career.

Management information systems are information processing systems used by organizations to support their daily operating activities and decision-making functions. The systems can be manual, but are most powerful when they are computer based. Management information systems integrate different subsystems according to a general information management plan. Data within the subsystems conform to the specifications of the integrated system, allowing easy sharing throughout the system.[55] Multiple users reach the management information system with terminals or personal computers (PCs). Users get a wide range of data, decision models, and database querying methods. Management information systems strongly support the analytical, strategic planning, and decision activities of an organization.

Decision support systems are computer-based systems designed to aid human decision makers' judgment. These systems do not automate an organization's decision processes; instead, they support those processes and help decision makers arrive at better decisions. Decision support systems are dynamic systems that change and evolve as a decision maker uses them. They can also be tailored to a decision maker's way of making decisions. An organization could have several decision support systems for different decision makers and classes of decisions. Contemporary uses of such systems include sales forecasting, cargo aircraft flight schedules, and medical decisions.[56]

Expert systems support decision making by simulating an expert's knowledge and decision process. An expert system designed to help medical diagnosis, for example, has a database of symptoms and a set of decision rules that guide a user through a diagnosis. Users access the interactive systems through a terminal or a PC. The users do not need to be experts in the area covered by the expert system.[57]

International Aspects of Decision Making and Problem Solving

The earlier description of the decision process phases applies most directly to decision making in the United States, Canada, and some European countries.[58] The behavior of a single decision maker, or those participating in each phase, varies depending on the culture in which the decision process happens. Because behaviors vary, decision makers from different cultures who must interact to reach decisions often have difficulty understanding each other's behavior.

Decision makers from different cultures bring different orientations to the problem identification and diagnosis phase of decision making. Some cultures focus on solving problems. Other cultures accept their situation and rely on providence to take care of the future. U.S. decision makers, for example, often see problems as something to attack and solve. Malaysian, Thai, and Indonesian decision makers usually try to adjust to the problem and accept situations presented to them.

Evaluating and choosing alternatives differ dramatically across cultures. The person who makes the decision, the speed of the decision process, and the risk allowed in choosing alternatives all vary from culture to culture. Decision making is more centralized in Philippine and Indian organizations than in Swedish and Austrian organizations.[59] Decision making proceeds slowly in Egyptian organizations, but quickly in U.S. organizations. Decision makers in Singapore and Denmark are more likely to take bigger risks than decision makers in Portugal and Greece.[60]

Cultures also vary in the order in which decision makers assess alternatives. Decision makers in Japan and China usually consider all alternatives before choosing. Decision makers in the United States, Germany, and Canada typically use a serial process, rejecting alternatives along the way to a final choice.

Ethical Issues in Decision Making and Problem Solving

Decision-making and problem-solving processes in organizations raise several ethical concerns.[61] Ethical questions can arise not only when choosing among alternatives, but also when setting the goal for a decision, creating a set of alternatives, and assessing them. Other ethical questions arise when carrying out the decision.

An ethical decision maker willingly engages in an open and fair dialogue with all parties potentially affected by the decision.[62] The decision maker's responsibilities include giving information freely without deceiving others involved. The moral decision maker likely does not know the right answer for every ethical issue, but freely discusses all issues with affected parties.

A model of decision making and ethics has been proposed that tries to explain why unethical decisions happen.[63] The model proposes that decision makers who face ethical issues in a decision proceed in two phases. The first phase applies a decision rule that states a minimum cutoff for each dimension. An ethical rule in this phase could state, "We reject any alternative that creates a conflict of interest." When an alternative passes that rule, the decision maker then assesses it further by considering its benefits or costs weighted by its importance.

Research underlying this model suggests decision makers consider the ethical dimension with other dimensions when assessing alternatives. Positive benefits of dimensions other than the ethical one can overwhelm an undesirable ethical dimension. The ethical dimension also can have negative effects with little likelihood of happening. For example, the penalty is a large fine, but the organization is unlikely to be caught, which might lead decision makers to an unethical decision.

Summary

Decision making is the process of choosing among different courses of action using decision criteria. The criteria for choosing among alternatives can include cost, profit, danger, or pleasure.

Some decision-making models describe a process for problems with well-known alternatives, results, and decision rules (rational model). Another model describes a process for conditions of uncertainty and ambiguity (garbage can model). Each model gives different insights into organizational decision processes.

Managers can choose from different social processes for individual and group decisions. These approaches include processes involving a single individual, consultation with one or more people, or groups designed to reach consensus.

Decision makers use several heuristics or guidelines to simplify information processing during decision making. Such information processing strategies let decision makers move quickly through the process, but also limit the information they use, resulting in several judgment biases.

Decision makers can frame a decision in two different ways, with different effects on their decision behavior. People prefer to avoid risks in decisions framed as gains; they prefer to take risks in decisions framed as losses.

Decision makers often face a common dilemma: abandon a losing course of action or increase commitment to it. Evidence supports most decision makers being more likely to commit more resources, a process called escalation of commitment to a losing course of action.

Cohesive decision-making groups often develop groupthink, a phenomenon featuring excessive conformity to group norms that support agreement about decisions. Decision groups with groupthink are unable to critically assess alternative solutions to a problem.

Several human-based methods and computer-based methods exist for improving decision making in organizations. Human-based methods include brainstorming and techniques for increasing the information available to a decision maker (for example, the nominal group technique and the Delphi method). Computer-based methods include management information systems, decision support systems, and expert systems.

The international context of organizations adds complexities to organizational decision processes. Cultural variations in decision-making behavior and decision orientations suggest potential difficulties for multicultural decision-making groups.

An ethical decision maker has an open dialogue with all parties potentially affected by a decision and does not engage in deceptive behavior. A proposed model of decision making and ethics uses an explicit ethics decision rule.

Review and Discussion Questions

1 Review the decision-making process. Discuss each step in the process and the relationships among them.

2 Review the decision-making models described in this chapter. Which model do you think is closest to what managers do when they make decisions? Why?

3 Review the assets and liabilities of group decision making. Which methods of improving decision making in organizations help offset the liabilities? How? Why?

4 Have you experienced groupthink? Discuss the conditions under which it happened and how it could have been prevented.

5 Discuss the different methods of improving decision making in organizations. Which of these methods do you expect to find widely used in organizations? Discuss differences in how easy each it is to use method of improvement.

6 Discuss the culturally based differences in decision making and problem solving described in this chapter with students from countries other than your own or with students who have visited other countries. Have any students experienced the differences described? Discuss their reactions to those differences.

7 Review the discussion of ethics in decision making and problem solving. Discuss the value of explicitly considering the ethics of a decision.

Take Five: OB Alive: *Dr. Seuss' How The Grinch Stole Christmas* (2000)

Film director Ron Howard loosely adapted the original Dr. Seuss tale to the film screen. The Grinch (Jim Carrey) hates Christmas, but the Whos of Who-ville love it. Cindy Lou Who (Taylor Momsen) tries to convert the Grinch by inviting him to some Yuletide celebrations.

This scene begins in DVD Chapter 9, "Second Thoughts." The Grinch must decide about accepting Cindy Lou's invitation. The scene ends as he storms off screen while saying he will not go to the celebrations (Stop: 0 : 45 : 06).

Consider the following questions while viewing the scene: What are Grinch's options? What criteria does he use to choose among them? What steps does the Grinch follow in his decision process?

References and Notes

1. Koopman, P. L., and J. Pool. 1990. Decision Making in Organizations. In *International Review of Industrial and Organizational Psychology*, Vol. 5, ed. C. L. Cooper and I. T. Robertson. Chichester, UK: John Wiley & Sons, Chap. 4. Wilson, C. Z., and M. Alexis. 1962. Basic Frameworks for Decisions. *Academy of Management Journal* 5: 150–64.
2. Huber, G. P. 1980. *Managerial Decision Making*. Glenview, Ill.: Scott, Foresman, pp. 8–9.
3. Developed from Huber, *Managerial Decision Making*.
   March, J. G., and H. A. Simon. 1958. *Organizations*. New York: John Wiley & Sons, pp. 180–82.
   Vroom, V. H., and A. G. Jago. 1988. *The New Leadership: Managing Participation in Organizations*. Englewood Cliffs, N. J.: Prentice Hall.
4. Barnard, C. I. 1938. *The Functions of the Executive*. Cambridge, Mass.: Harvard University Press.
5. Developed from E. F. Harrison. 1975. *The Managerial Decision Making Process*. Boston: Houghton Mifflin, pp. 13–15.
6. March and Simon, *Organizations*, p. 137.
7. Simon, H. A. 1960. *The New Science of Management Decision*. New York: Harper & Row, pp. 5–6.

8. Developed from Koopman and Pool, Decision Making in Organizations.
   Harrison, *The Managerial Decision Making Process*, Chap. 2.
   Huber, *Managerial Decision Making*, Chap. 2.
9. Abelson, R. P., and A. Levi. 1985. Decision Making and Decision Theory. In *The Handbook of Social Psychology*, Vol. 1, ed. G. Lindzey and E. Aronson. Reading, Mass.: Addison-Wesley, Chap. 5.
10. Barnard, *The Functions of the Executive*.
11. Developed from March and Simon, *Organizations*.
    Simon, H. A. 1997. *Administrative Behavior: A Study of Decision-Making Processes in Administrative Organizations*, 4th edn. New York: Free Press.
12. Developed from March and Simon, *Organizations*, Chap. 6.
    Simon, *Administrative Behavior*.
13. March and Simon, *Organizations*, p. 141.
14. Koopman and Pool, Decision Making in Organizations.
    Mintzberg, H., D. Raisinghani, and A. Theoret. 1976. The Structure of "Unstructured" Decision Processes. *Administrative Science Quarterly* 21: 246–75.
    Newell, A., and H. A. Simon. 1972. *Human Problem Solving*. Englewood Cliffs, N. J.: Prentice Hall.
    Simon, *The New Science*.
15. Mintzberg, Raisinghani, and Theoret, The Structure of "Unstructured" Decision Processes, pp. 250–51. (Emphasis in original.)
16. March and Simon, *Organizations*, pp. 140–41.
17. Mintzberg, Raisinghani, and Theoret, The Structure of "Unstructured" Decision Processes, pp. 263–66.
18. Soelberg, P. O. 1967. Unprogrammed Decision Making. *Industrial Management Review* 8: 19–29.
19. March, J. G., and J. P. Olsen, eds. 1976. *Ambiguity and Choice in Organizations*. Bergen, Norway: Universitetsforlaget.
    March, J. G., and J. P. Olsen. 1986. Garbage Can Models of Decision Making in Organizations. In *Ambiguity and Command: Organizational Perspectives on Military Decision Making*, ed. J. G. March and R. Weissinger-Baylon. Cambridge, Mass.: Ballinger, pp. 11–35.
    A recent summary of research appears in N. Takahashi. 1997. A Single Garbage Can Model and the Degree of Anarchy in Japanese Firms. *Human Relations* 50: 91–108.
20. Pfeffer, J. 1982. *Organizations and Organization Theory*. Marshfield, Mass.: Pitman Publishing.
21. Developed from F. C. Brodbeck, R. Kerschreiter, A. Mojzisch, and S. Schulz-Hardt. 2007. Group Decision Making under Conditions of Distributed Knowledge: The Information Asymmetries Model. *Academy of Management Review* 32: 459–79.
    George, E., and P. Chattopadhyay. 2008. Group Composition and Decision Making. In *The Oxford Handbook of Organizational Decision Making*, ed. G. P. Hodgkinson and W. H. Starbuck. Oxford, UK: Oxford University Press, Chap. 19.
    Gist, M. E., E. A. Locke, and M. S. Taylor. 1987. Organizational Behavior: Group Structure, Process, and Effectiveness. *Journal of Management* 13: 237–57.
    Hare, A. P. 1992. *Groups, Teams, and Social Interaction: Theories and Applications*. New York: Praeger Publishers, p. 4.
    Maier, N. R. F. 1967. Assets and Liabilities in Group Problem Solving: The Need for an Integrative Function. *Psychological Review* 74: 239–49.
    Nemeth, C. J., and B. Nemeth-Brown. 2003. Better than Individuals? The Potential Benefits of Dissent and Diversity for Group Creativity. In *Group Creativity: Innovation through Collaboration*, ed. P. B. Paulus and B. A. Nijstad. New York: Oxford University Press, Chap. 4.
    Pate, S., W. E. Watson, and L. Johnson. 1998. The Effects of Competition on the Decision Quality of Diverse and Nondiverse Groups. *Journal of Applied Social Psychology* 28: 912–23.

Vroom and Jago, *The New Leadership*, Chap. 3.
Wagner, J. A., III, C. R. Leana, E. A. Locke, and D. M. Schweiger. 1997. Cognitive and Motivation Frameworks in U.S. Research on Participation: A Meta-Analysis of Primary Effects. *Journal of Organizational Behavior* 18: 49–65.
West, M. A. 2003. Innovation Implementation in Work Teams. In *Group Creativity: Innovation through Collaboration*, ed. P. B. Paulus and B. A. Nijstad. New York: Oxford University Press, Chap. 12.

22. Alper, S., D. Tjosvold, and K. S. Law. 1998. Interdependence and Controversy in Group Decision Making: Antecedents to Effective Self-Managing Teams. *Organizational Behavior and Human Decision Processes* 74: 33–52.

23. Black, J. S., and H. B. Gregersen. 1997. Participative Decision-Making: An Integration of Multiple Dimensions. *Human Relations* 50: 859–78.

24. Developed from V. H. Vroom and A. G. Jago. 1974. Decision Making as a Social Process: Normative and Descriptive Models of Leader Behavior. *Decision Sciences* 5: 743–69.
Vroom, V. H., and P. W. Yetton. 1973. *Leadership and Decision-Making*. Pittsburgh, Pa.: University of Pittsburgh Press.
Vroom and Jago, *The New Leadership*.

25. Pasewark, W. R., and J. R. Strawser. 1994. Subordinate Participation in Audit Budgeting Decisions: A Comparison of Decisions Influenced by Organizational Factors to Decisions Conforming with the Vroom–Jago Model. *Decision Sciences* 25: 281–99.
Vroom and Jago, *The New Leadership*, Chap. 6.

26. Field, R. H. G. 1982. A Test of the Vroom—Yetton Normative Model of Leadership. *Journal of Applied Psychology* 67: 523–32.
Field, R. H. G., and R. J. House. 1990. A Test of the Vroom–Yetton Model Using Manager and Subordinate Reports. *Journal of Applied Psychology* 75: 362–66.
Vroom, V. H., and A. G. Jago. 1978. On the Validity of the Vroom–Yetton Model. *Journal of Applied Psychology* 63: 151–62.

27. Ettling, J. T., and A. G. Jago. 1988. Participation under Conditions of Conflict: More on the Validity of the Vroom–Yetton Model. *Journal of Management Studies* 25: 73–83.

28. Tversky, A., and D. Kahneman. 1973. Availability: A Heuristic for Judging Frequency and Probability. *Cognitive Psychology* 5: 207–32.

29. Kahneman, D., and A. Tversky. 1972. Subjective Probability: A Judgment of Representativeness. *Cognitive Psychology* 3: 430–54.
Kahneman, D., and A. Tversky. 1973. On the Psychology of Prediction. *Psychological Review* 80: 237–51.

30. Nisbett, R. E., and L. Ross. 1980. *Human Inference: Strategies and Shortcomings of Social Judgment*. Englewood Cliffs, N.J.: Prentice Hall.
Tversky, A., and D. Kahneman. 1974. Judgment under Uncertainty: Heuristics and Biases. *Science* 185: 1124–31.

31. Bazerman, M. H. 1994. *Judgment in Managerial Decision Making*. New York: John Wiley & Sons, Chap. 2.
Tversky and Kahneman, Judgment under Uncertainty.

32. Bazerman, *Judgment in Managerial Decision Making*, p. 24.

33. Kahneman, D., and A. Tversky. 1979. Prospect Theory: An Analysis of Decisions under Risk. *Econometrica* 47: 263–91.
Kuhberger, A. 1998. The Influence of Framing on Risky Decisions: A Meta-Analysis. *Organizational Behavior and Human Decision Processes* 75: 23–55.
Levin, I. P., S. L. Schneider, and G. J. Gaeth. 1998. All Frames Are Not Created Equal: A Typology and Critical Analysis of Framing Effects. *Organizational Behavior and Human Decision Processes* 76: 149–88.
The classic treatment of framing effects appears in A. Tversky and D. Kahneman. 1981. The Framing of Decisions and the Psychology of Choice. *Science* 211: 453–58.

34. Kahneman, D., and A. Tversky. 1984. Choices, Values, and Frames. *American Psychologist* 39: 341–50.
Whyte, G. 1991. Decision Failures: Why They Occur and How to Prevent Them. *Academy of Management Executive* 5: 23–31.

35. Whyte, Decision Failures.

36. Bazerman, *Judgment in Managerial Decision Making*, p. 61.
Nutt, P. C. 1993. The Formulation Processes and Tactics Used in Organizational Decision Making. *Organization Science* 4: 226–51.

37. Staw, B. M. 1981. The Escalation of Commitment to a Course of Action. *Academy of Management Review* 6: 577–87.
Staw, B. M., and J. Ross. 1987. Behavior in Escalation Situations: Antecedents, Prototypes, and Solutions. In *Research in Organizational Behavior*, Vol. 9, ed. B. M. Staw and L. L. Cummings. Greenwich, Conn.: JAI Press, pp. 39–78.

38. Keil, M., B. C. Y. Tan, K.-K. Wei, T. Saarinen, V. Tuunainen, and A. Wassenaar. 2000. A Cross-Cultural Study on Escalation of Commitment Behavior in Software Projects. *MIS Quarterly* 24: 299–325.

39. Edwards, W. 1954. The Theory of Decision Making. *Psychological Bulletin* 51: 380–417.

40. Summarized in J. Ross and B. M. Staw. 1993. Organizational Escalation and Exit: Lessons from the Shoreham Nuclear Power Plant. *Academy of Management Journal* 36: 701–32.
Staw and Ross, Behavior in Escalation Situations.
Whyte, G. 1986. Escalating Commitment to a Course of Action: A Reinterpretation. *Academy of Management Review* 11: 311–21.

41. Whyte, G., A. M. Saks, and S. Hook. 1997. When Success Breeds Failure: The Role of Self-Efficacy in Escalating Commitment to a Losing Course of Action. *Journal of Organizational Behavior* 18: 415–32.

42. McConnell, M. 1987. *Challenger: A Major Malfunction*. New York: Doubleday.

43. Janis, I. L. 1971. Groupthink. *Psychology Today* (November), pp. 43–46, 74–76.
Janis, I. L. 1982. *Groupthink: Psychological Studies of Policy Decisions and Fiascoes*, 2nd edn. Boston: Houghton Mifflin. Janis, I. L. 1989. *Crucial Decisions: Leadership in Policymaking and Crisis Management*. New York: Free Press.
Janis, I. L., and Mann, L. 1989. *Decision Making: A Psychological Analysis of Conflict, Choice, and Commitment*. New York: Free Press.

44. George and Chattopadhyay, Group Composition and Decision Making.
Turner, M. E., and A. R. Pratkanis. 1997. Mitigating Groupthink by Stimulating Constructive Conflict. In *Using Conflict in Organizations*, ed. C. K. W. De Dreu and E. Van de Vliert. London: Sage Publishing, Chap. 4.

45. Aldag, R. J., and S. R. Fuller. 1993. Beyond Fiasco: A Reappraisal of the Groupthink Phenomenon and a New Model of Group Decision Processes. *Psychological Bulletin* 113: 533–52.
Esser, J. K. 1998. Alive and Well after 25 Years: A Review of Groupthink Research. *Organizational Behavior and Human Decision Processes* 73: 116–41.
Kerr, N. L., and R. S. Tindale. 2004. Group Performance and Decision Making. *Annual Review of Psychology* 55: 623–65. See p. 640 for a summary of groupthink research.
Longley, J., and Pruitt, D. G. 1980. Groupthink: A Critique of Janis's Theory. In *Review of Personality and Social Psychology*, ed. L. Wheeler. Newbury Park, Calif.: Sage Publishing, pp. 507–13.
Park, W. 1990. A Review of Research on Groupthink. *Journal of Behavioral Decision Making* 3: 229–45.

46. Bouchard, T. J. 1971. Whatever Happened to Brainstorming? *Journal of Creative Behavior* 5: 182–89.
Litchfield, R. C. 2008. Brainstorming Reconsidered: A Goal-Based View. *Academy of Management Review* 33: 649–68.
Osborn, A. F. 1963. *Applied Imagination: Principles and Procedures of Creative Thinking*, 3rd edn. New York: Charles Scribner's Sons.

Rickards, T. 1999. Brainstorming Revisited: A Question of Context. *International Journal of Management Reviews* 1: 91–110.

47. Dennis, A. R., and M. L. Williams. 2003. Electronic Brainstorming: Theory, Research, and Future Directions. In *Group Creativity: Innovation through Collaboration*, ed. P. B. Paulus and B. A. Nijstad. New York: Oxford University Press, Chap. 8.
Gallupe, R. B., and W. H. Cooper. 1993. Brainstorming Electronically. *Sloan Management Review* 35 (Fall): 27–36.
Gallupe, R. B., A. R. Dennis, W. H. Cooper, J. S. Valacich, L. M. Bastianutti, and J. F. Nunamaker, Jr. 1992. Electronic Brainstorming and Group Size. *Academy of Management Journal* 35: 350–69.
Kerr and Tindale, Group Performance and Decision Making, pp. 627–28.
Nunamaker, J. F., Jr., R. O. Briggs, and D. D. Mittleman. 1996. Lessons from a Decade of Group Support Systems Research. In *Information Systems: Decision Support and Knowledge-Based Systems*, Vol. 3, ed. J. F. Nunamaker, Jr. and R. H. Sprague, Jr. Washington, D.C.: IEEE Computer Society Press, pp. 418–27.

48. Bartunek, J. M., and J. K. Murninghan. 1984. The Nominal Group Technique: Expanding the Basic Procedure and Underlying Assumptions. *Groups and Organizational Studies* 9: 417–32.
Cook, C. W. 1980. Nominal Group Methods Enrich Classroom Learning. *Exchange: The Organizational Behavior Teaching Journal* 5: 33–36.
Delbecq, A. L., and A. H. Van de Ven. 1971. A Group Process Model for Problem Identification and Program Planning. *Journal of Applied Behavioral Science* 7: 466–92.
Rickards, Brainstorming Revisited.
Van de Ven, A., and A. L. Delbecq. 1971. Nominal versus Interacting Group Processes for Decision-Making Effectiveness. *Academy of Management Journal* 14: 203–12.

49. Dalkey, N. C. 1969. *The Delphi Method: An Experimental Study of Group Opinion*. Santa Monica, Calif.: RAND Corporation.
Dalkey, N. C., D. L. Rourke, R. Lewis, and D. Snyder, eds. 1972. *Studies in the Quality of Life: Delphi and Decision-Making*. Lexington, Mass.: Lexington Books.

50. Cosier, R. A., and C. R. Schwenk. 1990. Agreement and Thinking Alike: Ingredients for Poor Decisions. *Academy of Management Executive* 4: 69–74.
Mason, R. O. 1969. A Dialectical Approach to Strategic Planning. *Management Science* 15: B-403–B-414.
Schwenk, C. R. 1984. Devil's Advocacy in Managerial Decision Making. *Journal of Management Studies* 21: 153–68.

51. Schweiger, D. M., W. R. Sandberg, and J. W. Ragan. 1986. Group Approaches for Improving Strategic Decision Making: Analysis of Dialectical Inquiry, Devil's Advocacy, and Consensus. *Academy of Management Journal* 29: 51–71.
Schwenk, C. R. 1990. Effects of Devil's Advocacy and Dialectical Inquiry on Decision Making: A Meta-Analysis. *Organizational Behavior and Human Decision Processes* 47: 161–76.

52. Churchman, C. W. 1971. *The Design of Inquiring Systems: Basic Concepts of Systems and Organization*. New York: Basic Books.
Cosier and Schwenk, Agreement and Thinking Alike.

53. Schweiger, Sandberg, and Ragan, Group Approaches.
Schweiger, D. M., W. R. Sandberg, and P. L. Rechner. 1989. Experiential Effects of Dialectical Inquiry, Devil's Advocacy, and Consensus Approaches to Strategic Decision Making. *Academy of Management Journal* 32: 745–72.

54. Cooperider, D. L. 1990. Positive Image, Positive Action: The Affirmative Basis of Organizing. In *Appreciative Management and Leadership: The Power of Positive Thought and Action in Organizations*, ed. S. Srivasta, D. L. Cooperider, and Associates. San Francisco: Jossey-Bass, Chap. 4.
Spence, L. J. 1989. *Winning through Participation: Meeting the Challenge of Corporate Change with the Technology of Participation*. Dubuque, Iowa: Kendall/Hunt Publishing Co.

55. McLeod, R., Jr. 1993. *Management Information Systems: A Study of Computer-Based Information Systems.* New York: Macmillan.
56. Antes, J., L. Campen, U. Derigs, C. Titze, and G.-D. Wolle. 1998. SYNOPSE: A Model-Based Decision Support System for the Evaluation of Flight Schedules for Cargo Airlines. *Decision Support Systems* 22: 307–23.

    Kuo, R. J., and K. C. Xue. 1998. A Decision Support System for Sales Forecasting through Fuzzy Neural Networks with Asymmetric Fuzzy Weights. *Decision Support Systems* 24: 105–26.
    McLeod, *Management Information Systems*, Chap. 13. Rao, G. R., and M. Turoff. 2000. A Hypermedia-Based Group Decision Support System to Support Collaborative Medical Decision-Making. *Decision Support Systems* 30: 187–216.
    Sprague, R. H., and E. D. Carlson. 1982. *Building Effective Decision Support Systems*. Englewood Cliffs, N. J.: Prentice Hall.
57. McLeod, *Management Information Systems*, Chap. 15.
58. Developed from the following and other citations throughout: N. J. Adler, with A. Gundersen. 2008. *International Dimensions of Organizational Behavior*, 5th edn. Mason, Ohio: Thomson South-Western, Chap. 8.
59. Hofstede, G. 2001. *Culture's Consequences: Comparing Values, Behaviors, Institutions, and Organizations Across Nations*, 2nd edn. Thousand Oaks, Calif.: Sage Publishing.
60. Ibid., Chap. 4.
61. Harrison, *The Managerial Decision Making Process*, pp. 131–37.
62. Bowen, M. G., and F. C. Power. 1993. The Moral Manager: Communicative Ethics and the Exxon Valdez Disaster. *Business Ethics Quarterly* 3: 97–115.
63. Fritzsche, D. J. 1991. A Model of Decision-Making Incorporating Ethical Values. *Journal of Business Ethics* 10: 841–52.

Chapter 5: Post-Reading Questions

The reading presents a number of different decision-making models.

1. Think of an organization of which you have been a part (employee, volunteer, participant, etc.) and identify which model they typically seem to use. Why do you think that is?
2. Do you think they would benefit by using a different model? If so, which one and why? If not, why not?
3. Review Table 5.8.1 and explain which approach to decision-making you favor and why.
4. Think of a time you experienced or witnessed "group think." Why do you think it occurred and how could it have been avoided?

CHAPTER 6

Critical Thinking

Empowerment

Empowerment Through Control and Responsibility

Locus of Control

Who controls your life? Are the good things and bad things that have happened to you mostly the result of the choices and decisions you have made, or are they more due to luck and fate? There is no way to prove it one way or the other, but some of us tend to attribute our life experiences more to external factors (luck, fate, etc.) and some of us tend to attribute them more to internal factors (effort, talent, etc.). Which type of person are you? When you do poorly on an exam, is your first instinct to blame the professor for writing a difficult exam or is your first thought that you should have studied harder? Of course it could be a little of both, and it might vary depending on the exam and the circumstances. Nevertheless, some of us have a strong tendency to view ourselves as having an internal locus of control, and others of us have a strong tendency to view ourselves as having an external locus of control. As you might imagine, having an *internal* locus of control tends to make one try harder. If you believe you have control over the outcome of your life, you will put more effort into exerting that control. If, however, you do not believe you have any control over the outcome of your life, you will feel powerless and will be much less likely to try. Seligman referred to this phenomenon as "learned helplessness." When it starts to feel like nothing you do will make a difference, you naturally give up. You surrender to your circumstances. You become pessimistic and depressed.

Personal Agency

A closely related concept to Rotter's Locus of Control, is Bandura's Self-Efficacy. Although you might have an internal locus of control and believe that it is possible to influence your future outcome, you might not believe you have the talent, ability, or skill to achieve what you desire. The belief in your own abilities and your chances of success is referred to as self-efficacy. Although believing you can do it does not guarantee that you will succeed, it sure helps. And not believing that you have the ability to do something almost guarantees that you will fail. Any athlete knows the necessity of believing in themselves if they want to win.

The Free Will Debate

The ideas of internal locus of control and self-efficacy beg the question: Do we have free will or are our lives predetermined? The classic behavioral view of Skinner and Watson is that we have no free will. Our behavior has been shaped over the years by a history of reinforcement and punishment. We are constantly presented with contingencies, and how we respond will determine whether we are rewarded or punished. And those rewards and punishments will directly increase or decrease the probability of our repeating such behavior in the future; thus, our decisions are under external stimulus control, not under our internal control. We will do exactly what we have been trained to do, regardless of whether or not we naïvely think that we are making conscious and deliberate choices.

What might be considered the antithetical point of view is existentialism. Existentialism promotes the idea that we really do have free will, and that gives us the power to shape our own lives and create our own destiny. We have the ability to consider our options and make conscious deliberate choices, and our choices do make a difference. No one can control us unless we allow them to control us. Now you might say in a given situation, "I had no choice! He put a gun to my head and said if I didn't do it, he would kill me!" That would be a pretty extreme circumstance, but even there, you have a choice. It isn't the choice or the options you would prefer, but you do have a choice. And a number of very brave and committed people have chosen to die rather than violate their firmly held principles. When you compare that extreme situation to your own, that might put things into perspective. When you say things like "I have no choice, my parents wouldn't allow it, my wife would leave me, my friends would abandon me, my kids wouldn't understand," I would respond that "Yes, these things could happen, but they might not happen. Regardless, you still have a choice!"

Responsibility

We tell ourselves we have no choice to avoid the painful responsibility of having to make the choice. But the fact is, even choosing not to make a choice is still a choice! Freedom from choice is an illusion. If we go through life avoiding making choices and instead let others make the choices for us, or wait until decisions are made through inaction, opportunities are lost and options are closed, all due to indecision; however, our lives and our situations are still the result of the choices we made (or chose not to make). In some ways this is an inescapable burden, to be held responsible for our actions, but it also can be liberating to realize we have choices when we thought we didn't. Consider the mistreated wife caught in a loveless marriage. She doesn't like what her husband has become and desperately wants to leave, but she feels she cannot because she has no money to support herself. She is going to college to get a degree so she will have the skills and credentials to get a job. But meanwhile, she feels she has no choice but to stay in this bad relationship until such time as she is in a better position to make changes. She is miserable and depressed. However, she takes this class and reads this module and realizes that she does have a choice! She could move out right now. She might have to sleep on a friend's couch, she might have to live in her car, she might have to speak with a financial aid counselor, and she might even have to drop out of school for a while, but these are all choices that other people in similar situations have made. She may not like any of these alternatives and thus decide to continue doing what she was doing, but something has changed. Before she said, "I have no choice but to stay in this bad situation until I graduate." Now she tells herself, "I choose to stay in this bad situation until I graduate." This may sound like a subtle semantic difference, but it represents a huge shift in attitude. She went from feeling helpless and out of control to feeling hopeful and in control. She has chosen to suffer further temporarily, but it is her choice. She is empowered. And she is free to change her mind about this situation at any point in time. She is no longer trapped.

So as much as we try to avoid taking responsibility by pretending we are not free to make choices, there is much to be gained by accepting responsibility. But we must caution the reader that responsibility has more than one meaning. Responsibility means obligation. When you feel responsible for someone, you feel an obligation to take care of them. We feel that you are responsible for your life. You have an obligation to make the best choices possible for yourself and for the others that your choices will affect! But the other meaning of responsibility refers to blame. When we say you are responsible for breaking the window, we mean you are to blame. When we say you are responsible for your life and your choices, some people incorrectly interpret that to mean that you are to blame for all that goes wrong in your life. That is not true. Bad stuff happens—even to good people who make good choices. There are things in our lives that we cannot control, but we can control how we react to them. So we don't want to blame the victim for their circumstances; however, if the circumstances of your life are not what you would want, then we think you have an obligation to make changes in your life. You can spend your life wallowing in self-pity and blaming other people for your situation, but all that blame and self-pity won't make your life any better. It will only change for the better when you accept the responsibility for making it better!

Summary

What we are arguing here are not facts. Whether or not we have free will is a subject that will be debated by great minds for many years to come, just as it has been debated from time immemorial. But while science may not be able to answer the question as to whether man has free will, psychologists have discovered that people that have an internal locus of control and a belief in their own self-efficacy do tend to make life choices more proactively. And people that make their life choices more proactively do tend to have greater life satisfaction. So on this basis, we advocate that you should believe in your ability to make positive changes in your life, and we advocate that you should take active steps to make the changes that you envision as you see fit! In short, we believe that you can *empower* yourself by taking *control* of your life and by taking *responsibility* for your life.

All this is a lead-in to what comes next in your steps to problem-solving. We will be generating a lot of potential solutions and courses of action for your challenge statement. The group will help you to think of new ideas and new strategies. We are asking you to keep an open mind and use your critical thinking and discussion skills. People in your group will invariably suggest things that will cause you to think "I could *never* do that!" or "I would *never* do that!" or "I should *never* do that!" Keep those thoughts to yourself (at least at this step). You'll have a chance to clean them up later. For now, anything goes. They're just suggestions. Everything is good, no matter how challenging, impossible, or even downright silly it might seem at first glance. Actually, to do this step justice, you should make sure you have a few silly suggestions. Studies of creative problem-solving have demonstrated that allowing yourself to be silly and consider all ideas, no matter how outrageous, is key to finding new and better solutions. You can't think out of the box if you place the burden of making sure all ideas are realistic and acceptable on the surface before you begin. Sometimes the most far-out ideas have a kernel of something very valuable and useful in them. But you can't get at the diamond in the rough if you throw out everything that looks like a rock at first glance.

Group Assignment

In this week's discussion, please remind everyone of your challenge statement and give three possible solutions (options, suggestions, courses of action) on how to solve, master, or overcome your challenge. Then give three suggestions to each of your group members on how to solve, master, or overcome their challenge. Thus everyone should end up with multiple possibilities (three times the number of members in their group). Try to offer unique ideas. Be helpful, but also playful. Everyone should end up with a wide range of ideas from the sublime to the ridiculous. You are not allowed to reject anyone's idea. It is helpful to use a blackboard, dry erase board, or poster paper to record the ideas as people brainstorm. Then individuals can take their poster paper home or take a picture of the board with their cell phone, so everyone walks away with a personal copy of possible courses of action for their particular issue.

Individual Assignment

Take the list of alternatives that people brainstormed for you and pick one alternative course of action offered by each of your group members (including one that you offered to yourself). Try to choose a set of options that leave you with the widest range of alternatives, not several choices that are more or less the same. List one good thing and one bad thing about each of these alternatives (i.e., Why would this be a good choice? What are some of the potential advantages of this choice? Why might this be a bad choice? What are some of the potential disadvantages of this choice?).

The Weekly Reading

Pre-Reading Questions

The reading for this chapter is on the role of creative thinking in effective problem-solving.

1. To what degree do you believe you are a creative thinker?
2. Do you think creativity can be taught or enhanced, or is it a trait that you are born with and cannot change?
3. Do you think the school system you went through encouraged and fostered creative thinking? Could they improve in this endeavor? If so, how?

READING 9

Creative Thinking and Problem Solving

Paris S. Strom and Robert D. Strom

Speculation has long been the most common source of information on creative behavior. Explanations about the inventive mind, original thinking, and novel ideas have generally been pejorative. Ancient people saw creative individuals as possessed, driven to their innovation and unconventional behavior by some unseen power that chose them as a means of revelation. That creative behavior could be an outcome of learning was seldom considered. Instead, inspiration was attributed to the gods and, because evil and good were considered to be in constant dispute, anyone who demonstrated creativity was suspect. Original thinking could be a deception by the forces of evil, particularly in situations where individuals challenged dominant beliefs of their time (Shenk, 2011).

During the twentieth century unfavorable impressions of creative people continued but their behavior was linked to a presumed relationship between imaginative thinking and mental breakdown. Creative persons were no longer viewed as the pawns of an unseen force. Instead, they were personally responsible for their deviation in ideas and behavior from societal norms. Creativity was recognized as being an internal function but unrelated to education. Mental illness afflicted few geniuses, but eminent examples were cited to make it seem as though the exceptions were the rule. There was little recognition that willingness of creative individuals to press their nature to its limit is the supreme test of sanity. Instead, those who failed in such attempts were singled out as evidence that giftedness comes at too high a cost to be desirable (Ludwig, 1995; Russell, 2012).

The goals for this chapter are to describe an empirical distinction between creativity and intelligence with an overview of creative abilities, priority for mental operations of thinking, and progressive steps that define the creative process. Discussion includes the way creative students are seen by educators often as being difficult to work with because they give off-beat answers, refer to concepts that appear irrelevant to conventional thinkers, show humor and sarcasm, and frequently resort to daydreaming. Emphasis is given to the relationship between asking questions and becoming a self-directed learner. Curiosity and doubt are portrayed as powerful sources of motivation to support critical thinking. Attention is also paid to the kinds of questions teachers ask and how these practices correspond with the school priority for higher order thinking.

Value of Imaginative Abilities

The way to value originality is by appreciation for imaginative thinking. Human beings are unique in being imaginative, that wonderful attribute that enables us to look beyond the moment and current set of circumstances. Imagination allows people to go back in time and revisit the past as well as look ahead by envisioning ways to create a more desirable future. No one can predict what will happen tomorrow, but actions, motivated and shaped by imagination, can impact the nature of what life will become. Mankind may be evolving biologically at the same rate as other living organisms; however, in cultural terms, people change much more rapidly. As far as we can tell, the cats and dogs that we care about do not change at a corresponding rate. Left to themselves, they appear to do what they have always done and concern themselves with the same things. There is no need to keep checking with them to find out what's new. On the other hand, something will always be new in humanity because imagination triggers creative thinking and innovation (Robinson, 2013).

Over the past decade, China, India, Japan, Singapore, Taiwan, and other nations have decided that priority for creative thinking in schools is the best method to increase national productivity, compete in the global market, and support mental health (Sahlberg, 2011). The Chinese are decentralizing curriculum to enable greater flexibility; Singapore is attempting to promote a creative environment reflected by the guiding principle of "Teach less, learn more." These efforts to innovate depart from the common paradigm that dominated education practices before 2000 with a nearly exclusive emphasis on linear, logical, and analytical thinking. Since then it has become apparent that memorization must be joined by understanding how to process information that can be more accurately stored by technology. The emerging conceptual age paradigm is based on the premise that preservation of healthy economies will depend on greater support for original and inventive thinking. Computing, calculating, diagnostics, and legal work skills will remain important but lose value. This is because any activity that can be reduced to a set of rules and instructions is likely to become a software program, such as TurboTax, which has replaced many accountants and migrated lower-order tasks to less developed countries. Sir Ken Robinson (2011) provides an animated overview of why nations are adopting new outlooks on education that acknowledge creative thinking (http://www.youtube.com—search RSA animate changing education paradigms).

There are conflicting impressions about how to arrange conditions that foster creativity. In *The World is Flat*, Thomas Friedman (2007) contends that location no longer has the impact on creative production than in the past. Technology has leveled the global playing field, making the world flat so that anyone can innovate without having to emigrate. A contrary view comes from Richard Florida (2012) in *The Rise of the Creative Class*. He developed lists of cities on every continent where creative individuals tend to move since their talents are more commonly accepted, collaborators for novel projects can readily be found, and people prefer to collaborate on interdependent projects. Florida suggests that innovation is best encouraged by the geographic concentration of creative persons, entrepreneurs who recognize they can count on one another to allow their ideas to flow freely, recommend possibilities to improve concepts and products, and implement innovation sooner because creators and financial backers are in close contact. A small number of communities and regions, such as the Silicon Valley in California, generate most of the innovative ideas and products that are used throughout the world.

Many adolescents realize that they are less creative than they were during childhood when others assigned high value to the imagination they applied during fantasy play. Creative thinking begins to decline in the early grades when schools and families urge children to disconnect from reliance on imagination (Kim, 2010). A more promising practice is to ensure that the students in every town and city are able to find acceptance of divergent thinking without having to move to specific places where more favorable reactions to new ideas are the norm. What is known about the future suggests that efforts are needed to ensure more children retain their creative abilities into adulthood. Creative individuals can adapt to new knowledge, cope with complex situations, and think of constructive alternatives to resolve arguments. They show greater ability to generate new ways to improve situations, can make independent decisions, and feel comfortable with ambiguity (Runco & Albert, 2010).

Need for Divergent Thinking

The need for schools and families to help students retain their creative abilities was initially described by Joy Paul Guilford (1950) in his presidential address to the American Psychological Association. Guilford, a professor of psychology at the University of Southern California, contended that the traditional ways of viewing mental development were focused too narrowly on *convergent thinking*, an emphasis on knowing a single correct answer for problems and giving speedy responses. While these aspects of achievement are important, they should not dominate conceptualization of cognitive functioning at the expense of other abilities that appear to be essential for creative behavior. Guilford referred to *divergent thinking* as the ability to generate alternative answers for problems where there might be more than one solution, and to perceive many possibilities in situations.

A few years later, in 1957, Russia launched Sputnik I, the first artificial satellite. There was a feeling of national embarrassment because the United States had lost the initial round in the space race. Navy Admiral Hyman Rickover (1959, p. 16), a nuclear scientist, put the blame on public schools, citing the "inability of our institutions to find a place for the creative expert and their persistence in believing that novel projects can be carried out using routine methods." Soon there was public agreement about the need to support creative thinking and improve the science curriculum so the nation could catch up. Within weeks, Congress passed the National Defense Education Act (1958), providing funding for research on ways to nurture creativity in schools. Paul Torrance (1965) defined *creative thinking* as the process of sensing difficulties, problems, gaps in information, and missing elements; making guesses or formulating hypotheses about these deficiencies; testing guesses, possibly revising and retesting them; and finally communicating the results.

Subsequent studies of creativity focused on establishing a common basis for collaborative efforts. However, it was first necessary to determine whether creative potential is measured by intelligence tests or if creativity constitutes a separate domain of mental functioning that requires alternative tools for measurement. There was also speculation regarding the cognitive processes creative people rely on when producing their work. Identifying progressive steps in the creative process would be useful in order to establish a practical orientation for students. The willingness of teachers to nurture creative abilities had to be assessed and educational objectives modified so the expectations of students would reflect the newly adopted goals of society (Ness, 2013).

Creativity and Intelligence

Michael Wallach, professor of psychology and neuroscience at Duke University, and Nathan Kogan, psychologist at the Educational Testing Service, are recognized for their seminal study that changed how educators think about creativity. Their purpose was to establish whether *creativity*, defined as the ability to produce many associations among ideas and many that are unique, is independent of individual differences in the domain of general intelligence (Wallach & Kogan, 1965). The researchers also wanted to find out whether creativity, in a similar way to Spearman's (1904) G concept of intelligence, has a large degree of generality across different types of verbal and visual tasks. The 151 subjects were fifth graders (10 and 11 year olds) who attended one suburban public school. These students (70 girls and 81 boys) completed creativity instruments that called for the production of idea associations. The tests resembled an earlier battery of measures devised by Guilford (1950), but the conditions of speed and evaluation were deemphasized. Instead, a game-like setting without time limits was allowed. For each instrument (all were oral), the number of unique associations and the total number of ideas served as the correlational variables (Wallach & Kogan, 1965).

For one task, students were asked to produce examples for a concept specified in verbal terms. For example, "Name all of the round things that you can think of." The number of unique responses for an item was defined as the number of associates given by only one child to the item in question. Thus, while "lifesavers" was a unique response for things that are round, "buttons" was not unique. Another task required generating possible uses for verbally specified objects. To illustrate, "Tell me all of the things that you can do with a shoe." A unique response was "Trap a mouse," but it was not unique to "Throw it at a noisy dog." A third task called for thinking of similarities between two objects. For the item "Tell me the ways milk and meat are alike," a conventional response was, "They come from animals," whereas a unique response was, "They are government inspected."

In addition to verbal tasks, there were abstract patterns and line stimulus drawings for which students were expected to produce meanings or interpretations. A third set of assessments included ten indicators of general intelligence, including the verbal and performance subtests of the Wechsler Intelligence Scale for children (WISC); verbal and quantitative aptitude tests that were drawn from the School and College Ability Tests (SCAT); and Sequential Tests of Educational Progress (STEP), a measure of achievement in various subjects (Carlson, Geisinger, & Johnson, 2014).

The measures of creativity and intelligence were first determined to be valid and reliable, and then the dimensionality of these indicators was examined to find the degree to which they were related, referred to as correlation. A correlation of .40 or higher between two measures is considered substantial. The measures of creativity were highly intercorrelated (average .40); similar internal consistency was found for the general intelligence tests (average .50). However, the degree of relationship between creativity and intelligence was low, as shown by a correlation of .10. This lack of association led to the conclusion that individual differences in the ability to generate many cognitive units and many that are unique is a cohesive realm and independent from what is referred to as general intelligence. Within an assessment context free of evaluative threat and time constraint, being able to produce unique ideas comes from a different source than intelligence as historically perceived. Consequently, it can be asserted that the ability of students to demonstrate creativity, as defined in the Wallach and Kogan (1965) investigation, has little to do with whether or not they reveal behaviors that produce high scores on measures of general intelligence. This result is even more significant when it is recognized that all the measures of creativity in this investigation were oral, calling for verbal facility, and verbal facility plays a major role in the assessment of general intelligence.

Wallach and Kogan's (1965) findings suggested that it might be possible to educate to a greater degree many students who have been unsuccessful in traditional classroom environments. Operationally, the term *intelligence* has included abilities needed for reading and mathematics, subjects not conspicuously demanding of creative behavior. It should be mentioned, however, that while the creativity and intelligence domains seem separate, a person might rate high in both sectors. One estimate is that, in a group of students who are highly creative or highly intelligent, 30% qualify in both categories (Torrance, 2000a, 2000b). Finally, the statistical independence of these two domains has been documented at a time in life (ages 10 and 11) that is well below the age at which maximum differentiation of types of cognitive performance would be expected. This means that even greater independence could appear at later ages. These considerations suggest that a concerted effort is warranted to continually educate students for creative behavior.

Conformity and Independence

Some observers of social networking and age-segregated communication patterns worry that the growing influence of peer groups in adolescence could undermine the development and expression of divergent thought. There is concern that when peer approval is the main source of identity status, motivation of students to participate in independent thinking is likely to decline. The impact of group opinions on conformity was initially explored by Solomon Asch (1952) of Swarthmore College in Pennsylvania. His experiments that led to the study of group dynamics demonstrated how peer pressure could alter personal opinion, even about obvious facts. Student teams of six were recruited to look at a line appearing on a card and then report aloud which of three other lines—each of a different size—were the same length as the first one examined. The first five persons to report were confederates of Asch who had been instructed ahead of time to state the same wrong answer for certain trials. A sixth person, the only real subject, was always asked last to give his judgment. The tasks ensured being confronted by a situation he had never experienced before. He found that the line he saw as equal in length to the standard line is not equal according to colleagues. His peers are in a position to know yet they all disagree with him.

The experience produced tension for the subject because it was a violation of a primitive belief; group consensus was in conflict with direct evidence provided by his own senses. Asch found that most subjects continued to make independent judgments in the presence of one or two dissenters. With a single opponent the subject disagreed with his own perceptions 3.6% of the time; with two opponents, the error rate rose to 13.6% of the time. Incorrect judgments increased significantly when three or more persons opposed the subjects. This indicated that the size of a majority opposing them had an effect on the subjects. When four opponents contradicted their personal perceptions, subjects gave up their own perceptions 35.1% of the time. The experiment continued for numerous trials after which the naive subjects were relieved to find out about the details of their tests of nonconformity (Asch, 1956).

Asch recognized that perception and judgment were implicated when subjects announced their decisions about which lines were the same length. He could not know that years later, these two cognitive functions would be found to be mediated by different circuits within the brain. In the past decade neuroscientists have been able to rely on MRI (magnetic resonance imaging) techniques to map the neurobiology of processes such as emotion, attention, and memory. The question of whether groups can alter what individuals see was overlooked until Gregory Berns and his team from Emory University wanted to assess how fear might distort perception as a variation of Asch's social isolation experiment (Berns, Chappelow, Zink, Pagnoni, Martin-Skurski, & Richards, 2005).

The premise was that if others in a social setting can change what we see or suppose we see, an MRI should detect change in the perceptual region of the brain. However, if conformity is triggered at the decision-making level, changes should be made visible in the frontal cortex brain region involving judgment. Most of the right-handed adolescents and the young adults who were recruited by Berns and his team (2005) were confederates who were instructed to carry out the same deception role as applied in the Asch experiments 50 years earlier. When the naive subject arrived in the lab, four other people were seen who he supposed would be facing the same tasks. Everyone was told that they would be completing visual perception tasks on the computer. Each individual would be shown the same rotating images and know the answers that were given by all their colleagues. The task was to decide which of two shapes were the same or different. In the warm-up practice, almost all answers given by the subjects were correct. Later, when the group gave the wrong judgment as seen on the computer screen, the subject rate of correct answers dropped to 59%.

The MRIs provided the explanation. One might not think of conformity as related to a visual process, but that is what was found. The group altered patterns of activation in the visual and parietal processing regions of the subjects' brains when the subjects went along with them incorrectly. Whenever a subject capitulated to the group, and the group was incorrect, greater activity was observed in the parietal cortex as if it was working harder. A plausible explanation is that the consensus wrong answers imposed a virtual image in the mind of the subject. In the case of conformity, this virtual image beat out the image originating from the subject's own eyes, causing the subject to ignore his own perceptions and accept the perception of the group. Similar changes were not evident in the frontal lobes implicating judgment. Instead, the amount of activity there decreased when a subject conformed, suggesting that the group's answers took some of the load off the decision-making process in the frontal lobe (Berns, 2010).

Even when subjects stood their ground and gave the correct answer in opposition to the unanimously wrong answer by the group, changes in brain activity were detectable. However, in these instances of nonconformity, brain changes were not observed in the perceptual region but in the *amygdala*. When the amygdala fires, a cascade of neural events is unleashed that prepares the body for immediate action as the first stage in the socalled fight or flight system. The end result of amygdala activation is a rise in blood pressure and in heart rate, more sweating and rapid breathing. Many events can trigger the amygdale, but fear is by the most effective. The amygdala activation during nonconformity reinforced the upsetting experience of standing alone, even if a person had no recollection of it. In many people, the brain would rather avoid activating the fear system related to social rejection and just change perception instead to conform to the social norm (Berns, 2010).

If a group is capable of changing our perceptions and to stand alone activates powerful unconscious feelings of rejection, creative behavior may be more vulnerable than has generally been supposed. Beginning in middle school, students collaborate in cooperative learning groups where consensus opinion often governs actions of all the members. In this context, students who are more capable of generating divergent ideas are often advised to demonstrate bravery and be willing to suffer rejection as the cost to avoid conformity. Creative persons frequently respond to this advice by wanting to work independently rather than work in groups that dismiss their ideas without reflection. Preparing students for teamwork requires encouragement of divergent opinions and recognition that sometimes one person may have a better solution than the majority of a group. Throughout history, creative people have always had to overcome resistance to new ideas.

The Creative Process

The support of student creativity as a priority in school and finding ways to develop this capacity are becoming prominent goals. Those who conduct research in this context admit that the creative thinking process is not fully understood. However, there is agreement that several specific stages precede invention. The stages of the *creative process* are (1) preparation, (2) incubation, (3) illumination, and (4) verification (Ghiselin, 1987). The four stages are illustrated in Figures 6.9.1 (preparation), 6.9.2 (incubation), 6.9.3 (illumination), and 6.9.4 (verification).

Preparation

Some people are surprised to learn that preparation is a vital aspect of creative thinking. Instead, they tend to suppose that inspiration just comes to certain individuals and not to others. This assumption makes it easier to avoid the struggle in which those who create are engaged. *Preparation* (see Figure 6.9.1) begins after creative persons experience vague insights

Figure 6.9.1 Stage 1 of the creative process—preparation. Search data, begin to question assumptions, brainstorm with a partner, and try to see the main pieces of the problem. This process typically takes the most time. Illustration by Paris Strom.

and set out to examine some particular problem or realm of difficulty by flooding themselves with the diverse impressions held by others. Many obstacles that undermine production characterize the preparation phase. First, the literature on a problem may be so extensive that the task seems overwhelming. This appears to be the case when many search engines can be applied to locate an enormous database for consideration. At this point the individual might decide to withdraw from further exploration and go on to some other concern that appears to be less complicated.

A second related danger is that side issues can capture attention and divert interest from the original purpose. This is a familiar shortcoming among people whose indiscriminate curiosity often causes them to leave the desired line of direction. They may be pursuing a particular area of inquiry but along the way web sites they explore present links that take them away from their intention. Staying focused is essential and can be difficult during searches on the Internet or in a library (Rosen, 2013).

Third, the impatience that causes students to grapple with a particular issue can destroy their chances for success if they prematurely reach conclusions about the data (de Bono, 2010). This is a widespread hazard in situations where rapid production is an expectation. Whenever teachers set deadlines that are too early, they encourage superficial consideration of data. The emphasis on doing everything in a hurry is not conducive to creative thinking. It is necessary to recognize that a fundamental aspect of the preparation phase is immersion in ideas and insights already expressed by others. Awareness of these impressions produces the material on which synthesizing ability will operate. Abandoning a problem or project is easier at this stage than later because little work has been invested and the degree of emotional involvement is minimal (Cain, 2012).

Many adolescents see themselves as lacking creative potential because novel ideas have not come to them without preparation. Reading about the lives of eminent individuals including their failures, successes, and courage can correct this perception. Courage is required to move alone toward uncertainties, counter to one's classmates, and to do battle with personal prejudices. It takes persistence to restart a task again and again. Persistence brings success and failure. More than most of us, the creative person experiences failure because he or she does not run from complex tasks. Many people do not fail because they are so easily discouraged and quit; at the same time, they can never fully succeed. Persistence enables a person to sustain a question, a problem, or task, and work it through to completion. The history of creative persons who have contributed the most to society is an account filled with persistence and courage (Ness, 2013).

Preparation is a difficult period for all creative persons. Those who underestimate the value of preparation typically end their search process too soon. Potentially creative students frequently give up because they suppose that inventive thinking is simple or beyond their reach. The fact is quite often what seems to be a creative achievement is actually a matter of being able to sort abundant information and organize it well.

Incubation

The second stage of the creative process centers on incubation (see Figure 6.9.2). During *incubation* there is an irrational, intuitive encounter with the materials gathered in the search process. At this stage, people experience unrest as they try to produce an ordering structure, a recombination of information that will merit their expression in some unique as well as practical form. They may be preoccupied to the point that they fail to attend to routine tasks that others expect of them. As they try to allow an intuitive idea to take conscious form, creative persons are dissatisfied with themselves and often difficult to be around. Sometimes conflicts ensue with relatives or friends who consider inattention to them as a deliberate insult (Cain, 2012).

During the incubation stage, self-doubt can pose a great hazard. Confidence is essential when unconscious activity brings up new possibilities for combination one after another. It is imperative that the conscious mind refrain from disapproving ideas as they emerge and defer

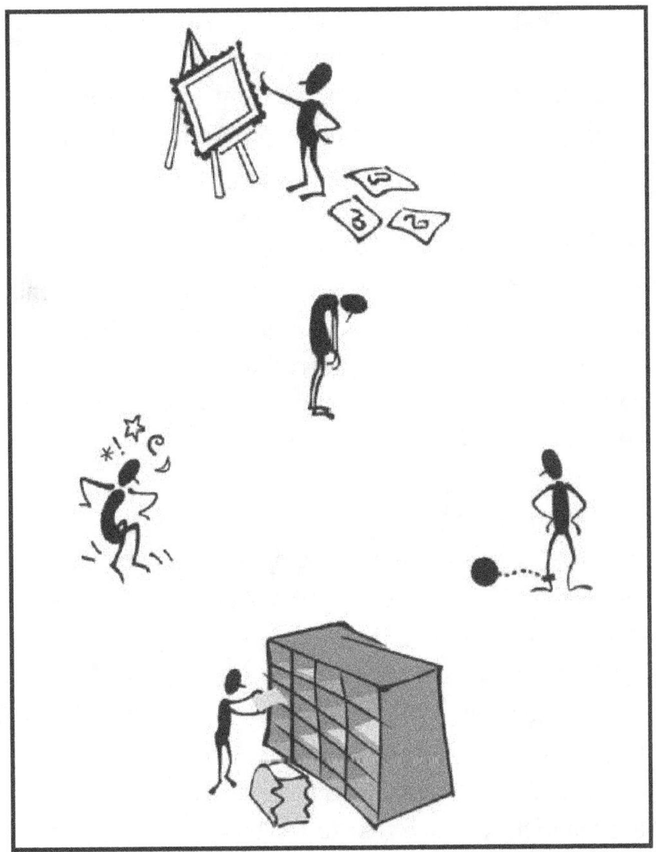

Figure 6.9.2 Stage 2 of the creative process—incubation. In-depth pondering, sketch or test ideas, get frustrated, recognize paradigm paralysis, look for one's niche. Illustration by Paris Strom.

judgment until a wide range of unconscious products become available. Feeling obligated to withhold judgment until the associative flow ends is a difficult and demanding task that requires a high tolerance for ambiguity and frustration. Mental health is usually delicate during the incubation phase, which can vary from a few minutes to months (Torrance, 2000b).

Students are often discouraged by their pace of production. Teachers and parents add to the frustration when they construe lack of speed as lack of ability, being slow as an indication of failure. It should be known that the time needed for production depends on the individual. The examples of Mozart and Beethoven represent a contrast in musical production. Mozart thought out quartets and symphonies in his head while traveling or exercising. Then, after coming home, he would write out the innovative melody in its entirety. On the other hand, Beethoven wrote his work note by note, fragments at a time recorded in a little booklet over a period of years. Often his initial ideas were so clumsy as to make someone wonder how, in the end, such beauty could emerge. Ernest Hemingway (1964, p. 154) admitted, "I didn't know I would ever be able to write anything as long as a novel. It often took me a full morning to write a paragraph." Later, he wrote a classic novel in six weeks.

During incubation, anything disruptive to concentration is likely to be rejected. There are some individuals for whom incubation can occur on and off over a lengthy period. For others, the attempt to produce ideas leads to excessive measures for sustaining touch with the unconscious in an environment that may be noisy and distracting. Not everyone seems to be psychologically capable of spending the same amount of time in the tension-producing phase of incubation. Yet creative persons usually prefer to work in long blocks of time so they can be fully engaged. This is without question the stage when peers, relatives, and teachers should be aware of the seeming self-punishment a person appears to experience. Giving up at this stage is done at great expense because creative persons typically consider not achieving the next stage, called illumination, as total failure (Hargrove, 1998). Albert Einstein observed, "The intuitive mind is a sacred gift and the rational mind is a faithful servant. We have created a society that honors the servant and has forgotten the gift" (in Ghiselin, 1987, p. 43).

Illumination

If the incubation stage presents creative persons with the situation Vincent Van Gogh identified as a "prison" where they are confined by internal conversation and debate, the phase of illumination may be analogous to a release from jail with a full pardon. *Illumination* (see Figure 6.9.3) is the inspirational moment the artist Paul Cezanne described as liberation, the mysterious becoming external, at the time when everything falls into place. It is the exhilarating triumph that creative persons like so much to relive, the time that is beyond words. Charles Darwin, whose search for the theory of evolution came to an end on a dusty lane, recalled the very spot on the road while traveling in his carriage that, to his joy and surprise, the solution occurred to him (Darwin & Wilson, 2005). Creative scientists, inventors, artists, and writers all look back with nostalgia at this brief, cherished moment and often refer to it as mystical. With illumination, the burden of tension is lifted and creative persons regain touch with those who are around them.

Figure 6.9.3 Stage 3 of the creative process—illumination. "Aha"—finding one's niche, loving the idea, taking the leap, and assembling the main pieces that fit well. Illustration by Paris Strom.

Some creative persons, especially those who have long awaited illumination, often make an effort to retain their joy by sharing it. Usually their accounts of how an idea occurred are less than exciting to others who perceive the quick shift from total preoccupation with the work and seeming depression to happiness and conscious delight as an additional sign of mental illness. They may wonder at the extremes in the creative person's behavior and especially at the sudden elation expressed over something that they may not understand or consider to be important. Further, in returning to a normal state of consciousness, some individuals cannot figure out why some people have become emotionally distant toward them during the interlude (Cain, 2012).

For some persons, the creative process ends with the illumination stage because they have achieved the tentative answer and shed their tensions. At this point, they may move ahead to confront another problem. Persons of this inclination seldom attain recognition or contribute as much as possible because they do not go on to make the form of their invention coherent to others who could enable its broader application or modify it to fit a wider range of prevailing situations (Ness, 2013).

Verification

The stage of *verification* occurs after an idea or plan has emerged from unconscious activity and must then be consciously evaluated (see Figure 6.9.4). Some creative persons find the need for verification difficult or impossible to accept because emotional certainty about worth of their idea or product precludes accepting any criticism or adaptation. Nevertheless, the pleasure of illumination must give way to rational judgment as the determinant of final production. If a writer is to communicate, the inspired work must become organized and edited. There must be a coherent flow so readers can share the message. Similarly, the successful experiment that elates a scientist must be clearly described (Oberkampf & Roy, 2010).

Unlike the brief illumination phase, verification is typically lengthy, arduous, and at times disappointing to a person whose patience declines because of eagerness to begin another project.

Figure 6.9.4 Stage 4 of the creative process—verification. Testing final idea to see/correct faults—"final editing," assessment by outsiders, experience closure and recognize success via individual or social judgment criteria. Illustration by Paris Strom.

The hazard that awaits many writers, scientists, and creators in technology and art is the temptation to avoid follow-through. This temptation has prevented good literature from ever becoming public knowledge. There are well-known writers like Samuel Coleridge and Percy Shelley, who left fragments of unfinished work because they could not revise it, feeling that inspiration could not be improved on and believing alteration would destroy the illumination. Hart Crane was an exacting author, and a look at his manuscripts reveals that revisions involved as much doubt as decision. In contrast, Gertrude Stein intensely disliked the drudgery of revision and the obligation to make certain of her writing projects intelligible (Malcolm, 2007). Being willing to seek and constructively interpret criticism from reviewers is essential at this stage. Sadly, most people have not been taught in school or at home to benefit from the criticism of others, and this presents an enormous obstacle to creativity. It means that growth is restricted since they rely on themselves only for criticism. Notwithstanding the attachment of certain writers to their work, insight during the revision process can usually improve organization, structure, and narrative flow (King, 2010).

Curiosity and Creativity

Role of Questions in Learning

The most visible evidence that someone lacks mental stimulation is failure to ask questions. Parents seldom recognize when this behavior begins to decline and therefore may not help their children become aware that generating questions is essential for self-directed learning and to get a good education. A common challenge of teachers is enabling students to feel comfortable in admitting confusion and being willing to seek guidance about lessons and concerns they do not understand. Solving problems often depends upon asking questions and then applying rational procedures to find answers. The French philosopher Voltaire (1694–1778) recommended that people "judge a man by his questions, not his answers." This advice implies that adults should help children retain their early sense of curiosity by regarding their questions as a form of achievement. By this strategy, students can be credited for their questions as well as answers (Redman, 1977).

Importance of Curiosity and Doubt

Presenting questions that motivate students to concentrate and think deeply was viewed by Plato as the foundation skill for teachers (Plato & Rowe, 2012). In *The Republic*, Plato (427–347 BC) described how Socrates would provide students a series of probing questions to engage them in critical thinking and eventually help them to attain understanding. The progression of steps, called the Socratic method, remains an approach used by teachers of all grade levels to evaluate student comprehension and identify lessons that have yet to be learned.

Fifteen hundred years after Plato's observations on the importance of questions, Pierre Abelard (1079–1142) established the University of Paris in France. By all accounts he was an extraordinary teacher whose students included 20 cardinals, 50 archbishops, and a pope (Celestin II). Abelard's assertion that reason and religious belief could coexist deviated from the prevailing authority worship of his era. A book he wrote entitled *Yes and No* presented 158 questions, all related to Bible verses (Abelard, 1120/2007). For each question, Abelard described conflicting views expressed by theological authorities. He explained that, regardless of the elevated status held by religious commentators, their words should not be believed without an examination of their logic. Because God is the creator of reason, then reason is the tool that he wants mankind to rely on rather than looking to celebrities for answers. Abelard felt that when the authorities disagree, deciding about the source to believe should not favor a speaker with the greatest reputation but instead the individual whose logic and reasoning is the most persuasive. Abelard suggested that the common people, most of whom could not read or write at that time, should reach their own decisions and recognize their potential to become critical thinkers, long before this expectation was thought to be possible or appropriate.

Abelard argued that truth cannot be at variance with itself. Because the truth of reason and revelation come from the same God, there must be a defect in the reasoning of mankind or some mistake in theological citations when the views expressed by religious authorities conflict. His *Yes and No* questions were considered offensive by the authority-loving scholars because it made transparent the confusion and irreconcilable statements made for most of the 158 biblical questions. It was also disquieting to conservative thinkers who did not foresee that reasoning was going to be on the side of revelation.

Abelard was persecuted for his position that doubt can be valuable because it motivates curiosity, questioning, and creativity. When people ask certain questions, they are more able to perceive the truth. Abelard looked at curiosity as a key for personal enlightenment. In contrast, the traditional view was that only authorities were in possession of the truth. Therefore, to doubt them was a sign of distrust, unacceptable to God and those representing him in the church hierarchy.

Unlearning and Cognitive Flexibility

In addition to the benefits that are motivated by doubt and curiosity, divergent thinking also depends on cognitive flexibility. Whenever new ways of doing things become necessary, it can be a short-term or lengthy challenge to leave behind habits that are usually well established. *Unlearning* is a willful activity that requires people to change their minds about ways of doing things that could be strongly habituated. In some cases, unlearning can be more difficult than new learning, and many people fail as they try to unlearn customary ways of responding. Table 6.9.1 identifies some of the behaviors students have usually acquired that they must unlearn and the replacement behaviors needed to perform more successfully in cooperative group work.

Table 6.9.1 Student Behaviors to Unlearn for the Transition to Collaborative Teamwork

TRADITIONAL BEHAVIORS	COLLABORATIVE BEHAVIORS
(1) Limit reading to content assigned by teachers.	Self-directedness means searching for materials without being told by the teacher.
(2) Passive listening without curiosity.	Asking questions should become a norm for everyone in an information-oriented society.
(3) Not questioning the views of authorities.	Critical thinking involves examination of logic for school policies, practices, and rules.
(4) Define education as in the classroom only.	Growing year-round, after graduation, while at work, in retirement, and until life ends.
(5) Leader and follower roles for group work.	Differentiated roles are assigned and knowledge merged to increase learning.
(6) Teachers are the main source of knowledge.	Students are accountable to share insights and knowledge with teammates.
(7) Over-reliance on use of textbooks for learning.	Textbook is augmented by electronic sources, teammates, and community input.
(8) Defensiveness when criticized by others.	Students learn to constructively process criticism to identify their needs for growth.
(9) Dependence upon extrinsic evaluation.	Students evaluate themselves and remain motivated without feedback of others.
(10) Gratuitous evaluation of performance for friends.	Students evaluate teammates in an authentic way as expected in the workplace.
(11) Ignoring the intended focus of a discussion.	Focus on pertinent issues and good time management reflects student accountability.
(12) Individual domination during discussions.	Learn to limit length and frequency of comments so that everyone can be heard.
(13) Team suppression of divergent thinking.	Peer encouragement of creative ideas is a necessary condition for group productivity.
(14) Inattention and distraction undermine discussions.	Concentrate on agenda, determine implications and solutions.
(15) Uninformed opinions are focus of discussions.	Cite credible references to support personal opinions during discussions.

Priorities for Thinking

Taxonomy of Educational Objectives

John Carroll (1963), at the University of Chicago, challenged the idea that the rate at which students acquire knowledge reflects their capacity to learn. He hypothesized that most students can learn whatever schools expect of them, but individuals differ in the amount of time and help that is needed to learn. Carroll speculated that if teachers were to allow enough time and made certain time is spent on a task, instructional goals could more often be attained. When all students are expected to learn in the same amount of time, those who are slow will be unable to meet goals. Benjamin Bloom, also on the University of Chicago faculty, found Carroll's premise appealing and incorporated it into the concept of performance objectives that formed part of his mastery learning theory. Bloom believed that it is possible to analyze any sequence of learning steps into specific objectives and teach them in a way that enables most students to develop their thinking capacity and meet school graduation requirements. Bloom and his colleagues devised the Taxonomy of Educational Objectives to serve as a conceptual outline for teachers to order and reorder their classroom and homework tasks to ensure that instruction and student thinking are not restricted to the lowest levels of the cognitive domain but also include exercise in higher-order thinking (Bloom, Englehart, Furst, Hill, & Krathwohl, 1956).

Lower- and Higher-Order Thinking

Bloom's six levels of performance objectives contained in the taxonomy include:

1. *Knowledge* is the lowest level of learning outcomes, defined as the ability of students to recall facts, names, dates, principles, or other information that is conveyed during class or in textbooks.

2. *Comprehension* goes beyond the recollection of knowledge in being able to translate meaning by explaining concepts, interpreting data, summarizing material, and predicting consequences.

3. *Application* refers to solving new and unfamiliar problems by recognizing the implications of specific rules, methods, concepts, principles, laws, or theories provided by comprehension.

4. *Analysis* requires recognizing relationships, organizational principles, and implications. These outcomes transcend comprehension and application because they require understanding of both the content and structural forms of knowledge.

5. *Synthesis* is the ability to reconstruct data by creating a new whole portrayal such as a unique communication (theme or speech), plan (research proposal), or set of relationships (scheme for classifying information).

6 *Evaluation* is the highest level of thinking, which requires the ability to assess the value of material (novel, statement, report) by using internal criteria (organization) or external criteria (relevance to a purpose). Evaluation outcomes are the highest in the taxonomy since they contain elements of all other categories plus conscious value judgments that are based on clearly defined criteria. The kinds of thinking that teachers encourage students to practice are reflected by classroom tests. When a test covers all cognitive levels of the taxonomy, students can demonstrate the full range of thinking abilities and reveal what they have learned.

After the death of Benjamin Bloom in 1999, scholars who assisted him in formulation of the taxonomy of educational objectives held meetings over a five-year time period to update the taxonomy to accord with prevailing conditions. The result was a book entitled *Taxonomy for Learning, Teaching and Assessing: A Revision of Bloom's Taxonomy of Educational Objectives* (Anderson, Krathwohl, Airasian & Cruickshank, 2000). The taxonomy presently receives more attention than when it was initially proposed (Krathwohl, 2002). One reason is that with rapid obsolescence of information, teaching and evaluation must go beyond recall of knowledge to include greater emphasis on the interpretation of knowledge, application of knowledge, analysis of knowledge, synthesis of knowledge, and evaluation of knowledge.

Patricia King, professor of higher education at the University of Michigan, has studied higher-order thinking for three decades. Her findings show that, even after four years of college, traditional age students are seldom able to demonstrate high levels of reflection, critical thinking, and sound judgment needed for evaluation. Most graduates believe that knowledge is mainly a matter of opinion with evidence playing a lesser role. Given the increasing amount of distraction, there is reason to doubt whether many students can become reflective, so evidence takes on greater importance than opinion (King & King, 2012).

Colleges traditionally have asked the public to trust them for knowing what it takes to be well educated and properly prepared for the workforce. However, the opposite message has been expressed by employers, who believe that college graduates are often unprepared for work. In a survey of employers by the Association of American Colleges and Universities (2013), over 40% of graduates were seen as not ready for their job. Employers also express concern about ever-rising grade point averages of college students that have the effect of masking their real value in the market. Stuart Rojstaczer at Duke University with Christopher Healy at Furman University (2012) examined grades of two million undergraduates at 200 colleges over a period of seventy years, from 1940 to 2010. They found that A's are 43% of all letter grades currently given to students, the sharpest increase since 1990. Private colleges assign a larger proportion of A's than public institutions. The researchers concluded that most institutions are gradually lowering standards. As a result, many employers no longer view grade point average as a reliable index of applicant potential (Supiano, 2013).

One alternative proposed to better judge the exit skills of students after completing four years of college is the *Collegiate Learning Assessment* (CLA), a new measure of critical thinking for seniors who can decide to use results to market themselves to potential employers. In 2014, about 200 colleges and universities administered the test, developed by the Council for Aid to Education to help protect employers from being fooled by good grades or misleading resumes. Large employers such as Proctor and Gamble, General Mills, and Google have developed their own assessments for making decisions about the prospect of job applicants because they have found grade point average (GPA) has little correlation to job success. The federal government has devised a new rating system to gauge performance of colleges based on exit data, what students know and the skills they possess at the time of graduation (Belkin, 2013).

Revision of Instructional Practices

Most educators agree that students should acquire higher-order thinking skills to meet the rising expectations of employers. However, projects that actually implement this goal are scarce. One exception is the long-term project led by Jerry Valentine, emeritus professor of educational leadership from the University of Missouri. Valentine developed the *Instructional Practices Inventory* (IPI) used in over 15,000 classrooms. The assessment process begins with collection of data to make known the ways students are cognitively engaged during instruction time. The customary strategy of schools to improve instruction has emphasized the observation of teacher behavior, but the focus of IPI centers on cognitive engagement of the students. Trained observers visit classrooms for some specified period, typically an entire day. The criteria used for coding observations describe whether students are engaged in higher-order deeper learning, knowledge and skill development, or not engaged in school learning at all (Valentine & Collins, 2011).

Observers systematically profile cognitive engagement of the students based upon the six categories defined in Table 6.9.2. The higher-order deeper thinking categories, listed as numbers 6 or 5 in the left column, represent desired forms of engagement. This cognitive activity is shown by critical thinking, problem solving, decision making from analysis, reflection, goal setting and strategizing, evaluation, synthesis, and creative and innovative thinking. Categories that are listed as numbers 4, 3, and 2 portray types of student engagement that are more passive than active. For example, this kind of engagement involves student development of knowledge and skills based on teacher-led discussions or lectures as well as independent and collaborative "seatwork" that implicates memorization, fact finding, simple understanding, and skills practice. Category 1 characterizes the amount of instruction time when students are not engaged in learning (Valentine & Collins, 2011).

Table 6.9.2 Instructional Practices Inventory Categories*

STUDENT ENGAGEMENT IN HIGHER-ORDER DEEPER LEARNING	
Student Active Engaged Learning (6)	Students are engaged in higher-order thinking and developing deeper understanding through analysis, problem solving, critical thinking, creativity, and/or synthesis. Engagement in learning is not driven by verbal interaction with peers, even in a group setting. Examples of classroom practices commonly associated with higher-order/deeper Student Active Engaged Learning include: inquiry-based approaches such as project-based and problem-based learning; research and discovery/exploratory learning; authentic demonstrations; independent metacognition, reflective journaling, and self-assessment; and higher-order responses to higher-order questions.
Student Verbal Learning Conversations (5)	Students are engaged in higher-order thinking and developing deeper understanding through analysis, problem solving, critical thinking, creativity, and/or synthesis. The higher-order/deeper thinking is driven by peer verbal interaction. Examples of classroom practices commonly associated with higher-order/deeper Student Verbal Learning Conversations include: collaborative or cooperative learning; peer tutoring, debate, and questioning; partner research and discovery/exploratory learning; Socratic learning; and small group or whole class analysis and problem solving, metacognition, reflective journaling, and self-assessment. Conversations may be teacher stimulated but are not teacher dominated.
STUDENT ENGAGEMENT IN KNOWLEDGE AND SKILL DEVELOPMENT	
Teacher-Led Instruction (4)	Students are attentive to teacher-led instruction as the teacher leads the learning experience by disseminating the appropriate content knowledge and/or directions for learning. The teacher provides basic content explanations, tells or explains new information or skills, and verbally directs the learning. Examples of classroom practices commonly associated with Teacher-Led Instruction include: teacher dominated question/answer; teacher lecture or verbal explanations; teacher direction giving; and teacher demonstrations. Discussions may occur, but instruction and ideas come primarily from the teacher. Student higher order/deeper learning is not evident.
Student Work with Teacher Engaged (3)	Students are engaged in independent or group work designed to build basic understanding, new knowledge, and/or pertinent skills. Examples of classroom practices commonly associated with Student Work with Teacher Engaged include: basic fact finding; building skill or understanding through practice, "seatwork" worksheets, chapter review questions; and multimedia with teacher viewing media with students. The teacher is attentive to, engaged with, or supportive of the students. Student higher-order/deeper learning is not evident.

STUDENT ENGAGEMENT IN KNOWLEDGE AND SKILL DEVELOPMENT	
Student Work with Teacher not Engaged (2)	This category is the same as Category 3 except the teacher is not attentive to, engaged with, or supportive of the students. The teacher may be out of the room, working at the computer, grading papers, or in some form engaged in work not directly associated with the students' learning. Student higher-order/deeper learning is not evident.
STUDENTS NOT ENGAGED	
Student Disengagement (1)	Students are not engaged in learning directly related to the curriculum.

**Remember: IPI coding is not based on the type of activity in which the student is engaged, but rather how the student is engaging cognitively in the activity. Examples provided above are only examples often associated with that category.* The *Instructional Practices Inventory* categories were developed by Bryan Painter and Jerry Valentine in 1996. Valentine refined the descriptions of the categories (2002, 2005, 2007, and 2010) in an effort to more effectively communicate their meaning. The IPI was developed to profile school-wide student engaged learning and was not designed for, nor should it be used for, personnel evaluation. The IPI Category descriptions provided herein are a part of the IPI Process for Collecting and Studying Student Engagement and permission to use the categories in any form must be obtained by the developer, Professor Emeritus Jerry Valentine, University of Missouri, at ValentineJ@missouri.edu. Reprinted with permission. See www.ipistudentengagement.com for more detailed information about the IPI Process and related research studies.

Aggregate data from the combined classroom observations are provided for the faculty to explore ways to improve their collective use of instructional time. Two decades of IPI data have revealed that student attentiveness to teacher-directed instruction accounts for about 40% of instructional time. Knowledge and skill development represents another 40%. As students grow older, their pattern of focus in learning time usually declines. The average disengagement time, when nothing is being learned, is 2–3% in the elementary grades, rises to 3–4% in middle school, and rises again to 6–8% in high school. Vocational/technical career schools commonly include hands-on experience that translates to a low degree of disengagement resembling elementary grades (Valentine & Collins, 2011).

IPI data processing has recently included recording of student application of technology, an addition to data gathering that is expected to provide new insights. Cumulative findings from past work indicate that passive student learning continues to dominate instructional time and less engagement time involves active thinking. Teachers still regard themselves as the main source of student learning, so there is less time scheduled for development of teamwork skills, acquisition of technology skills, and student sharing of knowledge that is acquired by Internet searching, journal or book reading, and conducting interviews with community resource agents outside school (Valentine & Collins, 2011). The Valentine training team provides school district, state, and regional workshops to prepare observers who are able to accurately collect engagement data and lead faculty collaborative learning discussions about student engagement at their school.

Assessment in the Classroom

Teacher Questions and Student Thinking

The questions that teachers ask have been a focus of many studies. Productive questions include Bloom's taxonomy levels of application, analysis, synthesis, and evaluation. Together these types of inquiry represent higher-order thinking. Presenting productive questions provides opportunities for students to create, apply, analyze, and evaluate. In contrast, use of reproductive questions emphasizes memory and comprehension, the lower-order thinking that often appears at the end of chapters in textbooks for purposes of content review.

The positive influence productive questions have on achievement has been examined. Generally, the impact ranges from 12–27 percentile points on norm referenced tests (NRT) by students whose teachers consistently rely on productive questions compared to those whose teachers do not regularly pose such questions. Meta-analyses have determined that a majority of questions asked by teachers at all grade levels are in the reproductive category. One study analyzed 18,000 teacher questions: 14,400, or more than 75%, excluded opportunities for students to show capacity for productive thinking (Tienken, Goldberg, & DiRocco, 2009).

Adoption of Goals for Thinking

Paul Torrance, director of the Bureau of Educational Research at the University of Minnesota, wanted to examine teacher goals for thinking. Secondary social studies teachers across the state of Minnesota (N = 1,297) were invited to submit a lesson including the three objectives they considered most important (Torrance, 1963). The objectives were then classified based on mental operations that students would have to engage in to attain each of them. These mental operations were originally described by Joy Paul Guilford (1959).

Table 6.9.3 lists and defines the five *mental processes* of cognition, memory, convergent thinking, divergent thinking, and evaluation along with proportion of emphasis each was given in the curriculum objectives of teachers that were submitted to Torrance. According to Torrance, little attention was given to divergent thinking (2.3%) or to evaluation (6.1%). These two mental operations are currently viewed as essential for productivity and self-direction. Recognizing that intelligence tests and classroom measures have focused mainly on cognition and memory, there is a need for traditional measures to be replaced by indicators of mental processes that accord with emerging demands of the workplace and reflect challenges that adolescents must be prepared to meet.

Table 6.9.3 Proportion of Emphasis on Mental Process Categories in the Curriculum Objectives of Secondary Social Studies Teachers (N = 1,297)

MENTAL PROCESS CATEGORIES[a]	DEFINITIONS	PROPORTION OF EMPHASIS IN CURRICULUM OBJECTIVES[b]
Cognition	Calls on students to recognize, be familiar with, aware of, know about, or appreciate.	65.9%
Memory	Includes remembering, knowing thoroughly, and acquiring knowledge.	5.2%
Convergent Behavior	Requires conforming to some behavior norms, adopting the proper attitude, and finding the single correct solution.	20.5%
Divergent Thinking	Consists of tasks that call for independent thinking, constructive thinking, creative thinking, original work, questioning, inquiring, and similar activities.	2.3%
Evaluation	Includes critical thinking, assessing, evaluating, judging, making decisions, comparing, and contrasting.	6.1%

[a]Adapted from Three faces of intellect, by J. P. Guilford, 1959. *American Psychologist, 14,* 469–479.

[b]Adapted from *Education and the creative potential* by P. Torrance, 1963, p. 5. Minneapolis, MN: University of Minnesota Press.

Solitude, Reflection, and Deliberation

Boredom has become more prevalent because of the significant increase in external stimulation provided by a broad array of technology sources. Imagination is a powerful remedy for boredom because it provides an internal source of stimulation when the external world of movies, videos, music, sports heroes, celebrities, Internet, teachers, social network friends, and family become boring. Creative people are rarely heard to complain about boredom during their discretionary time because they have an internal capacity to stimulate themselves. This asset can promote self-directed learning. Since *boredom* can often mean "not knowing what to do next," creativity is implicated. Persons who cannot think of what to do with discretionary time appear destined to become dependent on others to provide them with a sense of direction.

In a rush-oriented society there is a need to recognize that some goals cannot be attained quickly. Instead, students must learn at home and in the classroom to tolerate ambiguity. Persons who are strictly present-oriented often emphasize only short-term goals shown by their insistence on always receiving immediate feedback on any tasks they perform. However, for more complex learning and projects, there is a need to invest a significant amount of time and effort before an evaluation is appropriate. In this context, all students should have time alone, apart from peers, to reflect, evaluate, and dream while in school (Cain, 2012). Some families home-school children because of their belief that they can provide a more supportive environment for reflection.

Teachers can present an exercise and set a timer for five minutes while students reflect. This experience can help some individuals begin to acquire an appreciation for deliberation. Periods of reprieve should be built in to the schedule. Anyone engaged in the creative process recognizes that, after completion of a demanding project that required extensive preparation and emotional energy, there is a temporary need to establish more moderate expectations and time to partially withdraw to recover. Teachers who fail to honor this natural and necessary response pattern are not fulfilling their obligation to support the mental health of students.

Teacher Views of the Ideal Student

Most people are not highly creative although everyone needs to acquire problem-solving abilities for adjustment in an ever-changing environment. One context where the transformation should occur is teacher training. Teacher attitudes can be a powerful force in determining the kind of behavior expected of students. Some observers wonder how teachers and schools will respond to the emerging priority many societies are assigning to creative behavior. Some clues can be drawn from the 'ideal student' checklist that contains 62 characteristics discriminating between persons of high and low creativity. Torrance (2002b) provided this list, based on input from experts in creative learning to 1,000 teachers in the United States, India, Germany, Greece, and the Philippines. The educators were asked to place a check beside the characteristics that described the kind of person that they would like their students to become and cross out the characteristics they believed should be discouraged or punished.

Low correlations were found between the behaviors teachers favored and the behaviors that are usually exhibited by creative thinkers. Educators from all five countries were inclined to undermine creative thinking by encouraging only behaviors like obedience, memorizing what the teacher says during presentations, and accepting judgment of authorities. Students who presented questions, enjoyed speculating, became preoccupied with tasks, behaved like visionaries, and showed a willingness to take risks found most teachers discouraged these behaviors. This helps explain the assertion of Pablo Picasso that "Every child is an artist. The problem is how to remain an artist once we grow up" (Robinson, 2011, p. 48).

It seems natural that teachers would emphasize the cognitive skills reflecting their own competence. However, when expected to facilitate development of mental abilities that differ from their own assets, some teachers do so reluctantly, ineffectively, or not at all. Consequently, before most students become willing to risk involvement with creative thinking, some changes are necessary in teacher training. The primary need is to prepare educators who comprehend the importance of cognitive abilities they may lack themselves, understand ways to nurture long-term development of imagination, and try to recover some abilities they had as younger people.

Summary

Value of Imaginative Abilities

Creativity and intelligence have been determined to represent separate domains of mental ability. Accordingly, it seems that schools may be able to better educate many students who have been unsuccessful in mastering traditional curriculum. Divergent thinking can enable students to discover multiple ways of solving problems in situations where there is no convergent, single correct answer. The recognition that creativity and intelligence are separate domains of cognitive activity urges educators to nurture imagination and independent thinking to the same extent as other mental abilities. When student involvement with the full range of mental operations is in balance, thinking and learning become dual purposes for achievement.

The Creative Process

Inventive thinkers from diverse backgrounds report similar steps in the creative process they rely on for their extraordinary productivity. Nevertheless, although leaders in education state support for creativity, the organization and schedule of schools continue to ignore student need for preparation, incubation, illumination, and verification. Further, students are not made aware of their need to develop creative abilities, the need to spend time alone to engage in reflection, and ways peer norms can become more constructive.

Curiosity and Creativity

Student potential is commonly undermined by loss of curiosity. The sense of awe and wonder little children express by their frequent questions usually fades by the time students get to the secondary grades. The goal of educators to nurture self-directed learning can be reached if students remain motivated to ask questions and search for some answers on their own. The Taxonomy of Educational Objectives challenges schools to place more emphasis on divergent thinking and recognize the importance doubt plays in creative thinking and problem solving.

Priorities for Thinking

The Taxonomy of Educational Objectives can be used by teachers to assess how well their instruction contributes to higher order and lower order thinking of students. Research has found that college graduates are seldom able to demonstrate high levels of reflection, critical thinking, and sound judgment needed for evaluation. Contrary to the usual approach of observing teacher behavior, the *Instructional Practices Inventory* focuses on observation of how students are engaged during instruction time. This strategy to improve instruction identifies the proportion of times students participate in desired levels of thinking.

Assessment in the Classroom

Some people believe educators are no longer seen as models because students look to one another instead for guidance about norms of behavior. However, the kinds of questions teachers ask can directly influence the way that students approach problems. If teacher conversations, tests, and assignments focus on higher-order thinking instead of memorization of knowledge, the likely outcome is greater acceptance of uncertainty, reliance upon reflection, use of critical thinking, and better judgment.

Classroom Applications

1 Developing assignments that call on individuals and teams to generate alternative solutions for complex problems allows divergent thinking practice. This mental operation is often ignored in homework and project tasks but should become more prominent so that students can acquire the outlook and skills needed to deal with some of the complicated situations they will encounter.

2 Awareness that intelligence and creativity represent different domains of mental ability should caution teachers against reaching unfair conclusions about the performance students are capable of based solely on scores from intelligence tests. Such measures cannot identify students who are highly creative nor indicate which ones excel in creativity and intelligence. Schools intending to support creativity should use suitable tests to detect performance and track progress.

3 Acquaint students with progressive steps of the creative process and discuss how this process can be a guide for the way projects and tasks are scheduled, worked on, reviewed, and completed for the course. As students become aware of how your planning and class schedule support their engagement with the process, they should also recognize aspects of accountability expected of them.

4 Students who ask a lot of questions, enjoy speculating, tend to become preoccupied with tasks, act like visionaries, and show a willingness to take risks are often creative. Teachers should encourage them to sustain these behaviors, a departure from the tradition of discouraging them. In the effort to stimulate creative talents, teachers need to approve and support mental abilities that may be more prominent in students than in themselves.

5 Tell students that you expect them to enrich curriculum by searching the Internet or journals for ideas and materials that could augment content of the course. Their insights, drawn from self-selected, out-of-school sources of learning, should be shared with teammates or the whole class as arranged by the teacher. Teenagers who are

accountable for sharing learning with others soon appreciate the concept of interdependence, usually adopt a broader view of the student role, are recognized by peers for their leadership in helping them, and benefit from teammates who enrich their experience by assuming the same teaching function.

6 Express your creativity by combining visual and verbal methods in original ways to convey concepts. Students report that they are stimulated by the freedom that comes with being able to seek their own information on the web. The appeal of novelty and its favorable influence on motivation can be experienced by sometimes departing from a routine to have students engage in an unexpected activity or pause in a lesson to find out how students believe it could be applied. Such strategies help sustain interest and can often link academic lessons with real-life situations.

7 Students have greater opportunity to learn time management skills when they do not have to manage excessive homework that prevents them from using after-school time for other activities. When class projects involve due dates, it is appropriate to have planning discussions with students to decide on when aspects of their obligation should be completed. This monitoring ensures that procrastination is recognized as unacceptable. There is also merit in discussing the importance of balancing work and play for mental health, a guideline that should be respected by the faculty.

8 Students should adopt curiosity as an aspect of their lifestyle so they will remain learners after completing school. This is difficult because peers, beginning in early adolescence, discourage inquiry and make individuals feel conspicuous. Given the power of peer influence, teachers should try to use it to their advantage. During orientation of cooperative learning groups, specify that they are expected to encourage teammates to ask questions since making known what is not understood is necessary for learning. The active role students want requires this kind of behavior.

9 Creative students must feel comfortable when they work in groups or they tend to withdraw. One way to improve their status is encouraging them to help teammates with difficult tasks or concepts where there is lack of comprehension. When classmates begin to view the talented student as an asset to their team, the individual is usually recognized for leadership, is valued for willingness to act as a source of assistance, and becomes aware that communal achievement can make individual success more satisfying.

10 Categorize the kinds of questions that you plan to ask students for some unit of instruction. Pay attention to how these questions correspond with the Taxonomy of Educational Objectives to make sure that a significant portion of them enable students to demonstrate higher order thinking.

For Reflection

1. What aspects of the creative process should students practice more and better appreciate?
2. What are advantages and disadvantages of divergent thinking items on teacher-made tests?
3. In what ways do you see yourself as like and unlike persons identified as highly creative?
4. How do you intend to reconcile pressures for homework with needs for discretionary time?
5. What changes could help prospective teachers better support creative behavior of students?
6. What novel methods of instruction are appealing and something you want to use with your students?
7. What are some classroom situations that have turned you off since they produce boredom?
8. How do you feel about schools having creativity measures along with high-stakes testing?
9. How do you suppose teachers of your subject perceive students who are highly creative?
10. What can teachers do to help students become capable of seeing possibilities in situations?

Key Terms

Boredom
Convergent Thinking
Creative Process
Creative Thinking
Divergent Thinking
Illumination
Incubation
Mental Processes
Preparation
Unlearning
Verification

Explore These Web Sites

Link to these sites at http://www.infoagepub.com/strom-teaching

- Introduction to Creative Thinking
  http://www.virtualsalt.com/crebook1.htm

- National Health Museum, Two Forks Idaho
  http://www.accessexcellence.org
- RSA Animate—Changing Education Paradigms
  http://www.youtube.com
- Jay Walker: My Library of Human Imagination
  http://www.ted.com
- Amy Tan: Where does creativity hide?
  http://www.ted.com
- Susan Cain: Power of Introverts
  http://www.ted.com
- General Mills Total Mind Games—Comedy Skit about Total Blueberry Pomegranate Cereal
  http://tv.naturalnews.com/v.asp?v=851519FA1AC72A56F7205D2285CC66CF

Cooperative Learning Exercises and Roles (CLEAR)

EXERCISE 6.9.1: *Team Review*

Role: Reviewer

Team reviews of each chapter by all students can contribute to individual learning. This process begins outside class as each student underlines interesting and important comments in the text and class notes. Preparing for the team review requires each student to answer the following questions that will be the focus for discussion in class.

1. What are the main points and key issues presented in this unit?
2. Which ideas made a difference in how I think about this topic?
3. What insights from this lesson can I apply in teaching situations?
4. What aspects of a lesson are confusing or require more explanation?

The review is led by the team organizer who states the page and paragraph in the text s/he will read aloud in response to the first question. In turn, each teammate answers that same question. This process is repeated for each review question.

EXERCISE 6.9.2: *How Do You Do?*

Role: Improviser

In 1904, a few months before 25-year-old Albert Einstein (1879–1955) published his theory of relativity, he met 23-year-old artist Pablo Picasso (1881–1973), who would also soon receive worldwide recognition. When the two men came together at Lapin Agile, a cafe located in Paris, France, they attempted to educate each other about the world. The pair conflicted about values and meaning of life. The back-and-forth exchange of values in art and science is the theme of Steve Martin's provocative play entitled *Picasso at the Lapin Agile* (1996). Your exercise is to generate a list of famous persons you would like to observe as pairs having conversations about how they see the world. First, each teammate should take five minutes to devise a list, leaving out any persons who are remembered only for abusing others. When the team organizer says that time is up, every member should share their list of pairs and provide a rationale for teammates.

EXERCISE 6.9.3: *The Creative Process*

Role: Evaluator

1 Identify steps in the creative process that are most difficult for you and tell what can be done.

2 How should learning in the classroom change to provide more support for creative behaviors.

EXERCISE 6.9.4: *Dreams—The Story of Myself*

Role: Storyteller

Everyone has dreams they wish would come true. Sometimes these dreams provide a sense of direction, guide behavior, inspire perseverance, and motivate optimism. It is possible to better understand another person's motivation by hearing them tell about their dreams. Each person should choose one or more of these question they prefer as a focus to tell their personal story.

1 What are some dreams you have held onto for a long time?

2 What are some dreams that you have changed or given up?

3 Who listens to you when you try to describe your dreams?

4 What dreams do you have for other members of the family?

5 What happens when people quit dreaming about the future?

6. What dreams do you have that probably will not be achieved?
7. How important is it to be around people with similar dreams?
8. How do your dreams compare with dreams others have for you?
9. Which of your dreams are other people unwilling to support?
10. Which of your dreams have already started to come true?

EXERCISE 6.9.5: *Boredom and Stimulation*

Role: Discussant

1. Why do you suppose people express boredom more now than in the past?
2. What kinds of situations or events do you usually consider to be boring?
3. What things distinguish boring teachers from those who motivate you?
4. How does boredom affect the relationships you have with other people?
5. What are some methods you rely on to reduce possibilities of boredom?
6. How does boredom influence your involvement in watching television?
7. What are some of your own characteristics that others might find boring?
8. What things would you change about schools in order to reduce boredom?
9. Who do you interact with on a regular basis that is stimulating? Boring?
10. How are you trying to help other family members minimize boredom?

EXERCISE 6.9.6: *School Days*

Role: Generational Reporter

Parents want to have more conversations with adolescent daughters and sons but sometimes feel uncomfortable unless there is an agenda. Invite an adolescent to use the following guide to have a conversation with parents. S/he should write down the answers of both parties about their experiences in school and give you the interview notes to share anonymously with teammates or the class.

Directions: Education changes for every generation. Nevertheless, the classroom involves some experiences all age groups remember. Parents and students take turns answering each question.

1. What are some things about school that have been most pleasing for you?
2. What kinds of changes do you think are needed to improve schooling?
3. How are the students who misbehave at school punished by the faculty?
4. What kinds of peer pressure do you have to deal with daily at school?
5. What benefits have you gained from being in extracurricular activities?
6. How do friends make a difference in the way that you feel about school?
7. How can relatives be more helpful with your homework assignments?
8. What can be done to lower the rate of students who drop out of school?
9. What sorts of things have happened at school that bothered you most?
10. What kinds of help do you need that are not provided by the school?
11. How do you feel about computer aspects of learning at the school?

EXERCISE 6.9.7: *Boredom Reduction*

Role: Improviser

Teachers of all grades are concerned about a growing number of students who express boredom with their school experience. Prepare three side-by-side lists. In the first column, list some school practices you think contribute to boredom. In the middle column, list replacement practices that could reduce boredom. In the right column, list behavior changes students need to make within themselves to diminish their frequency of boredom.

EXERCISE 6.9.8: *Multiple Models*

Role: Evaluator

Life in an age-segregated society is sometimes portrayed as threatening adolescent development because teenagers are exposed to more pressure from peers. On the other hand, it is understood that peers can be a valuable source of emotional support and social support. Instead of supposing adolescents should imitate adults only, recognize that peers can also be beneficial models. Think about contexts and situations where adult or peer models offer greater benefits as models.

1. What lessons can teachers and parents model better than classmates?
2. What lessons can peers teach one another more effectively than adults?
3. How are peer and teacher instructional methods similar and different?

EXERCISE 6.9.9: *Collaboration and Unlearning*

Role: Storyteller

When new ways of doing things become necessary, the greatest challenge is often leaving old habits behind. Unlearning is a willful activity requiring that people change their minds about ways of doing things that are strongly habituated. In some cases, unlearning can be more difficult than new learning, and some fail in unlearning their customary responses. Reexamine Table 6.1 and identify behaviors you have acquired that should be unlearned in order to become a more productive member of a cooperative learning team.

EXERCISE 6.9.10: *Ideal Student*

Role: Discussant

The definition of an "ideal student" depends upon how success is defined. What attributes, skills, and knowledge do you intend to encourage and discourage for the students in your classes?

References

Abelard, P. (2007). *Yes and no.* Charlotte, VT: Medieval MS. (Original work published 1120)

Anderson, L., Krathwohl, D., Airasian, P., & Cruickshank, K. (2000). *A taxonomy for learning, teaching, and assessing: A revision of Bloom's taxonomy of educational objectives.* Boston, MA: Allyn & Bacon.

Asch, S. (1952). *Social psychology.* New York, NY: Prentice-Hall.

Asch, S. (1956). Studies of independence and conformity: A minority of one against a unanimous majority. *Psychological Monographs General and Applied, 70*(9), 1–70.

Association of American Colleges and Universities. (2013). *It takes more than a major: Employer priorities for college learning and student success.* Washington, DC: The Association.

Belkin, D. (2013, August 25). Colleges set to offer exit tests: Employers say they don't trust grade-point averages. *The Wall Street Journal.* retrieved from http://online.wsj.com

Berns, G. (2010). *Iconoclast: A neuroscientist reveals how to think differently.* Boston, MA: Harvard Business Review Press.

Berns, G., Chappelow, J., Zink, C., Pagnoni, G., Martin-Skurski, M., & Richards, J. (2005). Neurobiological correlates of social conformity and independence during mental rotation. *Biological Psychiatry, 58,* 245–253.

Bloom, B., Englehart, M., Furst, E., Hill, W., & Krathwohl, D. (Eds.). (1956). *Taxonomy of educational objectives: The classification of educational goals, Handbook I: Cognitive Domain.* New York, NY: McKay.

Cain, S. (2012). *Quiet: The power of introverts in a world that can't stop talking.* New York, NY: Crown.

Carlson, J., Geisinger, K., & Johnson, J. (2014). *Mental measurement yearbook.* Lincoln: Buros Center for Testing, University of Nebraska.

Carroll, J. (1963). A model of school learning. *Teachers College Record, 64*(8), 723–733.

Darwin, C., & Wilson, E. (Ed.). (2005). *From so simple a beginning: Darwin's four great books*. New York, NY: W. W. Norton.

de Bono, E. (2010). *Think! Before it's too late*. New York, NY: Random House.

Florida, R. (2012). *The rise of the creative class revisited* (2nd ed.). New York, NY: Basic Books.

Friedman, T. (2007). *The world is flat: A brief history of the twenty-first century*. New York, NY: Farrar, Strauss & Giroux.

Ghiselin, B. (1987). *The creative process*. New York, NY: New American Library.

Guilford, J. (1950, September). Creativity. *American Psychologist, 5*(9), 444–454

Guilford, J. (1959). Three faces of intellect. *American Psychologist, 14*, 469–479.

Hargrove, R. (1998). *Mastering the art of creative collaboration*. New York, NY: McGraw-Hill.

Hemingway, E. (1964). *A moveable feast*. New York, NY: Charles Scribner's Sons.

Kim, K. (2010). Measurements, causes and effects of creativity. *Psychology of Aesthetics, Creativity, and the Arts, 4*(3), 131–135.

King, M., & King, P. (2012). *Assessing meaning making and self-authorship*. San Francisco, CA: Jossey-Bass.

King, S. (2010). *On writing*. New York, NY: Pocket Books.

Krathwohl, D. (2002). A revision of Bloom's taxonomy: An overview. *Theory Into Practice, 41*(4), 216–218.

Ludwig, A. (1995). *The price of greatness: Resolving the creativity and madness controversy*. New York, NY: Guilford Press.

Malcolm, J. (2007). *Two lives: Gertrude and Alice*. New Haven, CT: Yale University Press.

Martin, S. (1996). *Picasso at the Lapin Agile*. New York, NY: Samuel French.

Ness, R. (2013). *Genius unmasked*. New York, NY: Oxford University Press.

Oberkampf, W., & Roy, C. (2010). *Verification and validation in scientific computing*. New York, NY: Cambridge University Press.

Plato, & Rowe, C. (Ed.). (2012). *The Republic*. New York, NY: Penguin. Original work written by Plato in 360 B.C.E.

Redman, B. (Ed.). (1977). *The portable Voltaire*. New York, NY: Penguin.

Rickover, H. (1959). *Education and freedom*. New York, NY: E. P. Dutton.

Robinson, K. (2011). *Out of our minds: Learning to be creative*. West Sussex, UK: Capstone.

Rojstaczer, A., & Healy, C. (2012). When A is ordinary: The evolution of American college and university grading, 1940–2009. *Teachers Collesge Record, 114*(7), 1–23.

Rosen, L. (2013). *iDisorder: Understanding our obsession with technology and overcoming its hold us*. New York, NY: Palgrave Macmillan.

Runco, M., & Albert, R. (2010). Creativity research: A historical view. In J. Kaufman & R. Sternberg (Eds.), *The Cambridge handbook of creativity* (pp. 3–19). New York, NY: Cambridge University Press.

Russell, E. (2012). *Creativity, mental illness, and crime* (2nd ed.). Dubuque, IA: Kendall Hunt Publishing.

Sahlberg, P. (2011). *Finnish lessons: What can the world learn from educational change in Finland?* New York, NY: Teachers College Press.

Shenk, D. (2011). *The genius in all of us: New insights into genetics, talent, and IQ*. New York, NY: Anchor.

Spearman, C. (1904). "General intelligence," objectively determined and measured. *American Journal of Psychology, 15*, 201–209.

Supiano, B. (2013, September). Students and employers at odds on how college can spark a career. *The Education Digest*, 79(1), 36–38.

Tienken, C., Goldberg, S., & DiRocco, D. (2009). Questioning the questions. *Kappa Delta Pi Record, 46*(1), 39–43.

Torrance, E. P. (1963). *Education and the creative potential.* Minneapolis, MN: University of Minnesota Press.

Torrance, E. P. (1965). *Rewarding creative behavior: Experiments in classroom creativity.* Englewood Cliffs, NJ: Prentice-Hall.

Torrance, E. P. (2000a). The millennium: A time for looking forward and looking backward. *The Korean Journal of Thinking and Problem Solving, 10*(1), 5–19.

Torrance, E. P. (Ed.). (2000b). *On the edge and keeping on the edge.* Westport, CT: Greenwood.

Valentine, J., & Collins, J. (2011, April). *Student engagement and achievement on high stakes tests. A HLM analysis across 68 middle schools.* Presented at the American Educational Research Association Annual Conference, New Orleans, LA.

Wallach, M., & Kogan, N. (1965). *Modes of thinking in young children of the creativity–intelligence distinction.* New York, NY: Wadsworth.

Chapter 6: Post-Reading Questions

1. How has this reading affirmed or changed your beliefs about whether or not creativity can be taught or enhanced?
2. The reading described four stages of the creative process, including possible impediments at each stage. Which stage do you think you struggle with the most and why?
3. Table 6.9.1 in the reading lists a number of things you need to unlearn in order to be better at collaborative teamwork. Which of these do you most need to unlearn to improve your abilities for collaborative teamwork?

CHAPTER 7

Communication

Doing the Right Thing!

Accepting Responsibility

In our last module, we suggested that you have a responsibility to take active control of your life and to engage in active problem-solving rather than wallowing inactively in blame and self-pity. You are responsible for your life, and if it is not the life you want, who suffers for it? You can blame all the people you want, and perhaps there is plenty of legitimate blame to be had, but in the end it is still your life, and you are the only one who has the power to change it.

If you accept the argument that you have the freedom and responsibility to make your life the kind of life you want to have, then the next question is "How?" How do you insure that you are making the best decisions, the *right* decisions, given that you are going to have to live with the consequence of those decisions? Before we answer that important question, let's explore the various methods people use to *know* what is right and true. Let's explore some theories of truth.

Correspondence Theory of Truth

Science teaches us that seeing is believing—that the ultimate test of truth is how well it holds up, or *corresponds*, to reality. We trust our senses. We see, hear, smell, touch, and taste the results of our experiments. And if the results are too subtle to be picked up directly by our senses, we use measuring tools to enhance our senses: microscopes, telescopes, microphones, amplifiers, computers, and various other tracking and recording devices to make the less accessible information more accessible. In the end, we know to be true that which we can demonstrate to be true. In the absence of evidence, we do not believe. "Prove it!" is the motto of the correspondence approach to truth. Although this approach is the basis of the scientific method, and although science has done a great deal to improve our lives and enhance our civilization, it is not without its shortcomings. For one thing, although seeing is believing, you can't believe everything you see. The fact is our senses cannot always be trusted, nor are our measuring devices infallible. Our sensory information is filtered through our perceptions. We see what we want to see. We interpret incoming information through the lens of our previous beliefs, our biases, and our cultural perspectives. We are subjective observers, and total objectivity probably can never be fully achieved.

Coherence Theory of Truth

The coherence theory of truth is the truth of the philosophers. An idea is right and true to the degree that it can be shown to be logically coherent and consistent. If it is free from logical error, then by definition it must be true. If you take a course in logic, you will learn that there is a list of rules, very similar to mathematics, on how to construct a bulletproof argument of truth. It's hard to argue with logic. However, the truth of the argument usually depends on the truth of the starting assumptions. Most of these discussions are in the form of: If A is true, then it must follow that B, C, and D are true; therefore, E, F, and G are also true, etc. The problem is often that it all rests on the premise, assumption A, which is often something that is not actually provable (or disprovable). And there have been a lot of situations where something that can logically be predicted just doesn't match the reality of what happened.

Consensus Theory of Truth

The consensus theory of truth suggests that something is right and true if we can all agree that it is so. It is sort of a democratic truth. Because people are fickle, and because people often disagree on so many things, this might seem on the surface to be the weakest standard, but it could be argued that this is the standard that is most often used in the world. When everyone is convinced that something is true, it is very hard to be the lone voice of disagreement. And in fact, many psychology studies, from Asch's conformity experiments to investigations of jury deliberations, suggest that people cave easily to the will of the group. Think of the last disagreement you had with someone where one of you looked up information in a book (or on the internet) to prove a point. We know that everything we read is not necessarily true, but I bet as soon as one of you saw it in writing, you felt the matter was settled. How often in political debates do we use opinion polls to see who is right? I would never say consensus is Truth (with a capital T), but I realize that for all practical purposes, if everyone believes something to be true, they will act as if it is true. And it will be very difficult to get them to believe otherwise. There are also those who argue that there is no ultimate Truth with a capital T—that all knowledge is provisional and contextual.

Pragmatic Theory of Truth

Finally, we will look at the pragmatic theory of truth which purports that truth is somewhat relative but can be judged by its usefulness. If believing something to be true solves a practical problem, then for all practical purposes, it is true. Sidestepping for the moment whether there really is an absolute Truth with capital T, we are going to proceed in this course using the pragmatic approach for pragmatic reasons. It is useful. When faced with a life dilemma ("What should I do about this issue/challenge/problem?") there probably isn't one solution that you can know in advance is the right thing to do. But some solutions are probably better than others, and you can probably determine the best course of action at this time given the set of facts as you understand them. This is all we can do. The approach draws on philosopher Jürgen Habermas' ideal speech situation. The truth for Habermas is what would be agreed upon in the ideal speech situation. What is that? Well it is similar to what we previously described under critical thinking and critical discussion. It is a situation where all ideas are both entertained and open for critical evaluation. There is no dogma; there are no preconceived ideas that cannot be questioned or challenged. Everything is open for consideration.

Using the Ideal Speech Situation in Steps to Problem-Solving

We have asked you to brainstorm possible solutions to your challenge statement. We asked your group members to offer ideas to help you expand your horizons and consider new ideas. We told you not to reject anything offered at this point so that all ideas will be considered. Now we must critically evaluate these ideas, but here too, we need an open mind as well as a healthy skepticism.

In this way, we hope to create the ideal speech situation, or what we call critical discussion, to make sure that the best ideas are considered and evaluated with a collectively open mind. We will not necessarily end up with any one of these options, at least not in the original form, but it should help to clarify our thinking and lead us to making the best possible decisions based on our current understanding of the situation. And this, we believe, is as close to making sure we do the right thing as we can possibly come.

Group Assignment

In the last chapter's individual assignment you narrowed down the list of alternatives for your challenge. Now present the narrowed down list to your group.

1. Pick one alternative course of action offered by each of your group members (including one that you offered to yourself). Try to choose a set of options that leaves you with the widest range of alternatives, not several choices that are more or less the same.

2. Look at the list of alternatives that your group members have selected for themselves, and comment on whether you think they have chosen the widest range of alternatives or stacked the deck to avoid dealing with certain options.
3. List one good thing and one bad thing about each of these alternatives (i.e., Why would this be a good choice? What are some of the potential advantages of this choice? Why might this be a bad choice? What are some of the potential disadvantages of this choice?).
4. Finally, list one good thing and one bad thing about each of their alternatives. Thus, everyone will end up with a list of several options (one from each group member, including themselves) and a list of good things and bad things for each option.

Individual Assignment

After considering all the good and bad things about the various options you selected for further analysis, can you think of a way to combine the best elements of several of your choices into a new critical and creative solution (or action plan)? In other words, do not just select one of your alternatives, but try to come up with a totally new (or slightly new) alternative that builds on the best of several alternatives.

The Weekly Reading

Pre-Reading Questions

The reading for this chapter is on effective interpersonal communication. It was written for nurses, but it is full of excellent ideas that are applicable to everyone in all walks of life.

Think about a time when you had a major miscommunication with someone. What happened? What were the detrimental ramifications that happened afterwards? Why do you think it happened?

READING 10

Effective Interpersonal Communication

A Practical Guide to Improve Your Life

Kathleen A. Vertino

Communication is an integral part of life; without it, we would not survive. Verbal and non-verbal communication begins at birth and ends at death. We need communication not only to transmit information and knowledge to one another, but more importantly, to relate to one another as human beings around the world in the context of relationships, families, organizations, and nations.

The how, what, why, and wherefore of communication can either edify or harm us, as individuals, cultures, religions, and governments of countries, as we attempt to coexist. ***What*** we say, ***how*** we say it, and ***what we mean*** by it are extremely important, and can be life-changing. I recollect two teachers in elementary school. To me, one was a kind, caring person; the other was mean and sarcastic. Students, especially children, are particularly vulnerable during their formative years. Adults, teachers, and other children have the power to either help us blossom as an individuals or to destroy our self-esteem, and thus impact our potential for life. How? A kind (or cruel) word, or facial expression, can mean the world to a child. These two teachers in my past were polar opposites, but both affected me deeply.

In our professional roles as nurses, we are responsible to care for persons who are ill. When ill, patients may be unable to speak or advocate for themselves. Vulnerable patients need our voices to speak for them. Due to our constant exposure to other human beings who are suffering, nurses are perfectly positioned to utilize effective interpersonal communication, and in doing so, support our own emotional, psychological, and spiritual development.

There is a well-established link between team communication, worker morale, and patient safety. Poor team communication has been directly linked to preventable

Kathleen A. Vertino, "Effective Interpersonal Communication: A Practical Guide to Improve Your Life," *Online Journal of Issues in Nursing*, vol. 19, no. 3, pp. 19–30.

medical errors, high nurse turnover rates, and low morale (Brinkert, 2010; Institute of Medicine, 1999; Vessey, DeMarco, & DeFazio, 2010). Low morale contributes to high levels of stress, burnout, poor job satisfaction, and an overall poor quality of life. Controlling stress and burnout is an ***essential component of a healthy lifestyle.***

Use of effective interpersonal communication strategies by nurses in both personal and professional settings, may reduce stress, promote wellness, and therefore, improve overall quality of life. This article briefly explores the concept of interpersonal communication as it relates to Maslow's hierarchy of human needs; describes personal variables and the interaction of internal and external variables that can impact communication; and discusses possible causes and consequences of ineffective communication. Drawing on both the literature and my experiences as a longtime provider of care in the mental healthcare field, I offer multiple strategies, with specific examples of possible responses for effective communication. Recommendations in this article are intended for nurses to consider as they seek healthy communication strategies that may be useful in both their personal and professional lives.

Interpersonal Communication and Maslow's Hierarchy of Human Needs

In 1943, Abraham Maslow developed a hierarchy of human needs wherein he described the basis of human behavior in terms of the priorities of survival (Figure 7.10.1). Oxygen, food, water, and shelter, our most basic needs, must be met first. Once these basic needs are met we can

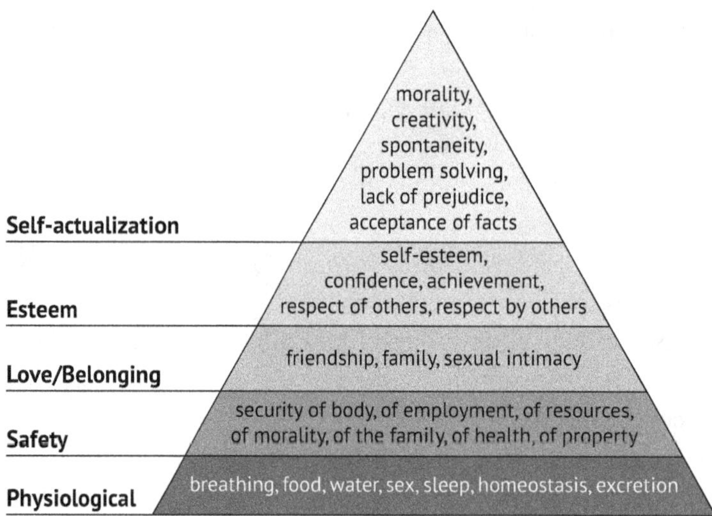

Figure 7.10.1 Source: Maslow's hierarchy of needs, n.d.

progress upward in the hierarchy toward fulfillment of needs for safety/security, love/belonging, and esteem. Finally, according to Maslow, the highest human needs revolve around finding one's purpose and realizing one's full potential, which culminate at the pinnacle of the hierarchy in self-actualization.

Maslow's hierachry of human needs can be applied to interpersonal communication. The concept of communication can be most appropriately considered in the context of three levels of the hierarchy: safety, love/belonging, and esteem. Of these, safety has the most intimate involvement with basic, "primitive" needs. For example, it feels very personal when one's safety is threatened by loss of any kind, whether it is a perceived or actual loss. A loss can invoke anger, grief, or fear in response to feeling helpless, powerless, unsafe, and vulnerable. Likewise, effective or ineffective communication may impact our ability to satisfy the needs of love and belonging, and also esteem.

Many would agree that interpersonal communication is an intimate, human activity that can weigh heavily on our overall psychological health and wellness, and therefore, warrants much discussion and attention. Despite this realization, the literature, especially in nursing, has not addressed this topic adequately. Although much has been written on workplace safety, lateral violence, and bullying to address issues that we face as professionals in the workplace, little has addressed how effective interpersonal communication can contribute to a healthy lifestyle in both the personal and professional life of the individual nurse. As each person seeks to meet his or her human needs, a number of variables, both internal (or personal factors) and external (or behavior of others) can combine to support effective or ineffective interpersonal communication. The next section will offer professional insight that I have gained in my nursing practice related to how multiple variables may impact communication. I offer this not as an exhaustive list of variables, but in the hope that it will provide some context for readers to reflect on their own unique mix of variables as they go on to read and consider the recommendations for effective communication.

Personal Variables: Internal Predisposing Factors

Human beings are complex creatures. We are composed of a plethora of variables that are continuously interacting with one another. Some of these personal variables are internal in nature; they are part of our makeup. Figure 7.10.2, developed by the author, is a simple representation of how variables might interact to produce a unique individual. In addition to our genetic makeup and gender, the variables (termed internal predisposing factors) consist of thoughts, feelings, and perceptions that are often learned early in life and shaped by childhood upbringing and experiences. In my clinical experience with patients, I have observed that early experiences can affect persons deeply, and perceptions of these experiences are not easily changed. Indeed, the impact of these experiences can cause a person to be rigid and inflexible. For example, a person who has been abused physically, verbally, or sexually by the opposite sex, and unhealed from this, can become unyielding in any future interactions with persons of that gender regardless of the situation or circumstances. However, all is not lost. In addition to factors that ***CAN*** be controlled and factors that ***CANNOT*** be controlled, there are factors that may change over time. Consider the variables listed in Figure 7.10.2. Which can be changed or controlled? Which cannot? Which are subject to change? These are important distinctions that will become clearer in the discussion of the following sections, as applied to interpersonal communication.

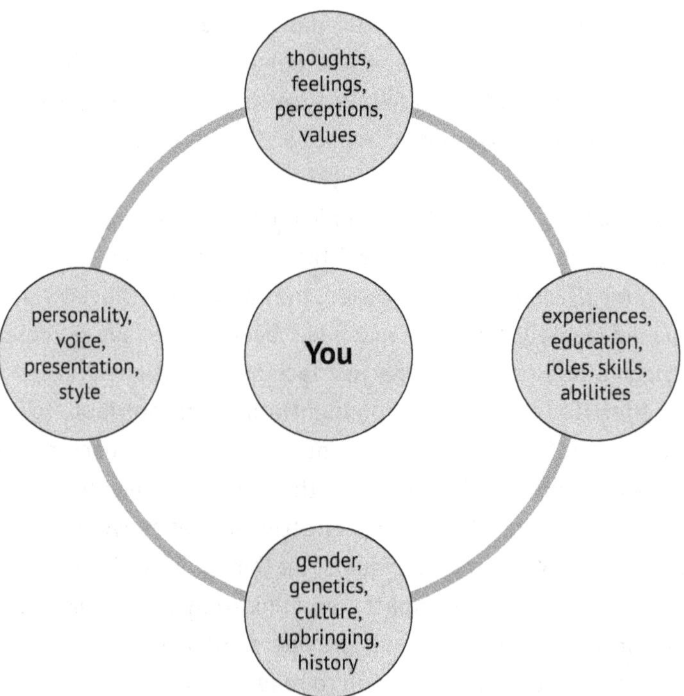

Figure 7.10.2 Personal variables: Internal predisposing factors (Source: Author)

Interaction of Internal and External Variables

Figure 7.10.3, developed by the author, represents how internal personal variables demonstrated in Figure 7.10.2 and external variables (behavior of others and situations) might interact. Further, consider how the interactions depicted in Figure 7.10.3 could influence the ***outcome and effectiveness*** of (our) interpersonal communication. Understanding and acceptance that one cannot control others and/or situations can create the psychological freedom necessary to develop insight into one's own behavior. That insight can be the first step toward positive change and improve communication. The next section will consider some causes and consequences of ineffective interpersonal communication, along with strategies and selected examples to support alternatives.

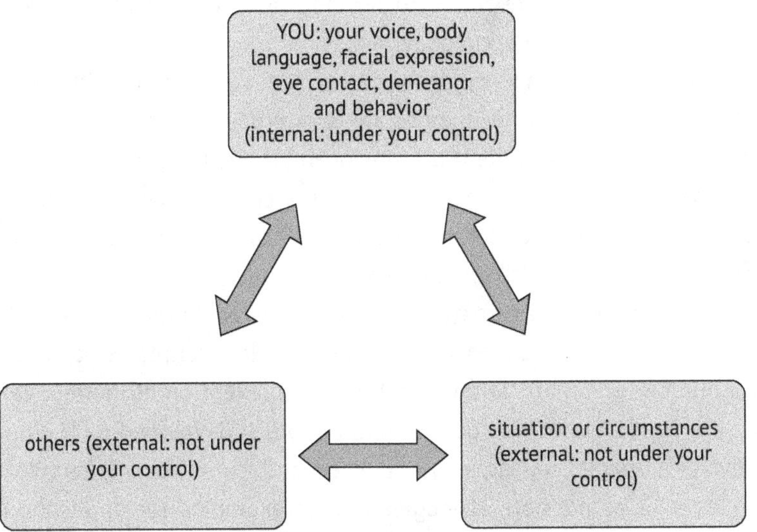

Figure 7.10.3 Interaction of Internal and External Variables (Source: Author)

Causes and Consequences of Ineffective Interpersonal Communication

Some consequences of ineffective interpersonal communication can be chaos, confusion, disorder, fear, conflict, inefficient systems, and wasted resources. Poor team communication has been cited as the number one cause of unnecessary patient deaths related to medical error since the 1990s (Institute of Medicine, 1999). Further, criticism has been directed at healthcare providers, including physicians, for their lack of study of interpersonal communication (Hull, 2007; Shapiro, 2011). Although numerous interpersonal communication theories exist, few have been applied to healthcare communication or utilized in any relevant manner by providers (Bylund, Peterson, & Cameron, 2012). Thus, a knowledge gap exists necessitating a frank discussion and pragmatic strategies for change. This section will offer selected strategies for effective communication for consideration, drawn from both literature and practice experience.

Personal life versus professional role calls us to develop and apply competent skills based on the specific situation, and adopt an appropriate demeanor and response. However, behavior based solely on role expectations may not always be appropriate. Here are some suggestions to begin to think differently. When applying what is discussed in this article to your personal and professional lives, think of yourself holistically. In other words, you cannot compartmentalize basic personality structure, or your personal way of relating to the world; you are who you are. Divorce yourself from antiquated acculturated role expectations of how women or men and nurses are ***supposed*** to behave. Strive to develop new ways of relating to support more rewarding interpersonal communication experiences.

One way to do this is to think in terms of the use of "self" versus "skills." Effective interpersonal communication is much more than techniques, skills, or procedures to be mimicked or parroted. Parroting or mimicking is generally viewed as insincere; if one behaves as a robot, most people will sense this. To say one must perform a certain skill or competency, in my opinion, diminishes our ability to have spontaneous human interactions that are meaningful. Techniques and skills can become too automatic and thus may limit your options.

Genuine human rapport requires creativity and flexibility. Best practice would dictate relating genuinely, human to human, and disregard of communication "scripts." Since new behavior can be risky and frightening, pragmatic strategies aimed at prevention of ineffective interpersonal communication are needed. With this goal in mind, Table 1, developed by the author, provides a brief overview of possible causes, consequences and cures for ineffective interpersonal communication, as well as possible strategies and/or examples for application. The section that follows elaborates on the information in Table 1 and offers additional discussion and/or practical guidance.

Table 7.10.1 Ineffective Interpersonal Communication: 12 Possible Causes, Consequences, Cures, and Examples for Effective Communication (Source: Author).

POSSIBLE CAUSES	POSSIBLE CONSEQUENCES OR INTERPRETATIONS	POSSIBLE CURES/ STRATEGIES	EXAMPLES OF POSSIBLE WORDING FOR EFFECTIVE COMMUNICATION
1. Social/Familial/ Organizational/ Cultural Taboos regarding "No Talk" Issues.	• Frustration • Helplessness • Lack of Trust • Substantive Issues are ignored	• Talk openly about the cultural taboos and how they may have contributed to a climate wherein people are reluctant to share or tackle difficult issues.	"I am not really comfortable bringing this up, but I feel we need to address it." "I am concerned about a patient safety issue that I want to bring to the attention of the team." "There is an issue that is bothering me, and I feel we need to discuss it."

POSSIBLE CAUSES	POSSIBLE CONSEQUENCES OR INTERPRETATIONS	POSSIBLE CURES/ STRATEGIES	EXAMPLES OF POSSIBLE WORDING FOR EFFECTIVE COMMUNICATION
2. Poor Conflict Management Skills	• Inappropriate and misdirected anger • Finger pointing • Blaming	• Learn how to respectfully disagree. • Become comfortable with affect (yours and others). • Remain calm and professional in all situations.	"I can see that you are upset. I would like to discuss this calmly and rationally." "Perhaps we can negotiate a compromise, middle ground?" "It looks like we may not agree on this, so let's table it for now and discuss again."
3. Poor Negotiation/ Problem-Solving Skills	• Knee jerk responses • Temporary or short-term fixes (sometimes referred to as "Band-Aids") • Focus is on "putting out fires" rather than vision	• Learn skills for collaboration. • Become comfortable with unfinished (long term) solutions. • Discover your strengths and those of others. • Assign or negotiate tasks/workgroups/ projects based on individual strengths and interests, versus a "we just need a warm body to complete this" approach.	"If you could do what you enjoy most, what would that be?"
4. Lack of Empathy/ Understanding of Others	• Poor team work/spirit • Lack of cooperation • Wasted time and resources	• Widen your perceptions and awareness of those around you and the environment.	It is very important to make eye contact and give undivided attention while the other person is talking.

(Continued)

Table 7.10.1 (continued)

POSSIBLE CAUSES	POSSIBLE CONSEQUENCES OR INTERPRETATIONS	POSSIBLE CURES/ STRATEGIES	EXAMPLES OF POSSIBLE WORDING FOR EFFECTIVE COMMUNICATION
		• Endeavor to be a team player. Large organizations, hospital units, work groups and families run best with a cooperative spirit among individuals. • Conversations and regularly scheduled FACE to FACE meetings are a must for development of rapport, negotiating and problem solving. • If your group prefers email for all communication, ask for a scheduled face to face, prepare an agenda and send it out in advance.	Do not take your phone to meetings unless you are expecting an urgent call. Acknowledge the other person's feelings. "I can see how tough this must be for you." "Based on looking around this room at all your faces, I can see the angst you are all feeling about this (patient, situation, issue)." "I know it has been hard on you to worry about scheduling issues all the time."
5. Unresolved Emotional Issues (e.g., history of physical or emotional abuse)	• Distorted perceptions of the world • Misinterpretation of the motives and messages of others • Distorted responses to communication of others	• Resolve your issues and do not focus on other peoples' issues; to do so takes time from looking at your own issues.	"I think there has been a misunderstanding here, I would like to discuss/clarify/clear this up." "I apologize if I was not clear; let me explain what I meant."

POSSIBLE CAUSES	POSSIBLE CONSEQUENCES OR INTERPRETATIONS	POSSIBLE CURES/ STRATEGIES	EXAMPLES OF POSSIBLE WORDING FOR EFFECTIVE COMMUNICATION
		• Seek to clarify and resolve the issue, if you feel the other person misinterpreted what you said or meant and as a result there is conflict or bad feelings. • Always own your own words and actions.	
6. Poor Self-Image/ Self-Esteem	• Perceived attacks • Perceived threats • Perceived losses • Fear of others or situations	• As above, in number 5. • If you feel threatened or attacked, step back, remain calm, and provide feedback to the other person(s). Allow yourself to be honest with your feelings.	"I am feeling like there is quite a bit of emotion in the room right now." "Sounds like this issue gets people fired up."
7. Poor Self-Image/ Negative Self-Talk	• Contributes to low self-image and lack of respect from others.	• As above, in number 6. • Do not refer to yourself in negative terms, such as, "I'm a mess." • Listen first, then respond. • Ask for a specific example.	When receiving feedback that may be helpful for your development–you can listen first, then respond with, "What I hear you saying is that I can become impatient at times. …" It may be helpful to ask for a specific example or incident of the behavior to enable you to have a fuller understanding of what may need to be changed. Try, "Can you provide an example of what you are referring to?"

(Continued)

Table 7.10.1 (continued)

POSSIBLE CAUSES	POSSIBLE CONSEQUENCES OR INTERPRETATIONS	POSSIBLE CURES/ STRATEGIES	EXAMPLES OF POSSIBLE WORDING FOR EFFECTIVE COMMUNICATION
8. Lack of Boundaries/ Inability to Set Limits	• Can be caused by history of abuse	• As above, in number 6. • Learn the difference between being a team player and being taken advantage of. • Do not agree to fulfil obligations, tasks, assignments that you are not fully competent to perform; or clearly qualified to do. • Do not agree to do anything outside your scope of practice or clinical privileges. • Know that it is ok to say NO. • Know that it is ok to say YES and ask how to do it.	"I have not been trained to perform that task, I would be happy to observe you at this time and learn." "Please walk me through this policy, process, procedure…." "I will check with my supervisor and inform you what I find out."
9. Lack of Insight	• Blindness to your faults and flaws robs you of opportunity for personal growth	• Be open to input from others. • Ask for honest feedback. • Be willing to take constructive criticism. • Work to develop the insight of a mature adult. Own your mistakes, apologize when you are wrong, and take action to correct any damage that has been done.	"I have been told I am impatient, do you agree with that observation?"

POSSIBLE CAUSES	POSSIBLE CONSEQUENCES OR INTERPRETATIONS	POSSIBLE CURES/ STRATEGIES	EXAMPLES OF POSSIBLE WORDING FOR EFFECTIVE COMMUNICATION
		• Resolve to learn from your mistakes and flaws and not to repeat the same behavior in the future. • Request feedback from trusted individuals.	
10. Physical or Mental Illness	• Pain, depression, or anxiety can affect one's ability to focus, listen, and respond	• Take care of your health, no one else will do this or should do this for you. • Request in simple terms the time you need to take care of yourself at work and at home.	"I am taking a nap/ bath/break do not disturb me for one hour." "I need to take Friday morning off for a medical appointment."
11. Hidden Agendas, Politics, Games and Tests	• Disdain and lack of trust for authority figures • Secrets create dis-empowerment and dependency which can lead to increased stress, burnout, lack of creativity and motivation	• Do not participate in gossip, rumors or back-stabbing. • Demonstrate integrity in all that you do. • Be honest. • Own your own mistakes. • Excuse yourself from or try to redirect the conversation if the discussion has turned from facts/problem solving to gossip or complaining.	"It seems we have strayed a bit from the original topic of the meeting….. can we get back to the agenda/ problem at hand?" "I believe the item we were discussing was. … and … the following solution(s) have been offered …"

(Continued)

Table 7.10.1 (continued)

POSSIBLE CAUSES	POSSIBLE CONSEQUENCES OR INTERPRETATIONS	POSSIBLE CURES/ STRATEGIES	EXAMPLES OF POSSIBLE WORDING FOR EFFECTIVE COMMUNICATION
12. Lack of Clear, Plain Speech or Writing (e.g., acronyms, codes, slang, hashtags, accents, culture, apps, jargon)	• Distancing strategy • Power move • You can appear uneducated	• Speak and present yourself in a professional manner at all times. • Never use slang or improper English in professional situations. • If you lack communication skills for appropriate speech and/or writing, learn them. • Use available software and computer technology to review/ correct anything submitted in writing. • Ask a colleague to proofread for you. Find the person on your team or work unit who enjoys details, and has the skill to find a misplaced semicolon. • Do not use acronyms, abbreviations, or other short-hand language unless everyone on the receiving end knows what they mean. If you do not know, ask for an explanation.	

Additional Insight about Barriers to Effective Communication: Thoughts from the Trenches.

The above table offers many "possibilities" to explain and address some common areas that may contribute to ineffective interpersonal communication. Below is some additional discussion and implications for practice to provide further insight into these concerns.

Cultural and Organizational Taboos/NO TALK Rules

It may be helpful to question "NO TALK" rules and communication taboos, such as the expression, "Children should be seen and not heard." In much of today's society, this may seem an absurd statement, but likely it was an accepted societal norm at some time in the past. But times have changed. In 2014, do not accept statements or situations at face value that do not make sense. You are entitled to an explanation and rationale when it is spoken or inferred that you should "not talk about" something. Find out why. If you are afraid to speak up, ask yourself why. If you are afraid or uncomfortable with conflict, then you must understand that fear of conflict can lead to poor conflict management and poor negotiation/problem solving skills (numbers 2 and 3 in the above table). NO TALK rules are often unspoken; in fact they are generally inferred, creating a more confusing situation. This can add to frustration, helplessness, lack of trust, and avoiding discussion about and problem solving of important issues. The only way around this frustrating barrier is to bring NO TALK issues forward and discuss them openly and honestly.

In the workplace, most nurses know that not reporting (i.e., not talking about) something that they know is wrong or against policy (or could bring harm to a patient) because "you don't want to get someone in trouble" is unethical behavior. A striking example of this is failure to report an impaired colleague. How might you talk about this NO TALK issue? Here are some suggestions that I have found helpful. Stick with the facts. Do not make judgments, or offer moralizing and/or solutions for fixing the problem. Go to the person's supervisor and ask if you can speak privately. If you are uncomfortable, say so. You might try saying, "I am not comfortable discussing this, but I feel it is my duty to report that I smelled alcohol on Fred when he gave me report this morning." Keep are cord of the date, time, and name of the person with whom you had this conversation. If the behavior is not addressed and occurs again, your next step is to go up the chain of command.

Poor Conflict Management

If you are not comfortable with conflict, chances are somewhere along the line you may have learned that conflict is "bad." Maybe you witnessed conflict that escalated into inappropriate aggression or violence, or you were not allowed to express negative feelings in order to solve conflict. The term "conflict management" that was coined years ago by the business world suggests that conflict must be managed or kept under control. This is not always true. Conflict often can provide the friction we need to discuss issues, consider alternative strategies and solve problems. Conflict in and of itself is not bad, but necessary. Opinions that differ from our own help us to learn and grow (Peck, 1978). Keep an open mind and discuss solutions respectfully when conflict arises. Remember, too, it is ok to disagree, and not all problems will be or can be solved. You do not have to fix everything.

Poor Negotiation/Problem-Solving Skills

In my experience, poor negotiation and/or problem-solving skills often happen when people are in a hurry to fix a problem, whether at home or in the workplace. A person may not take time to thoroughly think about the problem and possible solutions because we live in what I have heard described as a hurry-up, fix it now, instant mashed potatoes, just put out the fire culture. This "hurry up and fix it/get it away from me" ideology is sometimes due to discomfort with problems. Why? Because problems can evoke negative feelings within us, and we do not want to feel negative feelings. In my opinion, this is a real shame because "problems call forth our courage and wisdom; indeed they create our courage and wisdom" (Peck, 1978, p. 16).

It is common knowledge in present day healthcare that the population requiring care is growing and resources are shrinking. A hurry up, problem-avoidance mentality (one that I have often heard described in my years as a provider, especially recently) may deprive people of the opportunity to learn: 1) toleration for unfinished business; 2) creative problem solving; 3) flexible thinking; 4) coping; 5) spontaneity; 6) testing of boundaries; and most importantly 7) to sit with uncomfortable feelings. Emotional maturity is born of the foregoing experiences, and maturity is necessary to become skilled at negotiation and problem solving. Work to both develop negotiation and problem solving skills and also to ensure adequate time to allow for appropriate consideration of the problem at hand.

Lack of Empathy

If you live in a family or work on a team, empathy is a must; however, empathy requires a complex balance of well-developed boundaries, emotional stability, experience, and indeed, effective interpersonal communication. Helping professionals may find themselves on one end or the other of the emotional caring spectrum and err by being overinvested in or, conversely, detached from patients. Unfortunately, emotional detachment, a technique adopted by some providers, does not protect one from future or worsening burnout. For example, physicians have been criticized for their lack of empathy, whereas nurses have been hailed as owning the concept of caring (Spiro, Curren, Peschel, & St. James, 1996). If you lack empathy, you may have become hardened to the world for some reason. Perhaps you have been hurt or are burned out. Compassion fatigue, a term coined in the mid 1990s, describes a phenomenon wherein professionals working with traumatized clients were actually at risk for secondary traumatization due to over-identification with their clients' experiences (Sabo, 2006). This phenomenon occurs in all types of healthcare providers. Therefore, to maintain both physical and emotional health, it is important to strive to maintain the delicate balance between over and under caring.

Unresolved Emotional Issues

While an extensive discussion of this complex topic is beyond the scope of this article, some basic outcomes of unresolved emotional issues are commonly known by all. A disruptive or abusive childhood, adult victimization or trauma of any kind can leave emotional and psychological scars that can be difficult to heal. Survivors of abuse have trouble trusting, and as a result, can misperceive and misinterpret the motives of others. Mistrust of others can create distorted perceptions of the world, distorted communication patterns and general difficulty in personal and professional relationships. If you need professional help to resolve your own emotional issues, you owe it to yourself to do this. To support your own health, make the time and effort to get this help if you need it.

Poor Self–Image/Negative Self-Talk

A poor self-image, possibly combined with negative self-talk, can set the stage for ineffective interpersonal communication. Never degrade yourself or allow others to denigrate or be disrespectful to you. Never refer to yourself or your personal characteristics in pejorative terms. Make a decision to view these behaviors as unacceptable. If you want respect, you must demonstrate this by respecting yourself.

Sometimes we have to teach people how to treat us. For example, if you are spoken to in a disrespectful or condescending manner, by anyone, especially a co-worker, first know that this is unacceptable. You do not have to take verbal abuse from anyone, especially in the workplace. The expectation is for nurses, physicians, and all members of the healthcare team to behave professionally at all times. Should inappropriate behavior occur, you must make the decision to stand up for yourself. Even if it is hard, try calmly stating words such as, "Excuse me, but I would like to be addressed with courtesy and respect at all times" or "Please refrain from making pejorative remarks and focus on a solution to this problem."

All of us are a mix of positive and not-so-positive characteristics. Learn to appreciate the good qualities in yourself and others. It can be difficult to avoid judging yourself or others. You may find it helpful to pick one quality or character trait you would like to improve. Then, seek the wisdom of *a trusted* friend, counselor, or sage and ask for support and advice in order to accomplish your goal.

Lack of Boundaries/Inability to Set Limits

The inability to set limits is generally related to fear of rejection, people pleasing, or emotional insecurity. You may think, "They won't like me." Accept that you will not like everyone, and everyone will not like you, and that is okay. Assertiveness, or saying NO and setting limits appropriately is an ***ART*** that must be learned. Setting limits requires one to make simple, short statements in a calm, respectful manner. Focus on the positive and describe the **desired** behavior, as opposed to one that is undesired. Following this, describe the consequences for continuation of the undesired behavior. Do not argue, threaten, and attempt to intimidate, or show fear. State only the consequences that you have power to enforce, and that you will follow through upon. Do not promise what you cannot deliver. In your role as a nurse, you will deal with upset patients at times; however, you have the right and responsibility to set limits on inappropriate behavior. This is true both in your professional and your personal life. Table 7.10.1 provides selected examples of suggested verbal interventions that you might utilize to set limits.

Importance of Self Analysis and Insight

Since we do not live in a vacuum or in isolation, understanding yourself and developing insight into YOU is paramount to effective communication. Refer back to the personal variables in Figure 7.10.2. Consider how your upbringing may have influenced you. What was your home like? How were you treated and addressed by your parents and teachers? Was your family patriarchal (led by father) or matriarchal (led by mother)? Who delivered the discipline to children in your home? Who were the other significant adults in your life? How has your race, culture, and/or religion possibly influenced you? As an adult, how has your education and real world experience impacted you? Have you travelled to other countries? How have adult relationships such as spouse, children, and significant other influenced you? Have you been ill or lost someone close to you? It is important to understand how these factors have shaped and influenced you, and to what extent. These variables influence how you present, behave, and communicate in the world. Simply taking the time to engage in self-analysis to develop this type of personal insight can support the effective interpersonal communication necessary to maintain your health.

Physical or Mental Illness

Depression, anxiety, and alcoholism appear more likely to be high in professions with high stress, but there remain gaps in the research literature. Ross and Goldner (2009) conducted a review of the literature to examine stigma, negative attitudes and discrimination toward mental illness from a nursing perspective. They determined that although substance abuse among nurses has been studied, no such parallel examining nurses with mental illness could be found. The paucity of literature on the subject of nurses with mental illness is of concern. However, Ross and Goldner (2009) did find that nurses with mental illness are both stigmatized and stigmatizers; they judge themselves and others. In regard to ineffective interpersonal communication, Farrell (2001) reported that nurses who have mental illness often felt as though they were targets of bullying and lateral violence in the workplace.

Research supports that mental illnesses are biochemical brain disorders that are strongly genetically linked (Perese, 2012). Mental illness is not caused by weakness or lack of moral character. Ghaemi (2011) noted that some of the greatest leaders in history suffered from mental illness. Moreover, he purported that it was because of their suffering that these men (e.g., Lincoln, Churchill, Sherman) developed the personal characteristics necessary to become exceptional leaders during times of crisis.

Mental illness can be treated and should not be ignored. There is no shame in seeking the help of a mental health provider. Nurses seeking treatment for mental health disorders not only have the ability to improve their own health, but also by their actions may help to address perceived stigma associated with mental illness.

Hidden Agendas, Politics, Games, and Tests

Over a decade ago Horsfall (1998) addressed several important "personal" variables with respect to effective communication. Two of her foci addressed how power inequalities and personal prejudices affect communication. Even chosen seating in a meeting (i.e., who sits where) can be the subject of interpretation. Unfortunately much of what Horsfall discussed in 1998 has not changed in the present day. Unequal power structures, abuse of power, and feelings of powerlessness (including certain unspoken practices both within nursing, medicine and the world) prohibit equalization of power structures. For example, persistent use of patriarchal (or exclusively male led) systems still exist and contribute to the "inadequacy of mainstream nursing [and other] concepts of communication" (Horsfall, 1998, p. 78). Women, in particular, who communicate in a firm, assertive manner, may be subject to pejorative remarks in a male dominated environment. If there appears to be a gender barrier to effective communication, be firm anyway. Again, table 7.10.1 above offers information about how to address communication barriers due to these concerns, using neutral, nonthreatening, wording and actions.

Lack of Clear Plain Speech/Writing

Lack of clarity in speech and/or writing often contributes to ineffective communication. Avoid jargon, any kind of "isms," clichés, slogans and boring overused stories. If you have heard something before, it is likely that others have, too. Use others' work discriminately and give credit as appropriate. Be original. Shorthand, texting, hashtags, and social networking lingo should never be used in professional communication. Say what you mean and mean what you say. Use plain, straight-forward talk that addresses the issue at hand.

Do not always resort to email to communicate important messages; you can sometimes improve communication by asking for a face to face meeting. Email communication is indeed inappropriate in certain situations. According to a Forbes magazine article, *Do You Hide Behind Email?,* there are four times you should never use email: when you are mad, criticizing or rebuking; when there is a chance you could be misunderstood; when you are cancelling; or when apologizing (Warrell, 2012). Furthermore, when issues are delicate, sensitive, awkward, or negotiation is needed, they should always be discussed in person. Personal discussions facilitate trust and add to the richness of the experience by facial expression and body language (Warrell, 2012). Confident, mature individuals will speak with you face to face and will not hide behind email to communicate important information. Especially if a matter has escalated, make the time to talk in person to clarify concerns.

Conclusion

Effective interpersonal communication is necessary to negotiate the challenges of everyday living, whether in your personal or professional life. Because human beings are complex and each individual brings his or her own set of internal variables to every situation, the possibilities of interactional outcomes of any given communication can be exponential.

Although much has been written regarding workplace violence (e.g., bullying), practical strategies for addressing the mechanics of effective interpersonal communication are lacking. In order to address this, we need frank, open conversations regarding how our personal internal variables affect our interpretation of the world as we see it. This article has hopefully provided an opening dialogue in that direction with pragmatic discussion of common areas of concern. These recommendations are often ones that we, as nurses, offer to patients every day. Taking the time to consider them as they may apply in our professional and personal lives may go a long way to encourage healthy communication, and thus healthy nurses!

Author

Kathleen A. Vertino, DNP, PMHNP-BC, CARN-AP
Email: Kathleen.vertino@va.gov

Dr. Vertino received her DNP and MS degrees from the University at Buffalo. She holds dual national board certification as a PMHNP and CARN-AP. In addition to her role as a Nurse Practitioner in the Behavioral Health Clinic at the VA Western New York Healthcare System, she is involved in a number of scholarly, academic, and community service activities which include publishing and presenting. Due to her clinical expertise, leadership qualities, compassion for and understanding of patient care, and business acumen she has is sought by peers, colleagues and superiors for participation in numerous diverse task forces, academic and professional development programs, strategic planning initiatives and operations issues both within and outside the Veterans Healthcare Administration (VHA). She is a VHA Certified Mentor at the Fellowship level and has mentored staff with special projects. She is an active voice at the National level for Advanced Practice Nursing.

References

Brinkert, R. (2010). A literature review of conflict communication causes, costs, benefits and interventions in nursing. *Journal of Nursing Management, 18*, 145–156. Doi: 10.1111/j.1365-2834.2010.01061.x.

Bylund, C., Peterson, E., & Cameron, K. (2012). A practitioner's guide to interpersonal communication theory: An overview and exploration of selected theories. *Patient Education and Counseling, 87*(3), 261–267. Doi: 10.1016/j.pec.2011.10.006

Farrell, G. (2001). From tall grass to squashed weeds: Why don't nurses pull together more? *Journal of Advanced Nursing, 35*(1), 26–33.

Ghaemi, N. (2011). *A first-rate madness: Uncovering the links between leadership and mental illness.* New York, NY: Penguin Books.

Horsfall, J. (1998). Structural impediments to effective communication. *Australian and New Zealand Journal of Mental Health Nursing, 7*(2), 74–80.

Hull, R. (2007). Your competitive edge: The art of communication in professional practice. *The Hearing Journal, 60*(3), 38–41.

Institute of Medicine. (1999). *To err is human: Building a safer healthcare system.* Washington, DC: National Academy Press.

Kotter, J. (1996*). Leading change.* Boston, MA: Harvard Business School Press.

Maslow's hierarchy of needs. (n.d.). Retrieved May 30m 2014 from Wikipedia: http://en.wikipedia.org/wiki/File:Maslow%27s_hierarchy_of_needs.svg

Perese, E.F. (2012). *Psychiatric advanced practice nursing: A biopsychosocial foundation for practice.* Philadelphia, PA: F.A. Davis Company.

Peck, M., & Scott, (1978). *The road less travelled.* New York, NY: Touchtone Publishers.

Ross, C., & Goldner, E. (2009). Stigma, negative attitudes and discrimination towards mental illness within the nursing profession: A review of the literature. *Journal of Psychiatric and Mental Health Nursing, 16*(6), 558–567. doi: 10.1111/j.1365-2850.2009.01399.x.

Sabo, B. (2006). Compassion fatigue and nursing work: Can we accurately capture the consequences of caring work? *International Journal of Nursing Practice, 12*(3): 136–142.

Shapiro, J. (2011). Does medical education promote professional alexithymia? A call for attendance to the emotions of patients and self in medical training. *Academic Medicine, 86*(3), 326–332. doi: 10.1097/ACM.0b013e3182088833.

Spiro, H., Curnen, M., Peschel, E., & St. James, D. (Eds.) (1996). *Empathy and the practice of medicine: Beyond pills and the scalpel.* New Haven, CT: Yale University Press.

Vessey, J.A., DeMarco, R., & DeFazio, R. (2010). Bullying, harassment, and horizontal violence in the nursing workforce. *Annual Review of Nursing Research, 28*(1), 133–157. doi: 10.1891/0739-6686.28.133.

Warrell, Margie. (2012, August). *Hiding behind email? Four times you should never use email. Forbes.* Retrieved from: www.forbes.com/sites/margiewarrell/2012/08/27/do-you-hide-behind-email/

Chapter 7: Post-Reading Questions

The author suggests that we all understand and accept that one cannot control others and/or certain situations.

1. Are there certain people or situations that you find yourself habitually attempting to control to no avail?
2. What would be the benefits for you of letting go of your illusions of control?
3. Refer to the major miscommunication that you referenced in the Pre-Reading Questions section and analyze it in reference to Table 7.10.1. Use the table to categorize and identify what happened, what the consequences were, and what could have been done better.

CHAPTER 8

Identity Development

Identity Formation

Which one of the following statements best describes you?

1. I don't know yet what I want out of life, because I haven't given it much thought.
2. Finding direction and purpose in life was never a difficult thing for me, because I feel like I've always known what I wanted out of life.
3. I've given it a lot of thought, but I still haven't figured out where I'm going and what I want out of life.
4. After much consideration and deliberation, I've finally attained a sense of direction and purpose in my life.

Identity Statuses

In Erik Erikson's psychosocial theory of life-span development, life is geared toward developing a personal sense of identity which will guide you through adulthood. Once you figure out who you are, what you want to be, and what you want out of life, the rest is a matter of fulfilling those roles, goals, and values that you have determined will give your life the direction and purpose you are seeking. James Marcia operationalized some of Erikson's concepts surrounding the development of identity. Marcia suggested that people can be categorized into one of four identity statuses, depending on where they are in the identity formation process. These statuses are based on the degree to which we have explored our identity options and the degree to which we have committed to certain choices.

Diffusion

We all begin in the diffusion status. We have not yet committed to an identity as we have not yet even begun to explore our options. For young adolescents to be unsure of what they want to do when they grow up and unsure of exactly what they want out of life is quite normal. They are going to school because they have to, and generally doing what they are told, but they haven't yet begun to tackle those big questions because they don't have to. They have not yet taken full responsibility for their lives. When a 30-year-old is unsure of what s/he wants to do and, worse, is not actively trying to figure it out, this may be viewed as more problematic. Adults in diffusion tend to be drifters, moving from job to job, relationship to relationship (superficial ones at that), without making firm commitments to any life plan.

Foreclosure

For most of us who don't get stuck in diffusion, the next natural step is to start exploring identity options, to figure out what we believe in and what we want to do with our lives. However, some people commit prematurely without looking at all the possibilities. This is sort of like trying to solve the challenge you have chosen to work on in this class without first generating a lot of options to consider. You would just do the first thing that comes to mind. Many of these people uncritically accept an identity that was assigned to them, usually by their parents. Our parents often have a vision for what they want us to become, and part of being a teenager often involves questioning and challenging parental notions. Most kids want to decide things for themselves, but not all. Some, for various reasons, swallow whole their parents' values and life goals without thinking about whether they are really right for them. They become a doctor or a lawyer because "Daddy told me to," not because it is their heart's desire. Foreclosed people prefer to follow the directions of authority figures in general. They don't like having to think for themselves, and they don't like their commitments to be challenged. Some people enjoy a good debate, but people in foreclosure generally do not. Not having given a great deal of thought to their beliefs and life choices, they are not in a good position to defend them. "Because I say so" or "None of your business" is a fine answer for them.

Moratorium

For those of us who do not foreclose, the next step is to explore. The word moratorium implies taking a time out, and that is what people in the active state of exploration are doing. They have decided to take a time out and wait before making identity commitments. They are giving themselves time to figure out what is best for them. These are people who like to question and challenge the status quo. They have an investigative nature and they are in a state of experimentation. They want to make sure they will be making the right decision before they commit. College is an excellent time to engage in the exploration process of moratorium. Young people have many of the freedoms of being an adult and perhaps living on their own, without the full obligations of having to work and pay the bills (thanks to loans, grants, and parents). These particular people are free to take different courses (both for personal and professional reasons), to pursue different majors and career paths, and to get involved in various curricular and extra-curricular activities until they figure out what is right for them. Moratorium can be a fun time of limitless possibility, but it can also be a time of intense anxiety and distress as we are faced with so many choices that we feel overwhelmed, unable to decide, and fearful that we will make the wrong decision. These feelings might be intensified as graduation and other life markers of elapsing time start looming closer and closer, imploring for decisions to be made.

Achievement

After a thorough exploration and critical examination period in moratorium, hopefully we are ready to make some commitments to certain roles, goals, and values, which we expect will bring us life fulfillment. Once we have made those commitments—"This is who I am, This is what I believe in, This is what I want to do with my life"—we have an internal map for what is to come. This map will stabilize us and help us to navigate the future, as well as give meaning to the past. People who have achieved a sense of identity tend to be more stable. They are better able to deal with adversity, and they are able to achieve deeper and more intimate relationships (it is very difficult to share yourself with another person if you are not sure who you really are).

Foreclosure Revisited

A cautionary note is due here, because it is worth noting that there is some cultural bias going on here. In our Western, mainstream American culture, we value independence and becoming your own person. We are expected to find ourselves and achieve our identity. However, other cultures place a higher value on respecting authority and living up to obligations to others. Our society values the freedom to choose what you want to believe and what you want to do with your life. In some other cultures roles and obligations are placed on you from birth; and you will dishonor yourself, your family, and your community if you reject these roles, goals, and values. Our society is more individualistically oriented, while others are more collectively oriented. We will discuss this further in another module, but for the moment it is worth noting that foreclosure is not necessarily bad, and in some cultures it is more highly valued than in others. My own research shows that foreclosed individuals can be every bit as well adjusted psychologically as people who explore and achieve their identity. It may be as problematic to try and achieve an independent identity in a culture that values foreclosure as it is to be foreclosed in a culture that values identity achievement.

Where Do I Go from Here?

Erikson said that the psychosocial identity crisis occurs in adolescence. Research has shown that it often (perhaps even usually) is not completely resolved until well into young adulthood. In fact, recent trends show that it is taking people a lot longer on average to get established career-wise and otherwise. Economic forces, a decrease in apprenticeships, and the lack of entry-level positions in general (you need experience to get the job, but you can't get experience without the job) are causing people to delay their career establishment, and with that comes a general feeling of not being fully in the adult world. Even if people do establish a career path, they may still have other areas of their life that are unresolved. For instance one person could be achieved in career choice, in moratorium in regard to what they want out of a romantic relationship, foreclosed in regard to religion, and diffused in regard to political beliefs. In other words, just because one area of our life is resolved, doesn't mean that we don't still have other areas on which we can work.

In addition, just because we are achieved in some areas doesn't mean we will always stay achieved. We might need to revisit those old commitments. For instance, we might have done a thorough exploration and chosen a career, but several years down the road we decide that the career is not nearly as fulfilling as we had hoped. Or perhaps we didn't want to change careers but we found that we weren't as successful as we had hoped and we were forced out of our job or, perhaps, out of the field itself. There are many other reasons for questioning our identity commitments. Severe life-threatening traumas often cause us to question and re-evaluate our lives. Midlife and other existential crises may lead us to make drastic changes. Some identity researchers refer to this as a MAMA cycle. MAMA stands for Moratorium-Achievement-Moratorium-Achievement. It refers to the questioning and loosening of previous commitments followed by a new period of exploration, resulting in new commitments. In other words, the original moratorium leading to achievement was followed by a second moratorium which led to a second (new and improved!) achievement.

In this course we have asked you to look at your life. We began this course by asking you to consider your life goals, where you are headed, where you want to go, and where you don't want to go. We are trying to encourage you to think about your life and the choices you have been making (or avoiding). We are attempting to move those in diffusion or foreclosure into moratorium, and we are trying to help those in moratorium to move toward achievement. For those in achievement, they might want to develop a previously underdeveloped area. Whether this is your first moratorium to achievement, your third MAMA cycle, or you are just fine-tuning your achievements, it is our hope that this class will give you the tools to make your life more satisfying and meaningful. We have identified a single issue to work on, but hopefully the skills you are developing will continue to serve you well as you generalize them to other issues in your life. This is why we have been more focused on the process than the end point. As Gandhi said, "Give a man a fish, and he eats for a day, but teach him to fish, and he eats for a lifetime."

Group Assignment

In the last chapter's individual assignment, you created a new alternative that should have combined the best ideas of the other alternatives, maximizing the advantages and minimizing the disadvantages. Share this new alternative with your group and explain how it is an improvement over any of the previous alternatives. Give each other feedback on their choices. If you are having difficulty coming up with a new synthesized alternative, use the group to help you complete this task.

Individual Assignment

Reflect on the group process. How helpful have they been in giving you new ideas and insights into tackling your issue? Are certain members more helpful than others? What role does each member play (e.g., leader, peace maker, clown/distractor, nurturer, antagonist, etc.). How do you feel about the progress you are making on your issue? Are you looking forward to trying out the ideas you have generated? Do you have any concerns or reservations? What are these reservations and why do you think you are having them?

The Weekly Reading

Pre-Reading Questions

The reading for this chapter is on identity. It will reiterate some of what was written above on identity status and go on to discuss ethnic, gender, and sexual orientation identity.

1. Reread the four statements at the beginning of this chapter and try to classify your identity status. Think about the different domains of your life (career, relationships, religious beliefs, sexuality, life goals, politics, moral values, etc.). Do you find yourself in different statuses depending on the domain?
2. Try to identify one domain that, for you, represents each status.
3. Although you can be in a different status for different domains of your life, you probably have one particular status that best describes your overall sense of identity, because certain domains are more important to some people than others. What are the particular domains that you find to be most important when thinking about your sense of identity?

READING 11

Identity

Marc Setterlund, Seymour Feshbach, Bernard Weiner, and Arthur Bohart

Chapter Outline

Source: FuzzBones/Shutterstock.com

In the previous chapter we considered the development and functions of the self. In this chapter we consider aspects of the development of identity.

Identity deals with that which we consider to be most basic to our sense of self—the things that identify who we are, both to ourselves and to others. It includes our most basic values and goals and our ethnic and gender identifications. As fans of science-fiction movies or amnesia victims know, there is nothing more terrifying than the sense of losing one's identity. Identity involves the fundamental sense of *continuity* in one's life: I am who I was yesterday, and I am who I will be tomorrow. It provides a framework for taking action in the future.

Self-concept and identity are closely related ideas. Both can provide answers to the question "Who am I?" Yet they differ. *Self-concept* is one's *description* of who one is. *Identity* is one's *definition* of who one is (Baumeister, 1986); it consists of those things that most basically define who we are. Something can be part of one's self-concept ("I am sloppy") but not part of one's identity ("I don't consider sloppiness an integral part of who lam"). Identity is defined by our connection to various aspects of our life, and it helps us locate ourselves in terms of who we are and where we belong (Lewis, 1990).

Many psychologists believe that adolescence is the key developmental time period for the formation of identity. While individuals begin to develop an identity in early childhood and may continue to modify their identities throughout their lives, adolescence is thought to be the most crucial organizational period for forming an identity. This view characterizes the perspectives of Erik Erikson, James Marcia, Dan McAdams, and those who have developed models of ethnic identity formation. However, gender identity, as we shall see, appears to develop considerably earlier.

Stages of Identity Formation: Erikson and Marcia

Erik Erikson has been the most influential theorist of identity. Erikson emphasized the ability to experience oneself as having continuity and sameness as an important aspect of identity. Identity includes one's bodily identity, the ability to sustain loyalties, and a sense of having a future. It also includes having a stable sense of self versus feeling self-conscious, being able to pursue a career versus feeling paralyzed in terms of work, being able to experiment with various roles versus rigidly locking oneself into a fixed role, feeling clear about one's sexual identity versus being confused about one's sexual identity, and having ideological commitments versus being confused about one's values.

Erikson believed that late adolescence was the time of identity achievement, although earlier developmental periods played a role. Identity achievement precedes the development of the capacity for intimacy, which occurs in early adulthood. However, Erikson theorized that this sequence is more characteristic of males than of females. For females, interpersonal aspects are at the core of their identity. Men therefore achieve identity first and intimacy second, while women achieve identity and intimacy concurrently, or intimacy first. Erikson also assumed that women do not complete an identity in adolescence because marriage and having children complete their identities.

James Marcia (1980), using an interview format, followed Erikson's ideas on the development of identity in adolescence. Others have subsequently developed objective measures based on Marcia's interview format (Grotevant and Adams, 1984). An example of items from one of these measures is given in Table 8.11.1.

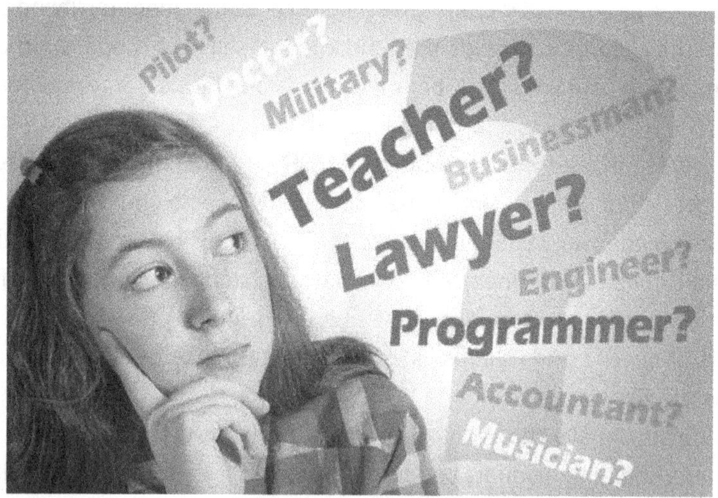

Determining an identity is a major task of adolescence. Choosing a career path is often a part of that identity.

Source: Hriana/Shutterstock

Table 8.11.1 Sample Items from the Objective Measure of Ego-Identity Status

STATUS	ITEM
Diffusion	I haven't chosen the occupation I really want to get into, but I'm working toward becoming a____until something better comes along. When it comes to religion, I just haven't found any that I'm really into myself.
Foreclosure	I guess I'm pretty much like my folks when it comes to politics. I follow what they do in terms of voting and such. I've never really questioned my religion. If it's right for my parents, it must be right for me.
Moratorium	I just can't decide how capable I am as a person and what jobs I'll be right for. There are so many different political parties and ideals, I can't decide which to follow until I figure it all out.
Identity-achievement	A person's faith is unique to each individual. I've considered and reconsidered it myself and know what I can believe. It took me a while to figure it out, but now I really know what I want for a career.

Source: Adams, Gullota, and Markstrom-Adams, 1994, p. 274.

Marcia's original research involved interviewing adolescents about their vocational plans and goals, and their values and beliefs. They were asked about the degree to which they had explored each of these areas and the degree to which they had made a commitment in each area. In early versions, the identity interview focused on vocational achievement. Later, to correct for this bias, interpersonal elements were added to the interview. Currently the interview includes questions about vocational plans, avocations, religious beliefs, political ideologies, gender-role orientation, sexuality, values, friendships, dating, marriage, parenting, family and career, setting priorities, and ethnicity.

Marcia identifies four identity *statuses* during adolescence: diffusion, foreclosure, moratorium, and identity achievement. These four statuses vary along two dimensions: commitment and exploration. **Identity diffusion** is characterized by low levels of both commitment and exploration. The person neither has a set of commitments to goals or values nor is actively struggling with the process of forming such commitments. **Foreclosure** is characterized by a high level of commitment and a low level of exploration. Individuals in this stage are most likely those who have adopted an identity from their parents or culture without actively exploring and choosing. **Moratorium** is what we typically think of as an identity crisis and is characterized by high levels of exploration but a low level of commitment. The person is in the process of exploring who he or she is and what he or she wants to be but has not come to any stable set of commitments yet. **Identity achievement** is arrived at through exploration which results in a personally chosen commitment to a set of values and goals for one's life. The different combinations can be seen in Table 8.11.2.

Table 8.11.2 The Two Dimensions of Marcia and the Four Alternative Identity Statuses

		COMMITMENT	
		YES	NO
EXPLORATION OF	Yes	*Identity achievement*	*Moratorium*
ALTERNATIVES	No	*Foreclosure*	*Identity diffusion*

In Marcia's scheme, identity achievement is the "highest" level, with moratorium the next, foreclosure third, and diffusion the lowest. However, a number of writers have noted that this order may be culturally biased. Only in Western society must one achieve an identity. In many other cultures, one attains one's identity from the culture and the role one plays in it (foreclosure). Therefore, for many cultures a foreclosed identity may be the healthiest. In fact, it has been found that for members of minority groups in the United States a foreclosed identity is more common than an achieved one. It has been argued that foreclosure may be a more functional identity for members of minority groups in a hostile society (Hauser and Kasendorf, 1983; Markstrom-Adams, Berman, and Brusch, 1993). Taking on an identity provided by one's group may be more adaptive than trying to individually achieve an identity in a society that blocks opportunities and conveys negative messages about one's minority status. This topic is discussed further in the section on ethnic identity.

Each of the four identity statuses can be thought of either as the state that a person is in or as a developmental stage. For some individuals, identity status remains relatively constant with time. In one study (Adams and Montemayor, 1988), constancy of identity status was found to occur for about 15 percent of the adolescents studied. For other individuals, the identity statuses form a kind of stage model, in which the individuals progress upwards through the four stages over time. About 50 percent of individuals were found to show steady progression over time. Still others showed an up and down pattern of progression and regression through the four statuses. A meta-analysis of 124 studies conducted by Kroger, Martinussen, and Marcia (2010) found that 49 percent of the adolescents in those studies remained stable in their identity, while 36 percent progressed to a higher identity status. Importantly, 15 percent regressed in their identity. Recognize that stability could be in any of the four identity statuses and that progress does not necessarily mean identity achievement.

Researchers have found a variety of correlates of the four identity statuses. Identity diffused individuals tend to show signs of poor psychological adjustment, such as feelings of inferiority and poorly articulated self-concepts. They are more likely to have parents who are rejecting or not affectionate and are more likely to have problems with substance abuse (Adams, Gullota, and Markstrom-Adams, 1994; Markstrom-Adams, 1992; Jones, 1992). Foreclosed individuals are more likely to be hardworking, quiet, obedient, respectful of authority, and industrious. They tend to come from families that are warm and supportive but that appear to stifle autonomous growth (Adams et al., 1994). Individuals in the moratorium status tend to be the most anxious, which is not surprising because they are in the midst of questioning their identity status. They appear to be high in self-directiveness while open to exploring alternative perspectives. They also tend to be introspective and emotionally responsive (Adams et al., 1994). Their families are likely to be democratically organized, but there is liable to be strain between the adolescent and the parents (Fuhrmann, 1986).

Identity achieved students have been found in many studies to have high levels of self-esteem, moral reasoning, self-confidence, psychological integration, emotional maturity, and social adeptness. They are also most likely to have established strong intimate relationships (Adams et al., 1994; Waterman, 1992). As with adolescents in the moratorium status, they are likely to have come from democratic homes (Fuhrmann, 1986). However, while the vast majority of the evidence indicates that identity achievement is associated with positive qualities, the findings are not entirely uniform. Kroger (1992) reports that some studies have found a high percentage of identity achieved participants to be excessively self-sufficient or detached.

Differences between men and women have been a major focus of investigation. As we have noted, Erikson assumed that interpersonal issues were at the core of women's identity, suggesting that their identities might not be completely formed until the intimacy stage in early adulthood. Research indeed supports the idea that identity and intimacy tend to merge for many women, while for men they are separated, that is, identity first and intimacy second (Patterson, Sochting, and Marcia, 1992). However, these researchers also conclude that the task of identity *begins* in adolescence both for women and for men. Further, for nontraditional women, late adolescence is the optimal time for resolution of the identity, as it is for men. For traditional women, whom Erikson expected would complete their identities when they married and had children, the evidence suggests that marriage and children do not complete their identities. Rather, these women put their identities "on hold" until their children have grown up, when they resume the task of identity completion. Josselson (1988) has studied identity formation in women by interviewing them in college and again when they were in their mid-thirties. She found that identity development for women does involve issues of interpersonal connection.

In early research on identity status it was found that for men, identity achievement and moratorium were the most "healthy" patterns (e.g., high self-esteem, etc.), while for women identity achievement and foreclosure were the healthiest (Patterson et al., 1992). At the time, Marcia (1980) suggested that the foreclosure status might be adaptive for women because society did not provide support for women, as it did for men, to explore and choose their identities. He predicted that if society changed, so would the pattern of these early research findings. Making Marcia look like a prophet, recent findings show that for women, as well as for men, identity achievement and moratorium are the more adaptive patterns. Patterson and colleagues (1992) note that this might be due to the fact that the identity status interview was changed over the years to take interpersonal issues more into account. However, they think this shift is more likely due to societal changes that now provide more support for women to choose careers.

Beyond Four Statuses

There is significant heuristic value in using Marcia's four identity statuses, but recent research has suggested a more nuanced view. Luyckx and colleagues have suggested that as a person commits to an identity, there is then a further exploration as to whether that identity is a truly workable identity (Luyckx, Goossens, and Soenens, 2006; Luyckx, Goossens, Soenens, and Beyers, 2006). A recognizable experience would be selecting a college major (Luyckx, Teppers, Klimstra, and Rassart, 2014). The first step is to identify the possible majors; this would be considered the moratorium stage. Then the person would decide on a major, which they termed exploration in breadth. Finally, the person deeply examines whether that is the right choice for who he or she is as a person, which they term exploration in depth (Meeus, 1996). For many people, that is the process. However, some people find the exploration to be very difficult and stressful. These people will continue to consider and reconsider *and reconsider* identities; this style is termed ruminative exploration (Luyckx et al., 2008).

It is also useful to consider different reactions to the diffusion stage as marked by concern over the lack of identity, or a relatively carefree diffusion in which the person is unconcerned about a lack of identity. The carefree diffusion is typically observed in the youngest adolescents and tends to be less common as the cohort ages (Verschueren, Rassart, Claes, Moons, and Luyckx, 2017).

There are several problems with the research done on identity statuses from Marcia's perspective. One problem is that most of the research has been done on college students, typically between the ages of eighteen and twenty-two. There is less research on adolescents not in college. In one study, Morash (1980) examined working-class youths and college students. It was found that working-class youths were more likely to be either identity achieved or diffused, while college students were more likely to be in moratorium or foreclosure. Working-class youths were also more likely to have experienced shorter, more concrete moratoriums. It may be that being in college allows one the luxury of a more leisurely moratorium period in which one can explore one's identity before making commitments. However, much more research is needed on adolescents not in college.

From a feminist perspective, Archer (1992) has criticized the research on identity statuses. She argues that focusing on differences between the genders is not fruitful. Individual men and women vary among themselves enormously, and the differences that have been found between men and women as groups are minimal. She believes it is more interesting to look at the question of how *individuals* pattern their identity achievement rather than at group comparison of genders. For instance, some of her research has found that reasoning about identity is "domain specific." This means that an individual's reasoning about identity in one area, such as vocation, is not necessarily the same as his or her reasoning in another area, such as relationships.

One criticism of identity status theory and research has previously been mentioned. That is that the whole concept of achieving an identity has a distinctly Western flavor. Myers, Speight, Highlen, Cox, Reynolds, Adams, and Hanley (1990), working from an Afro-centric paradigm, have noted that in Western culture one must establish one's worth through one's activities, while in other cultures one is valued just because one is. They believe that the Western idea is a product of our cultural assumptions, which separate self from others and separate the material from the spiritual. As previously noted, the foreclosure stage, therefore, may not necessarily be a less developed stage than the identity achieved stage in many cultures.

In conclusion, Marcia's theory of identity statuses has led to research that has helped clarify the process of identity development in adolescence. At the same time many issues remain to be clarified.

Racial and Ethnic Identity

We now turn to an important specific component of identity: **racial and ethnic identity**. Racial and ethnic identity has to do with those aspects of one's identity that relate to one's identification with one's ethnic group. Not everyone has specifically worked out an ethnic identity. However, it is a particularly important issue for minority group members in our culture. Because ethnicity and race are closely related, and at times fully mixed, many researchers use ethnicity to refer to both race and ethnicity (Schwartz et al., 2014). We will use that convention here, as the effects of discrimination seem to be the same whether it is based on race or ethnicity (Oyserman, Coon, and Kemmelmeier, 2006).

Individuals who are members of minority groups in our society face a particularly complicated task in forming an identity. First, they are often confronted with conflicting messages concerning important life values. For instance, the particular minority culture may hold the value that an individual's choice of careers should be influenced by the family, while the dominant culture in the United States emphasizes individual choice. Second, we have already seen that different cultural groups hold different views of what a self is: is it a "we" interconnected with others, or is it an "I," a separate, autonomous entity? Third, such individuals are often confronted with the social devaluation of their minority group status. In various implicit and explicit ways they are told that they are "less than" because they are members of a particular minority group. This message might be conveyed, for instance, through stereotypic television portrayals or through the relative invisibility of their group in television shows. Fourth, they face some objective limitations to their hopes and aspirations because of their minority group status and various concomitants, such as economic inequality.

There are two interrelated aspects to the formation of an identity for ethnic minority members. First is the issue of forming a positive, proactive identification with one's ethnic group. This is the issue that most models of ethnic identity formation have focused on. A second issue is that of acculturation—the degree to which the individual attempts to integrate with the dominant culture or chooses to remain separate and identify exclusively with the minority culture.

Ethnic identity, according to Phinney (1990), includes one's sense of self-identification as a group member, attitudes and values in relation to one's group, attitudes about oneself as a group member, the adoption of ethnic behaviors and practices, and the extent of one's ethnic knowledge and degree of commitment to one's group.

There is a commonality to many models of ethnic identity development. This commonality is shared by models of identity development for nonethnic minority groups as well, such as for gays and lesbians. The models tend to describe the process as proceeding in five stages (Umaña-Taylor et al., 2014):

1. Pre-encounter, in which one is unaware of or unconcerned about differences
2. Experiences with others leading to awareness of differences
3. A period of conflict between the old unawareness and the new awareness
4. Resolution and habituation
5. Commitment to the group and identity

Phinney (Phinney, 1990; 1991; Phinney and Rosenthal, 1992) has proposed a model of ethnic identity development that is synthesized from other models but is also based on the work of Erikson and Marcia. The first stage is that of an unexamined ethnic identity, which could be likened to Marcia's either foreclosed or diffused status. The adolescent either adopts an unexamined commitment to his or her ethnicity from the parents and is therefore foreclosed, or has no clear sense of commitment to ethnic identity but is not exploring it either and is therefore in a diffused state. In the second stage, some event—perhaps some act of discrimination (Quintana, 2007)—triggers the adolescent's awareness of his or her ethnic identity, and he or she begins to think about it. This stage is equivalent to the moratorium stage in Marcia's model. Indeed, during adolescence, exploration of ethnic identity tends to rise (French, Seidman, Allen, and Aber, 2006). In the third stage of ethnic identity development, some kind of commitment to an ethnic identity occurs. This follows a process of resolving conflicts and contradictions involved in being a minority in a majority culture where minorities have often experienced discrimination. Phinney and Chavira (1992) studied the development of ethnic identity in minority youths between the ages of sixteen and nineteen and found movement from lower to higher stages, as predicted.

Using an ethnically diverse sample and statistical technique called cluster analysis, Yip (2014) found that the Marcia model fit her data well. Adolescents in the achieved category included ethnic identity across situations. The achieved adolescents showed higher levels of exploration and higher self-esteem. The achieved and moratorium adolescents reported being more aware of the ethnicity in their everyday life.

A fundamental question is whether ethnic identity status has a positive or negative impact on psychological adjustment. Phinney (1991) found that not all components of a positive ethnic identity correlated with high self-esteem, but the trend was that individuals with a strong ethnic identity were more likely to have high self-esteem. Having a developed ethnic identity appears to work as a defense against perceived discrimination, allowing healthier adaptation (Sellers, Copland-Linder, Martin, and Lewis, 2006).

With respect to acculturation, Berry and his colleagues (1989) have defined four modes of acculturation. Those who strongly identify only with their ethnic group are in a state of separation. Those who strongly identify only with the dominant culture are in a state of assimilation. Those who identify with both their own group and the dominant culture are considered to be bicultural. Finally, those who identify with neither are considered to be in a state of marginalization. In general, most theorists now hold that biculturation is the most adaptive mode. For instance, LaFromboise, Coleman, and Gerton (1993) have argued that biculturated individuals are those who have developed the competencies to function both in their culture of origin and in the larger majority culture. They are able to utilize the best of both cultures. Meta-analysis of 83 studies, which included 32,197 individuals, found that psychological and social adjustment tends to be higher in people who identify with two cultures (Nguyen and Benet-Martínez, 2013). In this sense, they will have also developed a more complex, differentiated, and integrated identity.

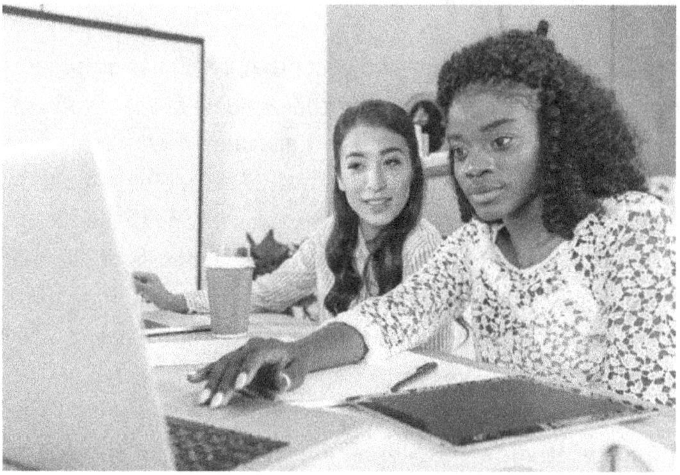

Having a sense of identification with one's own culture can have a positive influence on one's own identity.

Source: LightField Studios/Shutterstock

Sexual Orientation Identity Development

The process for forming identity for gay and lesbians has informed the models of race and ethnic identity, and been informed by those models as well. Unlike members of most race and ethnic groups, homosexuals are usually in the minority in their own families. Also, gays and lesbians can hide their identity, which members of many minority groups cannot do. There are two major theories of sexual orientation identity, and as we will see, they are similar, though not identical. Although both models were laid out to explain and understand the process for homosexuals, we can probably assume that the models work for other sexualities outside the mainstream.

Cass's model (1984) suggests that there are six stages to developing a sexual orientation identity that is different from the dominant model:

Stage 1: Identity confusion. A person starts to wonder if he or she may be homosexual. If that is accepted as a possibility, the person moves to the next stage.

Stage 2: Identity comparison. The person starts to compare himself or herself to homosexuals and nonhomosexuals.

Stage 3: Identity tolerance. The person starts to make more and more contacts with other homosexuals. The identity is tolerated, but not embraced.

Stage 4: Identity acceptance. A positive view of homosexuality starts to develop. However, disclosure of sexual orientation will be limited, and the person may often attempt to pass as heterosexual.

Stage 5: Identity pride. People will start to feel a great deal of pride about their sexual orientation. They will identify strongly with other homosexuals, and feel anger at the intolerance society directs toward homosexuals.

Stage 6: Identity synthesis. Roles models have typically helped the individual settle into the community and identity. The person feels comfortable in that identity, needing neither to hide nor flaunt the identity.

In this model, we see similarities to the moratorium and identity achievement stages that are key components of the Marcia model.

The other major model was laid out by Troiden (1988). This model includes typical ages at which the stage is experienced. He warns that the model is an ideal and simplified process. The real process is not linear and has many movements both forward and backward. Stages may overlap and be experienced more than once.

The first stage is sensitization. This is typically experienced before puberty. The child becomes aware that he or she is different from peers. Usually, this difference is not noted to be a sexual difference until after the onset of puberty.

The second stage is identity confusion. This stage is typically experienced in adolescence. The person realizes that he or she sexually different. Because most of the models to which the person is exposed are not homosexual, and because homosexuality is often stigmatized, this is often not a welcome recognition. Adding to the confusion is the general ease of arousal in adolescence that may lead to being aroused by either gender. At this point, the person can respond in several different ways. A person may deny or seek to change his or her sexual orientation. He or she may avoid situations that confirm desires. Among the forms of avoidance are the formation antihomosexual attitudes or escape via drugs or alcohol. A person may respond by redefining his or her desires—for instance, by claiming bisexuality, considering it a temporary stage, or describing it as a special case ("I'd only do this with you"). It is also possible that the person will accept the prospect and seek more information.

The third stage is identity assumption. This stage typically happens in the early twenties for men and somewhat later for women. At this point, the person will have included homosexuality into his or her self-concept. There is tolerance and acceptance of the identity, along with sexual experimentation and association with others in the community. Although a homosexual identity is developed, the identity is more tolerated than embraced.

The fourth stage is commitment. Homosexuality becomes a major part of the person's self-identity. The person usually enters into a same-sex love relationship. Typically, he or she finds it is much easier to live having adopted this identity than to continue to fight against it. As a result, personal happiness tends to increase.

Troiden's model has similarities to both Marcia's model of general identity development such as confusion and successful identity achievement. We also see aspects of the model of ethnic identity development with the experiences leading to awareness of differences, the resolution and habituation, and finally commitment to the group and identity.

Beyond the development of one's sexual orientation identity, members of the LGBTQ community must face another step: that is the process of coming out. The process of coming out can be a dangerous time, as there can often be an increase in prejudice and victimization directed at the person (Davison, 2005). Gay and lesbian youth show a suicide rate high above others of similar ages (Hottes, Bogaert, Rhodes, Brennan, and Gesink, 2016; Remafadi, French, Story, Resnick, and Blum, 1998), though legalizing same-sex marriage has been found to reduce the suicide rate in homosexual teens (Raifman, Moscoe, and Austin, 2017).

Legalization of same-sex marriage may reduce suicide rates for homosexual teens.

Source: Lisa F. Young/Shutterstock

Gender Identity, Gender Typing, and Gender Differences

Some of the most active current research in developmental psychology concerns the development of gender identity and the related issues of gender differences and gender typing. While gender identity has to do with individuals' self-perceptions of who they are as males or as females, gender differences have to do with the question of whether there are objective differences in psychological functioning between the two genders. The issue of gender-typing has to do with how males and females develop their masculine or feminine identities, attributes, or behaviors. The issue of whether there are gender differences and how gender-typing occurs are intimately related to the development of gender identity. We first examine gender identity, then consider the issue of gender differences, and finally reflect upon how gender differences and gender identity develop, i.e., the issue of gender-typing.

The convention that we use when describing the differences between males and females is to use the term **gender** for anything that might be due to culture and socialization and sex to refer to differences that are due to biology (Frieze and Chrisler, 2011). We need to be very careful about the term sex, as it is easy to confuse biological influences with social and cultural influences. We might look at something such as running a foot race as a sex difference where anatomical differences mean that males are faster than females. However, the current world record time for women in the 200-meter race (21.34 seconds) would have won every men's 200-meter Olympic final from 1900 to 1928. It might be argued that the reason is changes in training, and that is likely correct. But, think of training as something that is cultural. So, even in something that seems obviously to be based on a sex difference, culture matters.

Gender Identity

One of the most important components of identity is gender identity. In introducing his model of gender identity, Ashmore (1990), says that "it is assumed that sex and gender pervade most aspects of daily life and can shape many aspects of psychological structure and function" (p. 512).

One's **gender identity** is defined by how one's perception of gender influences or plays a role in other aspects of identity. It could be said to be the answer to the issue of what it means to the individual to be a man or woman. It is how one's view of oneself as male or female is interwoven with all the various other aspects of one's identity. According to Ashmore (1990), gender identity consists of five general content areas. The first is the biological and physical attributes associated with gender, including aspects of appearance and dress. The second area is "symbolic and stylistic behaviors," including how one walks, one's body bearing, and how one communicates nonverbally. The third area consists of the interests and abilities that one sees as relevant to and characteristic of one's gender. The fourth area is "social relationships," which includes images of how one will differentially relate to men and women as well as how one's sense of masculinity or femininity are organized and expressed in relationship with others. The fifth area is perception of one's personal and social attributes—for instance, one's personality traits and how these relate to masculinity and femininity.

Gender Differences

Many differences can be observed between boys and girls and men and women in terms of "typical" behavior. More boys play with blocks and fire trucks than do girls, who tend to play with dolls and paper cutouts more than do boys; boys prefer football, while girls prefer dramatic play. Gender differences in toy and activity preference can be observed early in development, well before the age of three (Lewis, 1987). Later in life, more men than women study to be architects and engineers, while more women become nurses and school teachers than do men. There are many exceptions and, although changes are occurring in traditional gender roles, there are still gender differences in preferred activities and in such diverse domains as child-care responsibilities, work roles, and occupations. These differences are most likely a reflection of the contrasting social roles ascribed to men and women. Comparable kinds of gender differences in social roles are observed in other societies, both modern and preliterate.

We know that these gender differences exist at the social level. The intriguing question is what they are related to at the psychological level. To what extent do boys and girls differ in intellectual abilities motivation social skills and other personality attributes? There are many common stereotypes concerning gender differences in personality. For example, males have been regarded as aggressive, rational, and ambitious, while females have been described as passive, emotional, and nurturant. These stereotypes are opinions and are in part responsible for the differential occupational roles, income levels, and statuses of the genders. But to what extent do these gender stereotypes have a basis in fact?

Gender-typing begins early in life.

Source: Stas Ponomarencko/Shutterstock

One task undertaken by psychologists has been to determine possible personality and cognitive attributes that distinguish the two genders and, in addition, to discern the age levels at which gender differences appear. This empirical task has proved to be far more complex than it initially seemed. First, one must assume that the samples of the genders studied are comparable on such variables as socioeconomic status and educational opportunity. It is also important to sample different ethnic and economic groups to establish that the findings are representative of boys and girls in general, rather than restricted to some particular segment of society. To add a further complication, as the culture undergoes economic and social change, there may be corresponding alterations in personality traits. For example, differences in dependency between the genders seem to have been greater in previous decades, indicating that gender differences reported at one time may not hold for another. Conversely, where there once were similarities, differences may suddenly appear. Finally, some of the psychological attributes distinguishing the genders are subtle and difficult to measure.

A second and even more challenging task for psychologists is determining how differences between the genders have come about, or how gender typing occurs. The role of biological versus social factors in determining behavioral differences between the genders is an especially interesting issue. It is evident from the extensive amount of research that has been conducted on gender differences that there is a great deal of overlap between the genders with regard to virtually any behavior. Because of individual variability within a gender and the overlap between genders, gender discrimination is psychologically, as well as legally, unjustified.

In the sections that follow, we consider research studies on gender differences and on the development of gender differences and gender identity.

Studies of Gender Differences

We are all aware that men and women are socialized to be different in a number of ways, such as in how they dress. However, are there basic *psychological* differences? A good deal of research has been done to determine whether there are such differences. In a classic review of the literature on human gender differences, Maccoby and Jacklin (1974) concluded that there were differences.

Research has indicated that men and women are now close to equal in the areas of both verbal and mathematical ability. In addition, even the finding that males are more aggressive appears to be just a moderate effect (Archer, 2004; Ashmore, 1990). Nonetheless, the data still indicate that men are more likely to be aggressive than women, although such a difference may depend on how aggression is measured (see the following discussion of how gender differences develop).

Ashmore's (1990) summary of research indicates that, overall, few psychological gender differences have been found that are of more than "small to moderate" size. There are differences between men and women in "social stylistic" behaviors, such as smiling and facial expressiveness. Women report themselves to be more empathic than men, although when empathy is objectively measured, only small differences are found. The largest differences found between men and women are in physical variables, such as in the distance to which they are able to throw a ball.

More recent findings have led to questions about some of these conclusions. For instance, early research on mathematical ability found differences between boys and girls; however, this difference has mostly disappeared in the United States (Hyde, Lindberg, Linn, Ellis, and Williams, 2008). Hyde (2014) reviewed the many meta-analyses that have examined the differences between the genders; many of the results of studies she reviewed are included in Table 8.11.3. A few of those meta-analyses she and her colleagues conducted, whereas others were conducted by other people as reported in her review.

Meta-analyses have been mentioned a few times so far in the text, and will be included several more times in the next chapters. **Meta-analysis** is a statistic process that allows an integration and analysis of multiple studies simultaneously. By doing this, the random variance that shows up in any one study is reduced, the impact of a single researcher's approach is reduced, and multiple methodologies can be combined. Meta-analysis is a uniquely powerful way of looking at research findings, and is one of the most trusted methods for confidently drawing conclusions about research. The product of a meta-analysis is the "effect size." In our table, the effect size indicates how much of a difference there is between males and females. By convention (Cohen, 1988), the absolute value of an effect size greater than .80 is considered large, near .50 is considered moderate, and near .20 is considered small.

It is worth noting that most gender differences are indeed quite small. Males report more interest in sex, but that is confounded with social demand characteristics (Fischer, 2007). Self-esteem differences build through adolescence, then become minimal in adulthood. Males do seem to be better at 3-D mental rotation, though even this may be due to practice effects in video games (Feng, 2007) and sports. The mental rotation effects do appear quite early (Quinn and Liben, 2008), which then might predispose boys to those activities.

Table 8.11.3 Gender Differences Effect Sizes from Various Meta-Analyses

TOPIC	EFFECT SIZE	TOPIC	EFFECT SIZE
Cognitive functions		Leadership effectiveness	−0.02
Mathematics	−0.05	*Temperament in childhood*	
Complex problem solving (HS students, 1990)	0.29	Inhibitory control	−0.41
Complex problem solving (HS students, 2008)	0.07	Negative affect	−0.06
3D mental rotation	0.56	Emotionality	0.01
Vocabulary	−0.02	*Personality traits*	
Reading comprehension	−0.03	Neuroticism facet anxiety	−0.27
Writing	−0.09	Extraversion facet assertiveness	0.49
Verbal fluency	−0.33	Agreeableness facet tender-mindedness	−1.07
Reading achievement U.S.	−0.26	Conscientiousness	−0.07

TOPIC	EFFECT SIZE	TOPIC	EFFECT SIZE
Math self-confidence	0.27	Sensation seeking	0.41
Math anxiety	−0.23	*Emotions*	
Interests		Guilt	−0.27
Engineering	1.11	Shame	−0.29
Science	0.36	Authentic pride	−0.01
Mathematics	0.34	*Aggression*	
Self-esteem		Physical	0.55
Elementary school	0.16	Relational	−0.19
Middle school	0.23	*Sexuality*	
High school	0.33	Masturbation	0.53
College	0.18	Use pornography	0.63
Post college adults	0.10	Number of sexual partners	0.36

Positive numbers mean males have larger scores; negative numbers mean females have larger scores. (Based on meta-analyses reported in Hyde, 2014.)

In general, most researchers believe that there are far fewer differences in basic psychological attributes between the genders than there are similarities. For instance, Hyde (1984) notes that gender accounts for about 5 percent of the variation in aggressive behavior in children, which means that about 95 percent of the variation in aggressive behavior is due to factors other than gender. As she points out, humans have 23 pairs chromosomes and only one is the sex chromosome, so we should expect more similarity than differences (Hyde, 2014, p. 378).

While there may be relatively few basic psychological differences between the genders, some differences in behaviors begin to develop very early. Boys between the ages of fourteen and twenty-two months already prefer trucks and cars to play with, while girls prefer dolls and soft toys (Smith and Daglish, 1977). Two-year-old girls prefer to play with other girls, and by age three boys prefer to play with boys (La Freniere, Strayer, and Gauthier, 1984).

Gender Typing: Development of Gender Differences and Gender Identity

There have been a number of different theories that try to account for differences that are observed between the genders. Biological theories hold that differences are based in biology and are observable as soon as children begin to interact and play with peers (around the age of two). Yet the role of biological factors is complex.

Evidence from primate studies indicates that male monkeys engage in more rough-and-tumble play than females do and that even male infants display more aggressive behavior when attacked than females do (Aldis, 1975; Devore, 1965). But whether these observations of monkey behavior are applicable to humans is uncertain. In humans in this culture, the process of treating males and females differently begins at birth, with pink and blue blankets. Girls and boys are not only differently identified through the use of different colors and clothing, but also reacted to with different expectations and behaviors. Thus, even these early differences in aggression may be attributed to social rather than biological factors.

Later in the book the question of gender differences in aggression and the role of biological and social factors are examined in more detail. At this point, it is useful to keep in mind that the greater aggressiveness noted in males is based on observations of direct physical and verbal aggression. Although the gender differences in direct aggression before the age of six have been questioned (Tieger, 1980), extensive evidence can be presented indicating that this difference is reliable (Maccoby and Jacklin, 1980) and can be observed in children as young as age three (Fagot, Leinbach, and Hagan, 1986). However, when one examines more indirect, subtle forms of aggressiveness, such as snubbing or ignoring peers or gossiping, there is some evidence that aggression is greater in females than in males (Feshbach, 1969; Lagerspetz, Björkqvist, and Peltorer, 1988). Indeed, the meta-analysis on relational aggression does indicate that girls use it more (Archer, 2004).

For the sake of completeness, we can include the psychoanalytic perspective. According to Freud, the process by which boys and girls develop sex differences and their gender identities is rooted in biology. For him, identification was the principal mechanism leading to sex typing. As a result of the process of identification, children acquire the attributes and orientations of their sex. The biological difference between boys and girls leads not only to their making a different choice of which parent to identify with, but also to a less satisfactory identification for females. Therefore, the process of identification has biological roots. Freud did recognize some influence of learning processes in the development of gender differences, however, and contemporary psychoanalysts acknowledge the importance of social variables to an even greater extent.

The social learning theorists stress the importance of the differential reinforcement boys and girls receive for "appropriately" imitating male and female models and for behaving in accordance with the norms and expectations of society. The behaviors that define the female and male roles are very much influenced by the culture in which a child is socialized. Gender role norms vary from society to society, but in each case children are rewarded for those behaviors that will help them fit the particular roles prescribed by society. This differential reinforcement begins very early. It is manifest in the disparate ways that males and females are handled by their parents, in the unequal rough-and-tumble play of fathers with boys versus girls, and in the reinforcements given for engaging in appropriate gender-typed activities. One of the earliest gender differences that is consistently observed is that a greater amount of physical stimulation and gross motor play is directed toward male infants than toward female infants (see Block, 1979; Parke and Suomi, 1980). Studies of child-rearing practices in this and other cultures (Antill, 1987; Block, 1973; Whiting, 1963) clearly indicate that parents have different expectations for boys and girls and respond differentially according to the gender of their child. It is inevitable that these socialization practices define and shape male and female behavior.

Children even act as enforcers of gender roles. Children will punish through statements or teasing of other children for playing with toys associated with the other gender (Langlois and Downs, 1980). Children know which other children act most often as the enforcers (McGuire, Martin, Fabes, and Hanish, 2007, as cited in Martin and Ruble, 2010). Thus, children learn to play only with gender "appropriate" toys or risk social sanctions. In adolescence, there is a continuation of this pattern, as adolescents report pressure from peers to act in gender-conforming ways (Kornienko, Santos, Martin, and Granger, 2016).

It should be noted that in many instances of gender differences it is very difficult to disentangle the influence of biological and social variables. Parental practices may reinforce and enhance subtle biologically based sex differences or may obscure them. Application of the twin method to the analysis of individual differences in masculine and feminine personality attributes enables one to at least partially separate the independent roles of biological and environmental influence. In one study, monozygotic and dizygotic twins ranging in age from eight to fifteen years were administered several questionnaire measures of **masculinity** and **femininity** (Mitchell, Baker, and Jacklin, 1989). These self-report measures are based on attributes which men and women believe to be more typical of and appropriate to males and to females. An example of a masculine item is "I am often the leader among my friends," and a feminine item, "I am a kind and gentle person." The relationships between monozygotic twins proved to be much stronger than that for dizygotic twins for both femininity and, especially, masculinity scores, thus providing evidence of a genetic influence. Analysis of the data also reflected significant environmental influences.

Children often expect other children to not play with toys associated with the other gender.

Source: LightField Studios/Shutterstock

It may be noted that masculinity and femininity are separate dimensions or traits rather than opposite ends of a single continuum. Thus, while boys tend to be higher in masculinity and girls higher in femininity, it is quite possible for a boy or a girl to obtain both high masculinity and high femininity scores. The original model of masculinity-femininity was unidimensional, meaning that as a person increased on one dimension, he or she necessarily decreased on the other dimension. The current conceptualization recognizes that individuals can have aspects of both dimensions as part of their personality.

The development of gender typing and gender-linked behaviors is a complex process in which maturational and cognitive factors are involved as well as gender and social influences. A study by Fagot and Leinbach (1989) illustrates the interaction of several of these factors. A sample of boys and girls and their parents were seen when the children were approximately eighteen months, twenty-seven months, and forty-eight months of age. At age twenty-seven months, half the children, designated as "early labelers," were able to successfully identify the gender of children and adults in photographs presented to them. The other half, who made several errors in identifying males and females, were designated as "late labelers." Differences between boys and girls, and between early and late labelers, in gender-linked behaviors at eighteen and at twenty-seven months are presented in Table 8.11.4. At eighteen months, there were no significant differences between the groups. However, at twenty-seven months, gender differences in male- and female-typed toy play and in aggressive behavior can be seen. In addition, these differences are strongly influenced by whether the child can successfully identify gender. The largest gender differences in gender-typed behaviors are between the boys and girls who can successfully identify gender (early labelers). Clearly, learning factors are entailed in the development of gender typing.

Table 8.11.4 Mean Percent of Time Children Spent in Gender-Stereotyped Behaviors

	BOY		GIRL	
CHILD ACTIVITY AND CHILD AGE	EARLY LABELER	LATE LABELER	EARLY LABELER	LATE LABELER
Male-typed toy play:				
18 months	4.1	6.8	.8	3.0
27 months	23.8	11.2	4.6	7.6
Female-typed toy play:				
18 months	2.7	4.7	4.5	4.1
27 months	1.9	5.1	20.8	10.2
Aggressive behavior:				
18 months	.8	2.5	1.1	.9
27 months	2.1	2.2	.4	1.9

Based on Fagot and Leinbach (1989).

Kohlberg proposed that children pass through three stages as they acquire an understanding of what it means to be a male or female. The first stage is that of "basic gender identity," which consists of acquiring the basic label of oneself as a boy or girl, usually achieved by about age three. The second stage is that of "gender stability." A number of researchers have found that very young children, even when they understand that they are boys or girls, do not understand that gender is a stable attribute that does not change over time. This developmental achievement occurs somewhat later, around five or six. The third stage is "gender consistency," which is the understanding that one's gender is stable across situations. That is, one's gender is not changed by dressing in clothes of the opposite gender or by engaging in play activities preferred by the opposite gender. This is typically achieved by age six to seven. Some research has found that the gender concept does indeed develop sequentially, passing through the stages, and that this sequence has been observed across cultures (Munroe, Shimmin, and Munroe, 1984).

An alternative to Kohlberg's view, Martin and Halverson (1981, 1987) have developed **gender schema theory**. They suggest that children develop a set of gender schemas, which are organized sets of concepts about males and females. Children begin very early to develop a basic gender identity based on a simple classification of toys and behaviors as "for males" or "for females." Using this basic categorization, they then begin to explore and gradually add more and more information to their gender schemas until they have developed a stable and consistent gender identity by about the age of seven. Of course, this does not signal the end of learning about gender, which continues throughout childhood and adolescence.

A study by Stangor and Ruble (1989) tested the gender schema model. One of the properties of a schema is that it selectively influences the kind of information one pays attention to and remembers. In this study, it was found that the proportion of pictures remembered by children that were consistent with their gender-role in contrast to pictures that were inconsistent with it, increased with age.

As we have mentioned, although gender-schema theory suggests that a stable and consistent basic gender identity is established by about age seven, new aspects of gender identity continue to develop as one grows older. Brown and Gilligan (1992) have showed that adolescence is an important time for socialization of certain aspects of the gender identity of girls. They studied how girls lose their "voice" during the transition from late childhood to adolescence. Nearly one hundred girls between the ages of seven and eighteen at a private girls' school were interviewed over a five-year period. It was found that as girls entered adolescence, they increasingly received pressure from their teachers and other adults to "be nice." They learned that in order to keep relationships, they had to lose an important part of relationships—authenticity. One of the girls says, "I do not want the image of a 'perfect girl' to hinder myself from being a truly effective human being, ... yet, I still want to be nice, and I never want to cause any problems" (p. 41). In sum, girls' gender identity during adolescence comes to include "being nice" at the expense of being authentic.

Androgyny

Is there such a thing as a "healthy" gender identity? We have already seen how young girls making the transition from childhood to adolescence are socialized to lose a part of themselves that has traditionally been considered to be masculine—their assertiveness. At the same time it is likely that boys are being trained to lose a "feminine" part of themselves. Would it be better if children were able to retain both their masculine and feminine sides? Precisely this issue has been raised in the study of **androgyny**.

In early research, it was assumed that masculinity and femininity were two opposite ends of the same pole. If one was high in masculinity (that is, possessed traits characteristic of the male stereotype), one could not be high in femininity. Bem (1974), however, asserted that masculinity and femininity were two separate dimensions, and, therefore, a person could be high in both masculinity and femininity. As part of their gender identities, individuals could have traits characteristic of both the stereotypical male and the stereotypical female. Bem assumed that individuals who were high in both masculinity and femininity would be more flexible and adaptive. Using an inventory designed to measure both masculinity and femininity, it was found that such "androgynous" individuals did exist. Several research studies also found that individuals who were androgynous did appear to be more well-adjusted. However, there are a number of methodological problems that have made it difficult to conclude at this point that androgyny is indeed uniquely associated with better psychological adjustment (Ashmore, 1990).

Conclusions on the Development of Gender Identity and Gender Typing

Ashmore (1990) has pointed out that the development of gender identity is a product of a number of different factors, including general cultural factors, specific interactions with specific individuals (e.g., parents, teachers, etc.), and one's own self-guided activities. The result is that individuals' gender identities will vary from person to person, and it may be meaningless to talk about "masculinity" and "femininity" as if they were global traits that individuals simply have more or less of. Ashmore suggests that culture has often been treated as if it were homogeneous, when in fact different subcultures in the United States may have different beliefs and expectations about the behavior of males and females. Individuals socialized in these subcultures may therefore have different concepts of male and female gender identities than do individuals socialized in the dominant or mainstream culture.

It is quite likely that gender typing and gender identity are functions of all the mechanisms that have been discussed: identification, selective reinforcement, cognitive labeling, and gender schemas. In addition, one cannot ignore the contribution of biological factors, even if they may be overridden by social reinforcement. In sum, gender typing and gender identity are the result of the interaction between social and biological processes, leading to personality differences between the genders and variations within each gender.

Narrative and Identity

Dan McAdams (1989; 2001) has focused on the **narrative identity**. Narrative identity is a person's internalized and evolving life story, integrating the past and future (McAdams and McLean, 2013). This reflects a recent more general trend toward viewing individual experience in terms of narrative constructions (Howard, 1991; Singer, 2004; Smith, 1988). What these views all have in common is the idea that people's personal realities are "constructed." How we construct our experiences of self, others, and the world determines the world we inhabit. Our constructions are significantly influenced by the cultures or subcultures in which we live. As we have seen, the self is constructed differently by different cultures. Even our experience of gender is now being seen as a social construction (Ashmore, 1990).

Mair, and others who adopt a narrative perspective, assumes that our constructions of reality take the form of stories:

> Stories are habitations. We live in and through stories. They conjure worlds. We do not know the world other than as story world. Stories inform life. They hold us together and keep us apart. We inhabit the great stories of our culture. We live through stories. We are *lived* by the stories of our race and place. It is this enveloping and constituting function of stories that is especially important to sense more fully. We are, each of us, locations where the stories of our place and time become partially tellable. (1988, p. 127)

Therefore, life experience is constructed along the lines of stories. Lives have plots and subplots, and main characters and minor characters. Paul Ricoeur, a French psychoanalyst, has argued that it is how we "emplot" our lives that provides meaning for the events in it. An event without being embedded in a "plot" has no meaning. He says:

> [A] story is made out of events to the extent that plot makes events into a story. An event, consequently, must be more than a singular occurrence, a unique happening. It receives its definition from its contribution to the development of a plot. A story, on the other hand, must be more than an enumeration of events in a serial order; it must make an intelligible whole of incidents. (1983, p. 152)

One's life can have a well-organized plot, a poorly organized plot, a plot that has few leads toward a productive future, or a plot poorly connected to the past.

The narrative perspective on personality is having an important influence on psychotherapy. Therapists representing psychodynamic, humanistic, and cognitive points of view have begun to view therapy as the "restorying" of an individual's life. Ricoeur (Smith, 1988) sees therapy as a process of reorganizing one's plot through sharing it with another. An important part of the healing process is the sharing of one's "untold" stories. What might be called "repressed experience" is really experience that has not previously been articulated and shared with another.

An example of how people can utilize narrative accounts to deal with a life problem is provided by Harvey, Orbuch, and Weber (1993). They studied hundreds of individuals dealing with traumatic experiences such as incest, armed combat, an airline crash, or the loss of a loved one. They argue that it is in developing an account of the incident that the victim learns how to cope with the event and to restore a sense of meaning to life. An *account* is a "story-like construction containing attributions, trait inferences, descriptions, emotional expressions, and related material regarding self and outside world" (pp. 1–2). Confiding in others as one develops the account appears also to be an essential part of the healing process. One study by Harvey and colleagues (1991) found that there was greater recovery if the individual engaged in account making through diary work, confiding in responsive, empathic others, or participating in support groups. Feelings of completion appear to be associated with accepting loss and appear to be crucial to recovery (Cox and McAdams, 2014).

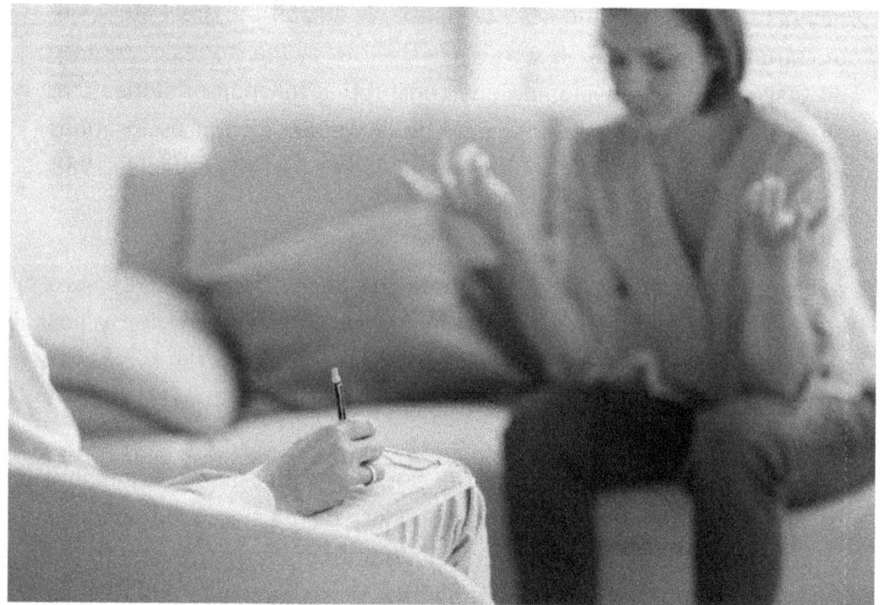

Psychotherapy can be seen as the process of restorying one's life.

Source: wavebreakmedia/Shutterstock

As we have noted, the narrative perspective has been applied to the study of identity by Dan McAdams (1989, 2001, 2013), who argues that identity is a narrative construction based on one's "life story." Our sense of ourselves, how we interpret events and experiences in our lives, comes from the sense of the "stories" we see ourselves as living. Further, our goals and motives only take on meaning in terms of our life story.

McAdams (1988) has researched this theory by collecting life stories from individuals. He had students enrolled in his developmental psychology courses complete "identity journals" in which they had to write about issues relevant to the class material. For instance, when the issue of consistency in personality was being discussed, students were asked to think about it in terms of themselves by trying to remember an incident in which they had done something completely out of character. McAdams has also interviewed midlife adults (see the interview format in Table 8.11.5). McAdams's research is a good example of the personological tradition of research in personality. That is, his interest has been in studying the life paths of whole individuals rather than in studying one aspect of behavior (say, achievement motivation) across large groups of individuals.

McAdams, like Erikson, argues that adolescence is the major period of identity and life-story construction, although one continues this process for the rest of one's life. Infancy contributes the "feeling tone" of the story—such as fundamentally hopeful or frightening—based on early experiences with caretakers. Early childhood contributes a variety of images (see Highlight 8.11.1). In late childhood, children are able to work with themes, and they begin to construct more truly story-like narratives about themselves and the events in their lives. During adolescence, individuals rearrange their past to develop a story of self that will help them face the future.

Table 8.11.5 McAdams's Life Story Interview Format

I.	Life Chapters
II.	Specific Scenes
	A. Peak Experience (High Point)
	B. Nadir Experience (Low Point)
	C. Turning Point
	D. Earliest Memory
	E. Significant Childhood Memory
	F. Significant Adolescent Memory
	G. Significant Adult Memory
	H. Significant Other Memory
III.	Important Persons
IV.	Future Script
V.	Stresses and Problems
VI.	Personal Ideology
VII.	Life Motif or Message
VIII.	Other

Source: McAdams, 1993.

Young children begin to develop their life stories by playing the role of fantasy characters.

Source: Oksana Kuzmina/Shutterstock

HIGHLIGHT 8.11.1

Early Childhood Roots of the Life Story

A turning point in my daughter's life was the day she saw *Snow White*. It was almost a year ago; she was three years old. The original Walt Disney version of the fairy tale was playing at a local theater, so I took the opportunity to escort Ruth Megan to her first full-length movie.

Since that day, my family has lived with Snow White and the Seven Dwarfs. All seven of the dwarfs ride with us in the car to nursery school—Grumpy, Happy, Doc, Bashful, Sleepy, Sneezy, and Dopey. The Wicked Queen, the Peddler Woman (who is the Queen in disguise), the Queen's Huntsman, and the Handsome Prince frequently show up for dinner. When she first met a classmate named William, Ruth told him that she lived in a little cottage (like the Dwarfs') tucked far away in the woods. (Incredulous, William told her she was crazy, and then reported that he would be traveling to nursery school next week in his flying car.) When William comes over for lunch these days, Ruth pretends that she is the Wicked Queen and he is the Queen's Huntsman, and the two of them terrorize her little sister, Amanda, who is 1 1/2 and cast in the pitiful role of Snow White. They steal her stuffed animals and threaten to lock her up, even kill her (William's idea, I am sure); they hide poisoned apples under her pillow. On other days, Ruth herself is Snow White, organizing regular birthday parties for Grumpy, her favorite dwarf, taping pink crepe paper all over the dining room, making birthday cakes out of sugar, pepper, oregano, and water.

My daughter is obsessed with the story of Snow White! Yet it is not so much the integrated story—from beginning to end—that so fascinates her. Rather, it is various pieces of the story, easily divorced from their coherent narrative context, that she appropriates into her daily life of fantasy, play, and fun. One day she is the Wicked Queen. The next day she is Bashful. Her identification with each of these characters is ephemeral and idiosyncratic. Recently she was Grumpy, rescuing three of the "Little Ponies" who were stranded on a cliff. Yet in *Snow White*, Grumpy never rescues anybody. And there are no ponies in the movie—they originate from a popular television show.

Although Ruth seems to recognize that stories have a certain canonical form, she does not insist that her own renditions conform to the canon. Her make-believe world is inconsistent, illogical, and very fluid. It is populated by a rich and ever-expanding repertoire of *images*. It is the images in stories—not the stories themselves—that Ruth zeroes in on. This is not to say that she cannot follow a story's plot or that she fails to appreciate the dramatic building of tension in narrative, the climax, and the denouement. Ruth has a pretty good sense of the whole story, from beginning to end, of Snow White and the Seven Dwarfs. But it is not the whole story that captures her imagination, for it is too big and complex, too systematic and progressive, to find its way *in toto* into her daily world of imagination and play. Instead, Ruth dwells on the images, reworking them daily into her own fantastical plots.

Source: McAdams, 1990.

As adults face obstacles and setbacks, the story takes a turn toward redemption. People whose life stories include themes of personal agency and exploration tend to show better psychological adjustment (McAdams and McLean, 2013). As individuals progress into adulthood, they have a number of different *imagoes*, or self-images, of themselves inside. This set of self-images acts like a Greek chorus commenting on and guiding behavior. McAdams (1988) found in his study of midlife adults that, although they were relatively normal individuals, their life story accounts were described as if they were "multiple personalities." In particular, they often had two conflicting primary self-images.

Some of the polarities in self-images found were: adventurer/housewife, humanist/barbarian, good citizen/bum, and worker/escapist. One subject, for instance, struggled with his two conflicting images, one of himself as an artist (with all its bohemian connotations) and the other of himself as a "successful, worldly moneymaker." Ultimately individuals integrate the various imagoes into one.

Summary

1. *Identity*, in contrast to self-concept, consists of all the things one identifies with—the things one considers to define who one is. An important component of identity is the sense of continuity in one's life.

2. Erikson felt that continuity and experiencing oneself are important aspects of identity. He believed that late adolescence is the time of much identity achievement. Marcia, extending the work of Erik Erikson, postulates that there are four different *identity statuses* during adolescence: diffusion, foreclosure, moratorium, and identity achievement.

3. Research has shown different patterns on how individuals move through the four identity statuses.

4. Erikson predicted that identity development would be more closely tied to the development of intimacy for women than for men. While some research has supported this, the results are complex and there are no clear patterns that characterize all or most of one gender in contrast to the other.

5. Ethnic identity development appears to pass through stages, going from a diffused or unquestioned state to a clearly defined and worked-out state. Strong ethnic identity appears to be associated with higher levels of self-esteem.

6. Biculturated individuals, who are able to flexibly utilize the best from both the majority culture and from their own minority culture, appear to be the healthiest psychologically.

7. There appear to be relatively few basic psychological differences between the genders, although members of the two genders are socialized to behave in different ways.

8. Biological theories of sex differences assume that these differences have a genetic basis. Psychodynamic theories focus on identification with the parent. Social learning theories focus on the reinforcement of gender-typed behaviors. Cognitive labeling and gender schema theories assume that children develop concepts about what behaviors characterize being a member of a given gender. Children then assimilate information to these concepts.

9. Narrative approaches to personality assume that people's lives are bound together by the stories they tell about themselves. McAdams's narrative approach to identity assumes that identity is a *life story*.

Thought Questions

1. Do you think your identity can be easily classified into one of the four major identity statuses: diffusion, foreclosure, moratorium, or achievement? Or do you think your identity may include components from more than one stage?
2. How have you struggled with the issue of your racial or ethnic identity, or sexual orientation identity?
3. What do you think accounts for differences between the genders?
4. In what way do you think you have constructed a "life story" that helps you make sense out of who you are?

Key Terms

androgyny A combination of high levels of both femininity and masculinity. (p. 185)
femininity The extent to which a person manifests characteristics typically associated with women. (p. 182)
foreclosure A person who has adopted an identity without consideration or exploration of alternative identities. (p. 168)
gender Aspects of oneself as male or female that may be due to culture and socialization. (p. 176)
gender identity One's inclusion of his or her gender as part of identity. (p. 176)
gender schema theory The idea that once a child has developed the idea that there are different genders, the world is then perceived through the lens of gender and what is appropriate for each gender becomes relatively fixed, thus changing behavior. (p. 184)
identity The goals, values, and roles that are the key descriptors of who we are to ourselves. (p. 166)
identity achievement Personally chosen commitment to a set of values and goals for one's life. (p. 168)
identity diffusion The status of a person who has low levels of both commitment and exploration to an identity. (p. 168)
masculinity The extent to which a person manifests characteristics typically associated with men. (p. 182)
meta-analysis A statistic process that allows an integration and analysis of multiple studies simultaneously. (p. 179)
moratorium The status of a person who is in the process of exploring who he or she is but has not committed to an identity. (p. 168)
narrative identity A person's version of his or her life story. (p. 186)
racial and ethnic identity Those aspects of one's identity that relate to one's identification with one's ethnic group. (p. 171)

References

Adams, G. R., Gullota, T. P., & Markstrom-Adams, C. (1994). *Adolescent life experiences.* Pacific Grove, CA: Brooks/Cole.

Adams, G. R., & Montemayer, R. (1992). *Patterns of identity development during late adolescence: A descriptive study of stability, progression, and regression*, 1988. Manuscript submitted for publication, as referenced in Adams, G. R., Gullota, T. P., & Markstrom-Adams, C. *Adolescent life experiences.* Pacific Grove, CA: Brooks/Cole.

Aldis, O. (1975). *Play fighting.* New York, NY: Academic Press.

Antill, J. K. (1987). Parents' beliefs and values about sex roles, sex differences and sexuality: Their sources and implications. In P. Shaver & C. Hendrick (Eds.), *Sex and gender: Review of personality and social psychology* (Vol. 7, pp. 294–328). Beverly Hills, CA: Sage.

Archer, J. (2004). Sex differences in aggression in real-world settings: A meta-analytic review. *Review of General Psychology, 8*(4), 291–322.

Archer, S. L. (1992). A feminist's approach to identity research. In G. R. Adams, T. P. Gullotta, & R. Montemayer (Eds.), *Adolescent identity formation* (pp. 25–49). Newbury Park, CA: Sage.

Ashmore, R. D. (1990). Sex, gender, and the individual. In L. A. Pervin (Ed.), *Handbook of personality* (pp. 486–526). New York, NY: Guilford.

Baumeister, R. F. (1986). *Identity: Cultural change and the struggle for self.* New York, NY: Oxford University Press.

Bem, S. L. (1974). The measurement of psychological androgyny. *Journal of Consulting and Clinical Psychology, 42*, 165–172.

Berry, J., Kim, U., Power, S., Young, M., & Bujaki, J. (1989). Acculturation attitudes in plural societies. *Applied Psychology, 38*, 185–205.

Block, J. H. (1973). Conceptions of sex role: Some cross-cultural and longitudinal perspectives. *American Psychologist, 28*, 512–529.

Block, J. H. (September 1979). Personality development in males and females: The influence of differential socialization. Paper presented as part of the Master Lecture Series at the meeting of the American Psychological Association, New York.

Brown, L. M., & Gilligan, C. (1992). *Meeting at the crossroads.* Cambridge, MA: Harvard University Press.

Cass, V. C. (1984). Homosexual identity: A concept in need of definition. *Journal of Homosexuality, 9*(2–3), 105–126.

Cohen, J. (1988). *Statistical power analyses for the social sciences.* Hillsdale, NJ: Lawrence Erlbaum Associates.

Cox, K., & McAdams, D. P. (2014). Meaning making during high and low point life story episodes predicts emotion regulation two years later: How the past informs the future. *Journal of Research in Personality, 50*, 66–70.

Davison, G. C. (2005). Issues and nonissues in the gay- affirmative treatment of patients who are gay, lesbian, or bisexual. *Clinical Psychology: Science and Practice, 12*(1), 25–28.

DeVore, I. (Ed.). (1965). *Primate behavior: Field studies of monkeys and apes.* New York, NY: Holt.

Fagot, B. I., & Leinbach, M. D. (1989). The young child's gender schema: Environmental input, internal organization. *Child Development, 60*(3), 663–672.

Fagot, B. I., Leinbach, M. D., & Hagan, R. (1986). Gender labeling and the adoption of sex-typed behaviors. *Developmental Psychology, 22*, 440–443.

Feshbach, N. D. (1969). Sex differences in children's modes of aggressive responses toward outsiders. *Merrill-Palmer Quarterly, 15,* 249–258.

Fisher, T. D. (2007). Sex of experimenter and social norm effects on reports of sexual behavior in young men and women. *Archives of Sexual Behavior, 36*(1), 89–100.

French, S. E., Seidman, E., Allen, L., & Aber, J. L. (2006). The development of ethnic identity during adolescence. *Developmental Psychology, 42*(1), 1–10.

Frieze, I. H., & Chrisler, J. C. (2011). Editorial policy on the use of the terms "sex" and "gender." *Sex Roles, 64*(11–12), 789.

Fuhrmann, B. S. (1986). *Adolescence. Adolescents.* Boston, MA: Little, Brown.

Grotevant, H. D., & Adams, G. R. (1984). Development of an object measure to assess ego identity in adolescence: Validation and replication. *Journal of Youth and Adolescence, 13,* 419–438.

Harvey, J. H., Orbuch, T. L., Chwalisz, K. D., & Garwood, G. (1991). Coping with sexual assault: The roles of account-making and confiding. *Journal of Traumatic Stress, 4,* 515–531.

Harvey, J. H., Orbuch, T. L., & Weber, A. L. (August 1993). *Restoring identity and control by account-making after major trauma.* Paper presented as part of a symposium on "Narrative Self-Interpretation," American Psychological Association Convention, Toronto, Canada.

Hauser, S. T., & Kasendorf, E. (1983). *Black and white identity formation.* Malabar, Florida: Robert E. Krieger Publishing Co.

Hottes, T. S., Bogaert, L., Rhodes, A. E., Brennan, D. J., & Gesink, D. (2016). Lifetime prevalence of suicide attempts among sexual minority adults by study sampling strategies: A systematic review and meta-analysis. *American Journal of Public Health, 106*(5), e1–e12.

Howard, G. S. (1991). Culture tales: A narrative approach to thinking, cross-cultural psychology, and psychotherapy. *American Psychologist, 46,* 187–197.

Hyde, J. S. (1984). How large are sex differences in aggression? A developmental meta-analysis. *Developmental Psychology, 20,* 722–736.

Hyde, J. S. (2014). Gender similarities and differences. *Annual Review of Psychology, 65,* 373–398.

Hyde, J. S., Lindberg, S. M., Linn, M. C., Ellis, A. B., & Williams, C. C. (2008). Gender similarities characterize math performance. *Science, 321*(5888), 494–495.

Jones, R. M. (1992). Ego identity and adolescent problem behavior. In G. R. Adams, T. P. Gullotta, & R. Montemayer (Eds.), *Adolescent identity formation* (pp. 216–233). Newbury Park, CA: Sage.

Josselson, R. L. (1988). *Finding herself: Pathways of identity development in women.* New York, NY: Jossey-Bass.

Kornienko, O., Santos, C. E., Martin, C. L., & Granger, K. L. (2016). Peer influence on gender identity development in adolescence. *Developmental Psychology, 52*(10), 1578–1592.

Kroger, J. (1992). Intrapsychic dimensions of identity during late adolescence. In G. R. Adams, T. P. Gullotta, & R. Montemayer (Eds.), *Adolescent identity formation* (p. 122–144). Newbury Park, CA: Sage.

Kroger, J., Martinussen, M., & Marcia, J. E. (2010). Identity status change during adolescence and young adulthood: A meta-analysis. *Journal of Adolescence, 33*(5), 683–698.

La Frenlere, P., Strayer, F. F., & Gauthier, R. (1984). The emergence of same sex affiliative preferences among preschool peers: A developmental ethological perspective. *Child Development, 55,* 1958–1965.

La Fromboise, T., Coleman, H. L. K., & Gerton, J. (1993). Psychological impact of biculturalism: Evidence and theory. *Psychological Bulletin, 114,* 395–412.

Lagerspetz, K. M., Bjorkgvist, K., & Peltoren, T. (1988). Is indirect aggression typical of females? Gender differences in aggressiveness in 11 to 12 year old children. *Aggressive Behavior, 14,* 403–414.

Langlois, J. H., & Downs, A. C. (1980). Mothers, fathers, and peers as socialization agents of sex-typed play behaviors in young children. *Child Development*, 1237–1247.

Lewis, M. (1987). Early sex role behavior and school adjustment. In J. M. Reinisch, L. A. Rosenbaum, & S. A. Sanders (Eds.), *Masculinity/femininity: Basic perspectives*. New York, NY: Oxford University Press.

Lewis, M. J. (1990). Self-knowledge and social development in early life. In L. A. Pervin (Ed.), *Handbook of personality* (pp. 277–300). New York, NY: Guilford.

Luyckx, K., Goossens, L., & Soenens, B. (2006). A developmental contextual perspective on identity construction in emerging adulthood: Change dynamics in commitment formation and commitment evaluation. *Developmental Psychology, 42*, 366–380.

Luyckx, K., Schwartz, S. J., Berzonsky, M. D., Soenens, B., Vansteenkiste, M., Smits, I., & Goossens, L. (2008). Capturing ruminative exploration: Extending the four-dimensional model of identity formation in late adolescence. *Journal of Research in Personality, 42*, 58–82.

Luyckx, K., Teppers, E., Klimstra, T., & Rassert, J. (2014). Identity processes and personality traits and types in adolescence: Directionality of effects and developmental trajectories. *Developmental Psychology, 50*, 2144–2153.

Maccoby, E. E., & Jacklin, C. N. (1974). *The psychology of sex differences*. Stanford, CA: Stanford University Press.

Maccoby, E. E., & Jacklin, C. N. (1980). Sex differences in aggression: A rejoinder and reprise. *Child Development, 51*, 964–980.

Mair, M. (1988). *Between psychology and psychotherapy*. New York, NY: Routledge.

Marcia. J. E. (1980). Identity in adolescence. In J. Adelson (Ed.), *Handbook of adolescent psychology*. New York, NY: Wiley.

Markstrom-Adams, C. (1992). A consideration of intervening factors in adolescent identity formation. In G. R. Adams, T. P. Gullotta, & R. Montemayer (Eds.), *Adolescent identity formation* (pp. 173–192). Newbury Park, CA: Sage.

Markstrom-Adams, C., Berman, R. C., & Brusch, G. (1993). *Identity formation among Jewish adolescents in dissonant and consonant community contexts*. Paper submitted for publication.

Martin, C. L., & Halverson, C. F., Jr. (1981). A schematic processing model of sex-typing and stereotyping in young children. *Child Development, 52*, 1119–1134.

Martin, C. L., & Halverson, C. F., Jr. (1987). The roles of cognition in sex-roles and sex-typing. In D. B. Carter (Ed.), *Current conceptions of sex roles and sex-typing: Theory and research*. New York, NY: Praeger.

Martin, C. L., & Ruble, D. N. (2010). Patterns of gender development. *Annual Review of Psychology, 61*, 353–381.

McAdams, D. P. (1988). *Power, intimacy, and the life story*. New York, NY: Guilford.

McAdams, D. P. (1989). The development of a narrative identity. In D. M. Buss & N. Cantor (Eds.), *Personality psychology: Recent trends and emerging directions* (pp. 160–176). New York, NY: Springer-Verlag.

McAdams, D. P. (1990). Unity and purpose in human lives: The emergence of identity as a life story. In A. I. Rabin, R. A. Zucker, R. A. Emmons, & S. Frank (Eds.), *Studying persons and lives* (pp. 148–200). New York, NY: Springer.

McAdams, D. P. (August, 1993). *Generative lives: Suffering, redemption, and personal destiny*. Paper presented at the American Psychological Association Convention, Toronto, Canada.

McAdams, D. P. (2001). The psychology of life stories. *Review of General Psychology, 5*, 100–122.

McAdams, D. P. (2013). *The redemptive self: Stories Americans live by* (Rev. and expanded ed.). New York, NY: Oxford University Press.

McAdams, D. P., & McLean, K. C. (2013). Narrative identity. *Current Directions in Psychological Science, 22,* 233–238.

McGuire, J., Martin, C. L., Fabes, R. A., & Hanish, L. D. (2007). The role of "gender enforcers" in young children's peer interactions. Poster presented at Biennial Meeting of the Society for Research in Child Development, Boston, MA.

Meeus, W. (1996). Studies on identity development in adolescence: An overview of research and some new data. *Journal of Youth and Adolescence, 25*(5), 569–598.

Mitchell, J. E., Baker, L. A., & Jacklin, C. N. (1989). Masculinity and femininity in twin children: Genetic and environmental factors. *Child Development, 60,* 1475–1485.

Morash, M. A. (1980). Working class membership and the adolescent identity crisis. *Adolescence, 15,* 313–320.

Munroe, R. H., Shimmin, H. S., & Munroe, R. L. (1984). Gender understanding and sex-role preferences in four cultures. *Developmental Psychology, 20,* 673–682.

Myers, L. J., Speight, S. L., Highlen, P. S., Cox, C. I., Reynolds, A. L., Adams, E. M., & Hanley, C. P. (1990). Identity development and worldview: Toward an optimal conceptualization. *Journal of Counseling and Development, 70,* 64–71.

Nguyen, A. M. D., & Benet-Martínez, V. (2013). Biculturalism and adjustment: A meta-analysis. *Journal of Cross-Cultural Psychology, 44*(1), 122–159.

Oyserman, D., Coon, H. M., & Kemmelmeier, M. (2002). Rethinking individualism and collectivism: Evaluation of theoretical assumptions and meta-analyses. *Psychological Bulletin, 128*(1), 3–72.

Parke, R. D., & Suomi, S. J. (1980). Adult male-infant relationships: Human and nonprimate evidence. In K. Immelmann, G. Barlow, M. Main, & L. Petrinovitch (Eds.), *Behavioral development: The Bielefeld interdisciplinary project.* New York, NY: Cambridge University Press.

Patterson, S. J., Sochting, I., & Marcia, J. E. (1992). The inner space and beyond: Women and identity. In G. R. Adams, I. P. Gullotta, & R. Montemayer (Eds.), *Adolescent identity formation* (pp. 9–24). Newbury Park, CA: Sage.

Phinney, J. S. (1990). Ethnic identity in adolescents and adults: A review of research. *Psychological Bulletin, 108,* 499–514.

Phinney, J. S. (1991). Ethnic identity and self-esteem: A review and integration. *Hispanic Journal of Behavioral Sciences, 13,* 193–208.

Phinney, J. S., & Chavira, V. (1992). Ethnic identity and self-esteem: An exploratory longitudinal study. *Journal of Adolescence,* 15, 271–281.

Phinney, J. S., & Rosenthal, D. A. (1992). Ethnic identity in adolescence: Process, context, and outcome. In G. R. Adams, T. P. Gullotta, & R. Montemayer (Eds.), *Adolescent identity formation* (pp. 145–172). Newbury Park, CA: Sage.

Quinn, P. C., & Liben, L. S. (2008). A sex difference in mental rotation in young infants. *Psychological Science, 19*(11), 1067–1070.

Quintana, S. M. (2007). Racial and ethnic identity: Developmental perspectives and research. *Journal of Counseling Psychology, 54*(3), 259–270.

Raifman, J., Moscoe, E., Austin, S. B., & McConnell, M. (2017). Difference-in-differences analysis of the association between state same-sex marriage policies and adolescent suicide attempts. *JAMA Pediatrics, 171,* 350–356.

Remafedi, G., French, S., Story, M., Resnick, M. D., & Blum, R. (1998). The relationship between suicide risk and sexual orientation: Results of a population-based study. *American Journal of Public Health, 88,* 57–60.

Ricoeur, P. (1983). Narrative and hermeneutics. In J. Fisher (Ed.), *Perspective on the work of Monroe C. Beardsley* (pp. 149–162). Philadelphia, PA: Temple University Press.

Schwartz, S. J., Syed, M., Yip, T., Knight, G. P., Umaña-Taylor, A. J., Rivas-Drake, D., & Lee, R. M. (2014). Methodological issues in ethnic and racial identity research with ethnic minority populations: Theoretical precision, measurement issues, and research designs. *Child Development, 85*(1), 58–76.

Sellers, R. M., Copeland-Linder, N., Martin, P. P., & Lewis, R. H. (2006). Racial identity matters: The relationship between racial discrimination and psychological functioning in African American adolescents. *Journal of Research on Adolescence, 16*(2), 187–216.

Singer, J. A. (2004). Narrative identity and meaning making across the adult lifespan: An introduction. *Journal of Personality, 72*(3), 437–460.

Smith, D. L. (1988). Psychotherapy and narration: The contribution of Paul Ricoeur. *The Humanistic Psychologist, 16*, 323–331.

Smith, P. K., & Daglish, L. (1977). Sex differences in parent and infant behavior in the home. *Child Development, 48*, 1250–1254.

Stangor, C., & Ruble, D. N. (1989). Differential influences of gender schemata and gender constancy on children's information processing and behavior. *Social Cognition, 7*, 353–372.

Tieger, T. (1980). On the biological basis of sex differences in aggression. *Child Development, 51*, 943–963.

Troiden, R. R. (1988). Homosexual identity development. *Journal of Adolescent Health Care, 9*, 105–113.

Umaña-Taylor, A. J., Quintana, S. M., Lee, R. M., Cross, W. E., Rivas-Drake, D., Schwartz, S. J., ... & Seaton, E. (2014). Ethnic and racial identity during adolescence and into young adulthood: An integrated conceptualization. *Child Development, 85*(1), 21–39.

Verschueren, M., Rassart, J., Claes, L., Moons, P., & Luyckx, K. (2017). Identity statuses throughout adolescence and emerging adulthood: A large-scale study into gender, age, and contextual differences. *Psychologica Belgica, 57*(1), 32–42.

Waterman, A. S. (1992). Identity as an aspect of optimal psychological functioning. In G. R. Adams, T. P. Gullotta, & R. Montemayer (Eds.), *Adolescent identity formation* (pp. 50–72). Newbury Park, CA: Sage.

Chapter 8: Post-Reading Questions

1. How important is your racial or ethnic identity to your sense of self?
2. Where would you rate yourself in the stage progression of ethnic identity as outlined in the chapter? Do you agree with this stage theory? Why or why not?
3. A stage theory was also presented in regard to sexual orientation development where the highest stage involves a "coming out" process. Given the levels of discrimination in certain societies (and families), coming out to others can sometimes be dangerous and even life threatening. Do you think it might be possible to feel fully developed in one's sexual orientation identity without coming out?
4. What role does sexuality play in your sense of identity?
5. Sexual orientation is part of identity, but other aspects of your sexuality (your likes and dislikes, your outward expression of sexuality, your code of sexual ethics, etc.) are also part of your sexual identity. Do you feel fully "achieved" in your sexual identity? Why or why not?

CHAPTER 9

Health and Happiness

Constructing a Plan

Perhaps this is a good time to recap what we have learned:

Empowerment

We talked about control and responsibility. Although philosophers and laypeople debate how much control we really have over our lives, we promote the value that it is better to believe you have control and deal with your issues proactively. While we can't prove that free will exists, we do know that people who believe they have control over their lives make decisions more proactively, and this leads to greater life satisfaction. You do not choose everything that happens to you, but you always have a choice on how you react to life circumstances. And although you can't control everything, you do have the power to make decisions, and the decisions you make do make a difference. So if you accept this reasoning, and we hope you do, then how do you make the best decisions? We think you do that by using critical thinking and discussion skills.

Critical Thinking and Discussion

We defined critical thinking as involving two somewhat opposing dispositions. The willingness to be open-minded and consider all potential ideas along with the willingness to question and challenge all potential ideas and hold them up to vigorous scrutiny. No idea is too wild to be considered, and no idea is too sacred to be challenged. And since we all tend to be masters of self-deception, if you want to really know whether you've been thinking critically and making the best decisions, then open it up to critical discussion. By sharing your thoughts and reasoning with others who you trust to call you out when they think you're fooling yourself, you can be sure that you're making the best possible decision given the set of circumstances, as best you and the others are able to understand them. And that's probably the best we can do. It doesn't guarantee a perfect outcome, but it does increase the odds that you'll get (or become) what you want.

So with an empowered stance of accepting responsibility for your life and taking active control of your future, and by using critical thinking to determine the roles, goals, and values, that you expect will give your life meaning and purpose, you are now ready to face the challenges and overcome the obstacles that might stand in your way. And this is where our steps to problem-solving (ICECRM) come in. Let's review the steps:

Steps to Problem-Solving

- **I** dentify the Problem
- **C** reate Alternatives
- **E** valuate Alternatives
- **C** onstruct a Plan
- **R** un the Plan
- **M** easure Your Success

So far, we have done the ICE, now we need to do the CRM. We've identified a problem, issue, or challenge. We have created a long list of alternatives for dealing with the challenge. And we have evaluated the list by first cutting it down to four or five solutions, and then evaluating the good and bad of each. Lastly, we tried to develop a new and improved and integrated solution that will maximize the positives and minimize the negatives of the choices you liked best. It is now time to construct your implementation plan.

A good plan is short-term, specific, and attainable. Let's examine each of these adjectives one at a time.

A Good Plan Is Short-Term

The journey of a thousand miles begins with the first step, and we should focus on taking that first step, not how far we need to go. The former is doable. The latter often seems formidable. As they say in Alcoholics Anonymous: "one day at a time." If we focus on trying to change our whole life and fix all our problems and stay clean and sober forever, it all seems overwhelming. But if we focus on just getting through the day without picking up a drug or a drink, perhaps we can manage. And by focusing just on today, the days add up into months, and the months add up into years. So too, your plan should not be about changing your life. It should be about what you can do this week that will be a first step toward implementing the solution you have selected for yourself. So for example, if you have decided to stop procrastinating, your plan for this week should not be an overhaul of your personality, but rather, it should be a commitment to do one small thing that you have been putting off. For another example, if you have decided to lose 30 lbs., it is probably not going to happen this week, but you can make a plan to exercise 3 times this week. Or you can make a plan to not eat after 8:00 p.m. this week, or no fast food this week. You are not committing the rest of your life, only this week. What can you do this week that will be the first step toward implementing your solution to your challenge statement?

A Good Plan Is Specific

Ever won a bet with someone and they tried to find a loophole to avoid paying up? Ever made a promise to yourself and then later found a way to technically keep the promise even though you broke the spirit of what you were committing to do? It is a natural tendency to look for ways to avoid living up to the responsibilities we have set for ourselves. So we promise to diet, and then we tell ourselves that we can eat that chocolate cake because we walked home from the store or that we can eat at 10:45 p.m. because it is still before 8:00 (in California!). When making your plan it is important to tell someone else about it. It will be harder to slip out of it if you will have to confess your failings to another person. We will use the group for this purpose. So you need to tell the group what you plan to do and exactly how you plan to do it. If your problem is social phobia and you have decided to face your fear of social situations by going to a party this week, you need to specify which party, how long you will stay, and how much time you will spend engaged in conversation with others. Otherwise you could walk in and walk out without saying a word to anyone and declare that you kept your word by "going to a party." Which is not to say that even walking in and out is not an accomplishment. For someone with severe social phobia, that simple act might be a big deal. But you need to specify in advance exactly what you are going to do, so we can all agree in the end that you did what you set out to do. So when you make your plan, make sure you specify who, what, when, where, and how. For instance, if you decide that you are going to work on being more assertive this week, it would not be enough to plan to stand up to someone. You need to specify what you are going to do. You might plan to go to a restaurant on Thursday with a friend, order a steak cooked medium rare, and then send it back because it is not cooked to your taste (too well or too rare, depending on which seems more plausible). As you look over your plan, and those of your group members, make sure everyone understands exactly what each person is committing to do. Be lawyers drawing up a contract, and make sure you've written it iron-clad!

A Good Plan Is Attainable

You want to be successful, especially on your first step. If you are wary of taking the journey and you fall on your first step, you will be at much greater risk of giving up. It would be better to make the first step, your plan for the first week, too easy than risk making it too hard. When you succeed, the thrill makes you want to try harder; when you fail, it becomes that much harder to try again. So don't bite off more than you can chew. If you have decided to face your fear of spiders, don't lock yourself in a closet full of tarantulas and let them crawl all over your body. Perhaps it would be better to start off your first week by planning to watch *Charlotte's Web.* Make it a bit of a challenge, so you do feel some sense of success, but only a small challenge, so the odds of success are in your favor.

Group Assignment

After reading "Constructing a Plan" presented above, use the group to help you to create a plan for what you are going to do next week to take the first step in implementing your selected solution. Go over everyone's plan for themselves and give them feedback. Ask them questions if you are unclear about any part of what they are intending to do. Let them know if you think their plan is short-term, specific, and attainable. You should know exactly what they will do, when they will do it, where they will do it, for how long they will do it, and with whom they will do it. If you have any doubts, express them. From the feedback you receive from others in regard to your plan, clarify anything they don't understand and feel free to modify your plan based on what they say. If you are having difficulty formulating your plan, ask your group for help. By the end of the group, everyone should be clear about their own and everyone else's plan of action.

Individual Assignment

Run the plan that you created in group and be prepared to discuss with them how it went.

The Weekly Reading

Pre-Reading Questions

The readings for this chapter are on self-worth and life satisfaction.

1. Do you feel that you live your life to the fullest and chase your dreams with gusto?
2. Do you wake up every morning with a sense of "carpe diem" (seize the day!)? If not, why not?
3. Do you have a strong sense of self-worth? Why or why not?
4. Are you satisfied with your life? Why or why not?

Rock the Boat

Robin Marvel

> "Men are afraid to rock the boat in which they hope to drift safely through life's currents, when, actually, the boat is stuck on a sandbar. They would be better off to rock the boat and try to shake it loose."
>
> —Thomas Szasz

Your life is not happening to you, it is responding to you. Your actions, the choices you make, your thoughts and the words you speak determine the quality of your of life. So then, who are you and how is your life treating you?

Figuring out who you are in truth will reveal so much about you and the path you are on. Every moment, every choice you make is directly related to how you see yourself, who you believe you are and what you think you are worth. These three factors determine everything—what you work to accomplish, whom you marry, your daily routine, how you limit and label yourself, how you treat others and all that you allow to take place in your life.

Life Check 1-1: Valuing the Self

- What do you think you are worth?
- How do you value yourself?
- Are you worth an amazing life, deserving to get all the things that you desire?
- Are you worth your dreams?
- Do you deserve the respect of yourself and others?

These are challenging questions that encourage you to really look at yourself, and you may not be able to answer them right now. However, by the end of this book you will see yourself, your relationships and your life with more value and you'll answer these questions with confidence and positivity.

In order to figure out who you are and how you value yourself, you must take a look at the real you. This is the person standing when you take away the job, the marital status, the family, the labels, the programmed beliefs: the true, down to the core individual. This is who speaks to you in silence and looks back at you from the mirror, giving you the chance to see yourself clearly.

If you are unable to see your worth, you will slowly lose your confidence and you'll begin to just exist. It is like a balloon that is full of air that gets a pinhole in it—it will slowly deflate until there is nothing left. The same thing happens in life if you don't value yourself. If this sounds like your situation, then I am sure glad you picked up this book so we can patch that pin hole and refill your balloon with a zest for life!

As you struggle with your self-worth, you may become stagnant, losing that inner spark and passion. Then life becomes routine, just going through the motions—get up, go to work, complain about the weather, complain about your job, what your spouse didn't do, your house, your kids, eat lunch, complain about co-workers, drive home, make dinner, put kids to bed, veg out on TV programs you idolize because the people are living with the excitement you crave but are scared to go after, go to bed and start over tomorrow.

When you are asked how your day is you are quick to respond with "so-so—you know, paying the bills." This is so common because it is always easier to stay in the comfort zone of your routine rather than walking outside that bubble and testing the waters. You always have that little bit of nagging doubt, the "what if" thoughts running around in the back of your mind. These thoughts may question if you are worth the great things in life, because you are totally focused on working so hard to make ends meet. You want to be comfortable, which can be a great thing but it becomes restricting when you lose sight of your passions and give up on yourself. Your life iPod gets stuck on playing the same two or three songs on repeat.

You no longer wake up in the morning saying, "Yes! Another amazing day to be alive!" Instead you become use to what is, settling because it is familiar and works, so why rock the boat. Well, I want you to stand up and rock your boat, dive back into life and regain your passion and purpose!

Life Check 1-2: Self-Critic

Pause for a moment and go look in the mirror. As you look at yourself,

- What thoughts pop into your head? Are they negative?
- Do you find yourself being a self critic? Be honest with yourself.
- Make the choice to stop the negative self chatter. Replace any negative words you are thinking about yourself with positive affirmations. The more you practice replacing negative thoughts with positive affirmations, the sooner they will leave. You are reprogramming the beliefs you hold for yourself.

So, now that you are taking a real, deep look at your genuine self, you will discover your self-worth, not the worth others have of you but what you really feel your value is.

Pay attention to the part of you that's visible when you shed the need to fit in, the fake image you project to others and the need for approval: the authentic you. Your life is created from the inside out, so when facing yourself you are able to really uncover the truth because you cannot lie. You can always step into the world with a smile and when asked "how are you" reply with a "great" but when you have to be honest there is no way to fool yourself. The truth is revealed and you cannot ignore it no matter how many masks you may wear in the outside world. You can walk around like you are on top of the world but if in the shadows of your truth you are lacking confidence, full of fear and worry, then you cannot truly experience a life of positivity, confidence and fearlessness—your genuine truth shines through in all aspects of your life. It is the real you. This is the you that was whole at one time, the you that unconditionally loved yourself and seen how beautiful you really are; the you that got excited and felt passionate.

Life Check 1-3: Passion

- Do you remember that person?
- When was the last time your spirit was on fire?

You are shaped by the positive and negative, internal and external events that you face throughout your daily living. The emotions and reactions you experience through each of these life circumstances creates your behavior and ultimately becomes how you deal with your life. It is imperative to take a look at those defining moments, positive and negative, to find the answers to why your life is how it is. As you experience negative moments you develop self doubt, fear and do not live your truth. This takes a toll on your self-worth. As you are experiencing positive moments you are strengthening your true self, empowering who you are to live an amazing life.

Unfortunately, life is not only full of positive moments but negative ones as well. Learning how to heal from old negative experiences and how to react to new negative experiences is the key to being in control of your life.

Life Check 1-4: Wounded Eye

- Think of negative events you have faced
- How did you react? Was your reaction healthy?

Believe it or not, there was a powerful, confident you before doubts crept in, before you developed a *wounded eye* from traumatic circumstances you have faced. There are many outside factors that have had an emotional impact on who you are today.

Let's take a look at some outside factors that may have affected you:

- Being bullied
- Abandonment
- Rejection of any kind
- Dealing with physical, mental, emotional abuse from others
- Self destruction with negative thoughts and words
- Loss
- Substance abuse of any kind

All these experiences slowly start to deplete your passion for life, creating self doubt and your get up and go energy, causing a wounded eye to form.

As you are encountering trauma, tragedy and hardship, you start to create your wounded eye, and if you aren't careful you can continue to live your life looking through it, carrying the emotion from each of these experiences into your daily living, defining yourself and your life from the negative emotion or wounded eye. Every time anything happens to you in the present, you relive the feelings of heartache that you experienced, using these old emotions as excuses for where you are in life now. It allows you to stay limited and stuck because you tell yourself that you have a good reason for being self destructive. Then society empowers you by giving you permission to stay wounded.

Life Check 1-5: Letting Go Excuses

- What experiences do you hold on to as an excuse for where your life is today?
- Are you ready to see clearly by healing your wounded eye?

How many times have you heard a story of someone who is exhibiting negative behavior like alcoholism, and then you hear yourself or others say, "That's so sad, but you know his mother died when he was fifteen so it makes sense." We as a society give permission to those who suffer trauma, creating an excuse and contributing to their wounded eye. I too have done that in the past until I realized I was encouraging self destructive behavior. It is important for you to stop making excuses for yourself and also for others. There is no reason to lose today by looking through the wounded eye of yesterday.

Have you ever seen the A&E network show *Intervention*? It is a great example of how common it is for people to live looking through their wounded eye. The majority of people on that show facing an intervention, no matter how old or what they are addicted to, always place blame for where they are now on something that happened 5, 10, or 15 plus years ago. Their lists include "my father never hugged me," "my parents divorced," "my dad was an alcoholic," "I was abused," "my mom abandoned us," "my sister stole my boyfriend" ... All of these are classic examples of someone living through their wounded eye. Their present life is in shambles, filled with addiction to fill the void created in the past when they experienced trauma, or had their feelings hurt or someone let them down. They are so quick to use this as an excuse to live through their wounded eye. Every experience they encounter in the present they react with the same behavior they had during the past trauma, creating a repetitive pattern. They see everything through the emotion of the past circumstance. This allows an excuse, as well as someone to blame for their present conditions.

I grew up with alcoholic, cocaine abusing parents. Their drug abuse ruled our life and left us homeless several times. I could easily choose to repeat the cycle and be an alcoholic or a drug abuser and blame it on my childhood. Society would defend me, claiming it makes sense because I had such an unstable childhood. I have made the choice to heal my wounded eye and not accept that as my truth, and I chose to break the cycle. Your rough past does not have to reflect on who you choose to be now. I am proof of that!

I am not saying that you have not faced hardships that can slow you down and change your course, what I am saying is that you have the choice to give your power away in the present to these past emotions or to release them and gain power. You can live looking through your wounded eye, or heal it. The choice is yours. You are solely responsible for how your life plays out.

Once you make the decision to clear your wounded eye, be prepared, it takes lots of work. It is not just a flip of the switch but an intense commitment to start taking personal responsibility for yourself. You need dedication to stop bringing your old wounds into your present. Look at it this way, if your past was so bad then why are you giving it so much space in your today? You are allowing these old emotions to rule your present and I know why. The reason you are losing so much of your present to the old stuff is because you need the excuse. If you are unhappy now, it is easier to blame it on something or someone else then to face it. That way it is not your fault. Well, it's time to wake up because no matter how many excuses you make, your life is yours and you are responsible for it.

You may not have been told this growing up, I know I wasn't. Growing up I learned that life happens to you, you are a victim of circumstance and you have no choice. Throughout my childhood and young adult days I always saw life as a struggle and felt there was nothing I could do to change that. This continued until I was twenty-three. I remember sitting in my living room and reading a book titled *Choosing Happiness: The Art of Living Unconditionally* (1991) by Veronica Ray and having a life changing experience. I learned that I was in control of my life. If I wanted to be happy then it was up to me, that for years I had been putting the burden of my happiness on my husband, the weather, my job, anything or anyone I could. Wow, that blew my mind! So I decided to put my newfound information into practice and it was game on! I made the choice to take personal responsibility for my life.

At first it was not easy because of course it was easier for me to blame others for where I was at. The more I committed myself to making personal changes, the more my life started to change for the positive. This choice changed every aspect of who I am today. I became more confident and started to create the life I desired, because if it was up to me, there was no way I was going to continue to sit on the sidelines and not participate in living. So here I am, telling you that in order to gain success in any area, you must take personal responsibility for where you have been and where you are going.

Life Check 1-6: Responsibility

- Are you taking responsibility for your life?
- If not, who are you giving that power to?
- What steps can you take today to start taking personal responsibility for your life?

You are the person who should be raising a hand when the questions arise: Why is my life the way it is? Whose fault is it that I am not happy?

You are in control of your life, you hold the key to where you are and where you are heading.

Taking personal responsibility includes looking at all the choices you are making. This goes from the daily choices like brushing your hair, going to work, what's for dinner, right lane/left lane, to life-shaping, important matters.

Your basic choices keep you living from day to day and are important to your self-worth. Making the choice to get up each morning and embrace the day impacts your entire life. Taking the time to care for yourself by brushing your hair and dressing for success empowers and motivates you. No matter what you do during your day, it is important to present yourself in a way that makes you feel good. Value yourself, you are worth it.

Life Check 1-7: Choices

- What basic choices are you making each day that empower you?
- Do you start each day with a positive attitude?
- How can you design your daily routine to include actions that will inspire you to look and feel good?

Let's look at the main event choices in your life. You know, the ones that have defined your life up to this point and those that you are making in the present that will shape your future. These choices include all areas of your life from your career to the people you surround yourself with, to where you choose to live. It is important when you are making these main event choices that they are your truth. That is, live the life you really want, rather than living a lie to please other people. The fact is that this is your life and it is not selfish to choose your happiness and be your number one priority.

If you spend your time basing your decisions on what others want for you, you are guaranteed to complain ten years from now about what you never did while blaming someone else, creating an excuse for yourself. You'll be talking about what you could have been if only you'd followed your passions instead of following the crowd.

You have the choice right now, no matter your age, your financial situation or your past, to become anything you desire. I have watched so many people limit themselves because they believe they are too old, too young, too small town, too big town and the list goes on and on. So, no more excuses, no more self imposed limits—today you make the choices that make you feel alive. Keep in mind that your choice may change. There is nothing carved in stone saying these main life choices cannot change with your personal growth and expansion. It is foolish to chain yourself to one way in a world that is so full of opportunity. Explore. Change your mind and be okay with it. If you are spending all your time stuck in a life choice that no longer serves you, then change it. You deserve to be happy and it is up to you how you get there.

Life Check 1-8: Dreams

- You get excited when thinking about this dream.
- You are where you are right now in life because you choose...
- What will you commit to right now to make your dreams come true? What steps can you take right now to move forward?

Bibliography

Ray, V. (1991). *Choosing happiness: The art of living unconditionally.* New York, NY: HarperCollins Publishers.

READING 13

The Pursuit of Happiness

Christine Vitrano

According to the life-satisfaction view, happiness is a state of satisfaction that implies nothing about the value of a person's life independent of her own perceptions. A person's happiness is proportional to how positively she views her life: the more favorable her impression, the happier she will be. But if happiness amounts to personal satisfaction, isn't it achieved simply by seeking to fulfill immediate desires? Doesn't granting people first-person authority with respect to their happiness preclude giving them advice?

I believe such concerns are unwarranted. Satisfaction does not render useless the value of advice, for present satisfaction does not ensure future satisfaction. A person's happiness attained unwisely may be only short-term, leading to unhappiness in the longer run. Happiness is also a degree notion. One may be happy, yet her level of satisfaction may be at the lower end of the scale. Thus, advising people about their choices can call attention to the shortsightedness of their goals or the limited intensity of their satisfaction. We don't have to deny that a person is happy in order to make suggestions about changes that could ensure future or greater happiness.

Consider Ted, who frequently skips school to hang out with his friends. His problem is that his happiness is only short-term. Eventually, he is going to fail out of school, severely limiting his prospects. Although he is satisfied now, he is jeopardizing his future happiness, trading it for some short-term pleasure. Granting that Ted is happy does not require us to approve of his lifestyle, nor does it preclude our providing him advice. We can seek to change his present behavior by appealing to his future prospects. We can also increase his chances for greater happiness by offering him strategies for increasing happiness that others have found effective.

Such strategies can take two forms. To distinguish them, consider Jaime, whose goal is to gain acceptance into a doctoral program in psychology. She has already applied to numerous departments but has been rejected by them all. Jaime is now unhappy and seeks help. One strategy consistent with the life-satisfaction view is to search for new means of achieving her goals. Therefore, we might suggest that Jaime apply to less prestigious schools, where she has a better chance of being accepted.

For that strategy to be effective, however, alternative means must be available that have not yet been tried. The strategy cannot help the person who clings to unreachable goals or faces insurmountable obstacles. For example, an aspiring actress or professional athlete may lack the talent needed for success. Such people are not guilty of lack of effort; rather, their goals are beyond their grasp, and seeking to achieve their dreams will lead only to unhappiness.

Other people suffer from bad luck. Consider a tennis player, moments away from winning her first championship, who suffers an injury that forces her to forfeit the match. She tries to compete again, but her injury affects her ability to play the game competitively. She never gets close to winning another tournament because her injury has essentially destroyed her career. As long as she holds on to the dream of being a professional tennis player, she will be unhappy.

A person's happiness, however, is not static. It is affected by not only external events but also internal changes in an individual's preferences. Recognizing people as dynamic beings, who are able to change their desires, goals, and values, enables us to appeal to a second strategy to alleviate unhappiness. Rather than seeking to change our external conditions, we can try to change our goals, modifying them or abandoning them altogether.

Let us imagine that Jaime, our aspiring graduate student, has tried every available means of achieving her goal. Unfortunately, she still has not been accepted into any doctoral programs, because her record in psychology is not strong enough. What else can she do? She can rethink why she likes psychology and then try to develop an alternative goal that is attainable. Perhaps she was drawn to the subject because she likes helping people. She might find professions that are equally fulfilling but do not require attending graduate school. In her fixation on becoming a psychologist, she had ignored these possibilities, but once she abandons her unrealistic goals and replaces them with more attainable ones, she may become satisfied with her life and achieve happiness.

One important implication of the life-satisfaction view is that each person controls her own happiness. People often see a gap between what they want and what they have and, believing this gap insurmountable, fall into despair. But goals can be altered, thereby creating new avenues toward satisfaction.

However, dissatisfaction is not always bad. If a person does not work up to her potential, or if alternative means for achieving goals can be found, then dissatisfaction is appropriate and can even be helpful. In such cases, experiencing unhappiness can motivate one to increased effort and greater resilience. Consider Leah, who receives a low grade on an important exam she expected to ace. She sees herself as an excellent student, but this exam was more challenging than she had anticipated, and she was overconfident about her mastery of the material. So the night before the exam when her friends asked her to go to the movies, she joined them rather than spending the extra time studying. As a result, she received a low grade and is unhappy.

Leah's unhappiness, however, does not result from desiring an unattainable goal. On the contrary, she is unhappy because she knows her aim was attainable. Had she studied sufficiently, she would have done well. Leah's dissatisfaction is reasonable, and, furthermore, her unhappiness may be good for her, because it may keep her from being overconfident in the future. Feeling dissatisfied need not imply viewing a situation as hopeless, nor must it condemn one to despair about the perceived gap between what we want and what we have. Instead, unhappiness can prevent a person from becoming complacent and inspire a search for new ways to achieve success.

Sometimes, however, what we seek is not within the realm of practical possibility. In such cases, dissatisfaction is self-destructive. Rather than motivating a person to try harder, the dissatisfaction results in hopelessness. In such instances, the life-satisfaction view implies that changing one's perspective can make happiness achievable.

One final point. Suppose someone asks you whether your life is happy. The answer depends on whether you look "upward," comparing your life to how good it might have been, or whether you look " downward," comparing your life to how bad it might have become. Looking upward is apt to lead you to say you are not so happy, because of the gap between your actual achievements and an ideal life. But if you look downward, you are likely to report increased happiness, considering your life in comparison to far worse possibilities. Although all the external features of your life remain the same, whether you compare your life to better or worse alternatives impacts your happiness. In other words, focusing on what you have achieved rather than on what you have failed to achieve can dispel dissatisfaction. Here is another way, according to the life-satisfaction view, that achieving happiness lies within your power.

These insights are reminiscent of the outlook of the Stoics. Recall their emphasis on changing one's mind rather than trying to change the world, for our minds are within our control, whereas events in the world are not. The Stoic outlook fits well with the life-satisfaction view of happiness.

Conclusion

Happiness transcends the barriers of race, religion, and culture. I may not understand the values of your society or share your language, customs, or beliefs, yet knowing you are happy tells me something important about your life.

I was struck by this power of happiness while traveling in East Africa, where I had the opportunity to visit a traditional Masai village in Kenya. Prior to the visit, our tour guide gave us a brief cultural lesson on the Masai. We were told that their lifestyle is nomadic and pastoral, revolving around their cattle. The Masai live in small huts made out of cow dung, and they sleep on beds made from cowhides. The cattle also provide food for the Masai, whose diet consists of cow meat, milk, and blood. The wealth of the Masai is measured in terms of their cattle, and to the Masai, amassing material possessions other than cattle is useless.

Our guide gave us a firm warning: "Do not feel sorry for these people. They are happy." Initially, this view was hard to understand. My initial reaction prior to meeting the Masai was, "Sure, *he* says they're happy, but they live in such poverty. How can they be happy?" My tendency was to focus on the Masai's lack of basic amenities and their unawareness of modern technology.

After visiting the Masai, however, I came to share our guide's outlook, for their satisfaction with their lives was obvious. They clearly took a lot of pride in their traditional lifestyle and were eager to share their customs with our group. The clothes of the Masai consisted of simple robes, but they were beautiful, their bright colors standing out dramatically against the arid, dusty landscape. Although the Masai lacked even such basic amenities as plumbing and electricity, most were educated and sent their children to school.

An outsider might be tempted to pity these people, as I initially did before meeting them, but this is a mistake. Although their lifestyle is different from ours, so too are their desires, and all of their needs are being met. They are not suffering, and their lives are filled with enjoyment. In short, the Masai are happy.

The life-satisfaction view can explain the happiness of people regardless of how different their lifestyles may be. It explains why the Masai, who possess so little, are nevertheless happy, as well as why some wealthy people in our own society, who possess so much, may still be deeply unhappy. Happiness is a state of mind. If over the course of your life you fail to appreciate what you have, you will never be happy. But if you can find satisfaction in your situation, whatever it may be, then happiness will be yours.

Chapter 9: Post-Reading Questions

1. Throughout the excerpt entitled "Rock the Boat," Robin Marvel provides a series of Life Check Questions. How did your answers to those questions affect your thoughts about the quality of your life and how it could be better?
2. Are you happy with your life? In "The Pursuit of Happiness," Christine Vitrano suggests that your answer to that question probably depends on your focus and where you are looking. Relate your answer to this question on where you focus. How might a different focus in your life change your answer to that question?

CHAPTER 10

Close Relationships

Making Relationships Work

This week is dedicated to running your plan. Everyone should be working on their own individual challenge; however, a number of you are probably dealing with relationship issues. Even if you have not selected a relationship issue to work on, we all can afford to improve the quality of our relationships (relationships are a very large part of what gives our lives meaning and purpose), and many of the issues we have been discussing in this book also have relevance to relationships. Let us begin by discussing one of the most important indicators of relationship quality: communication!

Quality of Communication

Much of these thoughts are taken from Jürgen Habermas' theory on the ideal speech situation. The communication between two or more people can be categorized into one of three types depending on what is going on in the conversation process.

Ordinary Communication

What characterizes most of our relationships and what allows us to carry on friendly discussions is a shared value system. When we are in agreement, we can have pleasant conversation on all nature of things. This is what we call ***ordinary*** communication. However, when there is disagreement, the true test of communication quality comes to light. The two people involved will probably attempt to come to some sort of agreement. They may start by discussing the pros and cons of each of their views, but it often disintegrates into a battle of who is right and who is wrong. The conversation has now moved from ordinary communication to strategic communication.

Strategic Communication

People use all nature of tricks to force the other person into surrendering to their view. We call this being ***strategic***. We define strategic communication as attempting to use force, power, intimidation, or manipulation to get an agreement when there really is none. The direct approach is using your power and intimidation. Threatening the other person in various ways (physically, verbally, emotionally, etc.) if they don't go along with what you demand, would be examples of this. Others use more subtle manipulation ("If you really loved me, you'd do it my way"). Some use the "silent treatment" by cutting off all communication until the other person comes around. Then there's the false agreement trick: "OK, you're right." In order to end the uncomfortable conflict, a person says they agree with you when clearly they do not. They are making it quite plain that they are saying they agree only to shut you up and end the conversation. All of these various attempts to reach agreement (and I'm sure you can think of some others) are what we call strategic. There must be a better way! (And there is.)

Critical Communication

Critical communication involves the same processes we previously discussed in regard to critical discussion. Each person in the conversation must be *open* to honestly considering the alternative point(s) of view. In addition, each person in the conversation must be willing to *challenge* all competing points of view. This includes being willing to have your opinions challenged by the other. It is relatively easy for most of us to challenge other points of view. It is much more difficult to allow our own point of view to be challenged and resist the temptation to get strategic (especially when you think you might be successful using such a route!). Just as a critical discussion can help to determine the best course of action for ourselves, critical communication can help us make the best group decisions and will allow all participants to feel that their opinions are valued. This brings us to our next (related) concept: participation in decision-making.

Quality of Participation

Who makes the decisions in your relationship? Does one of you usually get the final say? Does one person make the small decisions and the other make the big decisions? Does one person usually give in to the other person in order to "keep the peace"? In other words, are decisions made democratically or strategically?

Strategic Decision-Making

Just as communication can be strategic by using force, power, intimidation, or manipulation to force an agreement on who is right and who is wrong, one can also use these techniques to get their way when a couple (or group) needs to decide a course of action. Trying to force someone to do what you want, rather than trying to get them to freely agree that it is the best course of action, is being strategic. Going along with a course of action that you think is wrong (because you feel intimidated or you just don't think it is worth the argument) is also being strategic. Quality relationships don't have winners and losers. In a quality relationship, everyone is a winner!

Democratic Decision-Making

How can a couple use democratic decision-making if each person gets one vote? As discussed in a previous chapter, a democratic process is not judged by whether or not voting occurs. Many dictatorships hold annual elections. Everyone is encouraged to go out and vote; however, there is only one party on the ballot! Voting does not necessarily make a decision democratic. What makes it democratic is the equal opportunity to participate in the decision-making process. If a couple or a group have an open discussion about what to do, and they listen to and consider everyone's suggestion and finally come to a group (or couple) consensus on what to do, a vote may never have taken place, but the process was very democratic. On the other hand a small group of three may hold an election whereby two people agree to vote against anything the third person suggests, regardless of what it is. Despite the majority rule decision, the process was hardly democratic. What this means for your relationships is that everyone in the relationship should have an equal opportunity to influence the decisions that are made which affect the members of the relationship. Every member must be heard and given due consideration. There will be times where consensus cannot be reached and majority might rule, but participants are more likely to accept the will of the group if they feel the group took their opinions into serious consideration. We all want to be heard and respected. We don't always have to get our way. For a couple, voting won't help, but we might agree to something like, "this time we'll do it your way, and next time we'll do it my way." Other types of compromises are possible. The test is in the process of how the decisions are made, not necessarily what the final decisions turn out to be.

Mutuality of Shared Involvement

Another important issue in addition to the quality of the communication and the method of decision-making is the degree of mutual involvement in the relationship itself. Obviously all relationships are not equal. They vary in importance, function, and your level of commitment. Below are some different types of relationships:

Social/Casual Relationships

Many of the people we come in contact with are acquaintances. We see them on a regular basis because we travel in similar circles. These may include neighbors, fellow church members, parents of our children's friends, people we see at the gym, people we see at work, classmates, etc. We say, "Hi! How are you?" and make other small talk. Conversation might go on a little longer or go a little deeper, but it tends to lack genuine intimacy. These relationships are maintained as long as we keep running into each other, but if our circumstances change and we stop running into each other, we probably won't go out of our way to contact each other. Now this doesn't mean that the relationship can't change. Some casual relationships grow into deeper and closer friendships, but they don't have to. Many of our relationships can remain on this casual level for a lifetime.

Instrumental Relationships

Instrumental relationships can be closer than social/casual relationships, but they have an external motivation for the relationship. Typically we are working on a common goal that provides the purpose of our relationship. Thus, we might have to work with our co-workers on a project. We are no longer just saying hello as we pass in the hall or talking over lunch and breaks. We are now working together on a common cause. Similarly, we might have relationships that stem from serving on the same committee for a church, political party, or volunteer or civic organization. Once again, a relationship that starts off as instrumental may grow into something deeper, but it never has to. We can work for many years together, but when circumstances change the common cause, the purpose for the relationship fades and the relationship itself often slips away.

Personal/Intimate Relationships

But of course, not all relationships are casual, simply social, or instrumental. The relationships that give our life meaning and purpose are the personal and intimate relationships that we have with friends and family. These relationships have a deeper level of commitment and caring. These are the relationships we fight to maintain even when circumstances work to divide us.

Changes in Involvement

Most of us have all three of the above relationships. Not all relationships need to be personal and intimate. Those are special. But as I alluded to above, some relationships that start out as casual or instrumental blossom into an intimate relationship. The opposite can also be true. A romantic relationship can break up, but the partners may decide to remain casual friends. If it was a workplace romance, they might even be able to return to the instrumental relationship they previously had. The problem develops when one person wants the relationship to change, but the other does not. One person might want to get closer and take it to the next level, while the other is perfectly happy to leave the relationship at the level it is at. Alternatively, one person might want to stay close while the other wants to pull back.

How people react when they want the relationship to change, or when they want it to stay the same while the other wants it to change, is similar to what we just described under communication and decision-making. One option is to be strategic and try to force the relationship to become (or stay) how we want it. We can demand, threaten, intimidate, manipulate, beg, plead, nag, or use a host of other tricks to force the other person to do what we want. Or we can be democratic and have a critical discussion about what we want from the relationship and why. In the end, we need to accept that we cannot force another person to maintain an intimate relationship with us if they don't desire it.

Personal Responsibility

The last point we want to make is similar to one we made about working on your identified challenge. That is, whose responsibility is it? If you don't like the direction your life is taking, it is *your* responsibility to change it. You can blame others for your circumstances, but all the blame in the world isn't going to change your circumstances. It is your life; you're the one who suffers if it is not to your liking, and you are the only one who can make it more to your liking.

Our thoughts on relationships are similar. If you want to have quality relationships, it is your responsibility to make it so. If you find that your relationships are not satisfying enough and are not to your liking, then take responsibility to make a change. And we suggest that the best way to make changes is to use critical communication and democratic decision-making. Don't try to manipulate to get what you want, but talk about what you want. Find out if the other person wants the same thing, and if not, find out if you can work a compromise that will be mutually satisfying. If you cannot come to an agreement, then you might have to agree to part. You might lose some relationships—but the ones you keep will be better, and the ones you lose you probably would have lost eventually anyway. So resist the temptation to play games and manipulate. Lay your cards on the table and limit your involvement to people who are willing to do the same!

Group Assignment

This week people should be running their plans. You will discuss how it went next week. This week discuss your relationships in group. After reading the chapter entitled "Making Relationships Work," think about your various relationships and make a determination as to whether they are more strategic or more critical/democratic. Share some thoughts with your group members about this chapter and how it does or does not apply to your relationships. Are you satisfied with all of your relationships? Would you like to change the nature of some of them? How do you think you might be able to do that? Use the group to help give you ideas.

Individual Assignment

By now, you should have run your plan. How successful was it? If it was not 100 percent successful, why not? Get prepared to discuss your results in your next small group meeting.

The Weekly Reading

Pre-Reading Questions

The reading for this chapter is on interpersonal attraction. It is a long reading, so I have broken it up into two parts: one for this chapter and the rest for the next chapter.

1. What are the characteristics in others that inspire you to desire a closer relationship with them?
2. We have all experienced loneliness. To what degree is your loneliness related to the situation versus your behavior?
3. In times when you have felt lonely, were there things you might have done that could have reduced those feelings?

READING 14

Interpersonal Attraction and Close Relationships

Kenneth S. Bordens and Irwin A. Horowitz

Intimate relationships cannot substitute for a life plan. But to have any meaning or viability at all, a life plan must include intimate relationships.

—Harriet Lerner

Source: Max Kegfire/Shutterstock.

Key Questions

As you read this chapter, find the answers to the following questions:

1. What is a close relationship?
2. What are the roots of interpersonal attraction and close relationships?
3. What are loneliness and social anxiety?
4. What are the components and dynamics of love?
5. How does attachment relate to interpersonal relationships?
6. How does interpersonal attraction develop?

Kenneth S. Bordens and Irwin A. Horowitz, "Interpersonal Attraction and Close Relationships," *Social Psychology*, pp. 331–355.

7. What does evolutionary theory have to say about mate selection?
8. How can one attract a mate?
9. How do close relationships form and evolve?
10. How are relationships evaluated?
11. What is a communal relationship?
12. How do relationships change over time?
13. What are the strategies couples use in response to conflict in a relationship?
14. What are the four horsemen of the apocalypse?
15. What is the nature of friendships?

Both Gertrude Stein and Alice B. Toklas were born in California and lived in the San Francisco Bay area. Both eventually left the United States to live in Paris. The first visit between these two people on September 8, 1907, who would be lifelong friends and lovers, did not begin well. They had become acquainted the previous night at a Paris restaurant and had arranged an appointment for the next afternoon at Gertrude's apartment. Perhaps anxious about the meeting, Gertrude was in a rage when her guest arrived a half hour later than the appointed time. But soon she recovered her good humor, and the two went walking in the streets of Paris. They found that each loved walking, and they would share their thoughts and feelings on these strolls for the rest of their lives together.

On that first afternoon, they stopped for ices and cakes in a little shop that Gertrude knew well because it reminded her of San Francisco. The day went so well that Gertrude suggested dinner at her apartment the following evening. Thus began a relationship that would last for nearly 40 years.

The one was small and dark, the other large—over two hundred pounds—with short hair and a striking Roman face. Neither was physically attractive. Each loved art and literature and opera, for which they were in the right place. The Paris in which they met in the 1920s was the home to great painters (Picasso and Matisse) and enormously talented writers (Ernest Hemingway, F. Scott Fitzgerald). Gertrude knew them all. They began to live together in Gertrude's apartment, for she was the one who had a steady supply of money. Gertrude, who had dropped out of medical school in her final year, had decided to write novels. Soon, they grew closer, their walks longer, and their talks more intimate. They traveled to Italy, and it was there, outside Florence, that Gertrude proposed marriage. Both knew the answer to the proposal, and they spent the night in a 6th-century palace. They shared each other's lives fully, enduring two wars together. In 1946, Gertrude, then 70, displayed the first signs of the tumor that would soon kill her. Gertrude handled this crisis in character, forcefully refusing any medical treatment. Not even her lifelong companion could convince her to do otherwise. When Gertrude eventually collapsed, she was rushed to a hospital in Paris. In her hospital room before the surgery, Gertrude grasped her companion's small hand and asked, "What is the answer?" Tears streamed down Alice Toklas's face, "I don't know, Lovey." The hospital attendants put Gertrude Stein on a cot and rolled her toward the operating room. Alice murmured words of affection. Gertrude commanded the attendants to stop, and she turned to Alice and said, "If you don't know the answer, then what is the question?" Gertrude settled back on the cot and chuckled softly. It was the last time they saw each other (Burnett, 1972; Simon, l977; Toklas, 1963).

We have briefly recounted what was perhaps the most famous literary friendship of the last century, the relationship between Gertrude Stein and Alice B. Toklas. Stein and Toklas were not officially married. They did not flaunt their sexual relationship, for the times in which they lived were not particularly accommodating to what Stein called their "singular" preferences. Yet their partnership involved all the essential elements of a close relationship: intimacy, friendship, love, and sharing. Philosophers have commented that a friend multiplies one's joys and divides one's sorrows. This, too, was characteristic of their relationship.

In this chapter, we explore the nature of close relationships. The empirical study of close relationships is relatively new. Indeed, when one well-known researcher received a grant some years ago from a prestigious government funding agency to study love in a scientific manner, a gadfly senator held the researcher and the topic up to ridicule, suggesting that we know all we need to know about the topic.

Perhaps so, but in this chapter we ask a number of questions that most of us, at least, do not have the answers for. What draws two people together into a close relationship, whether a friendship or a more intimate love relationship? What influences attractiveness and attraction? How do close relationships develop and evolve, and how do they stand up to conflict and destructive impulses? What are the components of love relationships? And finally, what are friendships, and how do they differ from love? These are some of the questions addressed in this chapter.

The Roots of Interpersonal Attraction and Close Relationships

It is a basic human characteristic to be attracted to others, to desire to build close relationships with friends and lovers. In this section, we explore two needs that underlie attraction and relationships: affiliation and intimacy. Not everyone has the social skills or resources necessary to initiate and maintain close relationships. Therefore, we also look at the emotions of social anxiety and loneliness.

Affiliation and Intimacy

Although each of us can endure and even value periods of solitude, for most of us extended solitude is aversive. After a time, we begin to crave the company of others. People have a **need for affiliation**, a need to establish and maintain relationships with others (Wong & Csikzentmihalyi, 1991). Contact with friends and acquaintances provides us with emotional support, attention, and the opportunity to evaluate the appropriateness of our opinions and behavior through the process of social comparison. The need for affiliation is the fundamental factor underlying our interpersonal relationships.

People who are high in the need for affiliation wish to be with friends and others more than do people who are low in the need for affiliation, and they tend to act accordingly. For example, in one study, college men who had a high need for affiliation picked living situations that increased the chances for social interaction. They were likely to have more housemates or to be more willing to share a room than were men with a lower need for affiliation (Switzer & Taylor, 1983). Men and women show some differences in the need for affiliation. Teenage girls, for example, spend more time with friends and less often wish to be alone than do teenage boys (Wong & Csikzentmihalyi, 1991). This is in keeping with other findings that women show a higher need for affiliation than do men.

The needs for affiliation and intimacy motivate us to form and sustain relationships and close, affectionate relationships.

Source: Gianluca D. Muscelli/Shutterstock.

There is evidence that the affiliation motive operates on an implicit and an explicit level (Köllner & Schultheiss, 2014). The explicit need for affiliation is tied to more cognitive elements of affiliation, including self-concept and one's values, beliefs, and goals. The implicit system is more strongly related to the emotional aspect of affiliation (Köllner & Schultheiss, 2014). Köllner and Schultheiss conducted a meta-analysis of the literature on the explicit and implicit needs for affiliation and found a very small correlation between the two systems. This means that the two systems, like other implicit and explicit systems, are independent from one another and are related to different types of behavior. Additionally, they reported that the relationship between the explicit and implicit needs for affiliation is weaker for women than for men.

But merely being with others is often not enough to satisfy our social needs. We also have a **need for intimacy**, a need for close and affectionate relationships (McAdams, 1982, 1989). Intimacy with friends or lovers involves sharing and disclosing personal information. Individuals with a high need for intimacy tend to be warm and affectionate and to show concern about other people. Most theorists agree that intimacy is an essential component of many different interpersonal relationships (Laurenceau, Barrett, & Pietromonaco, 1998).

Intimacy has several dimensions, according to Baumeister and Bratslavsky (1999). One is mutual disclosure that is sympathetic and understanding. Intimate disclosure involves verbal communication but also refers to shared experiences. Another dimension of intimacy includes having a favorable attitude toward the other person that is expressed in warm feelings and positive acts such that the person is aware of how much the other cares.

The need for affiliation and intimacy gives us positive social motivation to approach other people. They are the roots of interpersonal attraction, which is defined as the desire to start and maintain relationships with others. But there are also emotions that may stand in the way of our fulfilling affiliation and intimacy needs and forming relationships. We look at these emotions next.

Loneliness and Social Anxiety

Loneliness and social anxiety are two related conditions that have implications for one's social relationships. Whereas the needs for affiliation and intimacy are positive motives that foster interpersonal relationships, loneliness and social anxiety can be seen as negative motivational states that interfere with the formation of meaningful relationships. In this section we shall explore loneliness and social anxiety.

Loneliness

Loneliness is a psychological state that results when we perceive an inadequacy in our relationships—a discrepancy between the way we want our relationships to be and the way they actually are (Peplau & Perlman, 1982). When we are lonely, we lack the high-quality intimate relationships that we need. Loneliness may occur within the framework of a relationship. For example, women often expect more intimacy than they experience in marriage, and that lack of intimacy can be a cause of loneliness (Tornstam, 1992).

Loneliness is common during adolescence and young adulthood, times of life when old friendships fade and new ones must be formed. For example, consider an 18-year-old going off to college. As she watches her parents drive away, she is likely to feel, along with considerable excitement, a sense of loneliness or even abandonment. New college students often believe that they will not be able to form friendships and that no one at school cares about them. The friendships they make don't seem as intimate as their high school friendships were. These students often don't realize that everybody else is pretty much in the same boat emotionally, and loneliness is often a significant factor when a student drops out of school.

Loneliness is a subjective experience and is not dependent on the number of people we have surrounding us (Peplau & Perlman, 1982). We can be alone and yet not be lonely; sometimes we want and need solitude. On the other hand, we can be surrounded by people and feel desperately lonely. Our feelings of loneliness are strongly influenced by how we evaluate our personal relationships (Peplau & Perlman, 1982). We need close relationships with a few people to buffer ourselves against feeling lonely.

Culture is also related to perception of loneliness. There is evidence that loneliness is a cross-cultural phenomenon (DiTommaso, Brannen, & Burgess, 2005). However, the way loneliness is experienced differs across cultures. For example, DiTommaso et al. found that Chinese students living in Canada reported higher levels of three types of loneliness than did Canadians. Additionally, Rokach and Neto (2005) compared Canadian and Portuguese individuals of varying ages on several dimensions relating to loneliness. They found that Canadians were more likely to point to their own shortcomings to explain their loneliness than were Portuguese individuals. Rokach and Neto suggest that this might be due to a greater disposition of North Americans to view loneliness as a form of social failure and to different family values and structures between the two cultures. Finally, cultural expectations about relationships can also affect the experience of loneliness. For example, in Western culture, greater importance is attached to romantic relationships than in non-Western cultures (Seepersad, Mi-Kyung, & Nana, 2008). Consequently, when not in a romantic relationship, members of a Western culture (Americans) experience more romantic loneliness than those in a non-Western culture (Koreans) (Seepersad, Mi-Kyung, & Nana, 2008).

As suggested earlier, loneliness can be associated with certain relationships or certain times of life. There are, however, individuals for whom loneliness is a lifelong experience. Such individuals have difficulty in forming relationships with others, and consequently, they go through life with few or no close relationships. What is the source of their difficulty? The problem for at least some of these people may be that they lack the basic social skills needed to form and maintain relationships. Experiences of awkward social interactions intensify these individuals' uneasiness in social settings. Lacking confidence, they become increasingly anxious about their interactions with others. Often, because of their strained social interactions, lonely people may be further excluded from social interaction, thereby increasing feelings of depression and social anxiety (Leary & Kowalski, 1995).

Beyond the psychological effects of loneliness, there are also physical and health effects. Within families, loneliness is associated with an increase in self-reported health problems and a higher rate of self-reported physical ailments (Segrin, Burke, & Dunivan, 2012). Hawkley, Burleson, Berntson, and Cacciopo (2003) report that lonely individuals are more likely to show elevated total peripheral resistance (a suspected precursor to hypertension) and lower cardiac output than nonlonely individuals. Loneliness is also associated with a higher risk for a heart condition in the elderly (Sorkin, Rook, & Lu, 2002). Loneliness and social isolation are also associated with higher levels of depression in older males (Alpass & Neville, 2003) and among male and female college students (Segrin, Powell, Givertz, & Brackin, 2003). In the Segrin et al. study, the relationship between loneliness and depression was related to relationship satisfaction. Individuals who are dissatisfied with their relationships tend to be lonely and, in turn, are more likely to experience depression. Lonely individuals get poorer-quality sleep (i.e., awaken more after falling asleep and show poor sleep efficiency) compared to nonlonely individuals (Cacioppo et al., 2002). This latter finding suggests that lonely people may be less resilient and more prone to physical problems

(Cacioppo et al., 2002). Finally, loneliness among older adults has been found to be a significant predictor of an early death over a six-year period (Luo, Hawkley, Waite, & Cacioppo, 2012).

Social Anxiety

Social anxiety is one of the most widely diagnosed anxiety disorders. Social anxiety (sometimes referred to as social phobia) arises from a person's expectation of negative encounters with others (Leary, 1983a, 1983b). Socially anxious people anticipate negative interactions and think that other people will not like them very much. These negative expectations then translate into anxiety in a social situation, using "safety behaviors" (e.g., avoiding eye contact and closely monitoring one's behavior) and underestimating the quality of the impressions made on others (Hirsch, Meynen, & Clark, 2004). Socially anxious individuals tend to see ambiguous social situations more negatively than individuals without social anxiety (Huppert, Foa, Furr, Filip, & Matthews, 2003). Additionally, socially anxious individuals tend to dwell on negative aspects of social interactions more than individuals who are low in social anxiety and also recall more negative information about the social interaction (Edwards, Rapee, & Franklin, 2003). According to Edwards et al., this pattern of findings is consistent with the idea that socially anxious individuals perform a negatively biased "postmortem" of social events.

There is a cluster of characteristics that define those with social anxiety. People who suffer from social anxiety tend to display some of the following interrelated traits (Nichols, 1974):

- A sensitivity to and fearfulness of disapproval and criticism.
- A strong tendency to perceive and respond to criticism that does not exist.
- Low self-evaluation.
- Rigid ideas about what constitutes "appropriate" social behavior.
- A tendency to foresee negative outcomes to anticipated social interactions, which arouses anxiety.
- An increased awareness and fear of being evaluated by others.
- Fear of situations in which withdrawal would be difficult or embarrassing.
- The tendency to overestimate one's reaction to social situations (e.g., believing that you are blushing when you are not).
- An inordinate fear of the anxiety itself.
- A fear of being perceived as losing control.

Interestingly, many of these perceptions and fears are either wrong or unfounded. The research of Christensen and Kashy (1998) shows that lonely people view their own behavior more negatively than do other people. Other research shows that socially anxious individuals tend to process disturbing social events negatively immediately after they occur and a day after the event (Lundh & Sperling, 2002). Social anxiety relates directly to this *post-event rumination.* However, social anxiety also operates through negative self-evaluation of social behavior and the inordinately high amount of attention that people with social anxiety focus on their negative self-image (Chen, Rapee, & Abbott, 2013). In other words, individuals with social anxiety tend to see their own social interactions with others as very negative and spend time reinforcing their image of themselves as socially inept.

Of course, real events and real hurts may be the source of much social anxiety. Leary and his colleagues examined the effects of having our feelings hurt in a variety of ways, ranging from sexual infidelity, to unreturned phone calls, to being teased (Leary, Springer, Negel, Ansell, & Evans, 1998). The basic cause of the hurt feelings and consequent anxiety is what Leary calls *relational devaluation,* the perception that the other person does not regard the relationship as being as important as you do. Perhaps the major source of social anxiety is the feeling that you are being excluded from valued social relations (Baumeister & Tice, 1990). Having one's feelings hurt, however, leads to more than anxiety. People experience a complex sense of being distressed, upset, angry, guilty, and wounded. Leary and colleagues (1998) examined the stories written by people who had been emotionally hurt. They found that unlike the old saying about "sticks and stones," words or even gestures or looks elicit hurt feelings, last for a long time, and do not heal as readily as broken bones. Teasing is one example of what appeared to be an innocent event—at least from the teaser's point of view—that in reality imprints long-lasting hurt feelings for many victims. The males and females in the study did not differ much in their reactions to hurt feelings or to teasing.

The people who do these nasty deeds do not realize the depth of the damage that they cause, nor do they realize how much the victims come to dislike them. Perpetrators often say that they meant no harm. No harm, indeed.

STUDY BREAK

The preceding sections introduced you to the definition of interpersonal attraction and the factors that can facilitate or inhibit relationship formation. Before you go on, answer the following questions:

1. What is the need for affiliation?
2. What is the need for intimacy, and how does it differ from the need for affiliation?
3. What is loneliness, and how does it relate to the number of friends a person has?
4. How can social anxiety interfere with the formation of relationships?
5. What are the characteristics of social anxiety?

Love and Close Relationships

Psychologists and other behavioral scientists long thought that love was simply too mysterious a topic to study scientifically (Thompson & Borrello, 1992). However, psychologists have become more adventuresome, and love has become a topic of increasing interest (Hendrick & Hendrick, 1987). This is only right, because love is among the most intense of human emotions.

Love's Triangle

Robert Sternberg (1986, 1988) proposed a **triangular theory of love**, based on the idea that love has three components: passion, intimacy, and commitment. As shown in Figure 10.14.1, the theory represents love as a triangle, with each component defining a vertex.

Passion is the emotional component of love. The "aching" in the pit of your stomach when you think about your love partner is a manifestation of this component. Passion is "a state of intense longing for union with the other" (Hatfield & Walster, 1981, p. 13). Passion tends to be strongest in the early stages of a romantic relationship. It is sexual desire that initially drives the relationship. Defining passion simply as sexual desire does not do justice to this complicated emotion. It is not improbable that people may love passionately without sexual contact or in the absence of the ability to have sexual contact. However, as a rough measure, sexual desire serves to define passion (Baumeister & Bratslavsky, 1999).

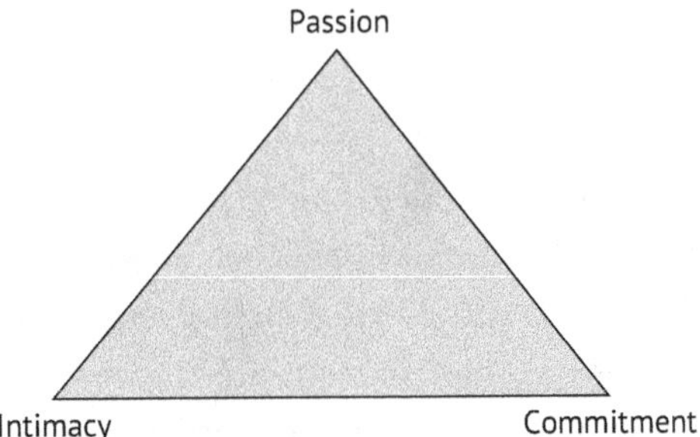

Figure 10.14.1 Robert Sternberg's triangular theory of love. Each leg of the triangle represents one of the three components of love: passion, intimacy, and commitment.

From Sternberg (1986).

Intimacy is the component that includes self-disclosure—the sharing of our innermost thoughts—as well as shared activities. Intimate couples look out for each other's welfare, experience happiness by being in each other's company, are able to count on each other when times are tough, and give each other emotional support and understanding (Sternberg & Gracek, 1984).

The third vertex of the triangle, *commitment*, is the long-term determination to maintain love over time. It is different from the decision people make, often in the heat of passion, that they are in love. Commitment does not necessarily go along with a couple's decision that they are in love. Sternberg defined various kinds of love, based on the presence or absence of intimacy, passion, and commitment. Table 10.14.1 shows each of these kinds of love and the component or components with which it is associated.

According to Sternberg (1986), the components of love need not occur in a fixed order. There is a tendency for passion to dominate at the start, for intimacy to follow as a result of self-disclosure prompted by passion, and for commitment to take the longest to fully develop. However, in an arranged marriage, for example, commitment occurs before intimacy, and passion may be the laggard.

Table 10.14.1 Triangular Theory and Different Love Types

KIND OF LOVE	LOVE COMPONENT		
	INTIMACY	PASSION	COMMITMENT
Non-love	No	No	No
Liking	Yes	No	No
Infatuated love	No	Yes	No
Empty love	No	No	Yes
Romantic love	Yes	Yes	No
Companionate love	Yes	No	Yes
Fatuous love	No	Yes	Yes
Consummate love	Yes	Yes	Yes

Baumeister and Bratslavsky (1999) studied the relationship between passion and intimacy and suggested that one may be a function of the other. These scholars argued that rising intimacy at any point in the relationship will create a strong sense of passion. If intimacy is stable, and that means it may be high or low, then passion will be low. But when intimacy rises, so does passion. Passion, then, is a function of change in intimacy over time (Baumeister & Bratslavsky, 1999). Research generally shows that passion declines steadily in long-term relationships, particularly among women, but intimacy does not and may increase in the late stages of the relationship (Acker & Davis, 1992). Positive changes in the amount of intimacy—self-disclosures, shared experiences—lead to increases in passion at any stage of a relationship. Finally, the relationship between relationship length and the components of love's triangle can be complex. For example, couples who are casually dating report lower levels of passion and intimacy than engaged couples. However, married couples report lower levels of passion and intimacy than engaged couples. Commitment, on the other hand, increases with relationship length (Lemiuex & Hale, 2002).

Levels of passion, intimacy, and commitment are also related to relationship satisfaction (Madey & Rodgers, 2009). Madey and Rogers found strong positive correlations between all three components and overall relationship satisfaction. They also found that intimacy and commitment showed the strongest correlations with relationship satisfaction. Additionally, they reported that individuals with a secure attachment experience higher levels of passion, intimacy, and commitment than those with a less secure attachment. Finally, intimacy and commitment mediate the relationship between attachment security and relationship satisfaction. That is, a secure attachment is related to higher levels of intimacy and commitment. In turn, these higher levels of intimacy and commitment are related to higher relationship satisfaction.

Types of Love

What, then, are Sternberg's types of love? Probably the most fascinating is **romantic love**, which involves passion and intimacy but not commitment. Romantic love is reflected in that electrifying yet conditional statement, "I am in love with you." Compare this with the expression reflecting consummate love, "I love you." Romantic love can be found around the world and throughout history. It is most likely to be first experienced by members of diverse ethnic groups in late adolescence or early adulthood (Regan, Durvasula, Howell, Ureno, & Rea, 2004). Additionally, concepts of romantic love are almost universally positive with characteristics such as trust and fulfilling emotional needs. One of the only negative characteristics that emerged as a "peripheral characteristic" was jealousy (Regan, Kocan, & Whitlock, 1998).

Romantic love doesn't necessarily mean marriage, however, for two main reasons. First, whereas marriage is almost universally heterosexual, romantic love need not be. Second, although some elements of romantic love may be common across cultures, some are not (de Munck, Korotayev, de Munck, & Kaltourina, 2011). Research by de Munck et al. found, for example, that intrusive thinking, happiness, passion, altruism, and improved well-being of partner were common elements to the concept of romantic love among Americans, Russians, and Lithuanians. On the other hand, there were some differences. Americans included the elements of friendship and comfort love as important to romantic love for the U.S. sample, but Russians and Lithuanians did not. Russians and Lithuanians said that romantic love was temporary, unreal, and a fairytale. Third, it is still an alien idea in most cultures that romance has anything to do with the choice of a spouse. In fact, there are still some cultures (e.g., some Indian sects) that practice arranged marriages in which commitment comes first, followed by romance. Interestingly, these arranged marriages appear to be just as satisfying as love-based marriages (Reagan, Lakhanpal, & Anguiano, 2012). Even in U.S. culture, the appeal of marrying for love seems to have increased among women in recent years, perhaps because women's roles have changed, and they no longer have so great a need to find a "good provider" (Berscheid, Snyder, & Omoto, 1989).

The importance of passion in romantic love is clear. Romantic lovers live in a pool of emotions, both positive and negative—sexual desire, fear, exultation, anger—all experienced in a state of high arousal. Intense sexual desire and physical arousal are the prime forces driving romantic love (Berscheid, 1988). One study confirms the physical arousal aspect of romantic love (Enzo et al., 2006). In this study individuals who had recently fallen in love were compared to single individuals and individuals in a long-term relationship. Enzo et al. found that the "in-love" participants showed higher levels of nerve growth factor (NGF) in their blood than single individuals or those involved in a long-term relationship. Interestingly, those "in-love" couples showed a drop in NGF if they remained together for 12 to 14 months. In fact, their blood levels of NGF were comparable to those who were in long-term relationships—perhaps providing evidence for the old adage that romance (passion) burns hot, but burns fast.

As noted, romantic love and sexual desire are likely to be seen as going together and being inseparable. This may be true in some cases. However, there is evidence that romantic love and sexual desire are two separate entities that can be experienced separately (Diamond, 2004). It is possible to experience the passion of romantic love without experiencing sexual desire. There may even be different physiological underpinnings to the two experiences (Diamond, 2004). For example, hormones associated with strong sexual desire have nothing to do with the intense bond experienced in romantic love (Diamond, 2003). Additionally, higher levels of norepinephrine and dopamine are more associated with sexual lust (i.e., the desire for sex with a willing partner without love) than with romantic love (Dundon & Rellini, 2012). Physiological mechanisms underlying the formation of strong attachments are more closely associated with activity involving naturally occurring opioids in the brain (Diamond, 2004).

Tennov (1979) distinguished a particular type of romantic love, which she called *limerence* and characterized as occurring when "you suddenly feel a sparkle (a lovely word) of interest in someone else, an interest fed by the image of returned feeling" (p. 27). Limerence is not driven solely or even primarily by sexual desire. It occurs when a person anxious for intimacy finds someone who seems able to fulfill all of his or her needs and desires. For limerent lovers, all the happiness one could ever hope for is embodied in the loved one. Indeed, one emotional consequence of limerent love is a terror that all hope will be lost if the lover leaves us (Brehm, 1988).

Consummate love combines all three vertices of love's triangle: passion, intimacy, and commitment. These couples have it all; they are able to maintain their passion and intimacy along with a commitment to a lifetime together.

Although we may fantasize about romantic love and view consummate love as a long-term ideal, other types of love can also bring happiness. Many couples are perfectly happy with *companionate love*, which has little or no passion but is infused with intimacy and commitment. Such partners are "friends for life" and generally have great trust in and tolerance for each other. Although they may regret the lack of passion, they are pragmatic and are able to live happily within the rules or limits of the relationship (Duck, 1983).

Unrequited Love

A special and very painful kind of infatuated love is love that is unfulfilled. **Unrequited love** occurs when we fall deeply and passionately in love and that love is rejected. Almost all of us have had some experience with unrequited love. In one study, 98% of the subjects had been rejected by someone they loved intensely (Baumeister, Wotman, & Stillwell, 1993). The emotional responses to unrequited love are generally negative. This is true for heterosexuals (Baumeister, et al., 1993) and gay men (Manalastas, 2011).

What makes unrequited love so painful is that both individuals feel victimized (Aron, Aron, & Allen, 1998). Very often, unrequited love ostensibly starts as a platonic friendship, but then one of the individuals admits that it was never just friendship, that he or she was always secretly in love with the other (Baumeister et al., 1993). In many cases, the object of the unrequited love is often unable to express lack of interest in terms that are sufficiently discouraging. The unrequited lover takes anything as encouragement, sustains hope, and then finds the final rejection devastating. The object of unwanted love, after the initial boost to the ego, feels bewildered, guilty, and angry.

In a typical case of spurned love, a college woman took pity on a young man whom no one liked, and one night invited him to join her and some friends in a game of Parcheesi. He thought the invitation signaled something more than she intended. Much to her horror, he began to follow her around and told her how much he loved her. She wanted this to stop, but she was unable to tell him how upset she was, because she was afraid of hurting his feelings. He interpreted her silence as encouragement and persisted (Baumeister et al., 1993).

Men are more likely than women to experience unrequited love (Aron et al., 1998). This is because men are more beguiled by physical attractiveness than are women. Men tend to fall in love with someone more desirable than they are. Interestingly, people report that they have been the object of unrequited love twice as many times as they have been rejected by another. We prefer to believe that we have been loved in vain rather than having loved in vain.

Unrequited love is viewed differently depending on one's perspective: pursuer or pursued. In one study those being pursued reported being the recipients of more unwanted courtship tactics, both violent and nonviolent, than they say they used as a pursuer (Sinclair & Frieze, 2005). Some interesting gender differences emerged in this study. For example, men tended to overestimate the extent to which their romantic advances were reciprocated. Women, on the other hand, were more likely than men to report multiple attempts to clearly reject unwanted advances.

Secret Love

If unrequited love is the most painful kind of love, then *secret love* may be the most exciting. In this form of love, individuals have strong passion for one another, but cannot or will not make those feelings publicly known. Secrecy seems to increase the attraction of a relationship. Researchers have found that people continued to think more about past relationships that had been secret than about those that had been open (Wegner, Lane, & Dimitri, 1994). In fact, many individuals were still very much preoccupied with long-past secret relationships. In a study of secrecy and attraction, subjects paired as couples were induced to play "footsie" under the table while they were involved in a card game with another couple (Wegner et al., 1994). The researchers found that when the under-the-table game was played in secret, participants reported greater attraction for the other person than when it was not played in secret.

Why does secrecy create this strong attraction? Perhaps it is because individuals involved in a secret relationship think constantly and obsessively about each other. After all, they have to expend a lot of energy in maintaining the relationship. They have to figure out how to meet, how to call each other so that others won't know, and how to act neutrally in public to disguise their true relationship. Secrecy creates strong bonds between individuals; it can also be the downfall of ongoing relationships. The sudden revelation of a secret infidelity will often crush an ongoing relationship and further enhance the secret one (Wegner et al., 1994).

The Formation of Intimate Relationships

The habits of the heart may be shaped by our earliest relationships. Developmental psychologists have noted that infants form attachments with their parents or primary caregivers based on the kinds of interactions they have (Ainsworth, 1992). These patterns of attachment, or attachment styles, evolve into **working models**, mental representations of what the individual expects to happen in close relationships (Shaver, Hazan, & Bradshaw, 1988). Working models are carried forth from relationship to relationship (Brumbaugh & Fraley, 2006). So, attachment patterns we use in one relationship are likely to be transferred to subsequent relationships. Attachment theory suggests that attachment styles developed in early childhood govern the way individuals form and maintain close relationships in adulthood. Three attachment styles have been identified: secure, anxious/ambivalent, and avoidant. Statements describing each style are shown in Table 10.14.2.

Table 10.14.2 Attachment Styles

ANSWERS AND PERCENTAGES		
	NEWSPAPER SAMPLE	UNIVERSITY SAMPLE
Secure		
I find it relatively easy to get close to others and am comfortable depending on them and having them depend on me. I don't worry about being abandoned or about someone getting too close to me.	56%	56%
Avoidant		
I am somewhat uncomfortable being close to others; I find it difficult to trust them completely, difficult to allow myself to depend on them. I am nervous when anyone gets too close, and often, love partners want me to be more intimate than I feel comfortable about.	25%	23%
Anxious/Ambivalent		
I find that others are reluctant to get as close as I would like. I often worry that my partner doesn't really love me or won't want to stay with me. I want to merge completely with another person, and this desire sometimes scares people away.	19%	20%

From Shaver, Hazan, and Bradshaw (1988).

Attachment styles relate to how relationships are perceived and how successful they are. According to research, people who identified their attachment style as secure characterized their lovers as happy, friendly, and trusting and said that they and their partner were tolerant of each other's faults (Shaver et al., 1988). Avoidant lovers were afraid of intimacy, experienced roller-coaster emotional swings, and were constantly jealous. Anxious/ambivalent lovers experienced extreme sexual attraction coupled with extreme jealousy. Love is very intense for anxious lovers, because they strive to merge totally with their mate; anything less increases their anxiety. This experience of love for anxious lovers is a strong desire for union and a powerful intensity of sexual attraction and jealousy. It is no accident that anxious lovers, more than any other style, report love at first sight (Shaver et al., 1988). Interestingly, the relationship between attachment style and relationship quality found with white samples applies to Spanish individuals as well (Monetoliva & Garcia-Martinez, 2005). In this study, a secure attachment was associated with positive relationship experiences. Anxious and avoidant attachments were associated with more negative relationship outcomes.

Given the working model of a partner and the expectations that anxious lovers have, it will not come as a surprise to you that individuals with this style tend to have rather turbulent relationships (Simpson, Ickes, & Grich, 1999). Research shows that anxious/ambivalents have relationships that are filled with strong conflicts. One reason for this, apparently, is that anxious/ambivalent individuals have *empathic accuracy,* the ability to correctly infer their partner's thoughts and feelings. Because of this ability, they are more threatened than are other individuals and feel much more anxious (Simpson et al., 1999). This is a case of knowing too much or, at least, placing too much emphasis on their partners' present moods and feelings that may or may not tell where the relationship is going. As you might imagine, Simpson and colleagues found that of all the couples they studied, the highly anxious/ambivalent partners were much more likely to have broken up within months. Finally, males and females with an anxious attachment react to hypothetical transgressions of their partners quite negatively. Typical responses included high levels of emotional stress, attribution patterns that are damaging to the relationship, and behaviors that escalate conflict (Collins, Ford, Guichard, & Allard, 2006).

Attachment Styles and Adult Love Relationships

Fraley and Shaver (1998) showed that the ways in which we respond to our earliest caregivers may indeed last a lifetime and are used when we enter adult romantic relationships. Where better to observe how adult individuals respond to the potential loss of attachment than at an airport? The researchers had observers take careful notes on the behavior of couples when one of the members was departing. After the departure, the remaining member of the couple was asked to complete a questionnaire determining his or her attachment style.

Those with an anxious working model showed the greatest distress at the impending separation and tended to engage in actions designed to delay or stop the departure, although in reality that was not going to happen. The anxious individuals would hold on to, follow, and search for their partner, not unlike a child would for a parent under similar circumstances. So attachment styles tend to be engaged particularly when there is threat (departure in this case) to the relationship. The effects seemed stronger for women than for men (Fraley & Shaver, 1998).

It is quite likely that the behavior of those airport visitors with an anxious working model was determined in great part by the level of trust they had in their partners. Mikulincer (1998) examined the association between adult attachment style and feelings of trust in close relationships. The results of this research suggest that those with a secure working model showed and felt more trust in their partners, and even when trust was violated, secure individuals found a constructive way to deal with it. For secure individuals, the main goal of the relationship was to maintain or increase intimacy.

In contrast, anxious working model individuals, although also desiring greater intimacy, were very concerned with achieving a greater sense of security in their relationships. Avoidant individuals wanted more control. But clearly, level of trust differs significantly among the three types of attachment styles. Anxious-style individuals continually have their sense of trust undermined, because they tend to fail at relationships. Sometimes, these individuals try to start relationships that are bound to fail. As you might suspect, the likelihood of someone falling in love with another who does not love them in return is dependent on one's attachment style. Arthur and Elaine Aron found that individuals with an anxious attachment style were more likely to have experienced unreciprocated love (Aron et al., 1998). Secure individuals had been successful in the past in establishing relationships, and avoidants were unlikely to fall in love at all. Anxious individuals place great value in establishing a relationship with someone who is very desirable but are unlikely to be able to do so. They tend to fail at close relationships and, therefore, they should experience more incidents of unrequited love; indeed, that is exactly what the research findings show (Aron et al., 1998). Finally, compared to individuals with a secure or avoidant attachment, individuals with an anxious attachment are more likely to engage in negative thoughts known as rumination (Reynolds, Searight, & Ratwik, 2014). Rumination is "a maladaptive process of self-reflection, featuring a hyper-focus on internal distress and the possible causes and consequences of these cognitive-affective experiences" (Reynolds et al., 2014, para 8). Reynolds et al. also found that individuals showing a higher level of rumination also report more anxiety associated with intimate relationships.

Are attachment styles a factor in long-term relationships? A study of 322 young married couples, all under age 30, found a tendency for those with similar attachment styles to marry one another (Senchak & Leonard, 1992). Attachment style is not destiny, however, as shown by the observation that people may display different attachment styles in different relationships (Bartholomew & Horowitz, 1991). None of these findings, however, come from long-term studies on the effects of attachment styles beyond childhood. Longitudinal research that follows individuals from infancy at least until early adulthood would give us more definitive information about whether early attachment styles really influence the way we respond in adult love relationships.

STUDY BREAK

This section introduced you to love relationships and different types of love. Before you begin the next section, answer the following questions:

1. What are the three legs of the triangular theory of love, and how do they relate to one another?
2. What is romantic love, and how does culture relate to its experience?
3. What is consummate love, and what are its components?
4. What are unrequited and secret love, and how do people react when they happen?
5. What is a working model, and how does it relate to relationship formation?
6. How do different attachment styles relate to adult relationships?

Determinants of Interpersonal Attraction

What determines why we are attracted to some individuals but not others? Social psychologists have developed a number of models addressing this question. Some specific factors identified by these models that play a role in attraction are physical proximity, similarity, and physical attractiveness.

Physical Proximity: Being in the Right Place

How did you and your best friend first meet? Most likely, you met because you happened to be physically close to each other at some point in your life. For example, you might have been neighbors or sat next to each other in elementary school. The idea that you are most likely to become friends with another person you happened to be physically close to suggests that those with whom you form friendships is more happenstance (chance) than providence. Confirmation for this idea was found in a study by Back, Schmukle, and Egloff (2008). Back et al. randomly assigned freshman students to seats in a classroom at the beginning of the school year. Then the students rated each other one at a time. A year later, students were given photographs of the other students and were asked to rate the strength of their friendship with each student. Back et al. found that students who sat next to another indicated stronger friendships than those who sat in the same row or had no physical relation to each other. As this and other studies show, physical proximity, or physical immediacy, is an important determinant of attraction, especially at the beginning of a relationship.

The importance of the **physical proximity effect** in the formation of friendships was also shown in a study of the friendship patterns that developed among students living in on-campus residences for married students (Festinger, Schachter, & Back, 1959). As the distance between units increased, the number of friendships decreased. Students living close to one another were more likely to become friends than were those living far apart.

Physical proximity is such a powerful determinant of attraction that it may even overshadow other, seemingly more important, factors. One study looked at friendship choices among police recruits in a police academy class (Segal, 1974). Recruits were assigned to seats alphabetically, and the single best predictor of interpersonal attraction turned out to be the letter with which a person's last name began. Simply put, those whose names were close in the alphabet and were thus seated near each other were more likely to become friends than those whose names were not close in the alphabet and were thus seated apart. The proximity effect proved more important than such variables as common interests and religion.

Why is proximity so important at the beginning stages of a friendship? The answer seems to have two parts: familiarity and the opportunity for interaction. To understand the role of familiarity, think about this common experience. You download some new music, but when you first listen to it, you are lukewarm about it. However, after repeated exposure, it "grows on you." That is, exposure to the new music seems to increase your appreciation of it. A similar effect occurs with people we encounter. These are examples of the *mere exposure effect,* in which repeated exposure to a neutral stimulus enhances one's positive feeling toward that stimulus. Since it was first identified in 1968 by Robert Zajonc, there have been over 200 studies of the mere exposure effect (Bornstein, 1989). These studies used a wide range of stimuli, and in virtually every instance, repeated exposure to a stimulus produced liking.

Physical proximity, in addition to exposing us to other people, also increases the chances that we will interact with them. That is, proximity also promotes liking, because it gives us an opportunity to find out about each other. Physical proximity and the nature of the interaction combine to determine liking (Schiffenbauer & Schavio, 1976). If we discover that the other person has similar interests and attitudes, we are encouraged to pursue the interaction.

Physical Proximity and Internet Relationships

Traditional social psychological research on the proximity effect has focused on the role of *physical closeness* in interpersonal attraction and relationship formation. However, evidence shows that more and more of us are using the Internet as a way to meet others (Rosenfeld & Thomas, 2012), which means that we must reevaluate the role of physical proximity in the attraction process. The Internet allows for the formation of relationships over great distances. One need no longer be in the same class, work at the same place, or live on the same block with another person to form a relationship. The Internet effectively reduces the *psychological distance* between people, even when the physical distance between them is great.

There is evidence that people are using the Internet to form relationships. For example, in one study 88.3% of male and 69.3% of female research participants reported using the Internet to form "casual or friendly" relationships with others. The study also found that 11.8% of men and 30.8% of women used the Internet to form intimate relationships (McCown, Fischer, Page, & Homant, 2001). In another study, 40% of college students reported using the Internet to form friendships. One of the main reasons for using the Internet in this capacity was to avoid the anxiety normally associated with meeting people and forming friendships. Finally, there was no gender difference in how the Internet was used to form relationships (Knox, Daniels, Sturdivant, & Zusman, 2001).

One concern related to the increasing use of the Internet to form friendships and other relationships is that it is somehow changing or even harming the entire concept of a friendship.

However, according to Amichai-Hamburger, Kingsbury, and Schneider (2013), this does not appear to be the case. If anything, using the Internet for social relationships appears to be stimulating the quantity and quality of the interactions among people and increasing relationship intimacy (Valkenburg & Peter, 2011). The Internet provides greater opportunity to seek out others who share our interests and attitudes (Amichai-Hamburger & Hayat, 2011), which is another important factor contributing to interpersonal attraction.

How do relationships formed via the Internet stack up against relationships formed the old-fashioned way? Apparently, they stack up quite well. McKenna, Green, and Gleason (2002) found that relationships formed on the Internet were important in the lives of those who formed them. This parallels what we know about relationships formed in a face-to-face situation. Further, they found that online relationships became integrated into the participants' lives, just as face-to-face relationships do. The Internet relationships formed were stable and tended to last over a 2-year period. Once again, this parallels more traditional relationships. Finally, McKenna et al. found that women found their relationships to be more intimate than men.

There are some differences between Internet relationships and offline relationships. Chan and Cheng (2004), using a sample of participants from Hong Kong, had participants describe the quality of one Internet relationship and one traditional, offline relationship. Their results showed that offline relationship descriptions tended to show that these relationships were more interdependent, involved more commitment, and had greater breadth and depth than Internet relationships. However, both types of relationships tended to improve over time, and fewer differences between the two types of friendships were noted as the relationship matured. Another study found that romantic relationships (e.g., dating and marital) formed offline lasted longer than those formed online (Paul, 2014). Paul also found that a smaller percentage of couples who met online went on to get married (32%) than those who met offline (67%).

So, it seems clear that the Internet is serving as a medium for the formation of meaningful interpersonal relationships. Is there any downside to this method of relationship formation? The answer is yes. One other finding reported by McKenna et al. (2002) was that individuals who felt that the "real me" was represented on the Internet were most likely to form Internet relationships. These individuals also tend to be socially anxious and lonely. It is these anxious and lonely individuals who are most likely to turn to the Internet as a way to form relationships that they find threatening offline. However, the relationships that socially anxious individuals form online may not be high quality. Tian (2013) found that compared to individuals with low levels of social anxiety, socially anxious individuals formed fewer new friendships, interacted with fewer existing friends, and had lower quality relationships with existing friends on the Internet. However, they did have higher quality relationships with new friends they made on the Internet. So, is lonely people's use of the Internet to form relationships a bad thing? It depends on what one means by loneliness. Weiss (1973) suggested that there are actually two types of loneliness. *Social loneliness* consists of the negative affect associated with not having friends and meaningful relationships. *Emotional loneliness* refers to an empty feeling tied to the lack of intimate relationships (Moody, 2001). A study conducted by Moody (2001) evaluated how face-to-face and Internet relationships related to these two forms of loneliness. Moody found that face-to-face relationships were associated with low levels of both social and emotional loneliness. However, Internet relationships were associated with lower levels of social loneliness, but higher levels of emotional loneliness. In Moody's words: "the Internet can decrease social well-being, even though it is often used as a communication tool" (p. 393). So, while Internet relationships can fulfill one's need for social contact, they may still leave a sense of emotional emptiness. Additionally, shyness has also been found to correlate with a condition called *Internet addiction*. The shyer the person, the more likely he or she is to become addicted to the Internet (Chak & Leung, 2004). Shyness is related to loneliness, with shy individuals being more likely to also be lonely (Jackson, Fritch, Nagasaka, & Gunderson, 2002). So, even though the Internet can help shy, lonely people establish relationships, it comes with an emotional and behavioral cost.

Although research shows that physical proximity is a strong predictor of relationship formation, more people are using the Internet for this purpose. The Internet reduces psychological distance, but not physical distance.

Source: GaudiLab/Shutterstock.

Similarity

Similarity between ourselves and others is another important factor in friendship formation. Similarity in attitudes, beliefs, interests, personality, and even physical appearance strongly influence the likelihood of interpersonal attraction. An interesting study conducted by Byrne, Ervin, and Lamberth (2004) demonstrated the effects of similarity and physical attractiveness on attraction. This study used a computer dating situation in which participants were given a 50-item questionnaire assessing personality characteristics and attitudes. Students were then paired. Some students were paired with a similar other and others with a dissimilar other. The pairs were then sent on a 30-minute date, after which they reported back to the experimenter to have their date assessed. Byrne et al. found that similarity and physical attractiveness, as expected, positively related to interpersonal attraction. So, there may be some validity to the claims of eHarmony.com, a company that purports to match people on a number of important dimensions, leading to successful relationships being formed!

Clearly, there are many possible points of similarity between people. Attitude similarity, for example, might mean that two people are both Democrats, are both Catholics, and in addition to their political and religious beliefs, have like views on a wide range of other issues. However, it is not the absolute number of similar attitudes between individuals that influences the likelihood and strength of attraction. Far more critical are the proportion and importance of similar attitudes. It does little good if someone agrees with you on everything except for the one attitude that is central to your life (Byrne & Nelson, 1965).

What about the notion that in romantic relationships, opposites attract? This idea is essentially what Newcomb called *complementarity*. Researchers have found little evidence for complementarity (Duck, 1988). Instead, a **matching principle** seems to apply in romantic relationships. People tend to become involved with a partner with whom they are usually closely matched in terms of physical attributes or social status (Schoen & Wooldredge, 1989).

Different kinds of similarity may have different implications for attraction. If you and someone else are similar in interests, then liking results. Similarity in attitudes, on the other hand, leads to respect for the other person. In a study of college freshmen, similarity in personality was found to be the critical factor determining the degree of satisfaction in friendships (Carli, Ganley, & Pierce-Otay, 1991). This study found similarity in physical attractiveness to have some positive effect on friendships but not a large one.

Why does similarity promote attraction? Attitude similarity promotes attraction in part because of our need to verify the "correctness" of our beliefs. Through the process of social comparison, we test the validity of our beliefs by comparing them to those of our friends and acquaintances (Hill, 1987). When we find that other people believe as we do, we can be more confident that our attitudes are valid. It is rewarding to know that someone we like thinks the way we do; it shows how smart we both are. Similarity may also promote attraction because we believe we can predict how a similar person will behave (Hatfield, Walster, & Traupmann, 1978).

Limits of the Similarity-Attraction Relationship

The similarity-attraction relationship is one of the most powerful and consistent effects found in social psychology. This, however, does not mean that similarity and attraction relate to one another positively in all situations and relationships. Similarity is most important for relationships that are important to us and that we are committed to (Amodio & Showers, 2005). For less committed relationships, dissimilarity was actually more strongly related to liking and maintaining a relationship over time (Amodio & Showers, 2005). Also, in supervisor-subordinate relationships within organizations, dissimilarity is associated with greater liking on the part of the subordinate for the supervisor (Glomb & Welch, 2005). In organizations, dissimilarity is most likely to translate into positive interpersonal relationships when there is a commitment to diversity (Hobman, Bordia, & Gallois, 2004).

Along the same lines, Rosenbaum (1986) argued that it is not so much that we are attracted to similar others as that we are repulsed by people who are dissimilar. Further examination of this idea that dissimilarity breeds repulsion suggests that dissimilarity serves as an initial filter in the formation of relationships. Once a relationship begins to form, however, similarity becomes the fundamental determinant of attraction (Byrne, Clore, & Smeaton, 1986; Smeaton, Byrne, & Murnen, 1989). Thus, the effect of similarity on attraction may be a two-stage process, with dissimilarity and other negative information leading us to make the initial "cuts," and similarity and other positive information then determining with whom we become close.

There also appears to be a difference between relationships formed in laboratory studies and real-life relationships with respect to the impact of similarity. Researchers have made a distinction between perceived similarity and actual similarity. *Perceived similarity* is how much similarity you believe exists between you and another person. *Actual similarity* is the actual amount of similarity that exists. A meta-analysis of the similarity-attraction literature showed that perceived similarity is a strong predictor of attraction in both the laboratory and real-life relationships. However, actual similarity predicts attraction in laboratory studies, but not in real-life relationships (Montoya, Horton, & Kirschner, 2008). In an interesting study, Ilmarinen, Lönnqvist, and Paunonen (2016) explored the relationship between personality similarity and friendship formation in a group of Finnish military cadets. The cadets completed measures of the big-five personality model (extraversion, agreeableness, conscientiousness, neuroticism, and openness to experience) and two "dark personality traits" (manipulativeness and egotism). They also rated the likeableness of their fellow cadets. Ilmarinen et al. found that similarity only predicted liking for the dark traits, especially at the low end of these dimensions. A person who scores on the low end of the manipulativeness (representing honesty) and egotism (non-egotist) scales is attracted to others with the same levels of these traits. Ilmarinen et al. suggest that this shows that people value the trait honesty when deciding whom to like.

STUDY BREAK

This section discussed some of the factors relating to interpersonal attraction. Before you go on to the next section, answer the following questions:

1. How and why does physical proximity relate to interpersonal attraction?
2. How do Internet relationships compare to more traditional relationships?
3. How does similarity relate to interpersonal attraction?
4. What is the matching principle, and why is it important in attraction?
5. What are the limits of the similarity effect?

Physical Attractiveness

Physical attractiveness is an important factor in the early stages of a relationship. Research shows, not surprisingly, that we find physically attractive people more appealing than unattractive people, at least on initial contact (Eagly, Ashmore, Makhijani, & Longo, 1991). Moreover, our society values physical attractiveness, so a relationship with an attractive person is socially rewarding to us.

In their now classic study of the effects of physical attractiveness on dating, Elaine Hatfield and her colleagues led college students to believe that they had been paired at a dance based on their responses to a personality test, but in fact, the researchers had paired the students randomly (Hatfield, Aronson, Abrahams, & Rottman, 1966). At the end of the evening, the couples evaluated each other and indicated how much they would like to date again. For both males and females, the desire to date again was best predicted by the physical attractiveness of the partner. This is not particularly surprising, perhaps, because after only one brief date, the partners probably had little other information to go on.

Physical attractiveness affects not only our attitudes toward others but also our interactions with them. A study of couples who had recently met found that, regardless of gender, when one person was physically attractive, the other tried to intensify the interaction (Garcia, Stinson, Ickes, Bissonette, & Briggs, 1991). Men were eager to initiate and maintain a conversation, no matter how little reinforcement they got. Women tried to quickly establish an intimate and exclusive relationship by finding things they had in common and by avoiding talk about other people.

There are, however, gender differences in the importance of physical attractiveness. Generally, women are less impressed by attractive males than are men by attractive females (Buss, 1988a). Women are more likely than men to report that attributes other than physical attractiveness, such as a sense of humor, are important to them.

Despite the premium placed on physical attractiveness in Western culture, there is evidence that individuals tend to match for physical attractiveness in much the same way that they match on personality and attitudinal dimensions. You can demonstrate this for yourself. Look at the engagement announcements accompanied by photographs of the engaged couples. You will find remarkable evidence for matching. Beyond such anecdotal evidence, there is research evidence for matching for physical attractiveness. Shafer and Keith (2001) found that married couples (especially younger and older couples) matched for weight.

What accounts for this matching for physical attractiveness? It turns out that physically attractive people tend to have higher standards for what they consider another person's level of attractiveness to be. For example, in one study, participants of varying levels of objective attractiveness (as rated by others) rated the attractiveness of several target individuals. The results showed that more physically attractive participants rated the target individuals lower in attractiveness than less attractive participants (Montoya, 2008). Further, more attractive participants expected less satisfaction in a relationship with targets they rated as less attractive. Additionally, attractive participants showed less fear of rejection from an attractive other than less attractive participants and saw a relationship with a target person of similar attractiveness more probable. So, people may match for attractiveness because they expect a satisfying relationship with others of similar attractiveness, have less fear of being rejected, and view a relationship with an attractive potential mate as likely to happen (Montoya, 2008).

Dimensions of Physical Attractiveness

What specific physical characteristics make someone attractive? Facial appearance has been shown to strongly affect our perceptions of attractiveness through much of our life span (McArthur, 1982; Zebrowitz, Olson, & Hoffman, 1993). Moreover, various aspects of facial appearance have specific effects. One group of researchers suspected that people find symmetrical faces more attractive than asymmetrical faces (Cardenas & Harris, 2006; Thornhill & Gangestad, 1994). Cardenas and Harris had participants examine pairs of faces, asking them to indicate which was more attractive. They found that more symmetrical faces were chosen over less symmetrical faces. Interestingly, when the researchers added asymmetrical makeup decoration to a symmetrical face, it reduced the perceived attractiveness of the symmetrical face. Similarly, Thornhill and Gangestad took photographs of males and females, fed those photos into a computer, created computer versions of the faces, and made precise measurements of the symmetry of the faces. They then asked subjects to rate the computer-generated images for attractiveness. They found that people do judge symmetrical faces to be more attractive than asymmetrical ones. Thornhill and Gangestad also asked the photographed students to fill out questionnaires about their sex and social lives. Those with symmetrical faces reported that they were sexually active earlier than others and had more friends and lovers. Finally, Mealey, Bridgestock, and Townsend (1999) report that between identical twins, the twin with the more symmetrical face is judged to be more physically attractive.

Why should symmetry and facial features in general be so important? The answer may lie more in our biology than in our psychology, an issue we explore later in the chapter.

There is a body of research that suggests that people's facial appearance plays a role in how others perceive and treat them (Berry, 1991; Noor & Evans, 2003; Zebrowitz, Collins, & Dutta, 1998; Zebrowitz & Lee, 1999). Zebrowitz and her coworkers (1998) noted that there is a **physical attractiveness bias**, a "halo," whereby individuals who are physically attractive are thought to also have other positive attributes. One cultural stereotype is that what is beautiful is good. That is, we tend to believe that physically attractive individuals possess a wide range of desirable characteristics and that they are generally happier than unattractive individuals (Dion, Berscheid, & Walster, 1972) Not only do we find attractive individuals more appealing physically, but we also confer on them a number of psychological and social advantages. We think that they are more competent and socially appealing than the average-appearing person. Moreover, unattractive individuals may experience discrimination because of their appearance. A study by Noor and Evans (2003) confirms this. They found that an asymmetrical face was perceived to be more neurotic, less open, less agreeable, and less attractive than a symmetrical face. So, individuals with symmetrical faces are associated with more positive personality characteristics than those with asymmetrical faces.

Much of this attractiveness bias is probably learned. However, there is some evidence that the attractiveness bias may have a biological component as well. In one experiment, infants 2 or 3 months old were exposed to pairs of adult faces and their preferences were recorded (Langlois, Roggman, Casey, Riesner-Danner, & Jenkins, 1987). Preference was inferred from a measure known as *fixation time*, or the amount of time spent looking at one face or the other. If the infant prefers one over the other, the infant should look at that face longer. As shown in Figure 10.14.2, when attractive faces were paired with unattractive faces, infants displayed a preference for the attractive faces. It is therefore quite unlikely that infants learned these preferences.

Furthermore, a number of distinctly different cultures seem to have the same biases. This doesn't necessarily mean that these biases aren't learned; various cultures may simply value the same characteristics. Studies comparing judgments of physical attractiveness in Korea and in the United States found agreement on whether a face was attractive and whether the face conveyed a sense of power. In both countries, for example, faces with broad chins, thin lips, and receding hairlines were judged to convey dominance (Triandis, 1994).

Zebrowitz and her coworkers showed that appearances of both attractive people and people with baby faces (round faces, large eyes, small nose and chin, high eyebrows) affect how others treat them (Zebrowitz & Lee, 1999; Zebrowitz et al., 1998). Whereas attractive people are thought to be highly competent both physically and intellectually, baby-faced individuals are viewed as weak, submissive, warm, and naive. What happens when baby-faced individuals do not conform to the stereotype that they are harmless? In a study of delinquent adolescent boys, Zebrowitz and Lee (1999) showed that baby-faced boys, in contrast to more mature-looking delinquents, were punished much more severely. This is a contrast effect: Innocent-looking people who commit antisocial actions violate our expectations.

Although attractiveness and baby-facedness may have a downside when these individuals run afoul of expectations, the upside is, as you might expect, that the positive expectations and responses of other people shape the personalities of attractive individuals across their life (Zebrowitz et al., 1998). This is self-fulfilling prophecy, whereby attractive men who are treated positively because of their appearance become more socially secure as they get older. Similarly, Zebrowitz found that a man who had an "honest" face in his youth tended to be more honest as he got older.

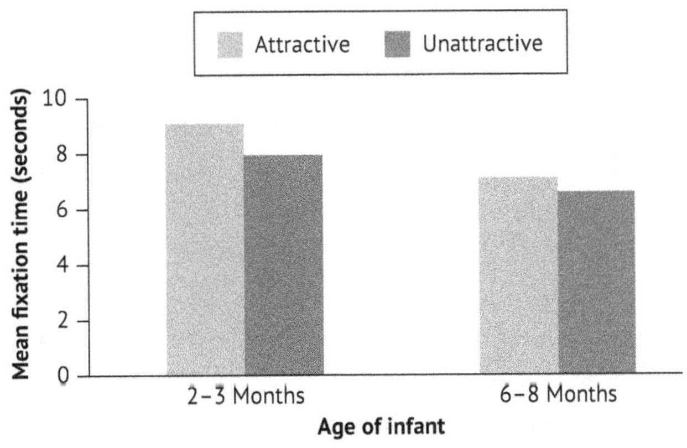

Figure 10.14.2 Infant fixation time as a function of the attractiveness of a stimulus face. Infants as young as 2 or 3 months old showed a preference for an attractive face over an unattractive face.

From Langlois and colleagues (1987).

For baby-faced individuals, the effect over time was somewhat different. These individuals become more assertive and aggressive over time, probably as a way of compensating for the stereotype of a baby-faced individual as submissive and weak.

However, Zebrowitz and colleagues (1998) did not observe such a self-fulfilling prophecy for women. That is, attractive young women do not become more attractive and competent socially as they age. Zebrowitz suggested further that less-attractive women may learn to compensate by becoming more socially able to counteract the negative image held of less-attractive women. This would explain the lack of significant differences in socially valued personality attributes between younger attractive and less-attractive women as they age into their fifties. Interestingly, women who had an attractive personality in their youth developed high attractiveness in their fifties, suggesting, according to Zebrowitz, that women manipulated their appearance and presentation (makeup, etc.) more than men did. It may be that this is due to women's greater motivation to present an attractive appearance because they have less power to achieve their social goals in other ways (Zebrowitz et al., 1998).

Physique and the Attractiveness Bias

Physique also profoundly affects our perceptions of attractiveness. Buss (1994) observed that the importance of physical attractiveness has increased in the United States in every decade since the 1930s. This is true for both men and women, although men rate physical attractiveness as much more important than do women. Western society has widely shared notions of which bodily attributes are attractive. We have positive perceptions of people who fit these notions and negative perceptions of those who do not. We sometimes even display discriminatory behavior against those who deviate too far from cultural standards.

People can be categorized by body type into *ectomorphs* (thin, perhaps underweight), *mesomorphs* (athletic build), and *endomorphs* (overweight). Positive personality traits tend to be attributed to mesomorphs and negative ones to people with the other body types (Ryckman et al., 1991). There is some ambivalence about ectomorphs, especially as societal attitudes toward thinness seem to shift, influenced by such factors as an increasing health consciousness and an association of excessive thinness with acquired immunodeficiency syndrome (AIDS). Perceptions of endo-morphs, in contrast, remain consistently negative. Of course, some people are more intensely attuned to physical appearance than are others. It appears that those people who are most conscious of their own appearance are the most likely to stereotype others on the basis of physique.

Certainly this is the case with regard to overweight individuals. Research confirms that obese individuals are stigmatized and are the target of negative stereotypes in our society. This bias cuts across genders. Obese men and women are likely to be stigmatized (Hebl & Turchin, 2005). These negative stereotypes exist on both the implicit and explicit level (Waller, Lampman, & Lupfer-Johnson, 2012; Wang, Brownell, & Wadden, 2004). In one study (Harris, 1990), subjects judged a stimulus person who was depicted as either normal weight or (with the help of extra clothing) obese. They evaluated "Chris," the stimulus person, along several dimensions including the likelihood that Chris was dating or married, her self-esteem, and her ideal romantic partner. The results, almost without exception, reflected negative stereotyping of an obese Chris compared to a normal-weight Chris. Subjects judged that the obese Chris was less likely to be dating or married compared to the normal-weight Chris. They also rated the obese Chris as having lower self-esteem than the normal-weight Chris and felt that her ideal love partner should also be obese.

Studies also show the practical consequences of these attitudes. For example, it has been shown that overweight college students are less likely than other students to get financial help from home (Crandall, 1991). This effect was especially strong with respect to female students and was true regardless of the resources the student's family had, the number of children in the family, or other factors that could affect parents' willingness to provide financial help. The researchers suggested that the finding might be largely explained by parents' negative attitudes toward their overweight children and consequent lack of optimism about their future. In a related domain, there is evidence that businesspeople sacrifice $1,000 in annual salary for every pound they are overweight (Kolata, 1992). Weight can also affect evaluations of employability (Grant & Mizzi, 2014). Grant and Mizzi found that an overweight potential job applicant was rated as less employable than a normal weight applicant. They also found that stereotypes about overweight people did not mediate the relationship between weight and employ-ability ratings. They did find, however, that a "rational bias" (e.g., customers would feel uncomfortable with the overweight employee) mediated the relationship.

Interestingly, the bias against overweight people is shown by children. Children between the ages of 2 and 5 were shown two line drawings of children. One of the drawings showed a child who was 23% larger than the other. The children were asked to ascribe various characteristics to the figures in the drawing. The results showed that the children were more likely to ascribe negative qualities to the larger figure (Turnbull, Heaslip, & McLeod, 2000). This finding should not be surprising since these stereotypic images of body image are portrayed in children's literature and movies (Herbozo, Tantleff-Dunn, Gokee-Larose, & Thompson, 2004). Just think, for example, about the Disney film *The Little Mermaid*, in which the mermaid Ariel is depicted as a slim, beautiful, young woman and the sea witch (the villain) is depicted as an obese, unattractive woman.

The bias against overweight people even extends into the world of health care. For example, Waller, Lampman, and Lupfer-Johnson (2012) found a stronger implicit bias against overweight people in a medical than nonmedical context. In another study, an implicit prejudice and implicit stereotypes were shown toward overweight people by health care workers, a majority of whom were doctors (Teachman & Brownell, 2001). There was, however, little evidence for an explicit prejudice. In another study, doctors showed more negative attitudes toward hypothetical obese patients than average-weight patients and that they would spend less time with an obese patient (Hebl & Xu, 2001). Physicians indicated that they would be more likely to refer obese patients for mental health care. The good news was, however, that doctors seemed to follow an appropriate course of action with respect to weight-unrelated tests.

The bias against obese people may be culturally related. Western culture seems to place a great deal of emphasis on body image (just take a look at the models [male and female] used in advertisements). One cross-cultural study using British and Ugandan participants showed that the Ugandan participants rated a drawing of an obese figure more positively than British participants (Furnham & Baguma, 2004). Another study conducted in New Zealand found that obese job applicants were evaluated more negatively than nonobese applicants (Ding & Stillman, 2005). The bias may also have a racial component as well. One study found that black males stigmatized an obese person less than white males and that black males are less likely to be stigmatized than white males (Hebl & Turchin, 2005).

One reason obese individuals are vilified is that we believe that their weight problem stems from laziness and a lack of discipline. If we know that an individual's weight problem is the result of a biological disorder and thus beyond his or her control, we are less likely to make negative judgments of that individual (DeJong, 1980). What we fail to realize is that most obese people cannot control their weight. There is a genetic component in obesity, and this tendency can be exacerbated by social and cultural factors, such as lack of information and an unhealthy lifestyle.

Attractiveness judgments and stereotyping in everyday life may not be as strong as they are in some laboratory studies. In these studies, we make pure attraction judgments: We see only a face or a physique. When we deal with people, we evaluate an entire package even if much of what we see initially is only the wrapping. The entire package includes many attributes. A person may be overweight but may also have a mellifluous voice and a powerful personality. In a laboratory study in which subjects were exposed to a person's face and voice, the perception of the person's physical attractiveness was affected by judgments about that person's vocal attractiveness and vice versa (Zuckerman, Miyake, & Hodgins, 1991). Gertrude Stein was a woman many people found attractive even though she weighed over 200 pounds. Her striking face and her powerful personality were the main attributes that people remembered after meeting her.

Beauty and the View from Evolutionary Psychology

It is obvious that we learn to associate attractiveness with positive virtues and unattractiveness with vice, even wickedness. Children's books and movies often portray the good characters as beautiful and the villains as ugly. As noted, in the Walt Disney movie *The Little Mermaid,* the slender, beautiful mermaid, Ariel, and the evil, obese sea witch are cases in point. Such portrayals are not limited to works for children. The hunchback of Notre Dame, the phantom of the opera, and Freddy Kruger are all physically unattractive evildoers.

Evolutionary psychologists suggest that perhaps beauty is more than skin deep. Recall the research on the attractiveness of symmetrical faces. It seems that it is not only humans who value symmetry but also a variety of other species. For example, Watson and Thorn-hill (1994) reported that female scorpion flies can detect and prefer as mates males with symmetrical wings. Male elks with the most symmetrical racks host the largest harems.

Mate Selection: Good Genes or Good Guys? Proponents of evolutionary psychology, a subfield of both psychology and biology, employ the principles of evolution to explain human behavior and believe that symmetry is reflective of underlying genetic quality. Lack of symmetry is thought to be caused by various stresses, such as poor maternal nutrition, late maternal age, attacks by predators, or disease, and may therefore reflect bad health or poor genetic quality. Thus, the preference for symmetry in potential mates, whether human or animal, may be instinctive (Watson & Thornhill, 1994). Indeed, even small differences matter. Twins with lower levels of symmetry are reliably rated as less attractive than their slightly more symmetrical counterpart (Mealey, Bridgstock, & Townsend, 1999).

The degree to which biology may control human mating preferences can be underscored by the finding that the type of face a woman finds attractive varies with her menstrual cycle. Perret and Penton-Voak (1999) reported a study that showed that when a woman is ovulating, she is more likely to prefer men with highly masculine features. In contrast, during other times, men with softer, feminine features are preferred. The researchers had numerous women from various countries—Japan, Scotland, England—judge male faces during different parts of their menstrual cycles. The researchers believe that these results are explained by the observation that masculine looks, in all of the animal kingdom, denote virility and the increased likelihood for healthy offspring. In a related finding, Gangestad and Thornhill (1998) reported a study that showed that females preferred the smell of a "sweaty" T-shirt worn by the most symmetrical males but only if the women were ovulating.

Of course, it is likely that more choice is involved in mate selection than would be indicated by these studies. In any event, most people do rebel against the notion that decisions about sex, marriage, and parenthood are determined by nothing more than body odor (Berreby, 1998).

Certainly we would expect those with symmetrical appearances to become aware of their advantages in sexual competition. For example, consider the following study by Simpson and his coworkers. Heterosexual men and women were told that they would be competing with another same-sex person for a date with an attractive person of the opposite sex. The experimenters videotaped and analyzed the interactions among the two competitors and the potential date. Men who had symmetrical faces used direct competition tactics. That is, when trying to get a date with the attractive woman, symmetrical men simply and baldly compared their attractiveness (favorably) with the competitor. Less-attractive (read as less-symmetrical-faced) men used indirect competitive methods, such as emphasizing their positive personality qualities (Simpson, Gangestad, Christensen, & Leck, 1999).

Gangestad and Thornhill (1998) have argued that physical appearance marked by high symmetrical precision reveals to potential mates that the individual has good genes and is, therefore, for both men and women, a highly desirable choice. These individuals, especially men, should have fared very well in sexual competition during evolutionary history. Why? Research suggests that greater symmetry is associated with higher survival rates as well as higher reproductive rates in many species (Simpson et al., 1999). In men, it seems that certain secondary sexual attributes that are controlled by higher levels of testosterone, such as enlarged jaws, chins, and so forth, may project greater health and survival capability (Mealey, Bridgstock, & Townsend, 1999). Indeed, symmetrical men and women report more sexual partners and have sex earlier in life than less symmetrical individuals. The more symmetrical the individual—again, especially males—the more probable the person will have the opportunity for short-term sexual encounters, and the more likely, as Simpson and colleagues (1999) found, they will use direct competitive strategies to win sexual competitions.

Of course, good genes are not enough. Raising human offspring is a complicated, long-term—some might say never-ending—affair, and having a good partner willing to invest in parenthood is important. Indeed, theorists have developed what are called "good provider" models of mate selection that emphasize the potential mate's commitment to the relationship and ability to provide resources necessary for the long-term health of that relationship (Gangestad & Thornhill, 1997; Trivers, 1972).

How to Attract a Mate David Buss, a prominent evolutionary social psychologist, suggested that to find and retain a reproductively valuable mate, humans engage in love acts—behaviors with near-term goals, such as display of resources the other sex finds enticing. The ultimate purpose of these acts is to increase reproductive success (Buss, 1988a, 1988b). Human sexual behavior thus can be viewed in much the same way as the sexual behavior of other animal species.

Subjects in one study (Buss, 1988b) listed some specific behaviors they used to keep their partner from getting involved with someone else. Buss found that males tended to use display of resources (money, cars, clothes, sometimes even brains), whereas females tried to look more attractive and threatened to be unfaithful if the males didn't shape up. Buss argued that these findings support an evolutionary interpretation of mate retention: The tactics of females focus on their value as a reproductive mate and on arousing the jealousy of the male, who needs to ensure they are not impregnated by a rival.

Jealousy is evoked when a threat or loss occurs to a valued relationship due to the partner's real or imagined attention to a rival (Dijkstra & Buunk, 1998). Men and women respond differently to infidelity, according to evolutionary psychologists, due to the fact that women bear higher reproductive costs than do men (Harris & Christenfeld, 1996). Women are concerned with having a safe environment for potential offspring, so it would follow that sexual infidelity would not be as threatening as emotional infidelity, which could signal the male's withdrawal from the relationship. Men, however, should be most concerned with ensuring the prolongation of their genes and avoiding investing energy in safeguarding some other male's offspring. Therefore, males are most threatened by acts of sexual infidelity and less so by emotional ones. Thus, males become most jealous when their mates are sexually unfaithful, whereas women are most jealous when their mates are emotionally involved with a rival (Buss, 1994; Harris & Christenfeld, 1996).

According to the evolutionary psychology view, males ought to be threatened by a rival's dominance, the ability to provide resources (money, status, power) to the female in question, whereas women ought to be most threatened by a rival who is physically attractive, because that attribute signals the potential for viable offspring. Indeed, a clever experiment by Dijkstra and Buunk (1998), in which participants judged scenarios in which the participant's real or imagined mate was flirting with a person of the opposite sex, showed that dominance in a male rival and attractiveness in a female rival elicited the greatest amount of jealousy for men and women, respectively.

Many of Buss's findings about human mating behavior are disturbing because both men and women in pursuit of their sexual goals cheat and frustrate their mates and derogate their rivals.

However, some of his findings are kinder to our species. For example, he points out that the most effective tactics for men who wish to keep their mates are to provide love and kindness, to show affection, and to tell their mates of their love. That sounds rather romantic.

Indeed, evidence suggests that women are driven, at least in long-term mate selection strategies, by behavior and traits represented by the good provider models. Although men are strongly influenced by traits such as youth and attractiveness, women tend to select partners on the basis of attributes such as social status and industriousness (Ben Hamida, Mineka, & Bailey, 1998). Note the intriguing differences between traits that men find attractive in women and those that women find attractive in men. The obvious one is that men seem to be driven by the "good genes" model, whereas women's preferences seem to follow the good provider models. This preference appears across a range of cultures. One study by Shackelford, Schmitt, and Buss (2005) had males and females evaluate several characteristics that could define a potential mate. The participants were drawn from 37 cultures (including African, Asian, and European). Their results confirmed that, across cultures, women valued social status more than men, and men valued physical attractiveness more than women.

The other difference, however, is that traits that make women attractive are in essence uncontrollable: Either you are young or you are not; either you are attractive or you are not. Modern science can help, but not much. Therefore, a woman who desires to increase her value has the problem of enhancing attributes that are really not under her control (Ben Hamida et al., 1998). Male-related attributes—status, achievement—are all, to a greater or lesser extent, under some control and may be gained with effort and motivation. Ben Hamida and his colleagues argue that the uncontrollability of the factors that affect a woman's fate in the sexual marketplace may have long-term negative emotional consequences.

Before we conclude that there is an unbridgeable difference between men and women and that men follow only the good genes model and women only the good provider model, we need to take into account a recent meta-analysis showing that physical attractiveness and good earning potential mediate mate preferences for both men and women (Eastwick, Luchies, Finkel, & Hunt, 2014). We should also consider the possibility that what one wants in the sexual marketplace depends on what one's goals are and what one can reasonably expect to get. In fact, it appears that when looking for a casual sexual partner, both men and women emphasize attractiveness, and when searching for a long-term relationship, both look for a mate with good interpersonal skills, an individual who is attentive to the partner's needs, has a good sense of humor, and is easygoing (Regan, 1998). In fact, Miller (2000), an evolutionary psychologist, argued that the most outstanding features of the human mind—consciousness, morality, sense of humor, creativity—were shaped not so much by natural selection but rather by sexual selection. Miller suggested that being funny and friendly and a good conversationalist serves the same purpose for humans as an attractive tail serves peacocks: It helps attract mates.

Regan (1998) reported that women were less willing to compromise on their standards. For example, although women wanted an attractive partner for casual sex, they also wanted a male who was older and more interpersonally responsive. Men wanted attractiveness and would compromise on everything else. In fact, a woman's attractiveness seems to overcome a male potential partner's common sense as well. Agocha and Cooper (1999) reported that when men knew a potential partner's sexual history and also knew that she was physically attractive, they weighed attractiveness as much more important in the decision to engage in intercourse than the probability of contracting a sexually transmitted disease as suggested by that sexual history. However, women and men are less willing to compromise when it comes to long-term relationships. The results conform to the idea that casual sex affords men a chance to advertise their sexual prowess and gain favor with their peer group but that long-term relationships are driven by quite different needs (Regan, 1998).

Finally, students often ask about any differences between heterosexual and same-sex orientation mate preferences. The available research suggests that mate selection preferences between these groups may not differ all that much (Over & Phillips, 1997). For example, a study of personal advertisements placed by heterosexual and same-sex orientation males and females was conducted by Kenrick, Keefe, Bryan, Barr, and Brown (1995). Kenrick et al. found that mate selection patterns for heterosexual and same-sex orientation men were highly similar and showed similar patterns of change with age. Both groups of men preferred younger mates, and this preference grew stronger with age. This finding was replicated in a similar study of personal ads conducted by Burrows (2013). She found that gay men advertised for partners who were on average 13 years younger than themselves (heterosexuals advertised for someone 14 years younger). Kenrick et al. found a slight difference between same-sex orientation and heterosexual women. Younger women in both groups expressed interest in same-aged mates. However, with age, same-sex orientation women were more likely than heterosexual women to desire a younger partner. In another study, same-sex orientation women were found to be more interested in visual sexual stimulation and less in partner status than heterosexual women.

STUDY BREAK

This section explored how physical attractiveness affects interpersonal attraction. Before you begin the next section, answer the following questions:

1. Overall, how and why is physical attractiveness important in attraction?
2. What characteristics of faces contribute to the perception of facial attractiveness?
3. What is the physical attractiveness bias, and what are some of its components?
4. How and why does a person's weight relate to perceptions of attractiveness and behavior?
5. How do evolutionary psychologists explain the effects of physical attractiveness on attraction?
6. What are the factors relevant to human mate selection, and how can one attract a mate?

Key Terms

consummate love Love that includes all three components: passion, intimacy, and commitment. (p. 231)

loneliness A psychological state that results when we perceive that there is an inadequacy or a deprivation in our social relationships. (p. 224)

matching principle A principle that applies in romantic relationships, suggesting that individuals become involved with a partner with whom they are closely matched socially and physically. (p. 240)
need for affiliation A motivation that underlies our desire to establish and maintain rewarding interpersonal relationships. (p. 222)
need for intimacy A motivation for close and affectionate relationships. (p. 223)
physical attractiveness bias The tendency to confer a number of psychological and social advantages to physically attractive individuals. (p 243)
physical proximity effect The fact that we are more likely to form a relationship with someone who is physically close to us; proximity affects interpersonal attraction, mostly at the beginning of a relationship. (p. 236)
romantic love Love involving strong emotion and having the components of passion and intimacy but not commitment. (p. 229)
social anxiety Anxiety tied to interpersonal relationships that occurs because of an individual's anticipation of negative encounters with others. (p. 225)
triangular theory of love A theory suggesting that love is comprised of three components—passion, intimacy, and commitment—each of which is conceptualized as a leg of a triangle that can vary. (p. 227)
unrequited love Love expressed by one person that is rejected and not returned by the other. (p. 231)
working model Mental representations of what an individual expects to happen in close relationships. (p. 233)

References

Acker, M., & Davis, M. H. (1992). Intimacy, passion and commitment in adult romantic relationships: A test of the triangular theory of love. *Journal of Social and Personal Relationships 9*, 21–50.

Agocha, V. B., & Cooper, M. L. (1999). Risk perceptions and safer-sex intention: Does a partner's physical attractiveness undermine the use of risk-relevant information? *Personality and Social Psychology Bulletin, 25*, 756–759.

Ainsworth, M. D. S. (1992). Epilogue. In D. Cicchetti, M. M. Greenberg, & M. Cummings (Eds.), *Attachment in the preschool years*. Chicago: University of Chicago Press.

Alpass, F. M., & Neville, S. (2003). Loneliness, health and depression in older males. *Aging and Mental Health, 7*, 212–216.

Amichai-Hamburger, Y., & Hayat, Z. (2011). The impact of the Internet on the social lives of users: A representative sample from 13 countries. *Computers in Human Behavior, 27*, 585–589.

Amichai-Hamburger, Y., Kingsbury, M., & Schneider, B. H. (2013). Friendship: An old concept with a new meaning?. *Computers in Human Behavior, 29*, 33–39.

Amodio, D. M., & Showers, C. J. (2005). "Similarity breeds liking" revisited: The moderating role of commitment. *Journal of Social and Personal Relationships, 22*, 817–836.

Aron A., Aron, E., & Allen, J. (1998). Motivations for unrequited love. *Personality and Social Psychology Bulletin, 21,* 787–796.

Back, M. D., Schmukle, S. C., & Egloff, B. (2008). Becoming friends by chance. *Psychological Science, 19,* 439–440.

Bartholomew, K., & Horowitz, L. M. (1991). Attachment styles among young adults: A test of a four category model. *Journal of Personality and Social Psychology, 61,* 226–244.

Baumeister, R. F., & Bratslavsky, E. (1999). Passion, intimacy, and time: Passionate love as a function of change of intimacy over time. *Personality and Social Psychology Review, 3,* 49–67.

Baumeister, R., & Tice, D. (1990). Anxiety and social exclusion. *Journal of Social and Clinical Psychology, 9,* 165–195.

Baumeister, R., Wotman, S., & Stillwell, A. M. (1993). Unrequited love: On heartbreak, anger, guilt, scriptlessness and humiliation. *Journal of Personality and Social Psychology, 64,* 377–394.

Ben Hamida, S., Mineka, S., & Bailey, J. M. (1998). Sex differences in perceived controllability of mate value: An evolutionary perspective. *Journal of Personality and Social Psychology, 75,* 963–966.

Berreby, D. (1998, June 9). Studies explore love and the sweaty t-shirt. *The New York Times,* B14.

Berry, D. (1991). Attractive faces are not all created equal: Joint effects of facial babyishness and attractiveness on social perception. *Personality and Social Psychology Bulletin, 17,* 523–528.

Berscheid, E. (1988). Some comments on the anatomy of love: Or what ever happened to old fashioned lust? In R.J. Steinberg & M. L. Barnes (Eds.), *The psychology of love* (pp. 359–374). New Haven, CT: Yale University Press.

Berscheid, E., Snyder, M., & Omoto, A. M. (1989). The relationship closeness inventory: Assessing the closeness of interpersonal relationships. *Journal of Personality and Social Psychology 57,* 792–807.

Bornstein, R. F. (1989). Exposure and affect: Overview and meta-analysis of research, 1968–1987. *Psychological Bulletin, 106,* 265–289.

Brehm, S. (1988). Passionate love. In R. J. Steinberg & M. L. Barnes (Eds.), *The psychology of love* (pp. 232–263). New Haven, CT: Yale University Press.

Brumbaugh, C. C., & Fraley, R. C. (2006). Transference and attachment: How do attachment patterns get carried forward from one relationship to the next? *Personality and Social Psychology Bulletin, 32,* 552–560.

Burnett, A. (1972). *Gertrude Stein.* New York: Atheneum.

Burrows, K. (2013). Age preferences in dating advertisements by homosexuals and heterosexuals: From sociobiological to sociological explanations. *Archives of Sexual Behavior, 42,* 203–211.

Buss, D. M. (1988a). Love acts: The evolutionary biology of love. In R. J. Steinberg & M. L. Barnes (Eds.), *The psychology of love* (pp. 100–118). New Haven, CT: Yale University Press.

Buss, D. M. (1988b). From vigilance to violence: Tactics of mate retention in American undergraduates. *Ethology and Sociobiology, 9,* 291–317.

Buss, D. M. (1994). *The evolution of desire: Strategies of human mating.* New York: Basic Books.

Byrne, D., Clore, G. L., & Smeaton, G. (1986). The attraction hypothesis: Do similar attitudes affect anything? *Journal of Personality and Social Psychology, 51,* 1167–1170.

Byrne, D., Ervin, C. R., & Lamberth, J. (2004). Continuity between the experimental study of attraction and real-life computer dating. In H. T. Reis & C. E. Rusbult (Eds.), *Close relationships: Key readings* (pp. 81–88). Philadelphia, PA: Taylor & Francis.

Byrne, D., & Nelson, D. (1965). Attraction as a linear function of proportion of positive reinforcements. *Journal of Personality and Social Psychology, 1,* 659–663.

Cacioppo, J. T., Hawkley, L. C., Berntson, G. G., Ernst, J. M., Gibbs, A. C., Stickgold, R., & Hobson, J. A. (2002). Do lonely days invade the night? Potential social modulation of sleep efficiency. *Psychological Science, 13,* 384–387.

Cardenas, R. A., & Harris, L. J. (2006). Symmetrical decorations enhance the attractiveness of faces and abstract designs. *Evolution and Human Behavior, 27,* 1–18.

Carli, L. L., Ganley, R., & Pierce-Otay, A. (1991). Similarity and satisfaction in roommate relationships. *Personality and Social Psychology Bulletin, 17,* 419–427.

Chak, K., & Leung, L. (2004). Shyness and locus of control as predictors of Internet addiction and Internet use. *CyberPsychology and Behavior, 7,* 559–570.

Chan, D., K-S., & Cheng, G. H-L. (2004). A comparison of offline and online friendship qualities at different stages of relationship development. *Journal of Social and Personal Relationships, 21,* 305–320.

Chen, J., Rapee, R. M., & Abbott, M. (2013). Mediators of the relationship between social anxiety and post-event rumination, *Journal of Anxiety Disorders, 27,* 1–8.

Christensen, P. N., & Kashy, D. (1998). Perceptions of and by lonely people in initial social interaction. *Personality and Social Psychology Bulletin, 24,* 322–329.

Collins, N. L., Ford, M. B., Guichard, A., & Allard, L. M. (2006). Working models of attachment and attribution processes in intimate relationships. *Personality and Social Psychology Bulletin, 32,* 201–219.

Crandall, C. S. (1991). Do heavyweight students have more difficulty paying for college? *Personality and Social Psychology Bulletin, 17,* 606–611.

de Munck, V. C., Korotayev, A., de Munck, J., & Kaltourina, D. (2011). Cross-cultural analysis of models of romantic love among U.S. residents, Russians, and Lithuanians. *Cross-Cultural Research, 45,* 128–154.

DeJong, M. (1980). The stigma of obesity: The consequence of naive assumptions concerning the causes of physical deviance. *Journal of Health and Social Behavior, 21,* 75–87.

Diamond, L. M. (2004). Emerging perspectives on distinctions between romantic love and sexual desire. *Current Directions in Psychological Science, 13,* 116–119.

Diamond, L. M. (2003). What does sexual orientation orient? A biobehavioral model distinguishing romantic love and sexual desire. *Psychological Review, 110,* 173–192.

Dijkstra, P., & Buunk, B. (1998). Jealousy as a function of rival characteristics: An evolutionary perspective. *Personality and Social Psychology Bulletin, 42,* 1158–1166.

Ding, V. J., & Stillman, J. A. (2005). An empirical investigation of discrimination against overweight female job applicants in New Zealand. *New Zealand Journal of Psychology, 39,* 139–148.

Dion, K., Berscheid, E., & Walster, E. (1972). What is beautiful is good. *Journal of Personality and Social Psychology, 24,* 285–290.

DiTommaso, E., Brannen, C., & Burgess, M. (2005). The universality of relationship characteristics: A cross-cultural comparison of different types of attachment and loneliness in Canadian and visiting Chinese students. *Social Behavior and Personality, 33,* 57–68.

Duck, S. W. (1983). *Friends for life.* New York: St. Martin's Press.

Duck, S. W. (1988). *Handbook of personal relationships.* New York: Wiley.

Dundon, C. M., & Rellini, A. H. (2012). Emotional states of love moderate the association between catecholamines and female sexual responses in the laboratory. *Journal of Sexual Medicine, 9,* 2617–2630.

Eagly, A. H., Ashmore, R. D., Makhijani, M. G., & Longo, L. C. (1991). What is beautiful is good, but ... : A metaanalytic review of research on the physical attractiveness stereotype. *Psychological Bulletin, 110,* 109–128.

Eastwick, P. W., Luchies, L. B., Finkel, E. J., & Hunt, L. L. (2014). The predictive validity of ideal partner preferences: A review and meta-analysis. *Psychological Bulletin, 140,* 623–665.

Edwards, S. L., Rapee, R. M., & Franklin, J. (2003). Postevent rumination and recall bias for a social performance event in high and low socially anxious individuals. *Cognitive Therapy and Research, 27,* 603–617.

Enzo, E., Politi, P., Bianchi, M., Minoretti, P., Bertona, M., & Geroldi, D. (2006). Raised plasma nerve growth factors associated with early stage romantic love. *Psychoneuroendocrinology, 31,* 288–294.

Festinger, L., Schachter, S., & Back, K. W. (1959). *Social pressures in informal groups: A study of human factors in housing.* New York: Harper & Row.

Fraley, R. C., & Shaver, P. R. (1998). Airport separations: A naturalistic study of adult attachment dynamics in separating couples. *Journal of Personality and Social Psychology, 75,* 1198–1212.

Furnham, A., & Baguma, P. (2004). Cultural differences in the evaluation of male and female body shapes. *International Journal of Eating Disorders, 15,* 81–89.

Gangestad, S. W., & Thornhill, R. (1997). Human sexual selection and developmental instability. In J. A. Simpson & D. T. Kenrick (Eds.), *Evolutionary social psychology* (pp. 169–195). Mahwah, NJ: Erlbaum.

Gangestad, S. W., & Thornhill R. (1998, May 22). Menstrual cycle variation in women's preferences for the scent of symmetrical men. *Proceedings of the Royal Society of London, 265,* 927.

Garcia, S., Stinson, L., Ickes, W., Bissonette, W. & Briggs, S. R. (1991). Shyness and physical attractiveness in mixed-sex dyads. *Journal of Personality and Social Psychology, 61,* 35–49.

Glomb, T. M., & Welch, E. T. (2005). Can opposites attract? Personality heterogeneity in supervisor-subordinate dyads as a predictor of subordinate outcomes. *Journal of Applied Psychology, 90,* 749–757.

Grant, S., & Mizzi, T. (2014). Body weight bias in hiring decisions: Identifying explanatory mechanisms. *Social Behavior and Personality, 42,* 353–370.

Harris, C. R., & Christenfeld, N. (1996). Gender, jealousy, and reason. *Psychological Science, 7,* 364–366.

Harris, M. B. (1990). Is love seen as different for the obese? *Journal of Applied Social Psychology, 20,* 1209–1224.

Hatfield, E. (Walster), Aronson, V., Abrahams, D., & Rottman, L. (1966). Importance of physical attractiveness in dating behavior. *Journal of Personality and Social Psychology, 4,* 508–516.

Hatfield, E. H., Walster, G. W., & Traupmann, J. (1978). Equity and premarital sex. *Journal of Personality and Social Psychology, 36,* 82–92.

Hatfield, E., & Walster, G. W. (1981). *A new look at love.* Reading, MA: Addison-Wesley.

Hawkley, L. C., Burleson, M. H., Berntson, G. G., & Cacioppo, J. T. (2003). Loneliness in everyday life: Cardiovascular activity, psychosocial context, and health behaviors. *Journal of Personality and Social Psychology, 85,* 105–120.

Hebl, M. R., & Turchin, J. M. (2005). The stigma of obesity: What about men? *Basic and Applied Social Psychology, 27,* 267–275.

Hebl, M. R., & Xu, J. (2001). Weighing the care: Physicians' reaction to the size of a patient. *International Journal of Obesity, 25,* 1246–1252.

Hendrick, S. S., & Hendrick, C. (1987). Love and sex attitudes: A close relationship. In W. H. Jones & D. Perlman (Eds.), *Advances in personal relationships* (Vol. 1). Greenwich, CT: JAI Press.

Herbozo, S., Tantleff-Dunn, S., Gokee-Larose, J., & Thompson, J. K. (2004). Beauty and thinness messages in children's media: A content analysis. *Eating Disorders, 12,* 21–34.

Hill, C. A. (1987). Affiliation motivation: People who need people ... but in different ways. *Journal of Personality and Social Psychology, 52,* 1008–1018.

Hill, C. T., Rubin, Z., & Peplau, L. A. (1976). Breakups before marriage: The end of 103 affairs. *Journal of Social Issues, 32,* 147–168.

Hirsch, C., Meynen, T., & Clark, D. M. (2004). Negative self-imagery in social anxiety contaminates social interactions. *Memory, 12,* 496–506.

Hobman, E. V., Bordia, P., & Gallois, C. (2004). Perceived dissimilarity and work group involvement: The moderating effects of group openness to diversity. *Group & Organization Management, 29,* 560–587.

Huppert, J. D., Foa, E. B., Furr, J. M., Filip, J. C., & Matthews, A. (2003). Interpretation bias in social anxiety: A dimensional perspective. *Cognitive Therapy and Research, 27,* 569–577.

Ilmarinen, V., Lönnqvist, J., & Paunonen, S. (2016). Similarity-attraction effects in friendship formation: Honest platoon-mates prefer each other but dishonest do not. *Personality & Individual Differences, 92,* 153–158.

Jackson, T., Fritch, A., Nagasaka, T., & Gunderson, J. (2002). Toward explaining the relationship between shyness and loneliness: A path analysis with American college students. *Social Behavior and Personality, 30,* 263–270.

Kenrick, D. T., Keefe, R. C., Bryan, A., Barr, A., & Brown, S. (1995). Age preferences and mate choice among homosexuals and heterosexuals: A case for modular psychological mechanisms. *Journal of Personality and Social Psychology, 69,* 1169–1172.

Knox, D., Daniels, V., Sturdivant, L., & Zusman, M. E. (2001). College student use of the Internet for mate selection. College Student Journal, 35, 158–161.

Kolata, G. (1992, November 24). After kinship and marriage, anthropology discovers love. *New York Times,* p. B9.

Köllner, M. G., & Schultheiss, O. C. (2014). Meta-analytic evidence of low convergence between implicit and explicit measures of the needs for achievement, affiliation, and power. *Frontiers in Psychology, 5* (Article 826), 1–20.

Langlois, J. H., Roggman, L. A., Casey, R. I., Riesner-Danner, L. A., & Jenkins, V. Y. (1987). Infant preferences for attractive faces: Rudiments of a stereotype? *Developmental Psychology, 23,* 363–369.

Laurenceau, J. P., Barrett, L. F., & Pietromanaco, P. R. (1998). Intimacy as an interpersonal process: The importance of self-disclosure, partner disclosure, and perceived partner responsiveness in interpersonal exchanges. *Journal of Personality and Social Psychology, 74,* 1238–1251.

Leary, M. R. (1983a). *Understanding social anxiety: Social, personality, and clinical perspectives* (Vol. 153, Sage Library of Social Research). Beverly Hills, CA: Sage.

Leary, M. R. (1983b). Social anxiousness: The construct and its measurement. *Journal of Personality Assessment, 47,* 66–75.

Leary, M. R., & Kowalski, R. M. (1995). *Social anxiety.* New York: Guilford.

Leary, M. R., Springer, C., Negel, L., Ansell, E., and Evans, K. (1998). The causes, phenomenology, and consequences of hurt feelings. *Journal of Personality and Social Psychology, 74,* 1225–1237.

Lemiuex, R., & Hale, J. L. (2002). Cross-sectional analysis of intimacy, passion, and commitment: Testing the assumptions of the triangular theory of love. *Psychological Reports, 90,* 1009–1014.

Lundh, L.-G., & Sperling, M. (2002). Social anxiety and the post-event processing of distressing social events. *Cognitive Behaviour Therapy, 31,* 129–134.

Luo, Y., Hawkley, L. C., Waite, L., & Cacioppo, J. T. (2012). Loneliness, health, and mortality in old age: A national longitudinal study. *Social Science & Medicine, 74,* 907–914.

Madey, S. F., & Rodgers, L. (2009). The effect of attachment and Sternberg's triangular theory of love on relationship satisfaction. *Individual Differences Research, 7,* 76–84.

Manalastas, E. J. (2011). Unrequired love among young Filipino gay men: Subjective experiences of unreciprocated lovers. *Social Science Diliman, 7,* 63–81.

McAdams, D. P. (1982). Intimacy motivation. In A. J. Stewart (Ed.), *Motivation and society.* San Francisco: Jossey-Bass.

McAdams, D. P. (1989). *Intimacy.* New York: Doubleday.

McArthur, L. Z. (1982). Judging a book by its cover: A cognitive analysis of the relationship between physical appearance and stereotyping. In A. Hastorf & A. Isen (Eds.), *Cognitive social psychology* (pp. 149–211). New York: Elsevier/ North Holland.

McCown, J. A., Fischer, D., Page, R., & Homant, M. (2001). Internet relationships: People who meet people. *CyberPsychology and Behavior, 4,* 593–596.

McKenna, K., Green, A., & Gleason, M. (2002). Relationship formation on the Internet: What's the big attraction? *Journal of Social Issues, 58,* 9–31.

Mealey, L., Bridstock, R., & Townsend, G. C. (1999). Symmetry and perceived facial attractiveness: A monozygotic twin comparison. *Journal of Personality and Social Psychology, 76,* 151–158.

Milkulincer, M. (1998). Attachment working models and the sense of trust: An exploration of interaction goals and affect regulation. *Journal of Personality and Social Psychology, 74,* 1209–1224.

Miller, G. (2000). Evolution of human music through sexual selection. In N. L. Wallin, B. Merker, & S. Brown (Eds.), *The origins of music* (pp. 329–360). Cambridge, MA: MIT Press.

Monetoliva, A., & Garcia-Martinez, J. M. A. (2005). Adult attachment style and its effect on the quality of romantic relationships in Spanish students. *Journal of Social Psychology, 145,* 745–747.

Montoya, R. (2008). I'm hot, so I'd say you're not: The influence of objective physical attractiveness on mate selection. *Personality and Social Psychology Bulletin, 34,* 1315–1331.

Montoya, R. M., Horton, R. S., & Kirchner, J. (2008). Is actual similarity necessary for attraction? A meta-analysis of actual and perceived similarity. *Journal of Social and Personal Relationships, 25,* 889–922.

Moody, E. J. (2001). Internet use and its relationship to loneliness. *CyberPsychology and Behavior, 4,* 393–401.

Nichols, K. A. (1974). Severe social anxiety. *British Journal of Medical Psychology, 74,* 301–306.

Noor, F., & Evans, D. C. (2003). The effect of facial symmetry on perceptions of personality and attractiveness. *Journal of Research in Personality, 37,* 339–347.

Over, R., & Phillips, G. (1997). Differences between men and women in age preferences for a same-sex partner. *Behavioral and Brain Sciences, 20,* 138–140.

Paul, A. (2014). Is online better than offline for meeting partners? Depends: Are you looking to marry or to date? *Cyberpsychology, Behavior & Social Networking, 17,* 664–667.

Peplau, L. A., & Perlman, D. (1982). Perspectives on loneliness. In L. A. Peplau & D. Perlman (Eds.), *Loneliness: A source-book of current theory research, and therapy* (pp. 1–18). New York: Wiley.

Perrett, D. L., & Penton-Voak, I. (1999, February 25). Reply. *Nature,* 397, 661.

Regan, P. (1998). What if you can't get what you want? Willingness to compromise ideal mate selection standards as a function of sex, mate value, and relationship context. *Personality and Social Psychology, 24,* 1294–1303.

Regan, P. C., Durvasula, R., Howell, L., Ureno, O., & Rea, M. (2004). Gender, ethnicity, and the timing of first sexual and romantic experiences. *Social Behavior and Personality, 32,* 667–676.

Regan, P. C., Kocan, E. R., & Whitlock, T. (1998). Ain't love grand: A prototype analysis of the concept of romantic love. *Journal of Social and Personal Relationships, 15,* 411–420.

Reagan, P. C., Lakhanpal, S., & Anguiano, C. (2012). Relationship outcomes in Indian-American love-based and arranged marriages. *Psychological Reports, 110,* 915–924.

Reynolds, S., Searight, H. R., & Ratwik, S. (2014). Adult attachment style and rumination in the context of intimate relationships. *North American Journal of Psychology, 16,* 495–506.

Rokach, A., & Neto, F. (2005). Age, culture and the antecedents of loneliness. *Social Behavior and Personality, 33,* 477–494.

Rosenbaum, M. E. (1986). The repulsion hypothesis: On the nondevelopment of relationships. *Journal of Personality and Social Psychology, 51,* 1156–1166.

Rosenfeld, M. J., & Thomas, R. J. (2012). Searching for a mate: The rise of the Internet as a social intermediary. *American Sociological Review, 77,* 523–547.

Ryckman, R. M., Robbins, M. A., Thornton, B., Kaaczor, L. M., Gayton, S. L., & Anderson, C. V. (1991). Public self-consciousness and physique stereotyping. *Personality and Social Psychology Bulletin, 18,* 400–405.

Schiffenbauer, A., & Schavio, S. R. (1976). Physical distance and attraction: An intensification effect. *Journal of Experimental Social Psychology 12,* 274–282.

Schoen, R., & Wooldredge, J. (1989). Marriage choices in North Carolina and Virginia, 1969–71 and 1979–81. *Journal of Marriage and the Family 51,* 465–481.

Seepersad, S., Mi-Kyung, C., & Nana, S. (2008). How does culture influence the degree of romantic loneliness and closeness. *Journal of Psychology, 142,* 209–220.

Segal, M. W. (1974). Alphabet and attraction: An unobtrusive measure of the effect of propinquity in a field setting. *Journal of Personality and Social Psychology, 30,* 654–657.

Segrin, C., Burke, T., & Dunivan, M. (2012). Loneliness and poor health within families. *Journal of Social and Personal Relationships, 29,* 597–611.

Segrin, C., Powell, H., Givertz, M., & Brackin, A. (2003). Symptoms of depression, relational quality, and loneliness in dating relationships. *Personal Relationships, 10,* 25–36.

Senchak, M., & Leonard, K. (1992). Attachment styles and marital adjustment among newlywed couples. *Journal of Social and Personal Relationships, 9,* 221–238.

Shackelford, T. P., Schmitt, D. P., & Buss, D. M. (2005). Universal dimensions of human mate preferences. *Personality and Individual Differences, 39,* 447–458.

Shafer, R. B., & Keith, P. M. (2001). Matching by weight in married couples: A life cycle perspective. *Journal of Social Psychology, 130,* 657–664.

Shaver, P., Hazan, C., & Bradshaw, D. (1988). Love as attachment: The integration of three behavioral systems. In R. Sternberg & M. Barnes (Eds.), *The psychology of love* (pp. 68–99). New Haven, CT: Yale University Press.

Simon, L. (1977). *The biography of Alice B. Toklas.* Garden City, NY: Doubleday.

Simpson, J. A., Gangestad, S. W., Christensen, P. N., & Leck, K. (1999). Fluctuating symmetry, sociosexuality, and intrasexual competition. *Journal of Personality and Social Psychology, 76,* 159–172.

Simpson, J. A., Ickes, W., & Grich, J. (1999). When accuracy hurts: Reactions of anxious-ambivalent dating partners to a relationship-determining situation. *Journal of Personality and Social Psychology, 76,* 754–769.

Sinclair, H. C., & Frieze, I. H. (2005). When courtship persistence becomes intrusive pursuit: Comparing rejecter and pursuer perspectives of unrequited attraction. *Sex Roles, 52,* 839–852.

Smeaton, G., Byrne, D., & Murnen, S. K. (1989). The repulsion hypothesis revisited: Similarity irrelevance or dissimilarity bias. *Journal of Personality and Social Psychology, 56,* 4–59.

Sorkin, D., Rook, K. S., & Lu, J. L. (2002). Loneliness, lack of emotional support, lack of companionship, and likelihood of having a heart condition in an elderly sample. *Annals of Behavior Medicine, 24,* 290–298.

Sternberg, R. J. (1986). A triangular theory of love. *Psychological Review, 93,* 119–135.

Sternberg, R. J. (1988). Triangulating love. In R. J. Sternberg & M. L. Barnes (Eds.), *The psychology of love* (pp. 119–138). New Haven, CT: Yale University Press.

Sternberg, R. J., & Gracek, S. (1984). The nature of love. *Journal of Personality and Social Psychology, 47,* 312–329.

Switzer, R., & Taylor, R. B. (1983). Sociability versus privacy of residential choice: Impacts of personality and local social ties. *Basic and Applied Social Psychology, 4,* 123–136.

Teachman, B. A., & Brownell, K. D. (2001). Implicit anti-fat bias among health professionals: Is anyone immune? *International Journal of Obesity, 25,* 1525–1531.

Tennov, D. (1979). *Love and limerence: The experience of being in love.* New York: Stein & Day.

Thompson, B., & Borrello, C. M. (1992). Different views of love: Deductive and inductive lines of inquiry. *Psychological Science, 1,* 154–155.

Thornhill, R., & Gangestad, S. W. (1994). Human fluctuating asymmetry and sexual behavior. *Psychological Science, 5,* 297–302.

Tian, Q. (2013). Social anxiety, motivation, self-disclosure, and computer-mediated friendship: A path analysis of the social interaction in the blogosphere. *Communication Research, 40,* 237–260.

Toklas, A. B. (1963). *What is remembered.* New York: Holt, Rinehart & Winston.

Tornstam, L. (1992). Loneliness in marriage. *Journal of Social and Personal Relationships, 9,* 197–217.

Triandis, H. C. (1994). *Culture and social behavior.* New York: McGraw-Hill.

Trivers, R. (1972). *Social evolution.* Meno Park, CA: Benjamin/Cummings.

Turnbull, J., Heaslip, S., & McLeod, H. A. (2000). Preschool children's attitudes to fat and normal male and female stimulus figures. *International Journal of Obesity, 24,* 705–706.

Valkenburg, P. M., & Peter, J. (2007). Preadolescents' and adolescents' online communication and their closeness to friends. *Developmental Psychology, 43,* 267–277.

Waller, T., Lampman, C., & Lupfer-Johnson, G. (2012). Assessing bias against overweight individuals among nursing and psychology students: An implicit association test. *Journal of Clinical Nursing, 21,* 3504–3512.

Wang, S. S., Brownell, K. D., & Wadden, T. A. (2004). The influence of the stigma of obesity on overweight individuals. *International Journal of Obesity, 28,* 1333–1337.

Watson, P. W., & Thornhill, P. (1994). Fluctuating asymmetry and sexual selection. *Trends in Ecology and Evolution, 9,* 21–25.

Wegner, D. M., Lane, J. D., & Dimitri, S. (1994). The allure of secret relationships. *Journal of Personality and Social Psychology, 66,* 287–300.

Weiss, R. (1973). *Loneliness: The experience of emotional and social isolation.* Cambridge, MA: The MIT Press.

Wong, M. Mei-ha, & Csikzentmihalyi, M. (1991). Affiliation motivation and daily experience. *Journal of Personality and Social Psychology, 60,* 154–164.

Zebrowitz, L.A., Collins, M. A., & Dutta, R. (1998). The relationship between appearance and personality across life-span. *Personality and Social Psychology Bulletin, 24,* 736–749.

Zebrowitz, L. A., & Lee, S. Y. (1999). Appearance, stereotype-incongruent behavior, and social relationships. *Personality and Social Psychology, 25,* 569–584.

Zebrowitz, L. A., Olson, K., & Hoffman, K. (1993). Stability of babyfaceness and attractiveness across the lifespan. *Journal of Personality and Social Psychology, 64,* 453–466.

Zuckerman, M., Miyake, K., & Hodgins, H. S. (1991). Cross-channel effects of vocal and physical attractiveness and their implications for interpersonal perception. *Journal of Personality and Social Psychology, 60,* 545–554.

Chapter 10: Post-Reading Questions

1. Where do most of your close relationships lie on Sternberg's Triangular Theory of Love?
2. Are you satisfied with the distribution of relationships across those categories? Why or why not?
3. What are your thoughts on the role of physical attraction in relationships as outlined in the chapter?

CHAPTER 11

Interpersonal Attraction

Measuring Your Success

Now that you have run your plan, it is time to measure your success. Was it a complete success, a partial success, or a complete disaster? Let's examine each possibility starting with the last.

A Complete Disaster

Before we accept the idea that it was a complete disaster, let's entertain the possibility that it might have been a partial success. Did anything go right? Did you do what you had planned but just not as long or not as well? If not, did you at least make an attempt? If you made a good-hearted effort, then perhaps you have accomplished something. Perhaps it would be better to label this as a partial success, just for trying, especially if you tried hard. Now, if you didn't even try—if you thought about it, but decided not to go through with it, or if you completely forgot to do anything—then it would certainly be a stretch to call it even a partial success, but that's still not a complete disaster. If you didn't go through with it, the important thing to do is evaluate why. Was it too frightening? Were you too busy? Were you too lazy? Analyzing why can give you the key to the problem and suggest a solution.

Finding the Real Problem

Being "too busy" or "too lazy" are really just excuses. The first is blaming the situation, the second is blaming yourself, but both are probably cover-ups for the real reason: deep down you just didn't want to do it. This is usually due to fear. It might be fear of failure, but it could also be fear of success. In these cases it would be helpful to analyze what is going on in your heart. What would it mean to you if you tried and failed? What would it mean for you if you succeeded? Sometimes our problems (e.g., procrastination, dependency, substance abuse) are ways of dealing with deeper fears or problems, and if we didn't have these negative coping strategies, we might have to face up to the deeper problems. This takes us back to the first step of problem-solving where we talked about the fact that the identified problem is often not the *real* problem. If we found some way to totally avoid attempting the plan (whether we "forgot" or consciously just didn't try), we should probably take a serious look at the possibility that the real problem is something deeper than that which we have been dealing with.

Taking Smaller Steps

Perhaps it wasn't something deeper. Perhaps it was just too frightening to face up to your fear. If your problem was fear of flying and your plan was to get on a plane, the fear might have gotten the best of you. If your problem was lack of assertiveness and your plan was to do something assertive, you might have wimped out when you got too anxious about it. In these cases, you probably tried to take a giant step when you should have started with a baby step. It is not easy to face our fears and confront our anxieties. We need to start small. If getting on a plane is too anxiety provoking, then just sit in the terminal and look at the plane. You want to invoke a little anxiety, but not too much. Sometimes it takes some experimentation to find that window. In addition to exposing yourself to anxiety-provoking situations a little at a time, you also need to learn coping skills and undergo relaxation training. This will give you the tools to endure the anxiety so you can master it. As you slowly expose yourself more and more to the situations that make you anxious, you will start to habituate and the anxiety will began to dissipate.

Avoiding Negative Consequences

Perhaps it was a complete disaster not because you failed but rather because it resulted in a negative consequence. For example, you faced your fear of dogs, but the dog bit you, and now you're even more traumatized. Or you acted assertively, but the other person got defensive and physically aggressive. If we had made a proper plan, we should have set it up so success was likely and negative consequences were highly unlikely. Thus let's start by analyzing the plan and seeing if we could have foreseen this happening. If yes, then we are in a better position to make a safer plan. It will be a little harder next time, but try to take comfort in the fact that you learned a lesson and will guard carefully against a similar outcome. If it was a totally unable-to-have-been-foreseen, fluke occurrence, it might be even harder to try again, but try we must. And perhaps we need to try harder in developing a new plan to rule out the possibility of other fluke occurrences.

A Partial Success!

Even if you didn't completely accomplish what you had planned, if you even partially succeeded, you should view it as a partial success and not as a complete or even partial failure. Once again you need to examine why you didn't completely succeed. Were the steps too big? Did you ask too much of yourself? Was it harder than you anticipated? That's OK. You can make a new plan that adjusts for the difficulties that you met. Make sure the new plan is a little easier and increases the likelihood of success. But at the same time, congratulate yourself for your efforts. Congratulate yourself for trying, for facing your fears, and/or meeting the challenge. Know that the greatest athletes, celebrities, and scholars are never successful all of the time. They became great by not giving up when the going got tough. They had to fall. They had to make mistakes. They had to fail a little before they could succeed. It is not about always being successful; it is about never giving up. That is the real key to success! So celebrate your partial accomplishment and figure out how to make your next attempt even more successful!

A Complete Success

OK, before your revel too much over your success, ask yourself honestly if your plan was too easy? Did you challenge yourself? Was it difficult? If not, be honest with yourself and try to push yourself a little harder next time. If it was a real challenge, but you did push yourself hard and manage to succeed, then good for you! Be proud and bask in the glory for you deserve it. Believe that you can face any challenge if you really put your mind to it. In a previous chapter we discussed self-efficacy beliefs and locus of control. If you believe in your own ability to change your life for the better, you are more likely to try. Belief spurs effort, and effort brings success. You've shown yourself that you can do it, so now do it again! Make a bigger challenge for yourself and try again.

Group Assignment

After reading this chapter, discuss your successes and failures in carrying out your plan. Tell your group members what went right and what went wrong. Tell them if it was a complete success, a partial success, a lack of success, or a complete disaster. If it was anything less than perfect, try to analyze why. If it was completely perfect, consider whether you were fully challenging yourself. Then give each other feedback. If your group members are feeling badly about their lack of success, encourage them to try again. If they were successful, congratulate them on their success. If you suspect they are not being completely honest with themselves, challenge them to dig a little deeper. Do NOT formulate a new plan. You will do that next week. This week you should just analyze what went right, what went wrong, and figure out why. Share your experience and show support for each other.

Individual Assignment

Re-assess your group process. How well is your group functioning? Why or why not? What role has each member played in its facilitation or hindrance? Have you given them feedback on how they are helping or hurting? If not, why not? How does this group fit the model proposed in the first reading for this course?

The Weekly Reading

Pre-Reading Questions

The reading for this chapter is the second half of the chapter you have been reading on close relationships, both romantic ones and friendships.

1. What prompts you to desire a closer relationship with someone?
2. What behaviors do you tend to engage in to achieve a closer relationship?

Interpersonal Attraction and Close Relationships

Kenneth S. Bordens and Irwin A. Horowitz

Dynamics of Close Relationships

We have discussed why people form close relationships and why they form them with the people they do. We turn now to the dynamics of close relationships—how they develop and are kept going, and how in some cases conflict can lead to their dissolution. But what exactly are close relationships? What psychological factors define them?

There appear to be three crucial factors, all of which we saw in the relationship between Gertrude Stein and Alice Toklas. The first factor is emotional involvement, feelings of love or warmth and fondness for the other person. The second is sharing, including sharing of feelings and experiences. The third is interdependence, which means that one's well-being is tied up with that of the other (Kelley et al., 1983). As is clear from this definition, a close relationship can be between husband and wife, lovers, or friends. Note that even when research focuses on one type of close relationship, it is usually also applicable to the others.

Relationship Development

Models of how relationships develop emphasize a predictable sequence of events. This is true of both models we examine in this section, the stage model of relationship development and social penetration theory. According to the stage model of relationship development, proposed by Levinger and Snoek (1972), relationships evolve through the following stages:

Stage 0, no relationship. This is a person's status with respect to virtually all other people in the world.

Stage 1, awareness. We become conscious of another's presence and feel the beginning of interest. When Stein and Toklas first met in the company of friends, their conversation suggested to each of them that they might have much in common.

Stage 2, surface contact. Interaction begins but is limited to topics such as the weather, politics, and mutual likes and dislikes. Although the contact is superficial, each person is forming impressions of the other. Stein and Toklas moved into this stage the day after their first meeting and soon moved beyond it.

Stage 3, mutuality. The relationship moves, in substages, from lesser to greater interdependence. The first substage is that of involvement, which is characterized by a growing number of shared activities (Levinger, 1988). A subsequent substage is commitment, characterized by feelings of responsibility and obligation each to the other. Although not all close relationships involve commitment (Sternberg, 1988), those that have a serious long-term influence on one's life generally do. We noted how Stein and Toklas began by sharing activities, then feelings, and then an increasing commitment to each other.

The first stages of Levinger and Snoek's model give us insight into the early stages of a relationship where people first meet. However, it does not tell us anything about *how* people meet each other, giving them a chance to form a relationship. Surprisingly, there has not been all that much research on this issue. One exception is a comprehensive study of relationship formation by Rosenfeld and Thomas (2012). In their study, Rosenfeld and Thomas studied how people meet each other and how methods of meeting others have changed over time. Figure 11.15.1 shows some of the ways that heterosexual and same-sex couples meet (based on data from Rosenfeld, 2010). As you can see, there are different ways that couples meet, and for some methods, there are striking differences between heterosexual and same-sex couples. Heterosexual couples are

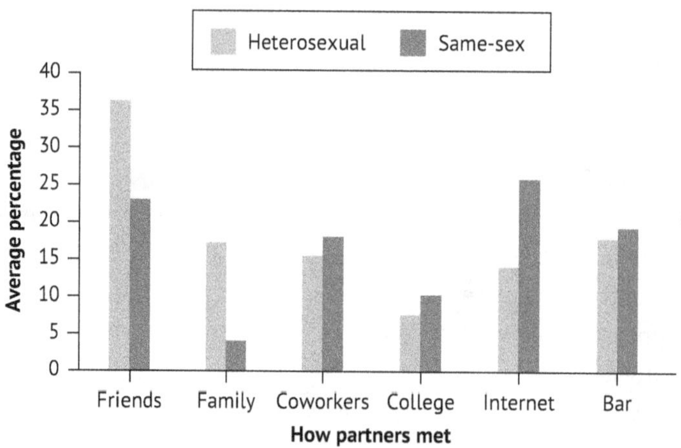

Figure 11.15.1 How couple's partners meet each other (average percent across relationship types). Based on data from Rosenfeld (2010).

more likely to meet through family members and friends. On the other hand, same-sex couples are more likely to meet via the Internet. Rosenfeld and Thomas report that some methods of meeting have shown a decline over the past decades, and some have shown an increase. For example, there has been a decline in couples (both heterosexual and same-sex) meeting via friends from 1980 to 2010. However, there has been a sharp increase in the percentage of couples who meet via the Internet from the late 1990s through 2010, especially for same-sex couples. Further, the gap between Internet use by heterosexuals and same-sex orientation individuals is even greater when you consider only couples who have met in the past 10 years of the study (Rosenfeld & Thomas, 2012). One reason why same-sex orientation individuals use the Internet more than heterosexuals is that the more traditional ways of meeting one's partner (e.g., family, friends, and church) have never been very useful for gays and lesbians. Consequently, they are likely to turn to the Internet because it represents the best possibility of meeting other gay or lesbian partners (Rosenfeld & Thomas, 2012). Interestingly, how couples meet is not related to whether or not they stay together (Rosenfeld & Thomas, 2012).

Once couples meet, their relationship progresses in terms of the communication patterns they show. A second model of relationship development, **social penetration theory**, developed by Altman and Taylor (1973), centers on the idea that relationships change over time in both breadth (the range of topics people discuss and activities they engage in together) and depth (the extent to which they share their inner thoughts and feelings). Relationships progress in a predictable way from slight and superficial contact to greater and deeper involvement. First the breadth of a relationship increases. Then there is an increase in its depth, and breadth may actually decrease. Casual friends may talk about topics ranging from sports to the news to the latest rumors at work. But they will not, as will more intimate friends, talk about their feelings and hopes. Close friends allow each other to enter their lives—social penetration—and share on a deeper, more intimate level, even as the range of topics they discuss may decrease.

Evidence in support of social penetration theory comes from a study in which college students filled out questionnaires about their friendships several times over the course of a semester and then again 3 months later (Hays, 1985). Over 60% of the affiliations tracked in the study developed into close relationships by the end of the semester. More important, the interaction patterns changed as the relationships developed. As predicted by social penetration theory, interactions of individuals who eventually became close friends were characterized by an initial increase in breadth followed by a decrease in breadth and an increase in intimacy, or depth.

An important contributor to increasing social penetration—or to the mutuality stage of relationship development—is *self-disclosure*, the ability and willingness to share intimate areas of one's life. College students who kept diaries of their interactions with friends reported that casual friends provided as much fun and intellectual stimulation as close friends but that close friends provided more emotional support (Hays, 1988b). Relationship development is fostered by self-disclosure simply because we often respond to intimate revelations with self-disclosures of our own (Jourard, 1971).

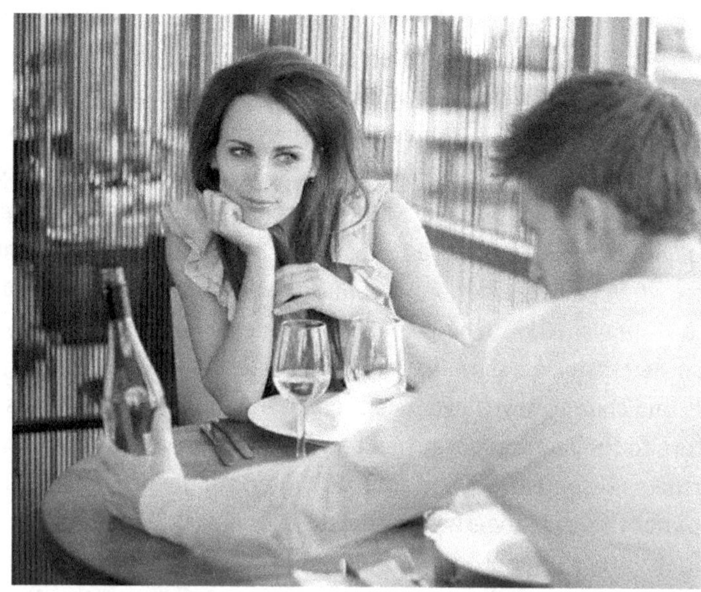

A dating script includes ideas about what a date should be like. Men and women have somewhat different dating scripts.

Source: Jacob Lund/Shutterstock.

Dating Scripts and Relationship Formation

Once people meet one another and enter into a relationship, what ideas do they carry into their relationships? Research on how people perceive relationships has focused on dating scripts. Cognitive psychologists define a script as our knowledge and memories of how events occur. For example, you may have a script concerning a basketball game in which 10 large, athletic individuals come onto a court and try to get a round ball through a hoop. A *dating script* is your concept of how a date should progress. That is, we have an idea about what we expect to happen on a date (for example, a "first date"). These scripts will guide our actions when we find ourselves in a dating situation and are derived from cultural and personal experiences (Rose & Frieze, 1989). Research shows that first-date scripts for men and women have many similarities but some important differences (Bartoli & Clark, 2006). Women, for example, have first-date scripts that are focused on the social interactions during the date. Men's first-date scripts are more action-oriented, which includes things like deciding what to do and when to initiate physical contact (Rose & Frieze, 1989). Generally, men's first-date scripts are proactive, and women's are reactive (Rose & Frieze, 1993). Additionally, men's dating scripts tend to place more emphasis on expecting sexual activity, whereas women's scripts are more likely to emphasize limiting such activity (Bartoli & Clark, 2006).

Recent research reveals some interesting things about dating scripts. First, dating scripts that conform to dominant gender-role stereotypes are seen more positively than those that do not (McCarty & Kelly, 2015). McCarty and Kelly had male and female participants rate a stereotypic (e.g., the man picks up the woman, holds the door open, etc.), counter-stereotypic (the female engaged in the behaviors depicted in the stereotypic date), or an egalitarian (none of the behaviors mentioned) date. McCarty and Kelly found that the stereotypic date was rated most positively. Additionally, the male in the stereotypic date was rated more positively (e.g., warmer, more appropriate) than in the other dating scenarios. Second, dating scripts of deaf individuals show some differences from traditional dating scripts of hearing individuals (Gilbert, Clark, & Anderson, 2012). Gilbert et al. compared the dating scripts of deaf individuals with those of hearing individuals (established in other studies) and found that a sexual outcome was not as strongly expressed among the deaf than among the hearing. In other aspects, however, the dating scripts of the deaf and hearing are very similar.

Culture provides a pretty clear set of scripts concerning heterosexual dating. There are countless movies, books, plays, and other sources of information providing a clear road map for heterosexual dating. The same does not appear to be true for dating scripts for same-sex relationships. There are differences in the dating scripts of gay men and lesbian women. The scripts of gay men tend to be more oriented toward sexual behavior and less toward emotion and intimacy. On the other hand, scripts of lesbians tend to be more oriented toward emotions (Klinkenberg & Rose, 1994). This difference parallels differences seen in heterosexual relationships, where men stress sexual and physical aspects of a date and women stress intimacy and emotion (Goldberg, 2010).

When we move from the realm of first dates and dating in general to more committed relationships, we again see that there are similarities and differences between same-sex and heterosexual couples. We must start this discussion with the fact that there are many more similarities than differences between same-sex and heterosexual couples in committed relationships (Roisman, Clausell, Holland, Fortuna, & Elieff, 2008). However, Roisman et al. report that lesbian partners work together better than partners in other relationships. Additionally, same-sex relationships tend to be more egalitarian than mixed-sex relationships (Shechory & Ziv, 2007). That is, in same-sex relationships, there is more equal distribution of household tasks and more liberal attitudes toward gender roles than in mixed-sex relationships. Generally, women in mixed-sex relationships feel less equitably treated in their relationships than women in same-sex relationships do (Shechory & Ziv, 2007). Additionally, partners in lesbian couples report a higher level of relationship quality than partners in either gay or heterosexual relationships (Kurdek, 2008). As a relationship progresses, partners in gay and lesbian couples show little change in reported relationship quality, whereas partners in heterosexual relationships show a decline in relationship quality that eventually levels off (Kurdek, 2008). Interestingly, partners in heterosexual relationships with children show two periods of declining relationship quality (Kurdek, 2008). Finally, couples in same-sex relationships are more likely to keep a romantic secret from their partners than couples in heterosexual relationships (Easterling, Knox, & Brackett, 2012).

STUDY BREAK

This section discussed how relationships form. Before you begin the next section, answer the following questions:

1. What are the stages of Levinger and Snoek's model of relationship formation, and what happens at each stage?
2. How do people tend to meet one another?
3. What dimensions underlie social penetration theory, and how do they relate to relationship formation?
4. How does self-disclosure relate to relationship formation?
5. What is a dating script, and how do scripts differ among people?

Evaluating Relationships

Periodically we evaluate the state of our relationships, especially when something is going wrong or some emotional episode occurs. Berscheid (1985) observed that emotion occurs in a close relationship when there is an interruption in a well-learned sequence of behavior. Any long-term dating or marital relationship develops sequences of behavior—Berscheid called these *interchain sequences*—that depend on the partners coordinating their actions. For example, couples develop hints and signals that show their interest in lovemaking. The couple's lovemaking becomes organized, and the response of one partner helps coordinate the response of the other. A change in the frequency or pattern of this behavior will bring about a reaction, positive or negative, from the partner. The more intertwined the couples are, the stronger are their interchain sequences; the more they depend on each other, the greater the impact of interruptions of these sequences.

Exchange Theories

One perspective on how we evaluate relationships is provided by **social exchange theory** (Thibaut & Kelley, 1959), which suggests that people make assessments according to rewards and costs, which correspond to all of the positive and all of the negative factors derived from a relationship. Generally, rewards are high if a person gets a great deal of gratification from the relationship, whereas costs are high if the person either must exert a great deal of effort to maintain the relationship or experiences anxiety about the relationship. According to this economic model of relationships, the outcome is decided by subtracting costs from rewards. If the rewards are greater than the costs, the outcome is positive; if the costs are greater than the rewards, the outcome is negative.

This doesn't necessarily mean that if the outcome is positive, we will stay in the relationship, or that if the outcome is negative, we will leave it. We also evaluate outcomes against *comparison levels*. One type of comparison level is our expectation of what we will obtain from the relationship. That is, we compare the outcome with what we think the relationship should be giving us. A second type is a *comparison level of alternatives*, in which we compare the outcome of the relationship we are presently in with the expected outcomes of possible alternative relationships. If we judge that the alternative outcomes would not be better, or even worse, than the outcome of our present relationship, we will be less inclined to make a change. If, on the other hand, we perceive that an alternative relationship promises a better outcome, we are more likely to make a change.

A theory related to social exchange theory—*equity theory*—says that we evaluate our relationships based on their rewards and costs, but it also focuses on our perception of equity, or balance, in relationships (Hatfield, Traupmann, Sprecher, Utne, & Hay, 1985). Equity in a relationship occurs when the following equation holds:

$$\frac{\text{Person A's Benefits (rewards} - \text{costs)}}{\text{B's Contributions}} = \frac{\text{Person B's Benefits (rewards} - \text{costs)}}{\text{A's Contributions}}$$

Rewards may include, but are not limited to, companionship, sex, and social support. Costs may include loss of independence and increases in financial obligations. The contributions made to the relationship include earning power or high social status. The rule of equity is simply that person A's benefits should equal person B's if their contributions are equal. However, fairness requires that if A's contributions are greater than B's, A's benefits should also be greater.

Thus, under equity theory, the way people judge the fairness of the benefits depends on their understanding of what each brings to the relationship. For example, the spouse who earns more may be perceived as bringing more to the marriage and, therefore, as entitled to higher benefits. The other spouse may, as a result, increase her costs, perhaps by taking on more of the household chores.

In actual relationships, of course, people differ, often vigorously, on what counts as contributions and on how specific contributions ought to be weighed. For example, in business settings, many individuals believe that race or gender should count as a contribution when hiring. Others disagree strongly with that position.

Has the fact that most women now work outside the home altered the relationship between wives and husbands as equity theory would predict? It appears, in keeping with equity theory, that the spouse who earns more, regardless of gender, often has fewer childcare responsibilities than the spouse who earns less (Steil & Weltman, 1991, 1992).

However, it also appears that cultural expectations lead to some inequity. Husbands tend to have more control over financial matters than wives do, regardless of income (Biernat & Wortman, 1991). Moreover, a study of professional married couples in which the partners earned relatively equal amounts found that although the wives were satisfied with their husbands' participation in household chores and childrearing, in reality there was considerable inequity (Biernat & Wortman, 1991). Women were invariably the primary caregivers for the children. Men spent time with their children and did many of the household chores, but they were not the primary caregivers. This may reflect a lack of equity in these relationships, or it may mean that women simply do not fully trust their husbands to do a competent job of taking care of the children.

What happens when people perceive inequity in a relationship? As a rule, they will attempt to correct the inequity and restore equity. If you realize that your partner is dissatisfied with the state of the relationship, you might try, for example, to pay more attention to your partner and in this way increase the rewards he or she experiences. If equity is not restored, your partner might become angry or withdraw from the relationship. Inequitable relationships are relationships in trouble.

In one study, researchers measured the level of perceived equity in relationships by means of the following question and scale (Hatfield, Walster, & Berscheid, 1978, p. 121): Comparing what you get out of this relationship with what your partner gets out of it, how would you say the relationship stacks up?

+3 I am getting a much better deal than my partner.
+2 I am getting a somewhat better deal.
+1 I am getting a slightly better deal.
0 We are both getting an equally good—or bad—deal.
−1 My partner is getting a slightly better deal.
−2 My partner is getting a somewhat better deal.
−3 My partner is getting a much better deal than I am.

Respondents were grouped into three categories: those who felt that their relationship was equitable, those who felt that they got more out of the relationship than their partners and therefore were overbenefited, and those who felt that they got less than their partners and therefore were underbenefited.

The researchers then surveyed 2,000 people and found, as expected, that those individuals who felt underbenefited were much more likely to engage in extramarital sex than those who thought that their relationship was equitable or felt overbenefited (Hatfield, Walster, & Traupmann, 1978). Generally, couples who feel that they are in an equitable relationship are more likely to maintain the relationship than those who are less equitably matched (Hill, Rubin, & Peplau, 1976).

Communal Relationships Although the research just reviewed suggests that people make rather cold-blooded, marketplace judgments about the quality of their relationships, it is likely that they also have other ways of evaluating relationships. For example, a distinction has been made between relationships governed by exchange principles—in which, as we have seen, people benefit each other with the expectation of receiving a benefit in return—and relationships governed by communal principles—in which individuals benefit each other in response to the other's needs (Clark, 1986). In **communal relationships**, if one partner can put more into the relationship than the other, so be it. That is, people may deliberately underbenefit themselves for the sake of the relationship.

Love relationships are often governed by communal principles. Clark and Grote (1998) reviewed the research concerning how couples evaluate their relationships, and although some of the results show that costs are negatively related to satisfaction as exchange theories would predict, sometimes, however, costs are positively related to satisfaction. That is, Clark and Grote found evidence that, sometimes, the more costs a partner incurs, the higher the satisfaction. How might we explain this? Well, if we consider the communal norm as one that rewards behavior that meets the needs of one's partner, then we might understand how costs could define a warm, close, and affectionate relationship. As Clark and Grote noted, it may be admirable, and one may feel good about oneself if, having helped one's partner, one has also lived up to the communal ideal. By doing so, the helping partner gains the gratitude of the other, feels good about oneself, and these positive feelings then become associated with the relationship.

One way to reconcile the different findings concerning the relationship between costs and satisfaction is to note that the costs one bears in a communal relationship are qualitatively different than those we bear in a purely exchange relationship that may be deteriorating. For example, consider the following costs borne in an exchange relationship: "She told me I was dumb." This is an intentional insult (and cost) that suggests a relationship that may be going badly. Compare this to a communal cost: "I listened carefully to what he said when a problem arose, even though I was quite busy and had other things to get done." This communal cost served to strengthen the relationship (Clark & Grote, 1998). To state the obvious, there are costs and then there are costs.

Love Over Time

We have talked about how relationships get started and how the partners evaluate how that relationship is going. Now let's consider what happens to relationships over time. What factors keep them together and what drives them apart? Sprecher (1999) studied partners in romantic relationships over a period of several years. The measures of love, commitment, and satisfaction taken several times over the period of the research show that couples who maintained their relationship increased on all measures of relationship satisfaction. Couples who broke up showed a decrease in measures of relationship health just before the breakup. The collapse of the relationship did not mean that love was lost. In fact, the splintered partners continued to love each other, but everything else had gone wrong.

Sprecher's work as well as that of others suggests that intact relationships are perceived by the partners in idealistic ways and that the partners truly feel that their love and commitment grows stronger as time goes on. Intact, long-term couples are very supportive of each other and that makes it easier for them to weather difficult personal or financial problems (Gottman, Coan, Carrère, & Swanson, 1998). For example, couples who support each other during times of stress are much better able to survive periods of economic pressure that tend to cause much emotional distress in a relationship (Conger, Rueter, & Elder, Jr., 1999).

Some individuals are especially idealistic and affirm a belief that they have met the person that destiny provided. Knee (1998) examined the relationships of those romantic partners who believed in romantic destiny and those who did not. He found that he could predict the longevity of the relationship by two factors: One was belief in romantic destiny and the other was whether the initial interaction was very positive. As Figure 11.15.2 shows, individuals who believed in romantic destiny and had that confirmed by initial satisfaction tended to have longer relationships than those who did not believe in destiny. But if things don't go quite so well at first, those who believe in destiny tend to bail out quite quickly and do not give the relationship a chance (Knee, 1998).

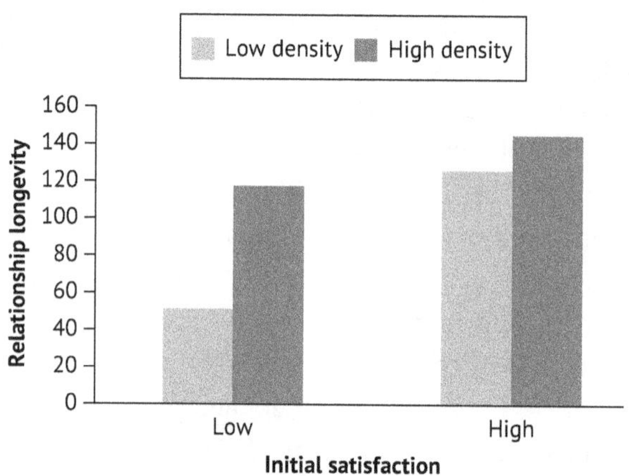

Figure 11.15.2 Relationship longevity as a function of belief in destiny and initial satisfaction with a relationship. Individuals who believed in romantic destiny and had initial satisfaction with the relationship tended to have longer relationships than those who did not. However, when initial satisfaction was low, individuals who believed in destiny tended not to give the relationship a chance and exited the relationship after a short time.

From Knee (1998).

Sculpting a Relationship

So we see that strong relationships are idealized and are able to withstand stresses because the partners support each other rather than work at cross-purposes. How do such relationships develop? Drigotas (1999) and his coexperimenters found that successful couples have an obliging interdependence in which each, in essence, sculpts the other, much as Michelangelo carved David out of the embryonic stone. This Drigotas aptly called the *Michelangelo phenomenon* (Drigotas, Rusbult, Wieselquist, & Whitton, 1999). In a series of four studies, these researchers showed that each partner tended to become more like the ideal self that their partner envisioned for them. In other words, each partner supports the other's attempts to change. This partner affirmation of each other is strongly associated with ongoing, well-functioning couples.

Of course, one reason that successful couples have similar views of each other is that individuals tend to search for people who are similar to them. There are two types of similarity that are relevant to relationship sculpting: actual similarity and ideal similarity. Actual similarity refers to the degree to which partners possess similar traits. For example, Klohnen and Mendelsohn (1998) reported research that showed that individuals pair up with partners of approximately equal value and attributes. Note that this is in line with exchange theories discussed earlier. Therefore, people with positive self-images tend to have more positive descriptions of their ideal partner as compared to those with lesser self-images. Ideal similarity refers to "the extent to which a partner possesses attributes and traits that are part of *(a)* one's ideal self standards, or *(b)* one's ideal partner standards" (Rusbult, Kumashiro, Kubacka, & Finkel, 2009, p. 62). Klohnen and Mendelsohn (1998) reported a significant similarity between one partner's description of the ideal self and his or her description of the partner. In fact, individuals tended to bias their views of their partner in the direction of the ideal self-concepts. Rusbult et al. evaluated the contributions of actual and ideal similarity to relationship sculpting and found that both were involved. However, each contributed independently to relationship sculpting. That is, ideal similarity accounted for sculpting processing over and above that accounted for by actual similarity. Additionally, Rusbult et al. found that the level of ideal similarity in a relationship relates to the longevity of the relationship. Relationships with lower levels of ideal similarity were more likely to end than those with a higher level.

It appears then that successful relationships require that each partner work to affirm his or her beliefs about the other partner. What happens when one partner, say, gets a nasty surprise and learns that her spouse, a competent individual in social situations with people he does not know, is an awkward mutterer with close family members? Certainly, she may be upset and disillusioned. Past research by Swann (1996) has shown that when individuals confront evidence that goes against their firmly held views of themselves, they work very hard to refute or downgrade that evidence. Similarly, De La Ronde and Swann (1998) found that partners work hard to verify their views of their spouses. As Drigotas and colleagues (1999) suggested, we often enter into relationships with people who view us as we view ourselves. Therefore, we and our partners are motivated to preserve these impressions. Therefore, our surprised spouse will be motivated to see her husband as competent in social situations, as he sees himself, by suggesting perhaps that there is something about family gatherings that makes him act out of character.

There seems, then, to be a kind of unspoken conspiracy among many intact couples to protect and conserve the social world that the couple inhabits. The downside of this, of course, is when one of the partners changes in a way that violates the expectations of the other partner. For example, as De La Ronde and Swann (1998) suggested, if one partner, because of low self-esteem goes into therapy and comes out with a more positive self-image, the spouse holding the other in low regard in the first place is motivated, according to the notion of partner verification, to maintain that original negative image. Clearly, that does not bode well for the relationship.

Of course, having negative views of one's partner, as you might expect, is associated with decreased relationship well-being (Ruvolo & Rotondo, 1998). In fact, some people have a strong belief that people can change and, to go back to the example used here, that someone with a negative self-image can change for the better. Ruvulo and Rotondo (1998) measured the extent to which people involved in relationships believed that people can change. They found that when individuals had strong beliefs that individuals can change, then the views that they had of their partner were less likely to be related to the current well-being of the relationship. This means that if you saw that your partner had a negative self-image, but you were convinced that he or she could change for the better, that current image was not crucial to how you viewed the status of the relationship. However, for those individuals who did not feel that it was possible for people to change, the views of their partners were crucial to how they evaluated their relationships. So, if you believed that your partner's attributes and feelings were forever fixed, it makes sense that those views would be crucial to how you felt about the relationship. But, if things could change, probably for the better, well then these negative views won't last forever. Therefore, many successful couples behave in a manner that verifies initial images of each other.

STUDY BREAK

This section discussed a number ways that people evaluate their relationships and how relationships change over time. Before you begin the next section, answer the following questions:

1. How do exchange theories maintain that people evaluate relationships?
2. How does equity theory account for relationship evaluation, and what happens if a relationship is inequitable?
3. What is a communal relationship, and how does this approach differ from the exchange theory approach?
4. How do relationships change over time?
5. How do people go about sculpting a relationship? In your answer, describe the Michelangelo Effect.

Responses to Conflict

When relationships are deemed to be unfair, or inequitable, the result almost inevitably will be conflict. Conflict also can occur when a partner behaves badly, and everyone behaves badly at one time or another. The mere passage of time also makes conflict more likely. Couples are usually more affectionate and happier as newlyweds than they are 2 years later (Huston & Vangelisti, 1991). What happens, then, when conflicts arise? How do people in a relationship respond to conflicts? In this section we shall look at three responses to conflict: developing stories to explain conflict, accommodation, and forgiveness.

Developing Stories

Satisfied couples bias their impressions of their partner in ways that cause idealization of the partner and increase satisfaction in the relationship (McGregor & Holmes, 1999). Researchers have discovered that when satisfied couples confront a threat in the marriage due to something the partner has done (say, had a drink with another man or woman on the sly), individuals devise stories that work to diminish that threat. They construct a story to explain the event in a way that takes the blame away from their partner. The story puts the partner in the best light possible. McGregor and Holmes (1999) suggested that the process of devising a story to explain a behavior

Conflict in a relationship is inevitable. How couples handle conflict can determine whether the relationship continues or ends.

Source: Photographee.eu/Shutterstock.

convinces the storyteller of the truth of that story. Constructing the motives of the characters in the story (the partner and others) and making the story come to a desired conclusion—all of this cognitive work is convincing to the story's author, who comes to believe in its conclusions.

When reality is complicated, a story that is charitable, apparently, can go far in soothing both the offending partner and the storytelling partner (McGregor & Holmes, 1999).

Sometimes, instead of escalating the conflict, couples find ways to accommodate each other, even when one or both have acted in a negative or destructive manner (Rusbult, Verette, Whitney, Slovik, & Lipkus, 1991). Typically, our initial impulse in response to a negative act such as our partner embarrassing us in front of other people is to be hurtful in return. That is, we tend toward the primitive response of returning the hurt in kind.

Then other factors come into play. That initial impulse gets moderated by second thoughts: If I react this way, I'm going to hurt the relationship and I will suffer. What should I do? Should I lash back, or should I try to be constructive? Do I satisfy the demands of my ego, or do I accommodate for the good of the relationship?

Accommodation

These second thoughts, therefore, might lead to an **accommodation process**, which means that in interactions in which there is conflict, a partner does things that maintain and enhance the relationship (Rusbult et al., 1991). Whether a partner decides to accommodate will depend largely on the nature of the relationship. To accommodate, a person must value the relationship above his or her wounded pride. If the relationship is happy, if the partners are committed to each other, then they will be more likely to accommodate. People are also more likely to accommodate when they have no alternatives to the relationship. Interestingly, accommodation may occur spontaneously and very quickly after a negative event. In one study (Häfner & IJzerman, 2011), participants were shown a picture of either their partner's or a stranger's face showing a happy or angry expression. Participants' facial responses to the pictures were recorded. Häfner and IJzerman found that participants responded to the angry face of their partners with a smile within a second of seeing the picture. This finding was limited to participants who indicated that their relationship was strongly communal. An angry face of a stranger elicited an angry response.

Accommodation does not always mean being positive. Consistently reacting to a partner's negative behavior in positive ways may lessen the power that constructive comments can have under really serious circumstances. At times, it may be better to say nothing at all than to respond in a positive way. More important than being positive and agreeing with one's partner is to avoid being unduly negative (Montgomery, 1988). The health of a relationship depends less on taking good, constructive actions than on carefully avoiding insulting, destructive actions (Rusbult et al., 1991).

The way people in a committed relationship handle conflict, in short, is an excellent predictor of the health of the relationship. Relationship health correlates with handling conflict through accommodation, rather than ignoring conflict or focusing on negatives. Research shows a positive association between happiness in a relationship and a couple's commitment to discuss and not ignore conflicts (Crohan, 1992). Those couples who ignore conflicts report less happiness in their relationship.

Couples who tend to focus on negatives when dealing with conflict are more likely to end their relationship. An initial study showed that couples whose relationship was in difficulty tended to express negative feelings, sometimes even in anticipation of an interaction, and to display high levels of physiological arousal, whereas couples whose relationship was not in difficulty expected interactions to be constructive and were able to control their emotions (Levenson & Gottman, 1983). A follow-up study of most of the couples revealed that those couples who had recorded high physiological arousal were likely to have separated or ended the relationship (Gottman & Levenson, 1986).

As should be clear, conflict is not the cause of relationship breakup, nor is the lack of overt conflict a sign that a relationship is well. Rather, it is the way couples handle conflict that counts. Mark Twain mused that people may think of perhaps 80,000 words a day but only a few will get them into trouble. So it is with relationships. Just a few "zingers"—contemptuous negative comments—will cause great harm (Notarius & Markman, 1993). Consider the husband who thinks of himself as an elegant dresser, a person with impeccable taste in clothes. If, one day, his wife informs him during a heated exchange that she finds his clothing vulgar and is often embarrassed to be seen with him, she has struck a sensitive nerve. Her comment, perhaps aimed at damaging his self-esteem, may provoke an even more hurtful response and lead to growing ill will between the two—or to defensiveness and withdrawal. One zinger like this can undo a whole week's worth of loving and supportive interchanges.

Forgiveness

It is relatively easy to see how accommodation can solve conflict in certain situations. For example, if there is a disagreement over whether to buy a new Corvette or how to discipline the children, accommodation would be the most effective method of dealing with the conflict. However, there are events that occur in a relationship that might not be fixed by accommodation by itself. For example, an incident of infidelity may call for more than reaching an accommodation. Clinically speaking, infidelity presents one of the most serious challenges in a relationship and is one of the most difficult to handle in therapy (Gordon, Baucom, & Snyder, 2005). Infidelity is particularly damaging to an ongoing relationship when the transgressor is caught in the act or is discovered through an unsolicited third-party account (Afifi, Falato, & Weiner, 2001).

Given the potentially damaging impact of infidelity on a relationship, how can a relationship be repaired following such an event? One possibility is forgiveness, which makes conflict resolution and accommodation easier to achieve (Fincham, Beach, & Davila, 2004). In a case of infidelity the harmed partner will need to forgive the offender in order to begin the process of healing the relationship through conflict resolution and accommodation.

Most of us have some sense of what is meant by forgiveness. However, in order to study a concept like forgiveness empirically, we need a scientific definition. McCullough, Worthington, and Rachal (1997) define **interpersonal forgiveness** as changes involving a harmed individual showing decreased motivation to retaliate against one's relationship partner, a reduced tendency to maintain distance from the partner, and an increased tendency to express conciliation and goodwill toward the partner (pp. 321–322). McCullough et al. characterize forgiveness as the transition from negative motivational states (e.g., desire for revenge) to positive motivational states (e.g., conciliation) that help preserve a relationship. There are several ways in which interpersonal forgiveness can be expressed (see Table 11.15.1). Which method is used may depend on the nature of the relationship (e.g., married or dating) and the severity of the transgression (Sheldon, Gilchrist-Petty, & Lessley, 2014).

Table 11.15.1 Different Methods That Can Be Used to Give Forgiveness

FORGIVENESS METHOD	DESCRIPTION
Nonverbal	Using a nonverbal gesture to express forgiveness (e.g., a hug)
Conditional	Making forgiveness contingent on a change in behavior (e.g., I will forgive you if you don't see her any more)
Minimizing	Forgiving by minimizing the severity of the transgression (e.g., It really isn't that big of a deal that you stay out late)
Discussion-based	Changing the rules of a relationship, talking about the transgression or expressing emotions
Explicit	Overtly expressing forgiveness (e.g., stating "I forgive you")

Source: Sheldon, Gilchrist-Petty, & Lessley (2014).

As you might expect, a wronged partner's likelihood of forgiving his or her transgressing partner relates to the severity of the transgression. The more severe the transgression, the less likely forgiveness will be given (Fincham, Jackson, & Beach, 2005). The more severe the transgression, the less likely it is that the nonverbal and minimizing methods of forgiveness will be used (Sheldon, Gilchrist-Petty, & Lessley, 2014). Forgiveness is more likely if the infidelity is a one-time occurrence rather than a pattern of behavior and if an apology is offered for the infidelity (Gunderson & Ferrari, 2008). There is also a gender difference in how men and women respond to infidelity. Men, for example, are less likely to forgive sexual infidelity (e.g., your partner engaging in a passionate sexual relationship with another person) than emotional infidelity (e.g., your partner forming an intimate bond with another person) and would be more likely to terminate a relationship after sexual infidelity than after emotional infidelity (Shackelford, Buss, & Bennett, 2002). Conversely, women would be less likely to forgive an emotional infidelity than a sexual one and would be more likely to break up with a partner who engages in emotional infidelity. Forgiveness is also more likely to occur if there is a high-quality relationship between partners before the infidelity occurs (McCullough, Exline, & Baumeister, 1998).

What are the psychological factors that mediate forgiveness for infidelity? Forgiveness is related to whether empathy for the transgressing partner is aroused (McCullough, Worthington, & Rachal, 1997). McCullough et al. report that when a transgressing partner apologizes, it activates feelings of empathy for the transgressor and leads to forgiveness. Additionally, the type of attribution made for infidelity is important. For partners in a pre-transgression relationship that is of high quality, attributions for a transgression like infidelity are likely to be "benign" and arouse empathy, which will lead to forgiveness (Fincham, Paleari, & Regalia, 2002).

Love in the Lab

John Gottman has studied marriages in a systematic and scientific manner by using a variety of instruments to observe volunteer couples who agree to live in an apartment that is wired and to have their behavior observed and recorded. Results of research from what is known as the "love lab" suggest that there are three kinds of stable marriages (Gottman, 1995). The first type is the *conflict avoiding couple,* who survive by accentuating the positive and simply ignoring the negative; the second type is the *volatile couple,* who are passionate in everything they do, even fighting. Last is the *validating couple,* who listen carefully to each other, compromise, and reconcile differences (Gottman, 1995). All these styles work because the bottom line is that each style promotes behavior that most of the time is positive. What happens if partners in a relationship are mismatched for their styles? For example, what would happen if one person has a volatile style and the other an avoiding style? When mismatches occur, it does not bode well for the relationship, especially if one partner is volatile and the other is avoiding (Busby & Hollman, 2009). With this type of mismatch, partners are less satisfied with their relationship, experience more conflict, and are more likely to experience stonewalling (see next paragraph) than are matched or other mismatched couples (Busby & Hollman, 2009).

Gottman and Levenson (2002) have also found that the manner in which emotion is expressed in a marriage relates to how long a marriage lasts before divorce. Marriages with high levels of unregulated, volatile expressions of emotion (positive or negative) are shorter than those in which emotion is more neutral.

Gottman has been able to predict with uncanny accuracy the couples that are headed for divorce. He has identified four factors he refers to as the **four horsemen of the apocalypse.** These four factors are: complaining/criticizing, contempt, defensiveness, and withdrawal from social interaction (stonewalling). The last factor is the most destructive to a relationship and is a very reliable predictor of which couples divorce. There is no answer to stonewalling, but it means that communication has ceased and one partner is in the process of ostracizing the other by refusing to talk. Gottman suggested that there is a cascading relationship between the four horsemen of the apocalypse. Criticism may lead to contempt, which may lead to defensiveness and finally to stonewalling. The seeds of trouble in a marriage may be present very early in the marriage. Carrère and Gottman (1999) had newlywed couples discuss an instance of conflict that occurred in their marriages. They videotaped and analyzed how the couples interacted concerning the conflict. Carrère and Gottman found that couples who expressed negative emotion in the first three minutes of their conversation were more likely to divorce six years later than those who expressed positive emotion.

Most happy couples do not refuse to talk. Indeed, Gottman's observations in the love lab suggest that these partners make lots of attempts to repair a dispute to make sure the argument does not spiral out of control. These repair attempts, reaching out to the other, also include humor that works to defuse anger. Gottman (1995) noted that most marital problems are not easy to resolve. But happy couples realize that their relationship is more important than satisfying their own preferences and idiosyncrasies. For example, one spouse may be a "morning" person and the other is not. So when this couple goes on trips, they compromise. The "morning" person is willing to wait a bit later to start the day, and the "night" person is willing to wake up a bit earlier.

STUDY BREAK

This section introduced conflict in relationships and how conflict can be handled when it occurs. Before you begin the next section, answer the following questions:

1. How do couples use stories to handle conflict?
2. What is the accommodation process, and when is it most likely to be successful in reducing conflict?
3. How is interpersonal forgiveness used in cases of relationship infidelity, and when is it most likely to be successful?
4. What are the marriage styles described by Gottman, and how do they relate to the success or failure of a marriage?
5. What are the four horsemen of the apocalypse, and how do they relate to divorce?

Friendships

According to Sternberg's definition mentioned earlier, liking involves intimacy without passion. Given that liking involves intimacy, does liking lead to romantic loving? The answer to this question appears to be no. Liking evidently leads only to liking. It is as if the two states—liking and loving—are on different tracks (Berscheid, 1988). People may be fond of each other and may go out together for a long time without their affection ever quite ripening into romantic love. Can we say, then, that liking and loving are basically different?

Rubin (1970, 1973) thought that liking and loving were indeed essentially different. He constructed two separate measures, a liking scale and a loving scale, to explore the issue systematically. He found that although both friends and lovers were rated high on the liking scale, only lovers were rated high on the loving scale. Moreover, separate observations revealed that dating couples who gave each other high scores on the loving scale tended more than others to engage in such loving actions as gazing into each other's eyes and holding hands. A follow-up study found that these couples were more likely to have maintained the relationship than were those whose ratings on the loving scale were lower. Therefore, according to Rubin, we may like our lovers, but we do not generally love those we like, at least with the passion we feel toward our lovers.

However, even if liking and (romantic) loving are conceptually different, this does not necessarily mean that friendship does not involve love or that some of the same motives that drive romantic relationships are absent in long-term friendships. The friendships that we form during our lives can be loving and intimate and passionate. Baumeister and Bratslavsky (1999) suggested that passion can be just as strong in friendships except that the sexual component may be absent for a variety of reasons, the most obvious one being that the gender of the friend is wrong. The history of a friendship ought not to differ very much from that of a romantic relationship. When two individuals become friends, they experience attraction and affection and share disclosures and experiences. This rising intimacy leads to an increase in the passion of the friends, absent the sexual component (Baumeister & Bratslavsky, 1999).

Friendships can be either same-sex or cross-sex. Cross-sex friendships, of course, comprise a male and female friend. Although many people maintain both types of friendships, for most people same-sex friendships are more numerous than cross-sex friendships (O'Meara, 2006). O'Meara also found that men and women report having about the same number of cross-sex friends. Both same-sex and cross-sex relationships have their challenges. However, cross-sex relationships pose challenges not present in same-sex friendships. Cross-sex friendships may be fraught with sexual tension not present in same-sex friendships. Additionally, in American culture cross-sex friendships may not be seen as "normative," causing the friends to have to defend the relationship to others (O'Meara, 1989). O'Meara lists four challenges facing those in cross-sex friendships: determining the nature of the emotional bonds in the relationship, dealing with sexual tension, dealing with gender inequality within the relationship, and managing how the friendship looks to others. The good news is, however, that most people in cross-sex friendships successfully manage these problems and they become major issues in only a small percentage of cross-sex friendships (Monsour, Harris, Kurzweil, & Beard, 1994).

Gender Differences in Friendships

Female same-sex friendships and male same-sex friendships show somewhat different patterns (Brehm, 1985). Males tend to engage in activities together, whereas females tend to share their emotional lives. Richard and Don may play basketball twice a week, and while playing, they may talk about their problems and feelings, but that is not their purpose in getting together. Karen and Teri may have lunch twice a week with the express purpose of sharing their problems and feelings. Men live their friendships side by side; women live them face to face (Hendrick 1988; Wright, 1982).

The degree of this difference may be diminishing. In the last few decades, there has been a marked increase in the importance both men and women assign to personal intimacy as a source of fulfillment (McAdams, 1989). In fact, both men and women see self-disclosure as an important component in an intimate friendship. It is just that men may be less likely to express intimacy via self-disclosure (Fehr, 2004). Some research suggests that men and women self-disclose with equal frequency and perhaps intensity (Prager, Fuller, & Gonzalez, 1989). Additionally, both males and females place greater weight on the "communal" nature of friendship (i.e., friendship involving interpersonal closeness, intimacy, and trust) over the "agentic" nature (e.g., enhancing social status) of friendship (Zarbatany, Conley, & Pepper, 2004).

Men and women report having about the same number of close friends. Women tend to view their close friends as more important than men do, but men's close friendships may last longer than women's (Fiebert & Wright, 1989). Men typically distinguish between same-sex and cross-sex friendships. For men, cross-sex bonds offer the opportunity for more self-disclosure and emotional attachment. Men generally obtain more acceptance and intimacy from their female friends than from their male friends (Duck, 1988). However, for heterosexual men, cross-sex relationships are often permeated with sexual tension (Rawlins, 1992).

Women, in comparison, do not sharply distinguish among their friendships with males and females. They also see differences in their feelings for the various men in their lives. Some of their relationships with men are full of sexual tension, whereas other men may be liked, even loved, but sexual tension may be absent in those relationships.

Greater levels of interaction with females are associated with fewer episodes of loneliness for both men and women. Why? Interactions with women are infused with disclosure, intimacy, and satisfaction, and all these act as buffers against loneliness (Wheeler, Reis, & Nezlek, 1983). Women seem to make better friends than men do. It is telling that married men, when asked to name their best friend, are likely to name their wives. The expectations women have for friendship are often not satisfied by their spouse, and they tend to have at least one female friend in whom they confide (Oliker, 1989).

Friendships over the Life Cycle

Friendships are important throughout the life cycle. But they also change somewhat in relation to the stage of the life cycle and to factors in the individual's life. Sharing and intimacy begin to characterize friendships in early adolescence, as a result of an increasing ability to understand the thoughts and feelings of others. Girls have more intimate friendships in their early adolescent years than boys do, and this tends to remain true throughout life (Rawlins, 1992).

Why are boys less intimate than girls with same-sex friends? The reason might be that girls trust their friends more than boys do (Berndt, 1992). Girls tend to listen to their friends and protect their friends' feelings, whereas boys tend to tease or embarrass their friends when the opportunity arises. The more intimate the adolescent friendships, the more loyal and supportive they are. However, disloyalty and lack of support can sometimes result from pressure to conform to the peer group. Of course, these issues are not unique to adolescent friendships. Conflicts between intimacy and social pressure simply take on different forms as people get older (Berndt, 1992).

As individuals move into early and middle adulthood, the end of a marriage or other long-term intimate relationship can profoundly affect the pattern of a couple's friendships. When a woman experiences the breakup of a relationship, her friends rally around and support her (Oliker, 1989). Often, the couple's close friends will have already guessed that the relationship was in trouble. When the breakup occurs, they tend to choose one partner or the other, or to simply drift away, unable to deal with the new situation.

In later adulthood, retirement affects our friendships. We no longer have daily contact with coworkers, and thus lose a source of potential friends. With increasing age, new issues arise. The death of a spouse affects friendships perhaps as much as the breakup of a marriage. People who are recently widowed can often feel like "fifth wheels" (Rawlins, 1992). The physical problems often associated with old age can lead to a conflict between a need for independence and a need for help (Rawlins, 1992). As a result, older friends might have to renegotiate their relationships to ensure that both needs are met. Whatever the problems, friendships among the elderly are often uplifting and vital. This is well illustrated by the following statement from a 79-year-old widower: "I don't know how anyone would ever live without friends, because to me, they're next to good health, and all your life depends on friendship" (quoted in Rawlins, 1992).

STUDY BREAK

This section introduced different types of friendships and how they change over time. Before you read the Chapter Review, answer the following questions:

1. How do friendships differ from romantic relationships?
2. What are the rewards and challenges of same-sex and cross-sex friendships?
3. How does gender relate to friendships?
4. How do friendships change over the course of the life cycle?

Gertrude and Alice Revisited

Stein and Toklas are important because of their role in the vibrant literary world of Paris just after the end of World War I, a period that lasted well into the 1930s. However, aside from their historical importance, the relationship of these two individuals reflects and exemplifies the basic characteristics of close relationships. We saw how the need for intimacy overcame Alice's very strong feelings of social anxiety. Their relationship changed over time, of course, ending, finally, in a companionate one. However, they touched all the vertices of Sternberg's triangle of love: intimacy, passion, and commitment.

Chapter Review

1 What is a close relationship?
The essence of a close relationship is intimacy, friendship, sharing, and love between two people.

2 What are the roots of interpersonal attraction and close relationships?
Human beings possess positive social motives—the need for affiliation (the desire to establish and maintain rewarding interpersonal relationships) and the need for intimacy (the desire for close and affectionate relationships)—which influence us to seek fulfilling relationships. There are, however, motives that may inhibit the formation of social relationships, particularly loneliness and social anxiety, which arise because of a person's expectation of negative encounters with and evaluations from others. Another important factor in interpersonal attraction and close relationships is our earliest interaction with our primary caregiver, which shapes our particular attachment style. Attachment styles are patterns of interacting and relating that influence how we develop affectional ties with others later in life. Each of these styles evolves into a working model, a mental representation of what we as individuals expect to happen in a close relationship.

3 What are loneliness and social anxiety?
Loneliness is a psychological state that results when we perceive an inadequacy in our relationships. It arises when there is a discrepancy between the way we want our relationships to be and the way they actually are. It is not related to the number of relationships we have. The way loneliness is experienced varies across cultures and across age levels. Loneliness has been found to have psychological effects (e.g., feelings of social exclusion and depression) and physical effects (e.g., precursors to hypertension and heart ailments).

Social anxiety arises from a person's expectation of negative encounters with others. A person with social anxiety anticipates negative interactions with others, overestimates the negativity of social interactions, and dwells on the negative aspects of social interaction. Many of these negative assessments are not valid, however. Social exclusion and teasing are major factors in a person developing social anxiety.

4 What are the components and dynamics of love?
In Sternberg's triangular theory of love, love has three components: passion, intimacy, and commitment. Passion is the emotional component involving strong emotions. Intimacy involves a willingness to disclose important personal information. Commitment is the cognitive component of love involving a decision to maintain love long term.

Different mixes of these three components define different types of love. Romantic love, for example, has passion and intimacy; it involves strong emotion and sexual desire. Companionate love has intimacy and commitment; it is based more on mutual respect and caring than on strong emotion. Consummate love has all three components. Limerence is an exaggerated form of romantic love that occurs when a person anxious for intimacy finds someone who seems able to fulfill all of his or her needs. Unrequited love—love that is not returned—is the most painful kind of love. Secret love seems to have a special quality. Secrecy makes a partner more attractive and creates a bond between individuals.

5 How does attachment relate to interpersonal relationships?
During infancy, humans form attachments to their primary caregivers. These early attachments evolve into working models, which are ideas about what is expected to happen in a relationship. Working models transfer from relationship to relationship. Individuals with a secure attachment style characterized their lovers as happy, friendly, and trusting and said that they and their partner were tolerant of each other's faults. Those with an avoidant attachment style were afraid of intimacy, experienced roller-coaster emotional swings, and were constantly jealous. An anxious-ambivalent style is associated with extreme sexual attraction coupled with extreme jealousy. The ways in which we respond to our earliest caregivers may indeed last a lifetime and are used when we enter adult romantic relationships.

6 How does interpersonal attraction develop?
Several factors influence the development of interpersonal attraction. The physical proximity effect is an initially important determinant of potential attraction. The importance of proximity can be partly accounted for by the mere exposure effect, which suggests that repeated exposure to a person increases familiarity, which in turn increases attraction. Proximity is also important because it increases opportunities for interaction, which may increase liking. The advent of the Internet as a communication tool has led to a reevaluation of the proximity effect. Individuals who live far apart can now easily contact each other and form relationships. Research shows that Internet relationships are similar to face-to-face relationships: They are important to the individuals involved, they are incorporated into everyday lives, and they are stable over

time. However, face-to-face relationships tended to be more interdependent, involved more commitment, and had greater breadth and depth than Internet relationships. On the downside, individuals who use the Internet to form relationships tend to be socially anxious and lonely. These lonely individuals may still experience negative affect, despite having formed relationships over the Internet.

Another factor affecting attraction is the similarity effect. We are attracted to those we perceive to be like us in interests, attitudes, personality, and physical attractiveness. We tend to seek out partners who are at the same level of attractiveness as we are, which is known as the matching principle. Matching becomes more important as a relationship progresses. Similarity is most important for relationships that are important to us and that we are committed to. One hypothesis says that we are repulsed by dissimilar others, rather than being attracted to similar others. In fact, dissimilarity serves as an initial filter in the formation of relationships. Once a relationship begins to form, however, similarity becomes the fundamental determinant of attraction.

We also tend to be more attracted to people who are physically attractive, which is a third factor in interpersonal attraction. Generally, males are more overwhelmed by physical attractiveness than are females. Facial appearance, body appearance, and the quality of one's voice contribute to the perception of physical attractiveness. We tend to ascribe positive qualities to physically attractive people.

The downside to the physical attractiveness bias is that we tend to stigmatize those who are unattractive and ascribe negative qualities to them. In our society, obese people are particularly stigmatized and are portrayed negatively in art, literature, and films.

There is research evidence that the physical attractiveness bias is rooted in our biology: Even at 2 months, infants attend more to an attractive than an unattractive face. A new theory suggests that attractiveness, in the form of facial and body symmetry, may reflect genetic soundness. The physical attractiveness bias would thus have survival value for the species.

7 What does evolutionary theory have to say about mate selection?
Evolutionary theory suggests that symmetry (physical attractiveness) is reflective of underlying genetic quality. The preference for symmetry in potential mates may be instinctive. Physical appearance marked by high symmetry reveals to potential mates that the individual has good genes and is therefore, for both men and women, a highly desirable choice. Of course, good genes are not enough in a relationship. Successful relationships are long-term. "Good provider" models of mate selection emphasize the potential mate's commitment to the relationship and ability to provide resources necessary for the long-term health of that relationship.

8 How can one attract a mate?
Evolutionary theorists suggest that to attract a mate humans have developed love acts—behaviors, such as display of resources the other sex finds enticing, to attract a mate. Males tended to use displays of resources, whereas females tried to look more

attractive and threatened to be unfaithful to arouse jealousy. Jealousy is evoked when a threat or loss occurs to a valued relationship due to the partner's attention to a rival. Men and women react differently to infidelity. Men are more concerned with sexual infidelity, and women are more concerned with emotional infidelity. Even though men and women use different criteria for selecting a long-term mate (women look for resources, men for physical attractiveness), they have similar strategies for short-term relationships. When looking for a casual sexual partner, both men and women emphasize attractiveness.

9 How do close relationships form and evolve?

Models of how relationships develop emphasize a predictable sequence of events. One such model suggests that relationships develop across a series of stages involving an initial increase in shared activities followed by an increase in mutuality. That is, friends or lovers begin to share more intimate thoughts and feelings and become more and more interdependent.

Social penetration theory emphasizes that relationships change over time in both breadth (the range of topics people discuss and activities they engage in together) and depth (the extent to which they share their inner thoughts and feelings). Relationships progress in a predictable way from slight and superficial contact to greater and deeper involvement. An important contributor to increasing social penetration is self-disclosure, the ability and willingness to share intimate areas of one's life.

At some point, individuals begin to evaluate the status of their relationships according to the rewards and costs derived from them. According to social exchange theory, people evaluate a relationship against two comparison levels: what they think they should be getting out of a relationship and how the present relationship compares with potential alternatives. Equity theory maintains that people evaluate relationships according to the relative inputs and outcomes for each party in the relationship.

If inequity exists, the relationship may be in trouble. However, many love relationships are governed by communal principles, in which individuals benefit each other in response to the other's needs. In communal relationships, one partner can put more into the relationship than the other. That is, people may deliberately underbenefit themselves for the sake of the relationship.

10 How are relationships evaluated?

We periodically evaluate the status of our intimate relationships. Any interruption in the normal sequence of events in a relationship sends up a red flag. Social exchange theory suggests that relationships are evaluated according to the rewards and costs derived from a relationship. As long as rewards outweigh costs, a relationship is likely to continue. However, even if rewards outweigh costs, we may not continue the relationship. We use comparison levels to evaluate the outcomes we derive from a relationship. One comparison level is our expectation of what we will obtain from the relationship. Another comparison level involves comparing the outcomes of the relationship we are presently in with the expected outcomes of possible alternative relationships. If we conclude that alternative relationships would not be better or may even be worse than a current relationship, we will likely stay in our relationship. However, if we believe that an alternative relationship holds out the promise of better outcomes, we may end a current relationship.

Another theory is equity theory, which says that we evaluate our relationships based on their rewards and costs, but it also focuses on our perception of equity, or balance, in relationships. An equitable relationship is likely to be stable, whereas an inequitable one is likely to be unstable. Inequity leads people to try to restore equity to the relationship.

11 What is a communal relationship?
A communal relationship is a relationship governed more by communal principles than principles of exchange or equity. In a communal relationship, individuals benefit each other in response to the other's needs. In such a relationship, partners tolerate inequity. Love relationships are often governed by communal principles. In such relationships, high costs are often associated with relationship satisfaction. Making sacrifices for the sake of a relationship can strengthen the relationship.

12 How do relationships change over time?
Research shows that couples who maintained their relationship showed increased relationship satisfaction. Couples who broke up showed a decrease in relationship health just before the breakup. Long-term couples are very supportive of each other, and that makes it easier to overcome hardship. A belief in romantic destiny (i.e., that partners were made for each other) is positively related to relationship duration. In a sense, successful relationships involve partners sculpting a relationship by inducing changes in each other. Successful couples work hard at protecting the social structures that support their relationships.

13 What are the strategies couples use in response to conflict in a relationship?
One strategy for handling conflict is to construct a story to explain the event in a way that takes the blame away from their partner, showing the partner in the best possible light. This strategy, however, may just go so far to reduce conflict. Couples can also engage in an accommodation process, which means a partner focuses on positive things that maintain and enhance the relationship in the face of conflict. Accommodation is most likely in important relationships and when no potential alternative relationships exist. Couples who handle conflict via accommodation tend to have successful relationships. Dwelling on negativity harms a relationship.

There may be situations where accommodation is difficult to accomplish. For example, in a case of infidelity, accommodation may not solve a problem. In such cases couples may engage in interpersonal forgiveness. Forgiveness involves a decrease in the use of retaliation along with an increase in conciliation. Forgiveness involves a transition from a negative motivational state to a positive one. Forgiveness is made more difficult as the seriousness of a transgression increases.

14 What are the four horsemen of the apocalypse?
The four horsemen of the apocalypse are four steps identified by Gottman that can lead to the breakup of a relationship. They are complaining/criticizing, contempt, defensiveness, and withdrawal from social interaction (stonewalling). The last factor is the most damaging to a relationship and is highly predictive of marital divorce.

There is a cascading relationship between the four horsemen: Criticism can lead to contempt. Contempt can lead to defensiveness, which can lead to withdrawal. Gottman has observed that successful couples take steps to repair a dispute to make sure the argument does not spiral out of control.

15 What is the nature of friendships?
According to Sternberg, friendships are characterized by liking and involve intimacy but not passion or commitment. Friendships are based on an ongoing interdependence between people. There are some gender differences in friendships, although these differences may have decreased in recent years. Both males and females need the intimacy offered by friendships. However, females still seem to view friends as more important than males do, and females make better friends. Interactions with females are more likely to be characterized by disclosure, intimacy, and satisfaction, all of which act as buffers against loneliness. Friendships can be same-sex or cross-sex. Each type of friendship has its own rewards and challenges. Cross-sex relationships may involve sexual tension that must be dealt with.

Key Terms

accommodation process Interacting in such a way that, despite conflict, a relationship is maintained and enhanced. (p. 276)

communal relationship An interpersonal relationship in which individuals benefit each other in response to each other's needs. (p. 271)

four horsemen of the apocalypse Four factors identified as important in relationship dissolution: complaining/criticizing, contempt, defensiveness, and withdrawal from social interaction (stonewalling). (p. 280)

interpersonal forgiveness A harmed individual's decreased motivation to retaliate against and a reduced tendency to maintain distance from one's relationship partner, and an increased willingness to express conciliation and goodwill toward the partner. (p. 278)

social exchange theory A theory of how relationships are evaluated, suggesting that people make assessments according to the rewards (positive things derived from a relationship) and costs (negative things derived from a relationship). (p. 269)

social penetration theory A theory that relationships vary in breadth, the extent of interaction, and depth, suggesting they progress in an orderly fashion from slight and superficial contact to greater and deeper involvement. (p. 266)

References

Afifi, W. A., Falato, W. L., & Weiner, J. L. (2001). Identity concerns after a severe relational transgression: The role of discovery method for the relational outcomes of infidelity. *Journal of Social and Personal Relationships, 18,* 291–308.

Altman, I., & Taylor, D. A. (1973). *Social penetration: The development of interpersonal relationships.* New York: Holt, Rinehart & Winston.

Bartoli, A. M., & Clark, M. (2006). The dating game: similarities and differences in dating scripts among college students. *Sexuality & Culture, 10,* 54–80.

Baumeister, R. F., & Bratslavsky, E. (1999). Passion, intimacy, and time: Passionate love as a function of change of intimacy over time. *Personality and Social Psychology Review, 3,* 49–67.

Berndt, T. J. (1992). Friendship and friends' influence in adolescence. *Current Directions in Psychological Sciences, 1,* 156–159.

Berscheid, E. (1985). Compatibility, interdependence, and emotion. In W. Ickes (Ed.), *Compatible and incompatible relationships.* New York: Springer-Verlag.

Berscheid, E. (1988). Some comments on the anatomy of love: Or what ever happened to old fashioned lust? In R. J. Steinberg & M. L. Barnes (Eds.), *The psychology of love* (pp. 359–374). New Haven, CT: Yale University Press.

Biernat, M., & Wortman, C. (1991). Sharing of home responsibilities between professionally employed women and their husbands. *Journal of Personality and Social Psychology, 60,* 844–860.

Brehm, S. (1985). *Intimate relations.* New York: Random House.

Busby, D. M., & Holman, T. B. (2009). Perceived match or mismatch on the Gottman conflict styles: Associations with relationship outcome variables. *Family Process, 48,* 531–545.

Carrère, S., & Gottman, J. M. (1999). Predicting divorce among newlyweds from the first three minutes of a marital conflict discussion. *Family Process, 38,* 293–301.

Clark, M. S. (1986). Evidence for the effectiveness of manipulations of desire for communal versus exchange relationships. *Personality and Social Psychology Bulletin, 12,* 414–425.

Clark, M. S., & Grote, N. K. (1998). Why aren't indices of relationship costs always negatively related to indices of relationship quality? *Personality and Social Psychology Review, 2,* 2–17.

Conger, R. D., Rueter, M. A., & Elder, G. H., Jr. (1999). Couple resilience to economic pressure. *Journal of Personality and Social Psychology, 76,* 54–71.

Crohan, S. E. (1992). Marital happiness and spousal consensus on beliefs about marital conflict: A longitudinal investigation. *Journal of Social and Personal Relationships, 9,* 89–102.

De La Ronde, C., & Swann, W. B., Jr. (1998). Partner verification: Restoring the shattered images of our intimates. *Journal of Personality and Social Psychology, 75,* 374–382.

Drigotas, S. M., Rusbult, C. E., Wieselquist, J., & Whitton, S. (1999). Close partner as sculptor of the ideal self: Behavioral affirmation and the Michelangelo phenomenon. *Journal of Personality and Social Psychology, 77,* 293–324.

Duck, S. W. (1988). *Handbook of personal relationships.* New York: Wiley.

Easterling, B., Knox, D., & Brackett, A. (2012). Secrets in romantic relationships: Does sexual orientation matter? *Journal of GLBT Family Studies, 8,* 196–208.

Fehr, B. (2004). Intimacy expectations in same-sex friendships: A prototype interaction-pattern model. *Journal of Personality and Social Psychology, 86,* 265–284.

Fiebert, M. S., & Wright, K. S. (1989). Midlife friendships in an American faculty sample. *Psychological Reports, 64,* 1127–1130.

Fincham, F. D., Beach, S. R. H., & Davila, J. (2004). Forgiveness and conflict resolution in marriage. *Journal of Family Psychology, 18,* 72–81.

Fincham, F. D., Jackson, H., & Beach, S. R. H. (2005). Transgression severity and forgiveness: Different moderators for objective and subjective severity. *Journal of Social and Clinical Psychology, 24,* 860–875.

Fincham, F. D., Paleari, F. G., & Regalia, C. (2002). Forgiveness in marriage: The role of relationship quality, attributions, and empathy. *Personal Relationships, 9,* 27–37.

Gilbert, G., Clark, M., & Anderson, M. (2012). Do deaf individuals' dating scripts follow the traditional sexual script? *Sexuality & Culture, 16,* 90–99.

Goldberg, A. E. (2010). *Lesbian and gay parents and their children: Research on the family life cycle.* Washington, D.C.: American Psychological Association.

Gordon, K. C., Baucom, D. H., & Snyder, D. K. (2005). Treating couples recovering from infidelity: An integrative approach. *Journal of Clinical Psychology, 61,* 1393–1405.

Gottman, J. M. (1995). *Why marriages fail or succeed.* New York: Fireside.

Gottman, J. M., Coan, J., Carrère, S., & Swanson, C. (1998). Predicting marital happiness and stability from newlywed interactions. *Journal of Marriage and the Family, 60,* 5–22.

Gottman, J. M., & Levenson, R. W. (1986). Assessing the role of emotion in marriage. *Behavioral Assessment, 8,* 31–48.

Gottman, J. M., & Levenson, R. W. (2002). A two-factor model for predicting when a couple will divorce: Exploratory analyses using 14-year longitudinal data. *Family Process, 41,* 83.

Gunderson, P. R., & Ferrari, J. R. (2008). Forgiveness of sexual cheating in romantic relationships: Effects of discovery method, frequency of offense, and presence of apology. *North American Journal of Psychology, 10,* 1–14.

Häfner, M., & IJzerman, H. (2011). The face of love: Spontaneous accommodation as social emotion regulation. *Personality and Social Psychology Bulletin, 37,* 1551–1563.

Hatfield, E., Traupmann, J., Sprecher, S., Utne, M., & Hay, J. (1985). Equity and intimate relationships: Recent research. In W. Ickes (Ed.), *Compatible and incompatible relationships* (pp. 91–117). New York: Springer-Verlag.

Hatfield, E. H, Walster, G. W., & Berscheid, E. (1978). *Equity theory and research.* Boston: Allyn & Bacon.

Hatfield, E. H., Walster, G. W., & Traupmann, J. (1978). Equity and premarital sex. *Journal of Personality and Social Psychology, 36,* 82–92.

Hays, R. B. (1985). A longitudinal study of friendship development. *Journal of Personality and Social Psychology 48,* 261–273.

Hays, R. B. (1988b). The day-to-day functioning of casual versus close friendships. *Journal of Social and Personal Relationships, 5,* 261–273.

Hendrick, C. (1988). Roles and gender in relationships. In S. Duck (Ed.), *Handbook of personal relationships* (pp. 429–448). New York: Wiley.

Huston, T. L., & Vangelisti, A. L. (1991). Socioemotional behavior and satisfaction in marital relationships: A longitudinal study. *Journal of Personality and Social Psychology, 61,* 721–733.

Jourard, S. M. (1971). *Self-disclosure: An experimental analysis of the transparent self.* New York: Wiley.

Kelley, H. H., Berscheid, E., Christensen, A., Harvey, J. H., Huston, T. L., Levinger, G., McClintock, E., Peplau, L. A., & Peterson, D. R. (1983). *Close relationships.* New York: Freeman.

Klinkenberg, D., & Rose, S. (1994). Dating scripts of gay men and lesbians. *Journal of Homosexuality, 26,* 23–35.

Klohnen, E. C., & Mendelsohn, G. A. (1998). Partner selection for personality characteristics: A couple-centered approach. *Personality and Social Psychology Bulletin, 24,* 268–278.

Knee, C. R. (1998). Implicit theories of relationship: Assessment and prediction of romantic initiation, coping, and longevity. *Journal of Personality and Social Psychology, 74,* 360–370.

Kurdek, L. A. (2008). Change in relationship quality for partners from lesbian, gay male, and heterosexual couples. *Journal of Family Psychology, 22,* 701–711.

Levenson, R. W., & Gottman, J. M. (1983). Marital interaction: Physiological linkage and affective exchange. *Journal of Personality and Social Psychology, 45,* 587–597.

Levinger, C., & Snoek, J. D. (1972). *Attraction in relationships: A new look at interpersonal attraction.* Morristown, NJ: General Learning Press.

Levinger, G. (1988). Can we picture "love"? In R. J. Sternberg & M. L. Barnes (Eds.), *The psychology of love* (pp. 139–158). New Haven, CT: Yale University Press.

McAdams, D. P. (1989). *Intimacy.* New York: Doubleday.

McCarty, M. K., & Kelly, J. R. (2015). Perceptions of dating behavior: The role of ambivalent sexism. *Sex Roles, 72,* 237–251.

McCullough, M. E., Exline, J. J., & Baumeister, R. F. (1998). An annotated bibliography of research on forgiveness and related concepts. In E. L. Worthington (Ed.), *Dimensions of forgiveness: Psychological research and theological perspectives* (pp. 193–317). Philadelphia: Templeton Press.

McCullough, M. E., Worthington, E. L., Jr., and Rachal, K. C. (1997). Interpersonal forgiving in close relationships. *Journal of Personality and Social Psychology,* 73, 321–336.

McGregor, I., & Holmes, I. G. (1999). How storytelling shapes memory and impressions of relationships over time. *Journal of Personality and Social Psychology, 76,* 406–419.

Monsour, M., Harris, B., Kurzweil, N., & Beard, C. (1994). Challenges confronting cross-sex friendships: 'Much ado about nothing?'. *Sex Roles, 31,* 55–77.

Montgomery, B. M. (1988). Quality communication in personal relationships. In S. Duck, D. F. Hay, S. E. Hobfoll, W. Ickes, B. M. Montgomery (Eds.), *Handbook of personal relationships: Theory, research and interventions* (pp. 343–359). New York: Wiley.

Notarius, C., & Markman, H. (1993). *We can work it out: Making sense out of marital conflict.* New York: Putnam.

O'Meara, D. J. (1989). Cross-sex friendship: Four basic challenges of an ignored relationship. *Sex Roles, 21,* 525–543.

O'Meara, D. J. (2006). Cross-sex friendships: Who has more? *Sex Roles, 54,* 809–820.

Oliker, S. J. (1989). *Best friends and marriage: Exchange among women.* Berkeley: University of California Press.

Prager, K., Fuller, D. O., & Gonzalez, A. S. (1989). The function of self-disclosure in social interaction. *Journal of Social and Personal Relationships, 4,* 563–588.

Rawlins, W. K. (1992). *Friendship matters: Communication, dialectics, and life course.* New York: Aldine De Gruyter.

Roisman, G. I., Clausell, E., Holland, A., Fortuna, K., & Elieff, C. (2007). Adult romantic relationships as contexts of human development: A multimethod comparison of same-sex couples with opposite-sex dating, engaged, and married dyads. *Developmental Psychology, 44,* 91–101.

Rose, S., & Frieze, I. H. (1989). Young singles' scripts for a first date. *Gender & Society, 3,* 258–268.

Rose, S., & Frieze, I. H. (1993). Young singles' contemporary dating scripts. *Sex Roles, 28,* 499–509.

Rosenfeld, M. J. (2010). Meeting online: The rise of the Internet as a social intermediary. Retrieved from *http:// paa2010.princeton.edu/papers/100828*

Rosenfeld, M. J., & Thomas, R. J. (2012). Searching for a mate: The rise of the Internet as a social intermediary. *American Sociological Review, 77,* 523–547.

Rubin, Z. (1970). Measurement and romantic love. *Journal of Personality and Social Psychology, 16,* 265–273.

Rubin, Z. (1973). *Liking and loving: An invitation to social psychology.* New York: Holt, Rinehart & Winston.

Rusbult, C. E., Kumashiro, M., Kubacka, K. E., & Finkel, E. J. (2009). "The part of me that you bring out": Ideal similarity and the Michelangelo phenomenon. *Journal of Personality and Social Psychology, 96,* 61–82.

Rusbult, C. E., Verette, J., Whitney, G. A., Slovik, L. F., & Lipkus, I. (1991). Accommodation processes in close relationships: Theory and preliminary empirical evidence. *Journal of Personality and Social Psychology 61,* 641–647.

Ruvolo, A. P., & Rotondo, J. L. (1998). Diamonds in the rough: Implicit personality theories and views of partner and self. *Personality and Social Psychology Bulletin, 24,* 750–758.

Shackelford, T. P., Buss, D. M., & Bennett, K. (2002). Forgiveness or breakup: Sex differences in responses to a partner's infidelity. *Cognition and Emotion, 16,* 299–307.

Shechory, M., & Ziv, R. (2007). Relationships between gender role attitudes, role division, and perception of equity among heterosexual, gay and lesbian couples. *Sex Roles, 56,* 629–638.

Sheldon, P., Gilchrist-Petty, E., & Lessley, J. A. (2014). You did what? The relationship between forgiveness tendency, communication of forgiveness, and relationship satisfaction in married and dating couples. *Communication Reports, 27,* 78–90.

Sprecher, S. (1999). "I love you more today than yesterday": Romantic partners' perceptions of changes in love and related affect over time. *Journal of Personality and Social Psychology, 76,* 46–53.

Steil, J. M., & Weltman, K. (1991). Marital inequality: The importance of resources, personal attributes, and social norms on career valuing and the allocation of domestic responsibilities. *Sex Roles, 24,* 161–179.

Sternberg, R. J. (1988). Triangulating love. In R. J. Sternberg & M. L. Barnes (Eds.), *The psychology of love* (pp. 119–138). New Haven, CT: Yale University Press.

Swann, W. B., Jr. (1996). *Self-traps: The elusive quest for higher self-esteem.* New York: Freeman.

Thibaut, J. W., & Kelley, H. H. (1959). *The social psychology of groups.* New York: Wiley.

Wheeler, L., Reis, H., & Nezlek, J. (1983). Loneliness, social interaction, and sex roles. *Journal of Personality and Social Psychology, 45,* 943–953.

Wright, P. H. (1982). Men's friendships, women's friendships and the alleged inferiority of the latter. Sex *Roles, 8,* 1–21.

Zarbatany, L., Conley, R., & Pepper, S. (2004). Personality and gender differences in friendship needs and experiences in preadolescence and young adulthood. *International Journal of Behavioral Development, 28,* 299–310.

Chapter 11: Post-Reading Questions

1. When intuitively evaluating the quality of your relationships, do you believe you tend more to an "equity" or "communal" style as outlined in the reading? Explain how and why.
2. Looking at your closest relationship, how have your real and ideal selves grown and changed over the course of the relationship?
3. The reading discusses several strategies that people use when their partner engages in hurtful behavior. Which is your typical strategy? Why? Do you believe it is the best strategy? Why?
4. Which of the listed methods of forgiveness do you most tend to use? Do you believe it is the best method? Why?

CHAPTER 12

Managing Emotions

Constructing a New Plan

At this point you have constructed and run a plan, and you have evaluated its success. Based on that evaluation we want you to construct a new plan, so let's review your evaluation and how that should shape your new plan.

If the Plan Was a Complete Success

If the plan was a complete success, the first thing we want to consider is whether your plan was too easy. Did you truly challenge yourself? If not, then perhaps you should make your new plan even more challenging. Find a way to really push yourself to grow.

If the plan was not too easy, but rather you worked really hard to accomplish something, that's great. But you still need to push yourself even harder to continue growing. No pain, no gain, as they say. Find a further challenge to continue to deal with your issue.

If you feel the plan was so successful that your issue is completely solved, then I strongly suspect you chose a superficial issue—a small hurdle, rather than a major obstacle. Can you dig deeper? Can you find a bigger obstacle to overcome?

If the Plan Was a Partial Success

If you only had partial success, then you might want to consider trying the same thing again. But first, you should have evaluated why you weren't completely successful. Do you need to make the plan a little less challenging to insure success this time? Make sure this is a new plan that will be challenging on the one hand, but also make sure it is something you can accomplish with good effort. Be prepared to confront and conquer the obstacles that hindered you the first time.

If the Plan Was a Failure

If you really feel that you didn't even partially meet the challenge, you should have evaluated why you were not able to do it. We suggested three possibilities.

The Steps Were Too Big

If you were too anxious or resistant to do what you told your group you were going to do, then perhaps you bit off more than you could chew. In this case, tone it back. Make it easier. If, for example, you had planned to confront your father but, when the time came, you were too afraid to do it, then perhaps you need to make a new plan where you discuss a different topic with him; choose a topic that is a little stressful, but not as anxiety provoking as the original planned topic. If you are agoraphobic and your plan was to go out to the mall, your new plan might be to walk to the end of the street and back. Having failed your first attempt, you should have a better idea of how much anxiety you can withstand. You want to provoke enough anxiety to make it a challenge, but not so much that you set yourself up for failure.

It Wasn't the Real Problem

One of the possibilities we considered for failure was that there was a deeper problem than the one you focused on. The problem you chose was only a cover for, or a symptom of, the deeper problem. Now that you recognize that fact, it is time to begin dealing with the deeper problem. Your new plan should be a reflection of this recognition.

An Unforeseen Negative Consequence

Did your plan backfire? Did you try to face your fear of dogs only to be bitten? Did you try to be assertive and end up being threatened? Did some other unforeseen consequence interfere with the successful completion of your plan? In this case, it is time to revise your plan to insure that whatever interfered will not interfere again.

Constructing a New Plan

Obviously we cannot address every circumstance that might have happened to each of you, but hopefully you can apply the general framework laid out above to address the specific results of your first plan and to help you construct a new plan. Keep in mind that your new plan still needs to have the same qualities we discussed in formulating the original plan. A good plan is short-term, specific, and attainable.

Group Assignment

After reading this chapter on constructing a new plan, share your new plan for what you are going to do next week to take the next step in implementing your selected solution. Give each other feedback. Ask questions if you are unclear on any part of what someone in your group is intending to do. Let them know if you think their new plan is short-term, specific, attainable, and addresses what happened with the first plan. If you have any doubts, express them. From the feedback you receive from others in regard to your plan, clarify anything they don't understand and feel free to modify your new plan based on what they say. By the end of the group, everyone should be clear on their own and everyone else's new plans of action. Also, based on the last chapter's Individual Assignment, take some time for people to give each other feedback on the group process and everyone's role in helping or hindering the success of the group. Make sure to use I-Statements. Try to keep the feedback constructive, and try to take the feedback non-defensively.

Individual Assignment

Your individual assignment is to run the new plan you created in your group.

The Weekly Reading

Pre-Reading Questions

The readings for this chapter are on managing your emotions.

1. We all have ups and downs in our moods and emotions, but some of us experience more ups and some experience more downs, whereas others vacillate more quickly and frequently between ups and downs. Which best describes you?
2. Would you like to have better control over your emotions? Why?

READING 16

The Mood Elevator

Larry Senn

> *I know of no more encouraging fact than the unquestionable ability of man to elevate his life by a conscious endeavor. ... To affect the quality of the day, that is the highest of arts.*
>
> —Henry David Thoreau

Let me tell you a story about my friend John. I wonder whether you've ever known someone like him.

In many ways John is a lucky guy. He has a wonderful wife, two smart young kids, and an interesting job in the marketing division of a company we'll call Tip-Top Products. In the eyes of many people, John is on top of the world. But as our story begins, John is feeling very upset. He has just left his office at Tip-Top Products at closing time and is on his way home as usual, but he decides to stop for a few minutes at a nearby park to try to regain his composure.

John is troubled because of a conversation he had just a few minutes earlier with a colleague named Fran.

"Say, John," Fran remarked, poking her head into his office. "Have you heard the latest rumor about next year's budget? It's all over the company."

"Haven't heard a thing," John replied. "What's the scoop?"

"Well, it's just a rumor, of course, but the word is that the board is worried about this quarter's profit downturn. They're supposedly talking about downsizing. And from what I hear, your division might be on the chopping block."

John felt a knot beginning to form in his stomach. "Really? Who told you that?"

Fran shook her head. "I'm not supposed to say," she replied. "And it may turn out to be nothing, but I thought you'd want to know."

"Thanks, Fran," John answered. Suddenly his plans for the evening—enjoying dinner with the family followed by a football game on TV—seemed utterly inconsequential. Fears and worries flooded his mind as he left the office.

Now, sitting on a park bench a few minutes later, John thinks about the possibility of being laid off and the dire consequences that could have. What if he can't find another job? Will his kids be able to go to college? Will he lose his home? (A neighbor got laid off a year earlier and had to move back in with his parents—it can happen that easily.) Can his ego handle being fired? How will he break the news to his wife? Susie is such a worrier—and maybe she'll figure he must have done something wrong to deserve being let go. *She'll probably wish she'd married her old boyfriend Ben after all—isn't he a hotshot lawyer by now? And who could blame her? She deserves better than to be hitched to a failure like me.* John finds his mood rapidly plunging from anxious, to worried, to downright depressed.

Then his thoughts turn back to Tip-Top Products. He recalls all the years of hard work he's put in and the contributions he's made to the company's success. How had the bosses gotten the company into this position? And how did they decide that downsizing would be the solution? Was the decision made just to benefit the people at the top? *I bet those fat cats in the executive suite aren't facing any pay cuts—let alone layoffs,* John fumes. His feeling of depression gives way to a sense of resentment and self-righteous anger.

Suddenly he remembers Fran's words: "It may turn out to be nothing." That's true, isn't it? Rumors like this have circulated before and turned out to be just hot air. And Fran is always one of the first to spread the latest scuttlebutt—true or not. John's anxiety begins to lift. Heaving a sigh of relief, he says to himself, *It's probably not true at all! After all, one quarter of bad financial results is no big deal. I bet our profits are going to be back to normal in no time—and the board probably thinks so, too.* He gets up from the park bench and heads toward home.

Strolling through the park, John finds his thoughts going in a different direction. He says to himself, *Maybe this rumor is really a wakeup call for me. I've been trying to work up the courage to leave Tip-Top for the past year and look for something better—like a job at that high-tech startup my buddy Ron just joined. Maybe now is the time to do it.* He begins imagining the exciting changes that a new career path could bring—a higher salary, a bigger office, maybe a company car and a country club membership. Picturing the admiring expression on Susie's face when he brings home a handsome bonus check from his new employers, he becomes quite excited, even inspired. He vows to get to work on updating his résumé as soon as possible—maybe tonight!

John's buoyant mood is mellowed by the sight of two kids, about the same age as his own, climbing on a jungle gym. *After all,* he thinks, *isn't that what really matters—having a family you love?* There's a spring in John's step as he exits the park and heads for home, looking forward to some quality time with his wife and kids. As for the rumor about Tip-Top, that can wait till morning, when he will compare notes with his closest colleagues and figure out what's *really* going on.

***

You may have never had to deal with a downsizing rumor like the one that sent John into a tizzy that afternoon, but I'll bet you've experienced emotional ups and downs like he went through. It's a common, almost universal experience—especially in a world as full of unpredictable, uncontrollable changes and chances as ours. As you can tell from the story, John's emotional ups and downs simply followed his thinking. It's our thinking that takes us on this kind of wild ride in life.

I call this "riding the Mood Elevator"—but you might call it simply the human condition. It's our moment-to-moment experience of life. The Mood Elevator carries us up and down as we swing through a wide range of emotions. Those feelings play a major role in defining the quality of our lives, as well as our effectiveness in dealing with daily challenges.

We all ride up and down the Mood Elevator every day. So wouldn't it be great if we knew the right buttons to push to stay among the top floors? And wouldn't it be helpful if we knew how to make our visits to the lower floors less unpleasant and shorter in duration? Providing the keys that can help you control your rides on the Mood Elevator is the main purpose of this book.

Let's begin by looking at the Mood Elevator and the various floors it visits. The Mood Elevator map is based on my own experience, as well as input from hundreds of groups and tens of thousands of people who attended seminars designed or conducted by Senn Delaney and our client facilitators. In reality, we each have our own unique set of Mood Elevator floors, but most of the levels shown on the map are probably familiar to you—and it's likely you've visited them at one point or another in your life.

Think about your own travels on the Mood Elevator, beginning with your visits to the upper floors. These are moments, hours, or days when we are lighthearted. We are in touch with things we are grateful for in our lives; we feel secure, confident, creative, and resourceful. We are not easily bothered by people and situations and are less apt to "sweat the small stuff." We are more curious than judgmental and are inclined to see the humor in things. We tackle life's challenges with a sense of ease and grace, feel connected to the flow of life, and may even find ourselves able to tap into a source of universal wisdom or intelligence. At times like these, we are operating "up the Mood Elevator," and they are times we are likely to remember with a feeling of satisfaction and pleasure.

But being human means that we spend some time "down the Mood Elevator," as well. These are times when our lives don't look or feel as good, times when we feel insecure and worried. We find we are easily irritated and bothered by people or circumstances; we may feel judgmental, defensive, and self-righteous. Or we may feel vaguely "down," troubled, or depressed. When we are down the Mood Elevator, our emotions may range from quite passive (listless, lethargic, or blue) to very intense and active (resentful, fearful, or angry).

We'll use the Mood Elevator as our map of human experience throughout this book. It is simple and straightforward, and it fits well with my subjective perceptions of how my moods tend to shift. I am not claiming that the Mood Elevator has been scientifically validated; it is simply a tool that I have found very effective in my own life—and many others with whom I have shared it agree.

The Mood Elevator

Grateful
Wise/insightful
Creative/innovative
Resourceful
Hopeful/optimistic
Appreciative
Patient/understanding
Sense of humor
Flexible/adaptive
Curious/interested
Impatient/frustrated
Irritated/bothered
Worried/anxious
Defensive/insecure
Judgmental/blaming
Self-righteous
Stressed/burned-out
Angry/hostile
Depressed

To begin reflecting on the Mood Elevator and its role in your life, ask yourself the following questions:

- Which floors are most familiar to me as part of my normal day-to-day experience of life?
- Which floors most commonly define my temperament? On which floors would the people who know me best most often expect to find me?
- Which floors would I like to visit more often in my life? On which floors would I like to spend less time?
- Which floors do I most often get stuck on when I am having a bad day?
- Which floors do I tend to land on when my mood begins to drop?
- Which floors do I visit on days when I am feeling most productive, creative, and happy?

Everyone experiences the Mood Elevator in their unique way. For me, the feeling of gratitude tends to mark those moments when I'm on the very highest floor of my personal elevator. When I slow down, quiet my mind, and set aside the preoccupations and pressures of the day, I become aware of the gratitude I feel toward my wife, Bernadette, and our five children. The same sense of gratitude wells up in me when my teenage son, Logan, or one of my other kids gives me a hug and says, "I love you, Dad," or when I pause to experience a beautiful sunset that paints the sky with a multitude of amazing colors.

Good things seem to happen to me when I am on the upper floors of my Mood Elevator. I find myself feeling creative and resourceful. Ideas and answers come more easily, and solutions to problems seem more accessible. The feelings of love, hope, patience, and curiosity that I experience make my life richer and enable me to contribute more to my family and friends, to my church, and to my chosen life's work.

In fact, the pleasure I take from my days on the upper floors is what drove me to write this book—and also what enabled me to turn that desire into a reality. When I am on one of the lower floors, creative thoughts don't come at all. Frozen by writer's block, I find it hard to think of examples or stories to illustrate my ideas—and the ones I do manage to come up with appear silly and worthless. By contrast, there are days when metaphors and images come pouring out, as if I am connected to a source of inspiration and ideas greater than myself—some fount of universal intelligence and original thought that I only have to tap into.

One of the warning signs I've learned to recognize that tells me I'm heading down the Mood Elevator is when I notice myself becoming more impatient, more easily irritated or bothered. A minor inconvenience, mistake, or misunderstanding that I would ordinarily shrug off or laugh about seems to get under my skin, provoking annoyance or anger when I'm sinking toward those lower floors.

I am sure you can recall experiences from your travels on the Mood Elevator in your own life. Most people have a natural desire to experience life on the higher floors more often and more consistently. Who wouldn't want to worry less, feel less stress, and be irritated and bothered less often? Who wouldn't want to feel more gratitude, love, humor, and lightness? Who wouldn't want to experience a heightened degree of creativity, curiosity, flexibility, and resilience?

What's more, the benefits of life on the upper floors are long lasting and cumulative. The more time we spend at those higher levels, the better our lives tend to go—because the upper floors on the Mood Elevator are where we function at our best, thinking most clearly, making the smartest choices, and behaving most creatively. Think about it: Which floors would you rather be on when you are trying to build—or repair—an important personal relationship? When discussing a sensitive issue with someone you love? When tackling a complex problem at work? When making an important life decision?

For most of us, the answer is obvious. The higher levels on the Mood Elevator lead to more success with less stress—to healthier relationships, greater personal productivity, and a better quality of life. No matter how you personally define success—regardless of what realms of achievement and happiness are most important to you—the upper floors on the Mood Elevator are a better place from which to parent, to lead, and to build a career.

Just imagine how different your life, work, and relationships might be if you spent a lot more time on the upper floors—and if you knew how to minimize the negative impact on yourself and others from your inevitable visits to the lower floors.

When I talk with people about the Mood Elevator, almost everyone immediately recognizes the concept—yet very few have ever thought about their life experience in this way. That's probably because they assume that the Mood Elevator is "just the way life is," a basic truth of human existence that we can't change and that it's therefore pointless to think about.

It is true that being human means we all spend time riding up and down the Mood Elevator. We all will visit most of the floors at one time or another. But the time we spend at the various levels differs dramatically. Have you ever known someone who seemed to have permanently moved in to the floors labeled *impatient/frustrated, worried/anxious,* and *judgmental/blaming*? On the other hand, have you ever been lucky enough to know someone who was habitually in residence on the floors named *resourceful, hopeful/optimistic,* and *patient/understanding*? The choices we make can have a significant impact on which floors we spend the majority of our time on—and that, in turn, has a huge effect on the people we come in contact with and the quality of our lives.

There's much more to say about the Mood Elevator. The relationships among the different floors can be complex, and moving from one floor to another can sometimes be quite challenging. In the chapters to come, we delve more deeply into the realities of navigating life on the Mood Elevator.

For now, the key takeaway is this: The central purpose of this book is to provide you with some techniques you can use to increase the amount of time you spend up the Mood Elevator and reduce the duration and negative impacts of operating on the lower floors. The principles I share in the chapters that follow have already enabled countless people to spend more time on the upper floors, and I believe they can do the same for you.

READING 17

Pointers for Riding the Mood Elevator

Larry Senn

The happiness of your life depends on the quality of your thoughts.

—Marcus Aurelius

Living life up the Mood Elevator and at your best is based on a few fundamental premises.

Life happens, and it's not always pretty, but we have the choice to make of life what we will through our thinking. The first premise of living life up the Mood Elevator is to understand that our thinking creates our experience of life—and we have the power to direct it as we will.

The second premise is that we came into this world with what could be called *innate health*. That includes the whole system that gives us the ability to experience life through our thoughts and feelings. It also represents a set of built-in, inborn, God-given traits, including the fact that we are naturally loving, curious, and wise. Our innate health represents all the higher levels on the Mood Elevator.

Over time we all develop thought habits and unhealthy-normal thinking that takes us away from our natural state. This is inevitable because our thinking triggers our feelings, and our thinking varies from moment to moment and can be influenced by many things.

The teachings I have shared in this book are designed to help connect you to your innate health—the best of who you already are at your core. In some sense, you don't have to learn anything other than how to access that innate health, but to do that requires an understanding of the role of thought and the feelings that it generates. Only you can learn to ride the Mood Elevator in your own unique way, just as only you could learn to walk, beginning with those first few wobbly steps as a baby.

The pointers in this book will help you do just that:

- Know that at your core you have innate health and the ability to be at your best. This is a very reassuring idea—one you can turn to in times of doubt and anxiety.
- Know that to be human means you will ride the Mood Elevator and visit each and every floor.
- Look to your feelings as your guide to tell you when you are down the Mood Elevator. Carry a Mood Elevator pocket card as a daily reminder.
- Learn to recognize the feelings that accompany any unhealthy-normal thinking or thought patterns, and make them a loud bell.
- Use pattern interrupts to change your thinking and your feelings.
- Feed the thoughts you favor, not those that drop you to the lower floors on the Mood Elevator.
- Live in the world of mild preference—not a world of "have-to's" and "my ways."
- Take better care of yourself and remember to stretch and recover with exercise, sleep, and time off.
- Use breathing and self-awareness exercises to *be here now* and quiet your mind.
- Maintain a gratitude perspective; count your blessings daily and be grateful for life itself.
- Recognize and honor the separate realities we all live in. Be quick to understand others' perspectives and slow to blame or criticize.
- Remember that your thinking is unreliable in the lower mood states, so delay important conversations and decisions; don't act on your unreliable thinking, and don't take your lower mood state out on other people.
- Have faith that when you are down the Mood Elevator, this too shall pass—just like the weather. The sun is always up there; the clouds can obscure it, but they will pass, as will your low mood.

The greatest gift I received as a child was the message from my mother that my natural state was to be loving, wise, and capable—that I was born whole and complete and that anytime I doubted that, it was just an error in my thinking. My goal is to "pay it forward."

My hope is that the concepts in this book can put you on a path to finding that key and creating more love, joy, peace, inspiration, fulfillment, and success in your life.

Chapter 12: Post-Reading Questions

1. Larry Senn offers a list of strategies for attaining better control of the "mood elevator." Which of these do you think you might find to be of the most benefit? Why? To learn more about each of these strategies, you might want to read the whole book from which these two excerpts were taken.

CHAPTER 13

Conflict Resolution

Coping Strategies and Social Support

This week is dedicated to running your new plan. Everyone should be working on their own individual challenge; however, a number of you are dealing with issues related to coping. Even if you have not selected a coping issue to work on, we all can afford to improve our coping skills. In this chapter we will be discussing how we cope, how we should cope, how we should not cope, and how we can help others to cope.

How We Cope

There are many ways to cope with the various stresses we all face. We might try to distract our mind by reading a book, seeing a movie, or doing some meditation or relaxation exercises. We might get drunk or high, we might have sex, or we might pick a fight. We might blame ourselves for our problems and wallow in depression, or we might blame others and get enraged. We might use the steps of problem-solving we learned in this book, or we might get lost in fantasies about better times. We also might turn to friends and loved ones for emotional and social support.

Mapping Your Strategies

Think about the many things you do to cope when you are feeling stressed. Now, take a piece of lined paper and divide it in half lengthwise into two columns. Then divide the second and third columns in half, so you end up with one big fat column followed by four very thin columns. Then put in the following headings:

COPING STRATEGIES	+ OR –	FREQUENCY	POSITIVE	NEGATIVE

In the first column, list all the ways you cope with stress. Put down as many different ways as you can. Don't leave anything out. Once you have completed the first column, look it over and decide if each of these strategies is a positive/good way of coping (e.g., relaxation exercises) or a negative/bad way of coping (e.g., getting drunk). If you believe it is a positive strategy, then put a + sign in the second column. If you believe it is a negative strategy, then put a – sign in the second column. And yes, it can be both (put a + and a – in the box). An example of this might be that you read to distract your mind when you feel overwhelmed, which is basically positive, but often you get so engrossed in your books that you neglect your other obligations, which can be rather negative.

In the third column, mark the frequency with which you engage in each particular strategy. Give it one check for "occasionally," two checks for "often," and three checks for "all the time."

For the last two columns give yourself a score based on the previous two columns. If you had a plus and three checks, you would put a three in the "positive" column and leave the negative column blank. If you had a minus and two checks, you would put a two in the "negative" column and leave the positive column blank. In the case of a strategy that you rated as both positive and negative, your scores would be based on how often it is positive or negative. So for instance, with the reading example I gave above, you might read all the time which is mostly positive, but occasionally it becomes negative when it starts to interfere with other obligations. In this case you might put a 3 in the positive column and a 1 in the negative column as seen in the example below:

COPING STRATEGIES	+ OR –	FREQUENCY	POSITIVE	NEGATIVE
Relaxation exercises	+	√√√	3	
Get drunk	–	√√		2
Reading	+ / –	√√√	3	1
		Totals:	6	3

Then add up the positive column and add up the negative column and put the totals at the bottom of these two columns. This will give you a gross indicator of your relative distribution of positive to negative coping.

The Power of Non-Negative Coping

While it is important to have and use positive strategies to cope with life's stressors, you might be surprised to know that research has shown that it is even more important to avoid engaging in negative coping strategies. In fact the relationship between negative coping and poor psychological adjustment is much stronger than the relationship between positive coping and good psychological adjustment. Of course this is quite dependent on what you are doing and how bad it actually is for you, but we can all benefit by taking an overview of our habits and evaluating their costs. From the chart you have created, hopefully you can see the balance of your positive to negative coping. Use this information to think about some of the strategies you might want to use more often and some of the strategies you might want to use less often.

Social Support

One particular coping strategy that we hope you listed was some version of using social support. You may have written down "talk to my husband" or "go out with friends" or some other way of phrasing that you rely on the emotional support of friends and loved ones. Next we would like you to map out your Social Support Network.

Mapping Your Support Network

Take another sheet of paper and divide it into three columns—one big fat column, followed by two narrow columns—and write the headings as shown in the sample below.

PEOPLE IN MY LIFE	COULD GO	DID GO

Now, list all the significant people in your life. You might start with immediate family members, followed by extended family, then friends, co-workers, teachers, classmates, and anyone else with whom you have regular contact. List everyone you can possibly think of.

Next, go through the list you created and put a check mark in the "Could Go" column next to every person on that list that you would feel comfortable going to for support about a personal problem. It would probably vary depending on the problem or issue, as some people are better resources for certain issues than others, but at this point I don't want you to go to that level of detail. Just as a general question, ask yourself "Is this a person I feel I could talk to on more than a superficial level?"; it doesn't matter whether you have ever done so before or not.

Last, I'd like you to check off in the third column those people you actually have gone to with a personal issue or problem.

Finding Support

The first column represents your social network. It is also your potential social *support* network. Did you include your group members? If not, consider adding them. Some of these other people on your list you may have never considered going to for support, but think about them. Perhaps some of them would be receptive and supportive. And by opening up to them, you invite them to open up to you. You might move a superficial relationship into a closer relationship. And really, can anyone have too much social support? Some people think it is sufficient to have one really close friend that you can talk to about anything. But what if they're not around when you need them? And is it really fair to make someone your 24-hour on-call personal psychologist? It is great if they'll do that for you, but in the long run, you're probably better off if you share the wealth. As we suggested above, not everyone is an expert in all areas. As we've learned in group, there is great benefit to getting multiple perspectives on a particular issue. When it comes to social support networks, size matters, and more is better. Think of ways to expand your network!

Perceived vs. Received Support

Hopefully we are all aware of the benefits of talking to someone about our issues and problems; however, what you might not be aware of is that column 2 (Could Go) is actually more strongly related to good psychological adjustment than column 3 (Did Go). In other words, feeling like you have someone to talk to if you were having difficulties is far more important than actually talking to someone. This is not to minimize the importance of talking out your troubles, it is just that we will use the support system now and then as needed. But just knowing the support system is available is a constant source of well-being. It also means that if you see someone in your life going through a rough patch, you don't have to try to force them to talk to you about it. Just letting them know that you are there (e.g., "If you ever want to talk about it, I'll always be there to listen") can do them a world of good – even if they don't take advantage of the offer!

Emotion-Focused vs. Problem-Focused Support

And speaking of giving support to your significant others, I'd like to make a distinction between two types of support. Imagine a situation where a wife comes home and tells her husband about her difficult day at the office. Her husband, trying to be helpful, immediately comes up with a list of suggestions on what to do to solve or minimize the difficulties. Instead of feeling grateful for the suggestions, she feels hurt. Several thoughts run through her head: "He doesn't understand the severity of the problems. He thinks I can't solve my own problems. He thinks I'm too incompetent to think of those things myself!" Now, imagine instead if his response to her was "You poor thing. It must have been a really difficult day. Why don't you go relax and I'll run you a hot bath and fix you dinner." Suddenly she feels much better, not only because of the nice things he'll do for her but also because he has communicated understanding and empathy. He has validated her feelings. In the first instance he invalidated her feelings; he may not have intended to, but her feelings were invalidated nonetheless. This is the difference between emotion-focused (focusing on the feelings) and problem-focused (focusing on the solution) support. Both are important and helpful, but knowing what is needed and when is even more important. In this course we have focused intensely on helping each other problem-solve, but it can only be effective if it is done with empathic understanding. It is also a personality trait. Some of us tend to focus more on the details of the problem, and some of us focus more on the surrounding feelings. If you discuss this distinction with some of the important people in your life, then you can more clearly communicate your needs. Tell people when you are looking for empathy and when you are looking for solution-finding assistance. Ask them which they would prefer before you delve into the problem-solving phase. Soon you'll start to recognize the cues and you won't even have to ask. It is an important skill for a psychologist to gain, but it is just as important for a friend. As a rule of thumb, start with emotion-focus, display empathy, and validate the feelings before you move on to solving the problems.

Group Assignment

To give people time to run their plan, use group time to discuss coping. Hopefully, after reading the chapter above and doing the suggested exercises, you have learned a few things about yourself, how you cope, how you use social support, and how you might improve in this regard. Think about it and then use the group to share your thoughts. Comment on what others say about their coping styles. Encourage them to follow through on the positive changes they suggest for themselves, and suggest other ways that you think they might improve.

Individual Assignment

By now, you should have run your new plan. How successful was it? If it was not 100 percent successful, why not? Get prepared to discuss your results in your next small group meeting.

The Weekly Reading

Pre-Reading Questions

Conflict often arises when working in groups.

1. How do you typically deal with conflict?
2. Some people are particularly difficult to work with. How do you handle a difficult person? Do you have any typical strategies?
3. Sometimes people get angry with you. What ways, if any, do you have for de-escalating conflict in contentious situations?

How to Resolve Conflict and Defuse Contentious Situations

Verbal Judo and Other Communication Techniques

Scott A. Bonar

When I got out of the truck, I could see the man was extremely angry. His face was flushed, his eyes were wide open, and he approached me yelling insults and threats. I reached out my hand to shake his, but he refused it and continued yelling. The other biologists were in the truck, and people from nearby houses started to gather. They all looked angry and menacing. They were yelling that whatever the government, that is, "big brother," wanted to do to "their" lake was not okay with them, and they wanted us to get out of there right now. We were out of cell phone contact, out of radio contact, and it was important that we work on their lake, because it had the longest-term data set on outmigrating salmon of any small lake in western Washington—a critical component of our study.

The man left his pickup truck and came up to me screaming, "What the hell are you government people doing here? You have no right to bother us! Get the hell out of here! This is a private lake!" At that moment I had three choices: (1) I could yell at the man and the crowd and hope my anger would drive them back; (2) I could get back into the truck and get my crew out of there as quickly as possible; or (3) I could use "verbal judo" to try to smooth out the situation.

What if I had tried anger or the "mad" approach? Here is a likely scenario. I could have said, "Don't you threaten me! What the hell do you think you're doing! As an agency biologist, I've got the perfect right to sample fish in the lake. The law's on my side! Get out of my way, or I'll call the game wardens and get you arrested!" This response may have made me feel considerably better in the short term, because I could vent on the guy and I would not have let him "get away" with insulting me. I may have even made him back off a bit, because he might have been concerned that

Scott A. Bonar, "How to Resolve Conflict and Defuse Contentious Situations: Verbal Judo and Other Communication Techniques," *The Conservation Professional's Guide to Working with People*, pp. 21–47.

I would make good on my threat. However, this would have probably poisoned my relationship with him in the long term. He may have come back at me even angrier. At the very least, even if he backed off at that time, he would have probably felt justified about harassing us over the two-year period we had to work at the lake, maybe with words, maybe by vandalizing my truck. While some in the crowd were angry along with him, others were curious and just wondering what would happen. If I, a government employee, came back at him with extreme anger, it is likely that some, if not all, of the crowd would have felt compelled to defend him. If we would have made good on our threat to call in wildlife agents to get us out of the crowd, we probably would have been humiliated at work by not being able to handle the situation ourselves. We would have also damaged hope of a good relationship between those people and State Fish and Wildlife in the future. Furthermore, agency management would most likely have made us choose a different study site in order to avoid controversy in the future. The anger option could go very wrong, with little chance for success.

The other option I had was to back off, or the "sad" approach. As soon as the man approached yelling, I could have walked hurriedly back to the truck and said, "Let's get out of here!" We could have wheeled the trucks around quickly and avoided the wrath of the crowd. This could have given us the highest margin for safety. We would have avoided further verbal conflict that could have escalated. However, this would have been the most damaging choice for my self-esteem, as well as damaging the respect my crew had for me. It is unlikely we would have continued to use the lake, so we would have lost one of the best study sites for the project in western Washington. The crowd would have lost respect for government biologists, and in future encounters would have learned that meeting biologists with anger and disrespect would be the best way they could get what they wanted. Stories travel quickly among agency biologists, so my social standing in the agency could have also been affected.

Clearly, there are times both the "mad" and "sad" approaches work. If I needed to bluff my way out of a situation that I would not need to come back to, and the body language of the critic told me I could get away with it, a strong counterattack might have been the best approach. If we were accosted by camouflage-fatigued sociopaths carrying assault weapons, the flight approach would have been the option of choice. But for most situations, including this one, there is a third choice—verbal judo. I have found verbal judo (the "glad" technique) to be most effective in the majority of cases.

Verbal Judo

What is verbal judo? Verbal judo is using words to calm down and "disarm" your critic. The technique is analogous to a martial art in that you disarm your critic without running away or getting angry, and you work with your critic to use his or her own strength to solve the problem. Numerous excellent books and articles discuss the procedure.[1] While all have similar steps, I borrow most heavily from the process used by psychologist David Burns.[2]

Understand Your Critic

Before you can help your critic or develop a better relationship with him or her, you need to know from where he or she is coming. This can be done in two steps: ask questions to understand why they are criticizing you, and then demonstrate to them that you understand.

Ask Your Critic Questions to Draw Out the Real Problem

If the person is explaining the problem or venting, you actively listen, asking questions when appropriate to draw him or her out. In his book *Seven Habits of Highly Effective People,*[3] Steven Covey says to listen so you can be understood. This period of questioning and listening allows the other person to vent their anger and allows you to hear their point of view so you can effectively respond. How often have we jumped in to solve a person's problem, only to find out what we were trying to solve was not the thing they were upset about in the first place? Phrases to draw someone out might include:

> Wow, you sound upset. Is something bothering you, and if so, what is it?
>
> I appreciate you being candid with me. Please feel free to keep going.
>
> Can you tell me a bit more?

I had a supervisor at the Washington Department of Fish and Wildlife who used this technique masterfully. At Inland Fish Division meetings, the manager would ask agency biologists their opinions on different matters. All would have a chance to vent and blow off steam, and once this was over, problem solving could begin. I never saw the supervisor lose his temper, even though criticism of management staff and blunt comments were frequently aired by district and regional biologists.

David Burns, in his book *Feeling Good,*[4] suggests that specific questions are most important in getting to the root of the problem. For example, someone might say, "You Fish and Game biologists don't know your butt from a hole in the ground." This is a nebulous criticism that really doesn't tell you anything. You want to ask them specific questions to identify the underlying problem. Therefore, you might say, "Wow, you sound pretty unhappy with Fish and Wildlife biologists. What happened to make you so angry at us?" After this he may respond, "You jerks closed hunting in this area." Now you have a specific concern to address. Here are other examples of what you might say to get specific.

> Criticism: "Jones, you don't seem to get anything done."
>
> Your question: "I can see you are upset, Mr. Crabbus. What did I do that led you to that conclusion?"

> Critic: "You did not turn in the Fiplet Lake Water Quality Report. It was due yesterday." (Here is the underlying problem—now you are able to work to solve this problem.)

Sometimes it takes a couple of questions to draw out the real issue. Keep asking questions until you have something specific with which to work.

> Criticism: "The research unit is a waste of resources and never does anything worthwhile."
>
> Your question: "Wow, it seems like you don't have much respect for the research unit! Why do you feel that we don't do anything worthwhile?"
>
> Critic: "You guys seem pretty cocky and you don't work well with agency geologists." (Here, the geologist shows that they have had their feelings hurt in the past, and you can attack that specific problem.)
>
> Your question. "Thanks for letting me know. Is there something on which you think we didn't work well with you in the past?"
>
> Critic: "Yeah, when you were setting up that meeting to discuss soil management, and you know I am one of the experts in the agency on soils, and I wasn't invited. Why not?" (Now you have something with which you can work. More than likely the geologist has had his feelings hurt because he was not invited.)

It is critical that you actively listen and keep your cool during this period. If you can do this and effectively use the steps below, you can often turn a critic into a supporter.

Paraphrase What They Say to Demonstrate That You Understand Their Concerns

During the understanding stage, paraphrasing, or repeating back to the critic what they said in your own words, is wonderfully effective.

> Critic: "I work and work all day, and the government just wants to bury me in paperwork. How is a landowner expected to keep up with all of this? What a worthless bunch the State Wildlife Agency is!"

> Paraphrase: "What you're saying is that the government paperwork is way too time consuming to fill out, and it is really hard to keep up with all of it—is that right?"

Notice that this is not repeating word for word what the person says to you, which is parroting, and sounds artificial, but is repeating back to them what they said in *your own words*. Here are some more examples:

> Example: "I don't seem to get any recognition from you for what I do. You promised me a raise, and you never seem to deliver."
>
> Paraphrase: "It sounds like you're pretty frustrated because you feel that I don't recognize your good work, and you don't think I follow through on things, especially your raise. Correct?"

By asking at the end of the paraphrase if you are correct, you give the person the opportunity to correct any errors you might have made in paraphrasing his or her concerns.

Sometimes you don't need to ask questions because you are perfectly aware of what the other person is upset about. If this is the case, one option is to simply skip to the next stage.

The Verbal Judo Stage or Disarming Your Critic

Once you know the true nature of the problem, and the person has had a chance to vent if needed, it is time to advance to the disarming stage. There are three extremely effective techniques for disarming your critic and getting his or her to your side. Any one of them can be used individually, or they can be used in combination.

Agreeing in Some Form with What They Say

I knew an older professor who was a court advisor to Judge Boldt in Washington State. In the mid-1970s Judge Boldt ruled on probably the most significant court decision affecting salmon fisheries in the state of Washington. He had the task of interpreting Indian treaties made one hundred years previously to determine who had the right to catch certain segments of the salmon population. Before the mid-1970s the tribes had no special rights over and above those of anybody else. However, Judge Boldt ruled that the Medicine Creek Treaty of 1854 stated that the treaty-signing tribes were entitled to catch 50 percent of the salmon. After the decision, the tribes were allowed to fish for and keep about 50 percent of the salmon catch. This angered the Anglo gill netters who were used to catching and selling most of the fish, and had been doing so for generations. The ensuing controversy surrounding this decision was phenomenal, and my friend told me of many heated arguments. He was a mild-mannered individual who generally got along with people very well. I asked him how he could remain so popular and retain his composure in the face of so much stress and controversy. He said basically that he got along because if someone called him an SOB, he would find a way to agree with them.

Agreement stops a critic in their tracks. They have nowhere to go—the argument is over if you find a way to agree with them! Many of you might say, "No way, the critic's logic is so far off, his points so nutty, that there is no way I could agree." However, below are some examples that show a person, if creative, can agree with almost anything in some form without lying! This is a crucial step because the technique does not work unless what you say back to the critic is truthful. You will see in the examples below that no matter how outlandish the statement, I can always find a way to agree without lying.

Criticism: "Fish and game people are incompetent asses."

Agreement: "You're right; some of them are!"

Criticism: "These hunting regulations are bulls_t."

Agreement: "Many of them could certainly be improved."

Criticism: "All of you ivory tower professors need to start living in the real world."

Agreement: "You're right! I often think I would benefit from additional experience in the trenches!"

Criticism: "Scott, I felt you did a poor job on this report."

Agreement: "There are several parts of it that could probably be improved."

Criticism: "The endangered species act should be repealed."

Agreement: "There are certainly parts that could be improved."

Now let us try some incredibly outlandish statements to show you that you could take this as far as you want.

Criticism: "The sun is made out of snow."

Agreement: "You're correct in that there is a lot we do not know about the makeup of the sun."

Criticism: "Government biologists are just 'New World Order' people with their black helicopters trying to control the people."

Agreement: "I agree with you that sometimes it is incredibly frustrating working with the government."

Some of you might say, "I will not agree with someone when they are talking about nonsense and insulting me." This is certainly your choice. You are correct that you do not have to put up with someone who is abusive, condescending, or just plain wrong. You have the power to decide if you want to use this tool or not. However, using a tool like this can often allow you to work past the areas of conflict and get you to a state where there is mutual problem solving.

Empathy

The second technique for disarming the critic, and equally important as agreement, is empathy. Empathy is not necessarily agreement, but it is demonstrating that you understand where the other person is coming from or you put yourself in the other person's shoes. You can decide to use empathy with or without agreement. Most people just want to know that you understand them. The following examples show how empathy is used in response to criticism.

The Importance of Truth in Verbal Judo

To some people, verbal judo techniques might seem manipulative. However, you are trying to improve your relationships and ability to communicate with others using these powerful tools. Therefore, it is of utmost importance to be *truthful and honest* in all of your communications. A person lying in agreement statements, slathering on false flattery, or bending the truth to get their way might enjoy some short-term successes, but long-term communication with the parties and your credibility will be damaged. If you are not honest, these techniques will backfire. Approaching all techniques in this chapter and in this book with the sincere intent of improving communication between you and the other party in an honest, direct, straightforward manner will provide the greatest benefits.

Criticism: "Government biologists just want to take people's land."

Empathy: "I know just where you are coming from. My uncle (brother, cousin) was a farmer and he was often frustrated by government regulations."

> Criticism: "You guys in the headquarters office don't seem to have any appreciation for what we deal with in the regional offices."
>
> Empathy: "I know exactly how you feel. I worked one summer in a regional office for Smith Office Supplies. The guys at headquarters often didn't seem to understand what we did out there."
>
> Criticism: "I want to camp here for the night. Why are you busting my butt? I'm not hurting anything!"
>
> Empathy: "Hey, I know what you're talking about. It's a bummer hiking all day, pitching your tent, and then being asked to move."
>
> Criticism: "My class has waited six months for you to come over and give us a presentation on water conservation. I'm getting pretty fed up with the delay!"
>
> Empathy: "I hear you. It is so frustrating when you want to plan something like that and it doesn't work out rapidly."

Sometimes it is difficult to agree with a critic, and in these instances empathy alone is an effective technique. A media specialist from the Arizona Game and Fish Department warned me that agreement, used at a public meeting where the TV cameras were rolling, might have an unintended effect. In the interest of having a "sound bite" the cameras might just capture your agreement statement and not capture your actual point of view after the statement. An example might be the following:

> Criticism: "I understand the Arizona Game and Fish Department is stocking jaguars in southern Arizona. Why in the heck would they do something like that?"

See how empathy might work better than agreement in this case:

> Agreement: "The Arizona Game and Fish Department does stock a lot of things, mainly fishes. I want to make it abundantly clear that they have not stocked jaguars."
>
> Empathy: "I know how frustrating it can be to keep up with all of the activities of a government agency. I want to make it abundantly clear that they have not stocked jaguars."

If the cameras catch only "The Arizona Game and Fish Department does stock a lot of things" and leave out the rest, it could leave the impression on the news that jaguars were stocked. Another caution is when someone wants you to say something bad about a third party. Here is another case where empathy might work better than agreement.

> Critic: "Tribal gill netters just want to take half the salmon and waste it. They won't put it to good use like we (the Anglo) gill netters will."
>
> Agreement: "Some tribal gill netters might waste some of the salmon. The judge interpreted that the treaty clearly states that treaty tribes are entitled to 50 percent of the catch."
>
> Empathy: "I know exactly how frustrating it must feel to loose a major part of the salmon catch. My parents were small family farmers, and lost a major part of their livelihood when large agribusiness expanded. The judge interpreted that the treaty clearly states that treaty tribes are entitled to 50 percent of the catch."

If the tribal gill netters or the media only listen to the agreement statement without your later explanation, you could have difficulties. Here the empathy statement might work better and keep you out of trouble.

Don't Criticize, Condemn, or Complain—Use Strokes!

The compliment is a powerful tool for calming down a critic. Using this technique, you compliment the person criticizing you. This can work wonders for calming the situation down and earning an ally instead of an enemy. Here's how it works:

> Critic: "You people at Andrews Consulting are just a bunch of biostitutes! You don't care about the environment, but you just want to make money!"
>
> Compliment: "Thanks for your comments. First, I want to say I am impressed with your level of concern for the environment. Most people wouldn't take the time to come out on a rainy evening like this and express their viewpoint. You are to be commended for your interest and commitment! The reason we took this project is..."
>
> Critic: "Bass angling has always been an important economic driver of our economy. Why in the heck are you guys screwing with the regulations?"

Compliment: "Mr. Jacobsen, you certainly have a long-term knowledge base about this region and care deeply about environment. The reason we changed the regulations is..."

You do not have to invent false compliments when using this technique. *Everyone* does something well. I believe it is better to work hard to identify the person's strengths and compliment those, rather than to make up something that is not true.

Empathy, agreement, and compliments are some of the main reasons that this technique is called verbal judo. By using empathy, agreement, and compliments with people, you are able to immediately get them on your side, in a mutual problem-solving mode, instead of engaging them in a frustrating match of butting heads and trying to prove one's own point.

Abraham Lincoln—Master of the Compliment

Those of us in biology, conservation, or any area of government can often learn from legendary politicians. A master of the compliment or stroking technique was Abraham Lincoln. When someone told Lincoln that his secretary of war, Edmund Stanton, said he was a damned fool, Lincoln said, "If Stanton said I was a damned fool, then I must be one. For he is nearly always right, and generally says what he means. I will step over and see him."[5]

In another instance, Lincoln was to appoint Civil War General Joseph Hooker as head of the Army of the Potomac. Before his appointment, Lincoln heard that the general said both the army and the government needed a dictator. Lincoln could have beat him back down immediately and refused to nominate him. Instead, he wrote him a letter filled with not only compliments, but also advice. He stated "I believe you to be a brave and a skillful soldier, which, of course, I like. I also believe you do not mix politics with your profession, in which you are right. You have confidence in yourself, which is a valuable, if not an indispensable quality. You are ambitious, which, within reasonable bounds, does good rather than harm. But I think that during Gen. Burnside's command of the Army,

(continued)

Abraham Lincoln (continued)

you have taken counsel of your ambition, and thwarted him as much as you could, in which you did a great wrong to the country, and to a most meritorious and honorable brother officer. I have heard, in such way as to believe it, of your recently saying that both the Army and the Government needed a dictator. Of course it was not *for* this, but in spite of it, that I have given you the command. Only those generals who gain successes, can set up dictators. What I now ask of you is military success, and I will risk the dictatorship." Lincoln made his point and the letter reportedly touched Hooker with its fatherly tone.[6] Hooker was later placed in charge of some of the president's funerals, ending with the final procession in Springfield, Illinois. Stanton, although he condemned Lincoln initially, later became a strong supporter. In both these instances, Lincoln kept his cool and his respect, and worked through the problem with stroking to make his point and get an end result with which he was comfortable.

Diplomatically State Your Point of View

Understanding the other person, and agreeing, empathizing, or complimenting the person builds the foundation or "sets the stage" for you to share your point of view. The person should now be more prepared to listen to you. Now in a kind, matter-of-fact way you can state your point and often have it listened to!

Burns[7] points out that there are only three possibilities when stating your point of view: (1) You are completely correct; (2) You are partially correct and the critic is also partially correct; and (3) You are wrong. He suggests the following methods to state your point of view:

You Are Completely Correct

Here, you diplomatically state your point of view. If the person continues to disagree, keep repeating yourself until he or she tires out.

> Critic. "I don't like the fact that you store your microscopes on this table."
>
> You: "I store the microscopes here so they will be accessible to the technicians. They don't have keys to the back room."

Critic. "Yeah, but they should be stored somewhere else."

You: "I understand your concern. I store the microscopes here so they will be accessible to the technicians."

Critic: "Microscopes should not be kept out front."

You: "You certainly show a lot of concern for the equipment, and that's great. I store the microscopes here so they will be accessible to the technicians."

By going over and over on your point, it is likely that your critic will rapidly tire. I'm tired from just writing the above exchange!

Burns suggests that when possible, state your point of view with an acknowledgment that you might be wrong or in some other way that allows your critic to save face. For example, you might be certain the environmental laws state that the person you are talking with has to have a permit to build a dock on her shoreline. Using a face-saving comment you might say, "I seem to recall that the county ordinance states that you will need a permit for this dock, but I might be wrong. Let's check the regulations and see for sure." Then you check the regulations and find that indeed the person needs the permit for the dock. This type of statement allows the person to save face. Allowing a critic to save face when you can is extremely important to their self-esteem and often allows them to comply more easily with any request you might have.

You Are Partially Correct and the Critic Is Also Partially Correct

Here you can negotiate an outcome using the negotiation techniques presented in this book (chapter 6). However, you have already presented yourself favorably to the critic by using the understanding and the empathy/ agreement/strokes portion of verbal judo, which will help you constructively negotiate. For my current position as a professor I tried to get an electrofishing boat to start my lake studies in Arizona. I was negotiating with my future boss, who stated that the program just did not have the money to provide something like that, and hoped I would take the position anyway. I had already gotten favorable replies on other equipment and a higher salary. Instead of continuing to fight for the boat, I stated, "I certainly can appreciate that budgets are tight right now, and I really appreciate that you have worked so hard for a higher starting salary and other equipment for me. I certainly know how tough it can be working though all the government regulations on these things. Thanks very much! (empathy and strokes). I took the position, moved to Tucson, and about three weeks later, my new boss called me up to tell me they raised enough money to purchase an electrofishing boat for my program.

You Are Wrong

Assertively and quickly thank your critic for pointing out your mistake and apologize for any hurt you may have caused. Everyone is human and makes errors, and if you rapidly admit yours when they occur, you can impress your critic and others. During a workshop on freshwater fisheries management, a distinguished professor taught us a method to sample lakes. I spoke up to say I disagreed with the method and voiced my opinion that it was not statistically correct. The professor was very diplomatic but stated that the method was in fact valid. After class, I checked with some of our agency statisticians and found out that indeed the method was valid. I immediately called the professor and said, "Dave, I'm going to have to eat some crow big time! I was wrong about your method!" This admission of error, I believe, impressed the professor and to this day we have an excellent relationship. We are currently involved in a book project together. In addition, he has recommended me to others when other types of projects have come up.

Yes, But...

Here's a tip. When using the agreement strategy, try to minimize using the combination of words "yes, but." For example, "*Yes* you're right, you have modified your report quite nicely, *but* I think there are several parts that could be rewritten." Instead, when it is not too awkward, try substituting the word "and" or do not say anything at all during the transition. For example "*Yes* you're right, you have modified your report quite nicely. I think there are several parts that could be rewritten." Often if you use "but" after agreeing, you just negate the agreement.

Verbal Judo in Action—The Angry Man in the Truck

Now I will relate how I dealt with the angry man from the truck and the rest of the crowd at the lake where we wanted to sample. Following this actual exchange the crowd calmed down and we could continue our sampling. We were able to sample the lake for two years following this incident and made friends with many of the lakeside property owners. One was even a chief petty officer on a submarine who gave my crew and me a tour when the ship was in port! Another worked on antique steam locomotives for a hobby and we got to know him quite well. Immediately following the exchange, one of my research unit personnel was so impressed by how quickly the crowd calmed down; he told me, "Man, I'll follow you anywhere." Two instigators of the incident calmed down and went home, but they were not supported by the majority of the crowd any longer. The instigators said, "You slippery fish—you certainly talked your way out of this one!" While all incidents do not turn out like this, I was very proud of what happened. I did not have to back down, we were able to sample the lake, and the situation did not escalate. Using similar tactics may give you a way to work out of these types of situations. Here is the exchange that ensued.

I offered my hand to the angry man as soon as he got out of his pickup truck. He refused to take it and continued to yell at me. He was calling me and my agency names and was in general extremely angry.

> Scott: "I'm here to listen to anything you have to say, sir" (understanding and allowing the person to vent).
>
> Angry man: "What the hell are you doing here? This is a private lake and you have no right to be here. We don't want you here screwing up our lake" (he went on and on for about a minute or two, and I just let him go).
>
> Other members of the crowd: "Yeah, just what the hell are you doing? What right does Fish and Wildlife have to push us around and do whatever they want to our lake? We don't want you here!"
>
> Scott: "Folks, I can certainly appreciate that you are concerned with what happens to your lake. I definitely know where you are coming from. My mom and dad own a lake in Indiana, and you can bet they have a big say about what goes on there" (empathy). "Why don't you want us to sample fish in your lake?" (inquiry).
>
> Another member of the crowd continued to go on: "Why are you showing up after we told you we didn't want you here? We told you we wanted you to stay away!"
>
> Scott: "I can understand that you're pretty angry that we just showed up" (empathy). "I tried to contact you all time and time again to present to you what we would be doing at your lake. However, none of you would let us come out to talk with you. We finally worked with the folks on this side of the lake, and they are going to allow us to launch the boat over here."
>
> Angry man: "What good would it have been for you to show up and give us a talk? You would have just had your government 'yes men' planted in the

audience to agree with you and would have come out anyway whether we wanted you here or not."

Scott: "Okay, I know you're concerned" (empathy), "but here I'm standing, all alone, and my coworkers are in the truck. I don't have any government yes men here. You can ask me any question you want. Can you tell me specifically what you folks are so concerned about?" (second inquiry).

Other members of the crowd: "We heard about your study. You're just going to sample fish on this lake so you can poison it to kill all the fish that are eating the salmon."

(We have just gotten to the root of the problem—they think our team is here to poison their lake to kill the fish that are eating the salmon. They heard about the Lake Davis incident [see chapter 2] and they wanted to prevent the water in their lake from being treated.)

Scott: "Folks, you are all to be commended for caring what happens to your lake" (strokes). "We're here to investigate what the fish are doing in your lake. We picked your lake, not because we would like to poison it, but because there is a fish trap five miles downstream that can record the number of salmon leaving. Traps are extremely uncommon on lakes in western Washington. We want to find out what is going on with salmon–introduced fish interaction with western Washington in general, not your lake in particular. We aren't government agents in black helicopters. We're more like Marlin Perkins (*Mutual of Omaha's Wild Kingdom*, an old TV show that was kind of like *The Crocodile Hunter*). We're just like you" (empathy). "We want to protect the environment for your kids and grandkids, but to do so we really need your cooperation. Can you help us out? We have the legal right to work on your lake, but I really want to work with you folks, not against you" (diplomatically stating point of view).

People in the crowd: "Can you promise us no one from the State Fish and Wildlife will poison the fish out in our lake?"

Scott: "Again, I certainly understand your concern about having piscicide or some other chemical dumped into your lake" (empathy). "I cannot promise that your lake will not ever be treated for introduced fish. I hope you'll understand it's a large agency, and I don't make policy for it. I suggest that if that time ever comes, and we're certainly not here to do it, you take it up with the agency at that time" (diplomatically stating my point of view).

One person in the crowd to angry man (Bud) and female instigator (Val): "Val and Bud, I can't see any problem with what they are doing. Let's let them go ahead."

Another person in the crowd: "Okay, I guess it was just a misunderstanding. But we don't want Fish and Wildlife treating this lake with chemicals."

Scott: "Okay, I completely understand" (empathy). "We certainly don't have any plans to do that."

Now the crowd starts to disperse. A couple of interested homeowners come over to the electrofishing boat and we show them how it works. Val and Bud then come up to me.

Val: "You talked your way out of this one, you slippery fish. We'll be keeping our eye on you."

Scott: "I wish I could change your mind that we're really not here to do anything to hurt your lake. However, if you have any questions, please give me a call. We really do want to work with you" (diplomatically stating my point of view).

As you can see, there was not a rigid order of (1) understanding; (2) empathy/agreement/strokes; and then (3) diplomatically stating your point of view. While this order often works best, I used whatever communication technique or combination I thought was appropriate when each question or insult was aired. This flexibility allowed me to choose the appropriate strategy depending on where the crowd was coming from.

Communication In Crisis Situations

What if the crowd had not dispersed as easily as it did? Law enforcement officers have developed communication techniques that work under crisis situations. Here we will discuss a few tips from their profession.

Gundersen and Hopper Techniques

In their book *Communication and Law Enforcement*, D. F. Gundersen and Robert Hopper suggest three ways to avoid crises when tempers are escalating out of control.[8]

Cooling Off

This is the extreme action of separating the warring parties. In domestic violence incidents police officers immediately separate the husband and wife to prevent further violence. In barroom brawls, we are all familiar with people separating the two combatants. Separating the parties allows them to "count to ten" or cool off for a while before dealing with the problem. If the crowd in the lake incident would have gotten angrier, despite my best efforts, we could have gotten back in our trucks and left the area. This would have been less preferable to working the problem out at the lake, but if the temper of the crowd was too high, it would have allowed everyone time to calm down before we tried another way to work with the landowners.

Smoothing

This technique uses compliments, stroking, small talk, and the exchange of pleasantries to calm the parties. Often the combatants are told what they have in common with each other. We conducted some smoothing tactics at the lake. We took every opportunity to show the landowners how much we were like them. We told them they cared about the environment, just like us; we all wanted to ensure our kids would grow up in a healthy environment; and I said my parents lived on a lake just like them. We talked and joked with them even though the underlying tension remained present throughout the night of that first sampling trip. We showed some of the landowners the electrofishing boat and described how we caught fish. We always tried to talk with them with an upbeat attitude.

Captain Mbaye Diagne—A Master of Smoothing

In Rwanda, 1994, eight hundred thousand Tutsis and moderate Hutus were slaughtered by Hutu extremists in a genocide that lasted one hundred days. This was the fastest rate of mass killings in the twentieth century. Roughly 10 percent of the entire population of Rwanda was murdered. The United Nations was ordered not to intervene and the United States and other Western nations refused to get involved. Against direct orders, Captain Mbaye Diagne, a Senegalese army officer and unarmed UN military observer, took action. He saved the two sons of the prime minister from slaughter by hiding them in a closet as their mother was being killed, and he and other UN observers

(continued)

Captain Mbaye Diagne (continued)

brought hundreds of Tutsis, moderate Hutus, and others to safety. Getting these people to safety was an almost superhuman task. In one instance he found twenty-five Tutsis hiding in an extremely dangerous neighborhood in Kigali. He successfully ferried them to UN headquarters in his jeep, five at a time past twenty-three checkpoints, each manned by Hutu militia killers. He convinced the killers at each checkpoint to let all the Tutsis live.

How did he do it? Mbaye was later killed in a random mortar attack and was not interviewed about his technique. However, witnesses say his ability to charm his way past the killers was uncanny. He would smile, joke with them, give them cigarettes, and make them feel confident. Belgians were targeted for killing in Kigali because they were considered by the extremist Hutus to be pro-rebel. A BBC journalist and Mbaye were stopped in their car at a Hutu extremist checkpoint. One of the militia members leaned into the car, waved a Chinese stick grenade under their noses, and asked if the BBC man was a Belgian. A wrong answer would have probably resulted in death for everyone. Mbaye joked with the militia member and said, "No, no—I'm the Belgian. I'm the Belgian here, look—black Belgian." That joke broke the tension of the moment, and the militiaman relaxed his guard. Then Mbaye said in fact the guy was BBC and had nothing to do with the Belgians. Because of the break in tension, the militia allowed the vehicle to pass.[9]

By smoothing his opponents with small talk, smiles, and jokes, this tall officer with the broad toothy grin saved hundreds of lives, even though he was unarmed and had no real power. These techniques have continually helped people talk their way out of dangerous, volatile situations. Smoothing techniques are also extremely beneficial for the conservation professional when working with angry ranchers, farmers, developers, landowners, and members of other agencies. Sometimes it only takes a joke, smile, or small talk to break the tension and allow for constructive problem solving.

Reframing

Often you can put a problem into a new light, so solutions that were not readily apparent before can now be identified. When two people are quarrelling with each other over a park management strategy, they can be told that the intensity of the fighting shows how much each of them cares about the environment. The situation is "reframed" and the parties look at it in a new light.

In the incident at the lake, there was one lady who was flanked by her two children about ten to twelve years old. The lady was carrying signs against big brother (i.e., the government) working on her lake, and was showing her anger to us along with many of the other people. I reframed the situation by indirectly asking her about the example she was setting for her children. My statement "How can we protect the environment for your kids without your cooperation?" was directed at her. It allowed her to look at the confrontation in a new light, as a mother not setting a very good example in front of her children by accosting people who were concerned for their quality of living and the environment. After this statement she put down her sign, and they quietly went home.

Thompson Verbal Judo Methods

George Thompson was a former professor of English literature and a police officer. He analyzed interactions between adversaries, many of them between police and suspects, and advanced techniques where words were used to disarm adversaries to reduce use of guns, nightsticks, or mace. He has spoken to thousands of police officers across the United States about these techniques and was one week away from training four of the officers who were videotaped in the Rodney King beating. He claims that if these officers had taken his course, the beating may not have happened. Thompson recommends a five-step hard-style approach for handling a tough situation.[10]

Ask

If they are threatening you, or doing something you want to change, ask them to change their behavior.

> You: "Please do not take that prehistoric pot from that ruin."

Set Context

Explain to them why you are asking them to do this. Often our parents made the comment "You need to do this because I told you so!" However, both parents and agency personnel can often make people mad by taking this position. People have a deep desire to know why they are being asked to do something. In his police work, Thompson found that about 70 percent of people would comply after they were told why they were asked to do something. For the above example, a typical response might be:

> You: "If you take the pot from the ruin, other people won't get a chance to enjoy it, archeologists won't be able to study it, and you will be violating the law!"

Present Options

If they still seem like they do not want to comply, you can present them with options and the consequences of those options. The task of choosing an option is left with them. Allowing them to choose an option can often encourage compliance much more effectively than giving them a single order.

> You: "You seem like you still want to take that pot. You have a couple of options here. You can continue to take the pot and violate the law. It's a nice pot and probably *would* look good on your shelf. However, I and others here would have to report you and you could face a fine up to five thousand dollars, and potentially have to serve some jail time. You would likely lose your job for a felony conviction, lose a lot of money, and damage your relationships with your family, all for an old pot. The other option is that you put it back and go about your business. You don't spend any jail time, continue to have a nice wilderness experience, and save money and embarrassment. Which way would you like to go with this?"

Thompson is also a great believer in empathy. Statements like "Hey, I know exactly how you feel, that pot would look great on your shelf, wouldn't it?" (empathy). "However, is it worth all the trouble?"

Confirm

If the person still is insistent on his or her action at this time, you can give him or her one last chance to comply. Thompson recommends the statement "Is there anything I can say or do at this time to earn your cooperation?"

Act

Before you get to the act stage, most people would have done what you would have asked. However, if the action continues, rapid, decisive action is needed. Here without any further statements, you report the person for stealing the pot. Figuring out how you are going to act is important before you reach this stage.

Dealing With Hecklers—A Common Occurrence for Conservation Professionals

When I was a graduate student, I had to give a talk in an auditorium in front of a large national audience about the subject of my dissertation, grass carp. Grass carp are large plant-eating fish that are used for plant control. I was happy with my talk and when I reached the end, I asked for questions; a scientist with a national reputation for expertise in grass carp blurted out, "You're wrong. Grass carp don't behave like that!" I was crushed. Even though I had carefully designed my experiment and collected my data, I felt that I was a failure, and now so did everyone in the auditorium. It was one of my earliest dealings with a heckler in scientific meeting.

Since that first incident, I have dealt with numerous hecklers. They seem to be more of the rule than the exception at large public meetings. So having the ability to deal with hecklers is an important skill for any conservation professional or government official.

We are all familiar with how comedians handle hecklers. I remember Steve Martin's *A Wild and Crazy Guy* concert on tape. It was a huge hit when I was a teenager in the 1970s. In it Steve Martin is telling jokes to a large audience and you can hear a heckler in the back screaming something unintelligible. Martin ignores the man at first and then he quips "Yeah, I can remember my first beer, too." It shuts the heckler down and the audience gets a huge laugh.

In public meetings, the heckler can often be someone you will have to work with later, or someone in one of the groups that you are working with to try and get support. Therefore, humiliating the person in front of the audience, as tempting as it may be, will probably not serve your ultimate interests. According to David Burns, most hecklers share the following attributes.[11] They are intensely critical, but their comments are often irrelevant or inaccurate. They are often not well accepted among their peers, and their comments are expressed in an abusive style. Burns gives a short technique for handling hecklers that has often worked quite well for me. First, thank the heckler for the comments. Acknowledge that the points he or she brought up are important and emphasize that there is a need for more knowledge. You can encourage the critic to pursue meaningful research of the topic, or in the case of someone who goes on and on, you can encourage the critic to further share points of view after the meeting.

If you are often heckled, you might want to examine your speaking style to see if you might be contributing to the problem. Have you worked hard to make your presentation interesting? Are your points relevant and well thought out? Careful preparation and consideration of the audience's interest level in what you have to say can minimize heckling.

When the grass carp scientist told me I was wrong, I was inexperienced in handling hecklers. I asked him first to clarify what was wrong about my points. He said that grass carp in his study preferred to eat plant species in a different order than what I found in my study. I said something like "that's interesting, our data revealed something different." After my talk, we continued our conversation. Although our first couple of conversations were somewhat heated, it lead to further research investigating the effects of grass carp size and water chemistry of the lake on grass carp feeding preferences. We found that preference could indeed vary somewhat among sites and fish of different sizes. Later when I found out more about verbal judo, I gave the scientist compliments about his work. He opened up considerably after this, and I came to consider him a friend and an excellent source of information. This incident provided a valuable lesson in keeping my cool, acknowledging that other data might be correct, and giving compliments even in the face of criticism. Incidentally, I thought I would be humiliated in the eyes of my fellow scientists because of his comments. Interestingly enough, when I spoke with several of the other scientists following my presentation, they were actually angry at *him* for trying to embarrass a graduate student.

Conclusion

Used correctly, words can save lives, protect natural resources, make friends, and build reputations. I am unfamiliar with studies that have tested the effectiveness of these techniques in a statistically controlled manner. However, I have tried many techniques in communication and have found those discussed in this chapter to be among the most simple and powerful. Using these techniques for over twenty years has provided me with powerful, positive results, and I have also seen them successfully used by many other conservation professionals. Add these tools to your toolbox of communication techniques, and see what results they provide you.

Chapter Summary

- Verbal judo can be a powerful technique to turn a critic into a supporter. It consists of (1) *understanding* your critic's point of view by asking questions; (2) using *agreement* in some form, *empathy* or *strokes* to diffuse the situation; and (3) then diplomatically stating your point of view.
- In volatile confrontational situations, cooling off, which consists of separating the parties; smoothing, which consists of using small talk, jokes, or an exchange of pleasantries; or reframing, which puts the problem into a new light, have all been used successfully.
- Another method of deescalating high-conflict situations consists of (1) asking them to change their behavior, (2) explaining why you are asking them to change their behavior, (3) presenting them with options they can choose and the consequences of following your requests or not, (4) asking them one more time to follow your request, and (5) taking whatever action is needed.
- One can deal with hecklers by (1) thanking them for their comments, (2) acknowledging that their points are important, and (3) encouraging them to conduct meaningful research on the topic, or asking them to discuss it with you further after the meeting.

Notes

1 David D. Burns, *The Feeling Good Handbook* (New York: Plume, 1989); David D. Burns, *Feeling Good: The New Mood Therapy* (New York: Signet, 1980); Stephen R. Covey, *The Seven Habits of Highly Effective People: Powerful Lessons in Personal Change* (New York: Simon and Schuster, 1989); George J. Thompson and Jerry B. Jenkins, *Verbal Judo: The Gentle Art of Persuasion,* 2nd ed. (New York: Quill, 2004); Sam Horn, *Tongue Fu! How to Deflect, Disarm, and Defuse Any Verbal Conflict* (New York St. Martin's Griffin, 1996).

2 Burns, *Feeling Good Handbook;* Burns, *Feeling Good.*

3 Covey, *Seven Habits.*

4 Burns, *Feeling Good.*

5 Paul F. Boller Jr., *Presidential Anecdotes* (New York: Penguin, 1981).

6 Donald T. Phillips, *Lincoln on Leadership: Executive Strategies for Tough Times* (New York: Warner, 1992).

7 Burns, *Feeling Good.*

8 D. F. Gundersen and Robert Hopper, *Communication and Law Enforcement* (New York: Harper and Row, 1984).

9 PBS Frontline, *Ghosts of Rwanda* (2004 [cited October 29, 2005]); available from http://www.pbs.org/wgbh/pages/frontline/shows/ghosts/.

10 George J. Thompson and Jerry B. Jenkins, *Verbal Judo: The Gentle Art of Persuasion*, 2nd ed. (New York: Quill, 2004).

11 Burns, *Feeling Good.*

Chapter 13: Post-Reading Questions

1. Did you find the author's "verbal judo" techniques to be useful? Why?
2. Can you think of a time when you used such a technique? How did it go?
3. Can you think of a time when you probably should have used this technique but didn't?
4. How difficult would it be to use this technique more often in conflict resolution? Why?

CHAPTER 14

Finding Balance

Measuring Your Continued Success

Now that you have run your new plan, it is time again to measure your success. Was it a complete success, a partial success, or a complete disaster? Let's review the possibilities we previously discussed.

A Complete Disaster

Remember that we cannot call it a complete disaster if anything went right. If it wasn't quite as successful as we would have hoped, at worst, it is still a partial success. If this was a revision of your previous plan, you should have increased your odds of success. However, if your first plan went well and so you decided to increase your challenge, you might have run into some problems. Once again it would be important to analyze what went so terribly wrong and why. Mostly it should be related to not addressing the ***real*** problem, needing to take smaller steps, or avoiding unforeseen circumstances. All of these were addressed in a previous chapter, so I won't reiterate it here. The important thing is to find the problem so you can address it and move on.

A Partial Success

Even if you didn't completely accomplish what you had planned, if you even partially succeeded, you should view it as a partial success, and not a complete or even partial failure. Once again, you need to examine why you didn't completely succeed. Were the steps too big? Did you ask too much of yourself? Was it harder than you anticipated? That's OK. Your next plan can adjust for the difficulties that you met. Unfortunately, we won't have time in this course to make another new plan, but that doesn't mean you cannot continue on your own. You should continue making a new plan for each week until you feel that you have completely mastered your issue. So celebrate your partial accomplishment and figure out how to make your next attempt even more successful!

A Complete Success

OK, before your revel too much over your success, ask yourself honestly if your plan was too easy. Did you challenge yourself? Was it difficult? If not, be honest with yourself and try to push yourself a little harder next time. If it was a real challenge, but you did push yourself and managed to succeed, then good for you! Be proud and bask in the glory, for you deserve it. Believe that you can face any challenge if you really put your mind to it. You've shown yourself that you can do it, so now do it again and again. Keep increasing your challenge each week until there is no more challenge left for you to attempt in regard to this issue. Then find a new issue to work on so that you continue to improve yourself and fulfill your life goals.

Group Assignment

Let your group mates know about the successes and/or failures that you experienced in carrying out your new plan. Tell your group members what went right and what went wrong. Tell them if it was a complete success, a partial success, or a complete disaster. If it was anything less than perfect, try to analyze why. If it was completely perfect, consider whether you were fully challenging yourself. Give each other feedback. If your group members are feeling badly about their lack of success, encourage them to try again. If they were successful, congratulate them on their success. If you suspect they are not being completely honest with themselves, challenge them to dig a little deeper. Do NOT formulate any new plans. You will discuss that in the next group meeting. During this meeting you should just analyze what went right, what went wrong, and figure out why. Share your experience and show support for each other.

Individual Assignment

Think about the progress you have made on your issue. Are you pleased or disappointed? Why? Where do you think you are on the Stages of Change (Precontemplation, Contemplation, Preparation, Action, Maintenance) as compared to where you were when you started this course? How has the group progressed and changed since the start of this course? How have you changed as a group member from the start of this course? How have the other group members changed?

The Weekly Reading

Pre-Reading Questions

The readings for this chapter are on finding balance in our busy lives.

1. Do you frequently find that you have too much to do and too little time?
2. Do you struggle with apportioning your time to the activities that are most important to you? Why do you think that is?

READING 19

Introduction

Too Much to Do, Too Little Time

Brian Tracy and Christina Stein

Everyone today has too much to do and too little time. You often feel overwhelmed with your duties, tasks, and responsibilities. The challenge for you is to simplify your life in such a way that you spend more time doing the things that are most important to you and less time doing those things that are not important at all.

The best news is that you have the power, right now, to live a life with no regrets, where you feel fully engaged in your relationships and everything you do. You can choose to live a life where each day holds meaning and purpose and brings you joy. You can live a life that is focused, positive, and completely in balance with the person you really are deep inside.

The desire for peace of mind and the idea of living a balanced life are central to your happiness and well-being. When you start to live your life in balance as the very best person you could possibly be, you will enjoy the happiness you deserve and experience harmony among all the elements that make up a successful life for you, as you define it.

Your Balance Point

We are all unique individuals with our own values, vision, purpose, and goals. Each one of us has a different way of achieving true balance. Each person experiences true balance when she is operating at her own unique *balance point*. It is from your balance point that you experience the highest level of clarity, commitment, strength, and confidence to pursue your ambitions, both personally and professionally.

Brian Tracy and Christina Stein, "Introduction: Too Much to Do, Too Little Time," *Find Your Balance Point: Clarify Your Priorities, Simplify Your Life, and Achieve More*, pp. 1–9.

The key to success in any area is, first, to start from the right place, and second, to know what steps you need to take to get where you want to go.

In karate, this starting point is the *ready stance*. In ballet, it's *first position*. In painting, you *prime your canvas*. In baking, you *set the oven*. Every area of life has a correct point from which to start.

Finding Your Balance Point

Your greatest need is to understand how to identify your balance point, move to it at will, and automatically return to it whenever you want. You need to establish your balance point before you can set and achieve the goals that are important to you and live a life that is harmonious and truly balanced.

True Balance

True balance is what you experience when everything in your life feels as if it is in perfect harmony. When you enjoy true balance, you feel clear and focused. You go through your day with courage and confidence. You know what you want to accomplish, and you take the necessary steps to accomplish it. Physically, you feel calm and relaxed. You have the health and energy to do whatever you choose to do.

Emotionally, you feel grounded and happy. You feel connected to others and appreciate your own unique self. Your mind, body, and spirit are in perfect alignment. You feel at one with the universe. This is your goal.

The Inner Experience

True balance is something you experience deep inside. It can be achieved only when you are confident with your choices. Once you have identified what enables you to enjoy this feeling of true balance, it is easier to find and easier to maintain.

You are experiencing true balance when you feel inspired and fully engaged in everything you do. Everything you choose to invest your time and energy into has special meaning for you. True balance is never threatened or influenced by the choices of others because it is a state of mind that is unique to each person. Your requirements for true balance will be exactly what you alone want and need.

False Balance

Generally speaking, people are impatient. They want whatever they want, and they want it now, even if they didn't know that they wanted it one minute ago. As a result, they gravitate readily to the quick fix of getting back into balance with as little effort as possible. They can easily be attracted to activities that will bring them a sense of false balance rather than doing those things that are necessary for them to achieve true balance.

In our society, we quickly turn to consumption to feel better. We drink too much, eat too much, and buy too many things we don't need in search of an *external* means to achieve some form of relief or balance. These false balance options are usually just Band-Aids. They don't really change anything in our lives, except temporarily.

If you take a yoga class, you are not going to suddenly become more flexible. The flexibility you desire will require many weeks and even months of steady work on yourself.

If you spend two weeks on an extreme diet, you may drop a few pounds, but you will seldom achieve your ideal weight. And whatever weight you lose, you will quickly put back on again as you revert to your previous lifestyle.

If you go on a vacation but spend the majority of your time distracted by work and e-mails, you are not going to come home feeling refreshed or reconnected to your loved ones.

Too many people are seeking a magic pill that will solve their problems and help them achieve their goals quickly and easily. We want quick solutions to problems that have taken years to develop, and this is simply not possible.

Beware of Easy Answers

As it happens, numerous experts, coaches, psychologists, and counselors claim that they can help you find peace of mind and balance. Unfortunately, many of their methods are flawed. They don't work for two major reasons. The first reason is that most of the solutions offered by so-called authorities offer only a quick fix. They don't solve the root problem that is causing your unhappiness and imbalance in the first place.

The second flaw in their ideas is that what brings balance in the life of one person will not necessarily work for another.

You are unique. There never has been and never will be anyone exactly like you. You have had a unique set of experiences, starting in early childhood, that has made you the person you are today. You have made different choices and decisions throughout your life, tried different things, made different mistakes, and gone in different directions from anyone else. The person you are today is a sum total result of thousands of small actions, thoughts, feelings, decisions, regrets, and events that, in combination, no one else has ever experienced.

Because you are special and unique, there are no pat answers or simple solutions that you can take out of a box or a book and apply directly to your life to solve your problems and achieve your goals.

Just as with most medicines, any advice or insight that you acquire may have side effects and cause unexpected reactions. You should always keep an open mind when you hear new ideas and then think about which parts of these ideas might apply directly to your own personal situation.

Falling Victim to False Balance

Many people are lured into the trap of false balance because they are unfocused and feel so overwhelmed with being out of balance that they don't even know where to start their quest. They feel as if they are spending their lives treading water and hoping not to sink. They are often stuck in a comfort zone, doing the same things in the same way, and disconnected from the reality of what a balanced life looks and feels like.

Often, they don't like and respect themselves. They lack the confidence to make tough choices and to take the actions necessary to align their lives with what they truly value. They are unclear about what is important to them and what motivates them.

You often see this situation with people who look to others to determine how to achieve their own state of balance. They will compare themselves to someone else and emulate what they see in hopes of achieving what they perceive is balance and happiness. For example, a son who is unclear about his career choice decides to copy his father's choice of career in an attempt to gain his father's approval. He is unclear about what he wants personally, so he imitates his father because that choice is comfortable and safe. His attempt to achieve balance the way his father appears to have achieved his state of balance will result in the son's finding false balance because his career choice will not be a reflection of what he truly values.

When people are in a state of false balance, they feel disengaged and powerless to change the world around them. They often turn to buying things to feel better. They buy things they don't need, spend money they don't have, eat the wrong foods, and turn to alcohol and drugs to feel better. They are desperate to fill the hole inside them and regain some sense of clarity and control in their lives.

Clarity Is the Key to Finding Balance

When people do not feel in control of their lives, they lose focus and lack commitment. Instead of directing their own lives, they react and respond to the behaviors and opinions of others. They end up investing their time and energy in things that don't bring them joy.

For example, a woman who has two young children wants to start a business, but she keeps agreeing to take on volunteer projects at her children's school. As a result, she has no time to work on developing her business. She becomes overwhelmed with all her commitments and does not set aside any time to pursue her own ambitions. She feels out of control—or controlled by the people around her. This robs her of self-confidence. She feels frustrated and unhappy. She finds herself reacting to the needs of others because she is unclear about her own needs and her own direction.

Without clarity, you cannot design a plan, and without a clear plan, there is no way that you can know what specific actions to take and which direction to go. However, when you become clear about and committed to what is important to you, design a plan for your life, and ensure that your life on the outside becomes a reflection of your desired life on the inside, you will begin to operate from your balance point and begin to make tremendous progress in every area of your life.

For you to enjoy the kind of life you have imagined, and to achieve everything that is possible for you, you will probably have to make a series of positive and constructive changes to the way you think, feel, and react to the world around you. The good news is that at any time, you can resolve to make the rest of your life the best of your life. You can make a decision today to become everything you are capable of becoming. You can take complete control of your present and design your ideal future.

In this book, you will learn how to identify, achieve, and maintain your balance point. You will learn how to move smoothly and confidently through life, recognizing when you are out of balance and knowing exactly what you need to do to restore your balance point once more.

Clarifying Your Values

First, you will learn how to identify your values in life and become crystal clear about what is truly important to you. You will learn how to organize your life around your values. You will learn how to set boundaries and insist on living your life in alignment with your values, not compromising them at the request or demand of others.

In addition, you will learn how to create an exciting vision of your ideal life sometime in the future, as well as what you will need to do to make your perfect future life into your current reality.

You will also learn how to infuse your life with meaning and purpose and organize your activities so that you really make a difference in every part of your life.

Setting Goals and Being Proactive

You will learn how to set and achieve your goals and make sure that everything you do on the outside is in harmony with what is most important to you on the inside.

You will also learn to become proactive and choose where you invest your time and energy. Instead of reacting to the circumstances around you and spending your limited time and energy achieving the goals of others, you will focus your energies accomplishing what is most important to you.

Setting Priorities and Managing Your Time

You will learn how to take complete control over your time and your life, how to set priorities, and how to get more done, faster and more easily, than ever before. You will also learn that by setting priorities on your goals and activities, and managing your time effectively, you will both energize and simplify your life.

Operating from Your Balance Point

When you learn how to blend your values, vision, mission, purpose, goals, and priorities into a clear life plan that reflects all the aspects of your unique personality, you will be able to establish and operate from your own unique balance point.

When you operate from your own personal balance point, you will enjoy unshakable self-confidence and self-esteem. You will achieve complete balance between your personal and professional ambitions and know that you are making every day count. When you choose to live your life from your balance point—in harmony with your values, vision, purpose, goals, and priorities—you will be choosing to live a life with no regrets.

Our goal in writing this book is to give you the practical, proven steps that you can take immediately to clarify your priorities, simplify your life, and achieve all your hopes and dreams. Let's get started!

READING 20

Determine Your Values and Start from the Right Place

Brian Tracy and Christina Stein

In the pages ahead, you will learn how to discover who you really are; what values drive your beliefs, attitudes, and actions; and exactly what you need to do to create a plan that ensures a life of passion, purpose, and self-direction.

Clarity Is Essential

The starting point of designing a wonderful life is for you to develop absolute clarity about who you are and what matters to you. This means that you must be clear about your *values*. It seems that successful, happy people know what their values are and what they stand for, and they refuse to compromise them. Most of the great men and women of history have been admired because of their character, because of their adherence to a set of values that enabled them to overcome incredible adversity and go on to accomplish extraordinary things. And this can be true for you as well.

Everything happens for a reason. Success and happiness are not accidents. Failure and underachievement are not accidents either. There are definite reasons for everything that happens, and most of these reasons are contained within yourself.

Fortunately, you can control the things that you think, say, and do, and by controlling them, you can design the kind of life that you want and create the kind of future that is possible for you.

When you become clear about your values and what is truly important to you, it becomes easier to make a plan for your future. People who know what they want and are clear about what they are working toward feel engaged and inspired by their lives.

Brian Tracy and Christina Stein, "Determine Your Values and Start from the Right Place," *Find Your Balance Point: Clarify Your Priorities, Simplify Your Life, and Achieve More*, pp. 11–25. Copyright © 2015 by Berrett-Koehler Publishers. Reprinted with permission.

Developing clarity about your values is the essential first step to creating a happy life. When you become clear about these values, you will start operating from your own personal balance point.

What Are Values?

Your values lie at the core of your character and your personality. Values are the foundation of your self-concept. They are like the axle around which your entire life turns. They are the primary drivers and motivators that push you forward. They determine who you are and who you are not, what matters to you and what does not.

You've heard the saying "life is a journey." Let's use that idea to help illustrate the role that values play in your life. On your life journey you will travel to many destinations. Just as you wouldn't just jump in your car and drive or hop on a plane and fly off somewhere, you wouldn't start without a clear destination. Your values largely determine which destination you choose. Do you prefer warm weather or cool weather? A city vacation or a seaside holiday? Luxury or budget? Are you interested in museums and other cultural experiences? The destination you choose and the trip you take will be a reflection of what is important to you, very much a reflection of your values. These values lie at the core of the person you really are inside, your self-concept.

Your Self-Concept

Your self-concept is your bundle of beliefs and ideas about yourself and your world. It is how you think and feel about yourself and every part of your life. It is the central or master program of your subconscious computer. Your self-concept precedes and predicts your performance and effectiveness in everything you do.

According to humanistic psychologist Carl Rogers, your self-concept is made up of three parts, like three overlapping spheres, each touching the other. These are your *ideal self*, your *self-image*, and your *self-esteem*. Let's look at each of them in order.

Your Ideal Self

Your *ideal self* is a combination of all the values and virtues that you admire in yourself and in others. It is a picture of the perfect person that you would like to be at some time in the future. Your ideal self is your vision of the very best person that you could possibly become.

Your Self-Image

Your *self-image* is the second part of your self-concept. This is the person you see on the inside and think of yourself as being. It is often called your "inner mirror"—you always behave on the outside the way you see yourself behaving on the inside.

You might identify yourself by your physicality, by the social roles you play, or by your personality traits. All improvements in your outer life begin with an improvement in how you think about yourself—your mental and physical self-image.

Your Self-Esteem

The third part of your self-concept, your *self-esteem*, is perhaps the most important part of your personality. This is the "reactor core" of your personality, the energy source and center that determines the power of your personality. Your level of self-esteem is the foundation of your *self-confidence*, the most important quality of all for success in a busy, competitive world.

Your self-esteem is defined as "how much you like yourself." The more you like yourself, or even *love yourself*, the better you do at anything that you attempt. And the better you do at your work and in other areas of your life, the more you like and respect yourself. Each aspect feeds the other: the more you like yourself, the better you do, and the better you do, the more you like yourself, in a continuing upward spiral of higher performance and higher self-esteem.

Your self-esteem is greatly affected by the relationship between your self-image and your ideal self. The more consistent the person you see yourself as being today is with your ideal self—the person you would like to be in the future—the higher will be your self-esteem.

The greater the distance between the person you see yourself as being today and the person you want most to be, the lower will be your self-esteem and self-confidence. When you are clear about your values and your ideals and you live every day in a manner that is consistent with those values, your self-image will move closer toward your ideal self, your self-esteem will increase, and you will feel a tremendous sense of self-respect and personal pride. This is our goal for you throughout this book.

The link between your self-image and your ideal self is why it is said that all problems in your personal life can be solved by a return to values, to the very best that is in you.

Select Your Values

What are your values? This is a great question! How do you determine what your values are today, and how do you decide what values are most important to you going forward?

There are two ways to determine your current values. The first is to look at your behaviors or actions on a day-to-day, hour-by-hour, and minute-to-minute basis. Your true values and beliefs are most often expressed in your *actions*. What you say or hope or wish or intend to do or be in the future does not really matter. Only your actions in the moment tell you, and everyone around you, what you truly value and who you really are deep inside.

The second way to assess your values is to look at how you behave under stress. When you are under stress or pressure and you are forced to choose one action or another, your choice will express your true values.

For example, ask yourself, "If I found out today that I had only six months to live, how would I spend my time?" Your answer to this question will tell you what is most important to you in life at this moment.

You can also determine what you truly value by looking at what makes you the happiest and what qualities you most respect and admire in others.

Clarifying your true values is not easy. Some people choose to attend intensive, three-day seminars on the subject of values clarification to help them develop absolute clarity about what is important to them in every area of life. These seminars are often life changing for the simple reason that most people, even highly educated and intelligent people, are unclear and unsure about what their values really are or what they should be.

But once you are clear about your values, and their order of priority in your life, and you resolve to live consistent with these values, you will feel a tremendous sense of liberation and exhilaration. Life will become simple and clear. You will know what to do and what not to do. Decision making will become easier. You will feel that you are becoming the very best person you can possibly be.

Let's talk now about three different kinds of values: character values, life category values, and values around roles and identities.

Character Values

Following is a list of character values, also referred to as "virtues." Virtues are the admirable and desirable qualities and strengths that make up a person's character. They are usually developed early in life as the result of parental influence and example. Virtues can also be developed in adulthood by repetition and practice and by refusing to allow exceptions.

Read through this list and ask yourself, "What kind of person am I?" Circle those words that you believe best describe your character and guide your choices and actions today, or jot them down on a piece of paper. Also circle or write down those virtues and values that you would most like to develop in the future. This combination constitutes your ideal self.

Accepting	Accountable	Assertive
Brave	Cautious	Committed
Compassionate	Confident	Considerate
Content	Cooperative	Courageous
Courteous	Creative	Curious
Defiant	Dependable	Determined
Devoted	Diligent	Disciplined
Discrete	Eloquent	Empathic
Enthusiastic	Faithful	Flexible
Focused	Forgiving	Friendly
Frugal	Generous	Gentle
Graceful	Grateful	Helpful

Honest
Humble
Humorous
Idealistic
Impartial
Industrious
Innocent
Joyful
Just
Kind
Knowledgeable
Liberal
Loving
Loyal
Moderate
Modest
Obedient
Open-minded
Optimistic
Orderly
Passionate
Patient
Peaceful
Persistent
Pious
Prudent
Punctual
Purposeful
Rational
Resourceful
Respectful
Responsible
Righteous
Selfless
Self-sacrificing
Servicing
Sensitive
Sincere
Spontaneous
Steadfast
Strong
Tactful
Tolerant
Trusting
Trustworthy
Truthful
Vital
Wise
Zealous

Now, look at your selections and choose the one value that is most important to you. (This is not easy!) Continue through your selected values and decide which is your second most important value and then your third, fourth, and fifth. This is a great exercise and an excellent starting point.

Which are the most important values in your life today? (Write them here or on a piece of paper.)

1 Confident (3)
2 determined (2)
3 loving (5)
4 Strong (1)
5 Open-minded (4)

Identifying which values are most important to you, and their order of importance, helps you live a more successful, balanced life for three reasons. The first reason is that the values you admire and desire the most are unique and personal to you. To achieve balance in your life, you need to be clear and committed to what matters most to you.

The second reason is that the more your daily words and actions are consistent with your most deeply felt values, the higher will be your self-esteem and the more you will like and respect yourself. The more self-esteem you enjoy, the greater will be your self-confidence.

The more self-confidence you have, the more energy and determination you will have to move forward and achieve your goals. Nothing will stop you.

The third reason why clarity regarding your values is essential is that to determine how to set goals and priorities, you need to know what you really want and care about more than anything else.

Life Category Values

We are shaped and motivated by the qualities of our character and the values we place on each different part, or category, of our lives. In achieving balance in our day-to-day lives, it is usually the life category values where we strive to achieve balance the most.

Before you can achieve success in your personal and professional lives, you must first determine what "success" looks like for yourself. Finding your balance point requires that you decide what is most important to you among these categories and then where and how you should invest your time and energy.

Look through the following list and circle the words or phrases that describe the most important elements of your life, both present and in the future, or write them down on a piece of paper. You may select all of them or only a few; there is no right answer—only what is right for you.

Romantic partnerships
Children
Friends
Money
Career
Travel
Religion
Fitness
Spirituality

Family
Parents
Social life
Work
Home
Material things
Health
Education
Community

Which are your five most important categories, those areas that take up, or that you wish would take up, most of your time?

1 ____________________

2 ____________________

3 ____________________

4 ____________________

5 ____________________

Does your life reflect all the categories you listed? Are there certain categories that are important to your happiness and fulfillment but to which you are not devoting enough time and energy?

You may find that you selected many of the categories, but not all of them are of the same importance to you. Later we will discuss how to prioritize your values and live a life that accurately reflects the significance you give each one. In addition, you will learn how to establish your values and priorities and how they may change in importance throughout your life.

Role and Identity Values

When asked to describe themselves, people often mention the roles they play and the jobs they do. Just as certain virtues are more meaningful to us than others, we also place different degrees of importance on our various identities and activities. Each person usually has multiple identities, each of which is more or less important than the others.

One person may value creative expression and identify strongly with being an *artist*. That same person may identify her role as a *professional* to be more central to her overall identity. She would therefore describe herself first as a professional and second as an artist. For many women, this is a particularly challenging exercise. Often, women who establish themselves in a career and then stop to raise a family find themselves struggling between their role as a professional and their role as a mother. For these women, determining how to divide their time is absolutely essential to establishing their personal balance point and to feeling happy and confident about how they spend their time.

As you go through the following exercise, be aware that a significant characteristic of values, especially our values around roles, is that they are constantly changing and evolving. At some points in your life you may identify more strongly with one role and then at a later point you may find yourself or imagine yourself connected to another. Circle or write down on a piece of paper the roles that you identify with and that are important to you now or that may be important sometime in your future.

Child	Mother	Father
Grandmother	Grandfather	Wife
Husband	Friend	Teacher
Student	Leader	Employer
Employee	Partner	Artist
Professional	Stepmother	Stepfather
Aunt	Uncle	Sister
Brother	Citizen	Devout follower

Of the roles you selected, which one do you identify with the most? Second most? Third? Fourth? Fifth? You can list roles relevant to your life right now or a combination of the roles you play now and the roles you hope to play in the future.

1 ______________________________

2 ______________________________

3 ______________________________

4 ______________________________

5 ______________________________

Becoming clear about what drives you, what you value, and how you prioritize those values is essential to creating your personal life design and learning how to operate from your balance point. Without crystal clear awareness of what truly matters to you, your path will be unclear, your foundation will not feel solid, and you will never experience the true balance and harmony that is possible for you.

Once you take the time to think about the values discussed in this chapter and acknowledge how integral they are to your overall sense of happiness, you will probably want to change the way you live your life and get yourself back on track. You will see clearly what you need to change to begin operating from your own balance point. This clarity will enable you to feel more empowered to become the kind of person who can achieve any goal you set for yourself.

Prioritizing Your Values

You need to be clear about your values if you want to live a happy life. You must also be clear about the priority in which you organize your values. Which value is *most* important to you? Which value is *second* most important to you? Which value is *third*, and so on? This order of priority largely determines the structure of your personality—what you think and feel, what you say, and what you do—especially when you are forced to choose between one value and another.

Imagine that you know two people, one person who values *security* above all else and another person who values *opportunity* or new experiences above all else. Here's the question: Would there be a difference between these two people in terms of their character and personality? Would the difference be small or large? The answer is that the difference would be *enormous*. The two people would be completely different from each other in their beliefs, expectations, attitudes, and behaviors.

Two Examples

Imagine two men: one is a lawyer and the other is a salesman. The lawyer goes to work early in the morning and comes home late at night. He often has to work on projects during the weekend and has little extra time to spend with his two young sons. However, he loves his job and feels fully engaged at work. He feels proud of his accomplishments and knows that he is providing well for his family.

The salesman travels extensively for work and is often away from home several days at a time. When he is home, he divides his time between his family and professional projects he is working on. He too places tremendous value on his ability to provide for his family.

Both men highly value their careers, take pride in their achievements, and feel good about their accomplishments.

You may think that because both of these men spend the majority of their time working, their lives are out of balance. But the reality is that these men both enjoy their work and highly value their ability to provide for their families. They are actually living their lives in alignment with their highest values and are therefore in balance.

No two people operate from the same balance point. People are different and contribute in unique ways to society. No two are exactly the same.

Learning to operate from your balance point requires that you stop comparing yourself to others and start to appreciate the differences that exist among people. What is right for you and what is right for someone else do not have to be the same. When you are clear about your own personal values and you decide to live by them, without compromise, you can feel calm and confident no matter what others do or say. You can then find and maintain your own balance point.

Action Exercises

1. Every day for a week, ask yourself, "What do I value the very most in life?" Your first answers to this question may be automatic but not necessarily accurate. Keep asking, and let your thoughts go where they lead you. You may be surprised at your final answer.

2. Imagine that you could have two words inscribed on your tombstone to summarize the kind of person you became in your lifetime. What two virtues or qualities would you want inscribed after the words, "Here lies (you). He/She was (two qualities)."?

Chapter 14: Post-Reading Questions

The authors write about the ways we tend to find "false" balance in our lives.

1. What are some of the ways you create false balance? Why do you think you do that?
2. Complete all of the "top five list" exercises in the reading and evaluate your life accordingly. To what degree do your life activities reflect your values? Can you think of some things you might do to make them more in alignment?

CHAPTER 15

Summing It Up!

So Long, Farewell

Can you believe the semester is almost over? Where does the time go? I hope you have learned a few things about yourself and made some progress on your goals. We are all just works in progress, so we should all have plenty left to do. At this point it is a matter of figuring out where you want to go from here. But before we address that issue, let us review some of the major concepts that we went over in this course.

Steps of Problem-Solving

The Steps of Problem-Solving aren't magic. They won't solve your problems by themselves. They are just a tool to help you structure your issue so that you can make the best decisions possible given the set of circumstances as best you are able to understand and predict them. We have learned that the problem we are focusing on is often not the *real* problem; we often need to dig a little deeper. We also learned that there probably are many more possible solutions if we just think outside the box, and using other people to help us to problem-solve can expand our perceptual horizons. And lastly, we learned the importance of making plans, following our plans, and taking small steps to ensure success.

Critical Thinking and Discussion

Even more important than the steps of problem-solving is the idea of using critical thinking and discussion. These are not just skills but also attitudes toward life. When faced with a challenge, do you dig your heels in and try to do things the same way you've always done them or do you seek out new information, considering all perspectives and examining new possibilities? When faced with a disagreement, do you dogmatically argue that you have cornered the market on truth or do you listen to the other person's perspective with an open mind and consider the possibility that s/he might have something valid to say? At the same time that you are attempting to be open-minded, do you also question and challenge all competing ideas? There is no free pass, no unquestioned assumption, no 'sacred cow' that can go unchallenged (your most firmly held beliefs, if they are valid, will survive critical examination, so you should have nothing to fear). If you place a *value* on critical thinking and discussion, you will come up with better ideas, your relationships will improve, and you will even contribute to World Peace! The United Nations (and our Congress) could use more respectful critical discussion and less name-calling and pointing fingers.

Empowerment

We discussed the importance of control and responsibility. People who believe that they have control over their lives make decisions more proactively. And people that make decisions more proactively are more satisfied with their lives than people who believe they have no control and that life is just a matter of fate/luck, and therefore allow their decisions to be made by indecision. We have encouraged you to take active control of your life and accept responsibility for the decisions that you make. You cannot control everything, and the choices in front of you may not be the ones you wish you had, but you always have a choice, and your choices make a difference.

Group Assignment

On this your last group, tell your group what you have gained from the experience of this course and the group itself and discuss what you plan to do next to continue working on your goals. If you appreciate the help that they have given you, be sure to express it. Try to give each member individual feedback. Help them to see the strengths that they have, and encourage them to keep on progressing. Wish them all the best of luck in all their future endeavors. Comment on the feedback you received from each of your group mates. Wish them all, as I wish you, the best of luck in all future endeavors!

Individual Assignment

Think about your final group meeting. How do you feel about leaving the group? Did the final meeting help you to get a sense of closure? Do you believe you will be able to continue to work in a positive manner on your issue and maintain the changes you have already made?

Why or why not? Could the skills learned in this course be used to help you with other issues you might be having or might face in the future? How so?

The Weekly Reading

Pre-Reading Questions

The readings for this chapter are a continuation of the readings from the same book as last week on finding balance in your life.

1. In last week's readings we explored the disconnect between what we value and how we spend our time. Why do you think that disconnect exists?
2. What are some of the obstacles in the way of finding greater happiness and fulfillment in your life?

READING 21

Discover What Holds You Back

Brian Tracy and Christina Stein

Your values lie at the core of your personality, as we have said before. When you are living in harmony with your values, you can tell because you experience peace of mind, calmness, and even joy. When you are out of balance and off track, you feel the opposite. Negative emotions, unhappiness, and discontent of any kind are nature's way of telling you to return to your values. You can almost immediately restore your feelings of peace and happiness by returning to what is really important to you and then by refusing to compromise your values.

Everyone has had the experience of being in a stressful situation, an unhappy relationship, or a bad job. You knew deep inside that something wasn't right. The worse the situation became, the more you felt forced to compromise your values instead of doing what you knew was right for you and insisting on your own happiness and well-being. The longer you stayed in that bad situation, the more stressed, unhappy, and actually detached from life and other people you became.

Finally, however, you took a deep breath, mustered up your courage, and decided to "do the right thing." You walked away from the bad job, even though you didn't know what you were going to do and even though you had bills to pay. You walked away from the bad relationship, even though you had no idea how you might ever find another, better relationship.

And then something absolutely terrific happened! You felt *exhilarated*. You felt wonderful. You felt happy and relieved. You felt as though a great burden had been lifted off your shoulders. You felt truly happy and almost laughed out loud as you walked away.

Why was this? The answer is simple. Whenever you decide to return to your values and get back on track, nature rewards you by giving you a feeling of joy and happiness. The purpose of this joyous feeling is to encourage you to live your life by your values more often.

The Obstacles to Happiness

There is no question that your values are central to your life and to everything that happens to you. Living by your values is absolutely essential for success, self-esteem, happiness, and peace of mind. Every time that you deviate from or compromise your core beliefs and values, you feel uncomfortable, unhappy, stressed, and anxious and you suffer low self-esteem. You don't like and respect yourself as much. This is why we say that almost all problems in your personal life can be solved by a return to your values.

Why is it then that people get off track and compromise their values, leading to frustration, failure, unhappiness, and feelings of inferiority and worthlessness? There are several reasons, all mental and emotional. Fortunately, you can identify them and remove these obstacles from your pathway toward becoming the best person you could possibly be.

1. *People feel a sense of undeservingness.* This is one of the main obstacles to happiness in adult life. Many people feel that they do not deserve to be happy, to be popular, to be successful, and to be loved and respected by others. They do not feel that they deserve to be successful, healthy, and wealthy and to live wonderful, exciting lives.

2. *People are unclear about their values.* They have never taken the time to sit down and think through what is truly important to them, what they care about, and what takes priority over everything else in their lives. The minute they do and they begin to establish a path for their lives with clear direction, they suddenly feel happy and in control of their lives. They are no longer reacting to those around them. Instead, they are proactive. They make their own choices and decisions. Clarity is essential.

3. *People are so overwhelmed with the feeling of being unfocused and out of balance that they don't know where to start.* They are stuck in a comfort zone and disconnected from the reality of what a balanced life looks and feels like. As a result, their feeling of busyness, having no time for what's essential, causes them to make thoughtless and impulsive choices. They are often enticed by short-term pleasures and satisfactions that tempt them to compromise their values for a quick fix.

4. *People don't consider the long-term consequences of their behaviors.* Short-term thinking is a major source of unhappiness, failure, and frustration in life.

   The most successful and happy people practice long-term thinking. They project themselves forward into the future and become clear about where they want to be five and ten years from today. They then evaluate each behavior in the short term with regard to what they really want to achieve in the long term.

Developing a long-term vision of your ideal future dramatically improves the quality of your current decision making. The very act of taking a little time to think before you decide and act, and to be sure that your actions are consistent with the highest values to which you aspire, can improve your life dramatically.

5 *People desire the approval of others, and they feel that only by compromising their values will other people like them, respect them, hire them, promote them, pay them, or include them.* This desire can dominate the thinking, feelings, and behavior of adult individuals. They can become preoccupied with earning the approval of others and especially avoiding their criticism or disapproval.

Because the approval of the important people in your life, especially your boss or spouse, is closely associated with your feelings of security, and security is a key driving emotional factor, you can easily compromise your values in the search for this approval. But the truth is that the only person whose approval you need is your own.

Put Your Own Happiness First

The most respected people in every society are those who clearly and distinctively express their own unique personalities. They are sure and unequivocal about their values and beliefs, and they refuse to compromise them for anyone or anything.

Ayn Rand was famous for pointing out that the achievement of your own happiness should be your highest value or goal in life. She said that you can determine how successful you are by how happy you feel about yourself minute by minute and hour by hour. Your personal happiness should be the barometer by which you judge your actions and your behaviors and especially your values.

There is some confusion on this point. People are taught that seeking their own happiness is somehow selfish. We are supposed to seek to make others happy first. But the truth is that you cannot give away what you do not have. You cannot make someone else happy unless you are happy yourself. If you truly want to make others happy, become a truly happy person. There is no other way.

When you are clear about your values, goals, and priorities, you operate from your balance point. As a result, you feel happy, clear, and focused. You go through your day with courage and confidence.

Values, Authenticity, and Balance

You must choose to be true to at least one person: *yourself.* Having integrity and being authentic is the only way to succeed at establishing and operating from your balance point. As Shakespeare wrote, "To thine own self be true, and it must follow, as the night the day, thou canst not then be false to any man."

Remember that your balance point is completely unique to you. You may find that you share values with others and connect and relate with them based on those values, but you will also encounter many differences. Your goal is to find what is right for you and then have the strength and confidence to move through your life committed to living your own personal set of values.

Don't feel threatened or doubt your values based on comparing yourself to others. You need to do what is right for you and embrace the idea that other people are doing what is right for them. Remember, "Different strokes for different folks."

Three Sets of Values

Imagine three women. The first woman decided that she wanted to get married and have children right after college. She chose to build her career after her children were all in school. The second woman decided to establish her career after college and spent ten years working hard to build a solid reputation and achieve success in her chosen profession. Only then did she decide to have children. The third woman decided to do both—to build her career while also getting married and raising children. All three women shared the values of having a career and being a mother, but each of them pursued those goals in her own unique way. Each of the three ways was a reflection of one woman's values and the unique balance point that she had.

Decide today to live a wonderful life. Carefully examine each of the obstacles to happiness—the reasons that people give for compromising their true values and settling for less than they are really capable of.

Remember that each of these obstacles exists only in your mind, in your thinking. At any time, you can throw off your self-limiting ideas and become a fully functioning, fully mature, happy person. You can discard your limitations and liberate yourself to realize your full potential. You can determine your own balance point, your own set of values and goals, and return to it whenever you want.

Action Exercises

1 Select one self-limiting belief that might be holding you back from achieving the happiness and joy you deserve, and ask yourself, "What if this belief were not true; what would I do then?"

   Whatever your answer, act as if it were impossible to fail, and it shall be.

2 Imagine that you have no limitations on what you can be, do, or have in any area of your life. Imagine that you had all the money and resources, talent and ability, knowledge and experience, and people and contacts that you require to achieve anything you really want. What is the first thing you would do differently in your life and relationships?

READING 22

Contribute with Purpose

Brian Tracy and Christina Stein

At this point, you are clear about your values—what you believe in and care about at a deep level.

You now know the major obstacles to happiness.

You are also clear about your ideal vision—your perfect life at some time in the future.

Now it is time for you to answer the question *why.*

Why are you here? What gives your life meaning? Why do you do what you are doing rather than a thousand other things? What would have to happen for you to feel completely engaged and truly balanced? What really matters to you?

Your Reason for Existence

Mark Twain once wrote, "The two most important days in your life are the day you are born and the day you find out why."

Friedrich Nietzsche wrote, "He who has a *why* to live can bear almost any *how*."

Viktor Frankl, in his book *Man's Search for Meaning*, said that the most powerful desire of the human being is for a sense of meaning and purpose in life.

Albert Einstein was once asked, "What is the purpose of human life?" He thought for a while and then replied, "Only a life lived for others is the life worth while."

Exactly! We are here to serve others in some way. This is the primary source of meaning and purpose in our lives—service to others. We want to make a difference in the lives of other people.

It turns out that one of the requirements for self-esteem, self-respect, and personal pride is the deep-down feeling that you are making a contribution to others that is greater than what you are receiving from them. You feel that you are putting in more than you are taking out. What you do really matters to someone.

Deserving Our Lives

The fact is that we all make our livings and our lives by serving other people or something greater than ourselves in some way. Human beings are uniquely designed in such a way that we feel happy only when we are contributing, when we are somehow enriching the lives of others.

People who are not making a contribution, who are not serving anyone, who are taking without giving, are never happy. They suffer from low self-esteem and limited self-respect. They become resentful and jealous of those people who are busy and productive and who are making a difference of some kind. Each person craves connection to others. Creating something that helps people or providing a service of some kind is one of the best ways to feel connected to something bigger than yourself. How you decide to serve others is one of the most important decisions you can ever make.

Contribute with Purpose—Your Perfect Job

A job is an opportunity to serve, more than anything else. Not only does it provide a way to satisfy your financial needs, but when your job holds meaning to you, your emotional and spiritual needs will be met as well.

Some of the happiest and most productive people are those who love their work, enjoy their coworkers, and feel that what they are doing benefits and serves others in some way. They believe they are making a difference.

Imagine your ideal job. If you could be successful at any job at all, what would you choose to do? If you could select any job in our society, what would it be?

If you had $20 million in the bank and only ten years to live and you had to work at something, what would you want to do? What work would you choose?

Deciding upon your ideal work is one of the great responsibilities of adult life. It is very much up to you. No one else can decide for you.

Look into Yourself

How can you find what it is that you love to do, what you are meant to do, the ideal work for which you were designed by nature?

You were born with special talents and abilities that make you different from anyone else who has ever lived. As Wayne Dyer once said, "Each child comes into this world with secret orders."

Michael Jordan said, "Everyone has talent, but *ability* takes hard work." Even if you have natural ability in some areas, it may take many years of hard work for you to develop to your full potential.

The Right Work for You

Following is a list of seven indicators of the right work for you, the career where you will feel fully engaged and where you will be the happiest in serving other people.

1. The right work for you is something that you really enjoy doing, something that you love to do.
2. The right work for you is easy for you to learn and easy to do. In many cases, you learned it automatically, without thought or effort.
3. You love learning more and more about the work if it is the right work for you.
4. When you are engrossed in this work, the hours fly past. You forget what time it is, and later you are surprised to see how much time has passed.
5. The right work for you gives you energy when you are doing it. You can spend hours at this work, often forgetting to eat.
6. If it is the right work for you, you want to be excellent at it, and you are constantly striving to learn and improve in that area.
7. If it is the right work for you, you admire the top people in your field, the ones who are recognized as excellent, and you want to be around them and learn from them.

Think back to a time when you experienced some of these indicators. In what areas of your life were you the happiest and most fulfilled? What were you doing when you were totally engrossed in your work or activities? What has been most responsible for your success in your work or career to date? Did the feeling of satisfaction and contentment come from a paid job or something in your personal life?

Work to Live or Live to Work?

In keeping with the theme of balance and operating from your balance point, understanding the distinction between working to live and living to work is very important. Some people feel fully invested and totally engaged in their professional roles and paid jobs. They are most confident, happy, and energized when they are working. However, some people are very good at their paid jobs, but they find that they feel most engaged, confident, and happy in their lives outside of their jobs.

For people who find their work to be fully satisfying, it would make sense to say that they would be operating from their unique balance point when they are investing most of their time and energy in their work. On the flip side, those people who feel more fully engaged in their personal lives would be operating from their balance point when most of their time and energy is focused on areas other than their paid jobs.

You can achieve balance and feel fully engaged in both your personal and professional roles when you organize your life around your values. Then, you can determine where your contributions will have the most meaning for you and those you serve.

The Clock Test

Here is a way you can tell if you are in the right job and contributing in the right place. It is called the "clock test."

What does the clock *mean* to you? For people in the *wrong* jobs or those who don't feel inspired by their work, the clock is a stern taskmaster. It tells them when they must start work, or resume working, and when they can quit their work for the day. They resent the clock and often feel that the clock has stopped.

These people feel disengaged from their work and are easily distracted by a variety of factors. They arrive at the last minute and leave at the first chance they get. Their job is not a source of fulfillment, and they do not feel satisfied at their work.

For people in the *right* jobs for them, the people who feel energized by their work, the clock is a competitor that they race against. The clock tells them how much time they have left before they will have to stop doing the work they enjoy. They are always trying to get more work done in the time allotted to them.

Success Leaves Tracks

When you are doing the work that you are designed to do, you will be eager to learn, to study, to take courses, to improve—evenings, weekends, and whenever you have any spare time.

However, if you have no desire to learn and improve, your current job may be the wrong one for you. This does not mean that it is a bad job. It simply means that the person you are, the values you embrace, and the requirements of the job do not fit together comfortably. When we talk about being out of balance and falling off track, a great indicator that your life is out of balance is your not feeling engaged and inspired in any area of your life, especially your work.

What if you do not feel inspired by your work? You may be quite good at the job that you do and feel confident in your professional contributions, but your job may be not a source of joy and inspiration. When you consider what contributions hold the most meaning for you, the answer may be something you do outside of your paid job.

Contribute with Purpose—Family, Friends, Community

You can serve in many other areas of life where you can enjoy profound feelings of meaning and purpose that are not work related. In fact, most people desire to both contribute professionally and contribute to their families.

Historically, women were responsible for rearing the children and maintaining the home. Men were expected to financially support their families with their jobs. However, there has been a major shift over time, and things have changed considerably. Now many more women are supporting their families financially, and many more men are caring for the children and maintaining the home.

Raise Happy Children

Most parents find great satisfaction and meaning in raising children. It is perhaps one of the most important jobs in our society. When you choose to become a parent, you can decide what kind of mother or father you want to be, based on your values.

Women especially struggle with this question. Most women want to both have a satisfying career and also be happy, successful mothers. But everyone is different. Some women are fully involved in their careers and find great meaning in their professional ambitions. Other women choose to dedicate all their time and energy to raising children. Some men choose to put their whole hearts into their work during the week and then are fully committed to their families on the weekend. There are many ways for men and women to achieve the balance they seek.

Raising children, for mothers and fathers, is a profound form of service. Most parents consider "serving" their children one of the most joyous and satisfying activities of life.

Choose Where to Serve

Many people serve in churches, nonprofits, government, and other organizations and receive profound mental and emotional benefits from this form of activity. Being a part of a community, organization, or cause brings feelings of satisfaction and personal worth. Service to others gives one a strong sense of being connected to something bigger than oneself.

How you choose to serve others, in whatever capacity, is not as important as the attitude and spirit that you bring to your service. As long as your basic motives in serving are to enrich and enhance the lives of your customers, your clients, your patients, or your recipients or beneficiaries and serving these people gives you joy and satisfaction, you are doing the right thing for you. Your life will feel meaningful and balanced.

Look into Yourself

What gives you your greatest feelings of meaning and purpose in life? What do you love doing? Who are the people you care about, respect, and want deeply to serve?

How could you organize your life so that you are serving more and more of these people better and better?

Finding the answers to these questions is the key to happiness, personal fulfillment, and true balance.

Action Exercises

1. Identify the kind of work you most enjoy and would want to do even if you weren't getting paid for it. What actions could you take, starting today, to do more of this work and get better at it?
2. Identify the people, causes, and organizations that you feel most strongly about and where you would like to serve and make a difference. What one action could you take immediately to become more involved in one of these areas?

READING 23

Conclusion

Four Ways to Energize Your Life

Brian Tracy and Christina Stein

There are only four ways that you can change your life or your work to enable you to stay on track and align with your balance point. They are simple and powerful.

1. *You can do more of some things.* What should you be doing more of if you want to be happier and more effective? The answer is usually that you should be doing more of those things from which you are getting the best results, those things that make you the happiest and that give you the greatest feeling of well-being in your life and work.

2. *You can do less of other things.* What should you be doing less of? Obviously, you should be doing less of the things that are not working for you—that are not giving you good results and are causing you unhappiness and frustration.

3. *You can start doing something that you are not doing today.* This is usually the hardest change to make. For you to start doing something completely new and different re quires tremendous discipline and willpower. Everyone slips into a comfort zone, and becomes accustomed to doing certain activities, even if they are no longer working for the person.

   What do you need to start doing today to create a wonderful life for yourself at some time in the future? What new activities do you need to engage in? What new subjects do you need to learn? What new goals do you need to set for yourself and work on every day?

4. *You can stop doing certain things altogether.* This brings us back to zero-based thinking. What are those things in your life that you should

discontinue altogether so that you have more time to do the activities that are really important to you?

In time management and personal management, and whenever you feel frustrated or unhappy for any reason, ask yourself this great question: *"What should I do more of, do less of, start, or stop?"* You will always find the answers somewhere within yourself.

When you begin to follow these ideas each day, you will find your balance point, your center, and begin to achieve all the wonderful things that are possible you.

Good luck!

Chapter 15: Post-Reading Questions

1. The authors offer five self-limiting beliefs we hold which serve as obstacles to our happiness. Which one(s) most apply to you? How would you act differently if you didn't hold such beliefs?
2. After reading about the seven indicators that you are doing the right work, think back to a time when you experienced some of these. What were you doing? What actions could you take to do more of this?
3. Which of the four ways to change your life do you most need to do to find more balance and more fully energize your life?

CONCLUSION

The goal of this book was to apply psychological principles of personal and interpersonal growth to help you find a greater sense of direction and purpose in your life. I don't expect this one course to fully achieve that goal, but hopefully you learned some things that you can apply to your life which will move you closer to the goalposts. The readings in this book covered many common issues that contribute to people moving further from this goal. Struggles with stress, time management, procrastination, and managing emotions seem to be universal and ubiquitous. A host of suggestions and strategies were offered to help you deal with these struggles and to build life skills in areas such as communication, coping, and conflict resolution. Particular focus was placed on problem-solving and critical thinking as tools to identify and overcome the challenges to achieving your life goals. It is hoped that continued use of these tools, skills, and strategies will lead to improving your relationships and helping you to find yourself, find happiness, and find balance in your life! In short, this course was about empowering you to be the best version of you that you would like to be. I wish you the best of luck in your continued pursuit of your dreams!

CPSIA information can be obtained
at www.ICGtesting.com
Printed in the USA
FSHW010402240820
73192FS

9 781516 590032